The Communicative Ethics
Controversy

The Communicative Ethics Controversy

edited by Seyla Benhabib and Fred Dallmayr

The MIT Press, Cambridge, Massachusetts, and London, England

This book was set in Baskerville by DEKR Corporation and printed and bound in the United States of America.

Library of Congress Cataloging-in-Publication Data

The Communicative ethics controversy / edited by Seyla Benhabib and Fred Dallmayr.
    p.   cm.—(Studies in contemporary German social thought)
Includes bibliographical references.
ISBN 0-262-02305-9. — ISBN 0-262-52152-0 (pbk.)
    1. Communication—Moral and ethical aspects. I. Benhabib, Seyla.
II. Dallmayr, Fred R. (Fred Reinhard), 1928–   . III. Series.
P94.C573   1990   76/124
170—dc20   90-32918
                                                CIP

Contents

Sources and Acknowledgments

The essay by Jürgen Habermas was translated by Shierry Weber Nicholsen and Christian Lenhardt; all other essays were translated by David Frisby. Acknowledgment is made to the authors for permission to translate these essays from the following sources:

Karl-Otto Apel, "Ist die Ethik der idealen Kommunikationsgemeinschaft eine Utopie? Zum Verhältnis von Ethik, Utopie und Utopiekritik," in W. Vosskamp, ed., *Utopieforschung* (Frankfurt: Suhrkamp, 1985), vol. I, pp. 325–355.

Jürgen Habermas, excerpts from "Diskursethik: Notizen zu einem Begründungsprogram," in *Moralbewusstsein und kommunikatives Handeln* (Frankfurt: Suhrkamp, 1983). A complete translation is available in *Moral Consciousness and Communicative Action* (Cambridge, MA: The MIT Press, 1990).

Dietrich Böhler, "Transzendentalpragmatik und kritische Moral. Über die Möglichkeit und die moralische Bedeutung einer Selbstaufklärung der Vernunft," in Wolfgang Kuhlmann and Dietrich Böhler, eds., *Kommunikation und Reflexion: Zur Diskussion der Transzendentalpragmatik; Antworten auf Karl-Otto Apel* (Frankfurt: Suhrkamp, 1982), pp. 83–123.

Robert Alexy, "Eine Theorie des praktischen Diskurses," in Willi Oelmüller, ed., *Normenbegründung-Normendurchsetzung* (Paderborn: Schöningh, 1978), pp. 22–58.

Sources and Acknowledgments

Otfried Höffe, "Kantische Skepsis gegen die transzendentale Kommunikationsethik," in *Kommunikation und Reflexion*, pp. 518–539.

Karl-Heinz Ilting, "Der Geltungsgrund moralischer Normen," in *Kommunikation und Reflexion*, pp. 612–648.

Hermann Lübbe, "Sind Normen methodisch begründbar? Rekonstruktion der Antwort Max Webers," in Willi Oelmüller, ed., *Transzendentalphilosophische Normenbegründungen* (Paderborn: Schöningh, 1978), pp. 38–49.

Herbert Schnädelbach, "Bemerkungen über Rationalität und Sprache," in *Kommunikation und Reflexion*, pp. 347–368.

Albrecht Wellmer, "Praktische Philosophie und Theorie der Gesellschaft. Zum Problem der normativen Grundlagen einer kritischen Sozialwissenschaft," in Willi Oelmüller, ed., *Normen und Geschichte* (Paderborn: Schöningh, 1979), pp. 140–174.

The Communicative Ethics
Controversy

Introduction

Fred Dallmayr

Ethics is again high on the contemporary agenda—if not of actual human conduct at least of intellectual discussions inside and outside of academia. In pragmatic and political terms this resurgence of ethics derives from the battery of urgent problems confronting Western industrial societies, problems ranging from advances in biological and medical engineering to issues of nuclear deterrence. These and related practical challenges give rise to pressing policy choices and dilemmas—to whose resolution ethics is expected to make at least a partial contribution. On a philosophical or "metatheoretical" level, the resurgence can be traced to a number of intellectual developments which, though less tangible and clear-cut, are equally far-reaching in character. As many observers have noted, our period is marked by several "paradigmatic" or quasi-paradigmatic changes which all affect the status and meaning of ethics. Foremost among these changes is the move from positivism—with its privileging of "objective" empirical facts over "arbitrary" moral preferences—to modes of "postempiricism" more hospitable to different dimensions of reasoning and argumentation. This move, in turn, is buttressed by a relative shift of emphasis among the traditional branches of philosophizing: namely, from "theoretical" to "practical" philosophy, from the analysis of things to that of performance. Undergirding and overarching these shifts is a further, still more momentous change characterizing our era: from a focus on "subjectivity" or "consciousness" to one on language—a change frequently pinpointed by the phrase "linguistic turn." Singly and jointly, these developments have had the effect of recasting ethics as a metatheoretical enterprise.[1]

The present volume highlights a prominent metaethical perspective which, originating on the Continent, has become a topic of lively debate on both sides of the Atlantic and which illustrates the intersection of the mentioned changes: the perspective of "communicative ethics" or "discourse ethics." As the label indicates, ethics in this perspective is not simply a matter of individual conscience or subjective consciousness but rather a concern indissolubly connected with language and communication. Moreover, normative yardsticks or principles from this vantage are not simply the contingent outcome of communicative exchanges but are seen as premises or preconditions of intelligible language and communication as such. In terms of language philosophy, the perspective heralds a shift from syntax and (neutral-empirical) semantics to speech performance or communicative activity; hence the close connection of this ethics with the broader philosophical and linguistic programs of "transcendental pragmatics" and "universal pragmatics." The most obvious feature of communicative ethics, however, is its antipositivist or at least broadly postempiricist stance: countering all forms of emotivism, imperativism, or prescriptivism (fashionable during the heyday of positivism), its proponents insist on the cognitive "knowability" or rational decidability of ethical principles and metaprinciples—where cognition or knowability does not simply coincide with the knowledge of "facts" (of an empirical or transempirical-intuitive sort). In general terms, communicative ethics can be described as a "cognitive ethics of language," that is, as a type of cognitivism which, instead of stressing (factual or intuited) data, relies on insights garnered through participation in communicative or discursive exchanges. Such exchanges are viewed not as individual thought-experiments (akin to a fictive "original position") but as social or intersubjective engagements; yet, ethical insights are cognitive-rational only to the extent that they grasp or reflect the normative structure of language—a structure variously described as "ideal speech community" or "ideal community of communication." By exploring this structure, communicative ethics is concerned not so much with the formulation of concrete norms or values as rather with the grounding of normativity itself; its central focus is the so-called "*Begründungsproblematik*," that is, the problem of the rational validation or justification of (metaethical) principles, including the specification of appropriate validation procedures. Placed in the context of recent Anglo-American discussions, communicative ethics is profiled or silhouetted in several distinctive ways. By accentuating rational validation, the perspective inserts itself squarely into the cognitivist camp—though with important qualifications. As indicated, cognition here does not denote the intuition of transempirical values (G. E. Moore and his followers) nor the derivation of norms from biological or social-psychological states of affairs (ethical naturalism). Moreover, by relying on language and communication, the perspective differs from other rational-categorial versions of cognitivism, including approaches concentrating on the normative premises of human action (Alan Gewirth) or on a fictive-mental argumentation (John Rawls). On the whole, communicative ethics shows greatest affinity to the "good reasons" approach in Anglo-American thought (Kurt Baier, Stephen Toulmin); however, instead of being satisfied with contingent or habitual modes of reasoning, proponents stress the unavoidable and rationally necessary ("*nichthintergehbar*") premises of argumentation. The latter point signals also the main line of demarcation from neo-Aristotelian ethics and its focus on practical judgment (Alasdair MacIntyre) and also from hermeneutical concerns with the particularities of concrete situations. In championing reason or rationality, the perspective stands clearly opposed to ethical skepticism in all its forms or guises. Older, quasi-positivist modes of such skepticism embrace the reduction of norms to emotive preferences (Alfred Ayer) or their equation with imperative commands (Charles Stevenson). More recently, under the impact of "antifoundational" and postmetaphysical arguments, ethical skepticism has resurfaced in strong versions of contextualism and (neo) historicism and even in attacks on normative "theorizing" itself. In lieu of universal yardsticks or principles, defenders of these views tend to underscore the context-dependency of norms (Richard

Rorty) or the inevitable pluralism and diversity of moral judgments (Michael Walzer, Bernard Williams).[2] The aim of the present volume is twofold: first, to introduce the English-speaking audience to the main theses or arguments advanced by the proponents of communicative ethics; and second, to acquaint the reader with some of the chief debates or controversies surrounding the perspective primarily in its European setting. The selection of essays was guided by these objectives. The volume opens with two papers by the foremost spokesmen of communicative ethics: Karl-Otto Apel and Jürgen Habermas (both at the University of Frankfurt). Their statements are augmented and further fleshed out by two supporting papers written by Dietrich Böhler and Robert Alexy (at the universities of Berlin and Göttingen, respectively). The second part of the volume is devoted to "critical considerations"—that is, to objections, rejoinders, and afterthoughts deriving from a variety of vantage points ranging from cognitivism to skepticism and to the broad camp of "critical theory" itself. While Otfried Höffe (Fribourg) defends Kantian philosophy against its communicative or linguistic reformulation, Herbert Schnädelbach (Hamburg) takes recourse to Wittgenstein's conception of "language games" to counter the privileging of ethical rules or principles over rule application. The next two essays—by the late Karl-Heinz Ilting and Hermann Lübbe (Zurich)—veer in the direction of ethical noncognitivism: while the former stresses the dichotomy between knowledge and practical will, the latter asserts the difference or incongruence between cognitive justification and concrete-social validity (of norms). The concluding essay by Albrecht Wellmer (Konstanz) places the program of communicative ethics in a broader—Hegelian and Marxist—context, while simultaneously voicing skeptical doubts about the goal of ultimate justification. In her afterword, Seyla Benhabib explores and evaluates the "communicative ethics controversy" both as it is presented in this volume and as it has evolved in more recent times on both sides of the Atlantic. In the remainder of my introduction I shall summarize the main lines of thought developed in the following essays.

Both of the leading proponents start out by situating communicative ethics against the backdrop of skepticism and noncognitivism. In the case of Apel's essay, its title—"Is the Ethics of the Ideal Communication Community a Utopia?"—already reveals the author's guiding motivation or concern: the desire to vindicate the perspective against charges of utopianism (if not of chiliastic tendencies) advanced by spokesmen of *Realpolitik*. As Apel observes, the only acceptable "futurism" in our time seems to be the notion of scientific progress, that is, of the steady transformation of human life through technical imperatives—while moral and political vistas are chastised as dangerous or as part of a defunct metaphysics. On a practical-political level, the notion tends to be associated with "social engineering" and particularly with low-key forms of "piecemeal engineering" averse to broader visions. Countering this narrowly scientistic outlook, Apel insists that scientific-technological change enhances rather than decreases the importance of ethics and normative principles as yardsticks for judging the directions and consequences of "progress." Communicative ethics is introduced at this point as the most comprehensive and rationally grounded avenue for developing such yardsticks. Communication in this case must not be confused with contingent types of bargaining and especially not with the "strategic model" of negotiated compromises among conflicting particular interests. What is missing in strategic pursuits and rational-choice calculations is the recourse to ultimate normative justification and especially to a principle of "trans-subjective universalization" akin to Kant's "categorical imperative." In Apel's words: "The consensual-communicative discourse ethics views the Kantian principle as the formal internalization of the principle of *universalized reciprocity* which requires that concrete norms be justified where possible by an *agreement* upon the interests of all those concerned."

In invoking Kant and universal principles, however, communicative ethics seems to conjure up a basic quandary of rational justification—a problem opponents have termed a "logical trilemma" (in the sense that justification involves either an infinite regress, a *petitio principii*, or the dogmatic acceptance of a first axiom). As Apel acknowledges, the problem is indeed inescapable as long as justification is equated with deduction or induction on a purely epistemic level. From a "transcendental-pragmatic" vantage, by contrast, justification means an appeal to the normative premises implicit in communication itself, that is, to the unavoidability or "untranscendability" (*Nichthintergehbarkeit*) of these premises and thus to the "reflexive self-grounding" of reason. What is decisive in this case is not the issue of a "noncircular final proof" but rather the fact that the implicit principle cannot be denied by communicative agents without "pragmatic self-contradiction." By pursuing this course, transcendental pragmatics—as philosophical framework of communicative ethics—forms part of a long philosophical tradition concerned with the "ultimate justification" (*Letztbegründung*) of principles, a line stretching from Socrates over Descartes to Kant. However, according to the essay, it is only in the transcendental-pragmatic inquiry into the inescapable validity claims of language and speech that this reflective legacy achieves full "explicative self-transparency." At this point Apel returns to the issue of utopia and utopiansim. While recognizing that ethical yardsticks cannot simply or directly be implemented in real life (in violation of considerations of individual or collective self-preservation), he maintains that such yardsticks furnish *at least* a "regulative idea" in Kant's sense or a measuring rod for assessing concrete situations. Actually, however, given their unavoidability, communicative principles play a stronger and more ambitious role—in that real-life exchanges must always foreshadow and "counterfactually" presuppose the conditions of an "ideal communication community" as their implicit *telos*. "As linguistic beings constrained to share meaning and truth with fellow beings in order to be able to think validly," he concludes, "humans must at all times anticipate counterfactually an *ideal form of communication and hence of social interaction*."[3]

Habermas's essay pursues a similar goal of normative validation, though along a somewhat less Kantian or "foundational" path. Since several portions or sections are omitted in the present volume, it may be advisable to offer a succinct overview of the entire essay, including the omitted parts. The opening section draws attention to the contemporary context of ethical discussions, a context dominated by positivist and noncognitivist assumptions. To counter the positivist bifurcation of facts and values (is and ought). Habermas sketches a "phenomenology of the moral domain," thereby reminding ethicists of the character of their topic. Relying on Peter Strawson's linguistic phenomenology of experience, the section concludes that, far from being arbitrary or random data, moral phenomena are intelligible from the "performative" vantage of interactive agents and that moral justification of conduct differs crucially from the neutral assessment of "means-ends relations." On the basis of this finding Habermas criticizes and rejects prevalent "subjectivist" and noncognitivist approaches to ethics, including emotivist and imperativist construals as well as the reduction of norms to prescriptive decisions (R.M. Hare). As he adds, this rejection does not automatically vindicate cognitivist counterpositions—especially conceptions (like intuitionism) equating descriptive and normative propositions, factual truth and moral "rightness." In the field of ethics or metaethics, he notes, rational justification can only have the status of a "truth-analogous" validity claim, that is, a claim buttressed by validating reasons (which in no way detracts from its cognitive character). Once accomplished, specification of such a validating basis entails the defeat of two points typically advanced by skeptics: the radical nonidentity of facts and values, and the general undecidability of moral questions.

In an effort to specify this basis, the second part of the essay turns to the context of linguistic pragmatics and more particularly to the domain of moral argumentation or "practical discourse." According to Habermas, both theoretical (scientific) and practical discourses are argumentative enterprises in which truth and rightness claims, respectively, are systematically tested and contested through the invocation of validating reasons. Yet, the two discourses are not entirely congruent or symmetrical due to the cultural (nonnatural) status of ethics—which entails that factually prevalent norms may not be rationally justified or morally binding. Regarding validating reasons in practical argumentation, Habermas concurs with Apel on the inapplicability (or only partial applicability) of inductive and deductive procedures. Hence, to permit the assessment of concrete norms, (meta) ethics requires a kind of "bridge principle" which performs an equivalent role to induction in empirical science and deduction in logic. In terms of the essay, such a bridging or linking rule can be found in the "principle of universalization" which captures the basic intention of Kant's categorical imperative. "To enable consensus," we read, "the bridge principle must make sure that only such norms are accepted as valid which express the *general will* or, in Kant's steadily repeated formulation, which qualify as a 'universal law'." In Habermas's view, however, universalization should not be restricted to an abstract formalism and certainly not to a rule governing only *in foro interno;* rather, in conformity with the turn to pragmatics, the principle has a social or public function by prescribing impartiality and general reciprocity: "Impartial judgment reflects a principle which requires that, in assessing interests, every participant must assume the perspective of *all others*" (in a variation on George Herbert Mead's notion of "ideal role-taking"). Once universalization is accepted as proper argumentative rule, the way is cleared for a communicative or "discourse ethics" whose basic maxim Habermas formulates in these terms: "A norm can claim validity only if all those potentially affected can consent to this validity as *participants of a practical discourse.*" (An "excursus" inserted at this point differentiates discursive ethics—guided by a categorical maxim—from contingently negotiated compromises and especially from Ernst Tugendhat's conception of agreement as an equitable adjustment of interests.)[4]

The third part of the essay (included in this volume) is devoted to the issue of justification or the development of a "justification program" appropriate to discursive ethics. In response to doubts or objections voiced by skeptical noncognitivists, Habermas initially seeks to provide a more solid grounding for the proposed "bridge principle" of universalization. Turning specifically to the so-called "trilemma" of ethical validation, the essay invokes Apel's transcendental pragmatics as a viable justificatory strategy (and also as an antidote to charges of ethnocentrism). Apel's rebuttal of the trilemma involves recourse to the necessary premises of argumentation—premises which skeptics cannot deny without lapsing into "performative contradiction." In Habermas's words: "Opponents commit a performative contradiction if it can be shown that, by entering into argumentation, they necessarily accept certain inescapable preconditions of argumentative language games geared to critical analysis." By relying on necessary premises, he adds, Apel recaptures an Archimedean point in argumentation which is analogous to the "I think" or to "consciousness as such" in Kant's perspective; differently phrased: the rules of argumentation are "nontranscendable" (*nichthintergehlar*) in the same sense as is cognition in transcendental philosophy. Rigorously explicated or elaborated, these rules are noncontingent and thus universal or tanscendental in character and furnish the yardsticks for a—counterfactually anticipated—"ideal speech situation" free of repression and argumentative inequality. In real-life contexts, to be sure, discourses or argumentative language games need to be institutionalized or organizationally secured—a process infecting ideal standards with contingent conventions. Yet, institutionalization does not simply nullify counterfactual standards but remains tied to normative goals "inescapably embedded in argumentation as such." Relying on this transcendental-pragmatic strategy the essay restates the basic maxim of discourse ethics: namely, that "only such norms can claim validity which find (or could find) consensus among all concerned as participants of a practical discourse."

Although recognizing the importance and rigor of Apel's approach, Habermas mollifies or moderates the transcendental quality of justification (canceling in effect Apel's effort of "ultimate justification" or *Letztbegründung*). As he observes, specifying the inescapable rules of argumentation does not so much justify normative yardsticks as only demonstrate the "lack of alternatives" to these rules. More important, theoretical specification of argumentative premises does not have the same (transcendental) status as these premises themselves but only that of a "hypothetical reconstruction" which may be more or less adequate. "The *certainty* with which we practice our 'know how' of rules," Habermas writes, "does not translate into the *truth* of our reconstructive proposals regarding hypothetically universal premises" (a statement which seems to approximate discourse-ethical principles to hypothetical if not conventional rules). Notwithstanding this qualification of transcendentalism, the essay turns next against skeptics who wish to elude normative-discursive standards by refusing to engage in argumentation. According to Habermas, this "escapist" strategy is doomed to failure—since practical discourses are embedded in real-life interactions from which members cannot exit (without self-destruction) and which obey their own ineluctable premises or rules (seen as "prolongations" of discursive principles into the domain of action). The relationship between discourses and real-life interactions finally leads Habermas to a consideration of alternative ethical perspectives—like neo-Aristotelian hermeneutics and Hegelianism—which view ethics as a matter of practical judgment or of a life-conduct called *Sittlichkeit*. While granting the elusiveness of rules, the essay subordinates practical judgment to normative principles, insisting that concrete applications can "falsify the (universal) meaning of norms." Regarding the aspect of life-conduct emphasized by Hegel, Habermas—while conceding its significance—inserts the issue into a series of dichotomies, like reason-history, theory-praxis, *Moralität* and *Sittlichkeit* (thereby equating the latter with custom or convention and the former with principled reflection). "Within the context of a life-world," he writes, "practical judgments derive their concreteness and action-motivating power from their connection with taken-for-granted ideas of the 'good life', with institutionalized *Sittlichkeit* as such." On the level of morality, by contrast, judgment is "severed from local conventions and the historicality of particular life-forms," giving primacy instead to rationally validated principles of rightness.[5]

In his essay Dietrich Böhler—one of Apel's former students— corroborates the latter's justification strategy, including the aim of "ultimate justification" (*Letztbegründung*). For Böhler, Apel's transcendental pragmatics stands in the tradition of self-reflective reason which can be traced back to Socrates and Plato and which, in modern times, includes a line of thinkers stretching from Descartes over Kant to Husserl. Attentive to the "linguistic turn," however, he supports a communicative or speech-pragmatic reformulation of the reflective legacy. "The self-reference of the thinking subject," he writes, "which, from

Augustine via Descartes, Kante and Fichte to Husserl, was treated solipsistically as an unmediated 'I think', is realized only in the performative attitude"—which means that self-reference and reflective identity are possible only "by means of the virtual relation to others," a relation commonly established through "the communicative role in a language game." As in Apel's case, recourse to language and communication does not equate endorsement of contingent speech patterns. In Böhler's presentation, transcendental pragmatics captures the essential concern of "pure reason," namely, the uncovering of the universal, noncontingent preconditions of communicative interaction. To participate in such interaction while denying these inevitable or transcendental preconditions means to get entangled in a "pragmatic inconsistency" (what Apel calls a "performative contradiction"). Acceptance of these premises, on the other hand, entails acceptance of the normative yardsticks governing communication or argumentation: namely, of the validity claims implicit in arguments and of their possible redemption in a— counterfactually anticipated—"unlimited community of argumentation." In Böhler's view, reflection on the premises of communication reveals the intimate connection between argumentation and ethics and thus establishes transcendental pragmatics as an ethical theory. Fleshing out the notion of anticipation, the essay notes that the projection of a normative consensus also presupposes reciprocal interpretation and understanding among participants—with the result that the argumentative community must be supplemented by a community of understanding, transcendental pragmatics by a transcendental hermeneutics. In a "discourse-political" sense, the anticipated community has the character of a universal or global "public sphere" (öffentlichkeit) supported by a civic cosmopolitanism.

Although sympathetic to Apel's general strategy, Robert Alexy's essay defends a more open-minded or ecumenical approach to the problem of justification. Like Habermas, Alexy begins with a critique of prevalent modes of ethical theory— chiefly naturalism and intuitionism—as a steppingstone to the formulation of a discourse ethics. To avoid the "trilemma" of metaethics, he states, the accent of theorizing must be shifted from induction to the pragmatics of speech and specifically to the basic premises of rational argumentation. Alexy calls these premises broadly "pragmatic rules" and defines the aim of a theory of "practical discourse" as the establishment and justification of a coherent system of such rules. Regarding the justification of rules, the essay delineates and accepts an assortment of strategies, mainly four: a "technical" approach (showing the instrumental adequacy of rules to the pursuit of given ends); an "empirical" type (stressing the actual prevalence and acceptance of rules); a "definitional" or stipulative version (proposing an axiomatic model of rules); and finally a "universal-pragmatic" path of justification (focusing on the conditions of possibility of communication, basically along Habermasian lines). Noting the different stringency of these approaches but tolerantly embracing all of them, Alexy proposes a "discourse-theoretical discourse," that is, a discourse (itself rule-governed) about the appropriate rules of discourse and their (more or less stringent) justification. The remainder of the essay offers a tentative classification of discursive rules, broken down into six types. What Alexy calls "basic rules" capture basically the inescapable premises or preconditions of communication. "Rules of reason" pertain to the structure of communication and in many ways resemble the condition of Habermas's "ideal speech situation." Other rules specify the "burden of argumentation" and the different "forms" or genres of communicative interaction. Under the rubric of general "justification rules" we find the principle of "universalizability" (as articulated in different ways by Hare, Baier, and Habermas), while "transition rules" are said to govern the shift from one type of discourse to another. The conclusion of the essay discusses the various functions of discourse theory—as an instrument of critique, as a criterion of validation, as projection of an "ideal"—and the possibilities and limits of the institutionalization of discourses.

The series of critical rejoinders opens with Otfried Höffe's vindication of Kantian philosophy and especially of the categorical structure of Kantian ethics. Focusing on transcendental pragmatics, Höffe portrays Apel's perspective as a communicative "transformation" of Kant's teachings and ultimately as an attempt to recapture the ground of a "first philosophy" (*prima philosophia*). While applauding its methodical rigor and political connotations, he finds the transformation flawed as well as distortive of Kant's intentions. Against the charge of a prelinguistic individualism, Höffe emphasizes the social dimension of Kant's ethics and also its mixture of concrete and transcendental elements. The chief bone of contention, however, is the issue of ultimate justification (*Letzbegründung*)—where transcendental pragmatics allegedly corrects Kant's shortcomings. In Höffe's view, the reverse situation actually obtains: by stipulating "ideal discourse" as normative yardstick, Apel invokes a normative principle which is presupposed, but not furnished or justified by linguistic communication. Apel's ethics, he writes (pressing the point of logical circularity), "presupposes certain ethical principles as self-evidently valid, although discourse should in fact be that instance through which the ethical principles are first of all justified." Accordingly, appeal to discourse or communication cannot by itself be adequate for purposes of justification; instead, it requires a prior notion of ethical normativity—such as it is formulated in Kant's categorical imperative. By ignoring this requirement, transcendental pragmatics is said to reveal a "deficit in justification" and to regress in a sense below the reflective "level reached by Kant"—although communicative ethics remains parasitical on the categorical imperative by insisting on the "autonomy" of communicative agents and by elevating (ideal) discourse to a "universal law." Elaborating on Apel's critique of Kant's ethics, Höffe notes that the so-called "fact of reason" points to the reality of moral consciousness rather than establishing (mistakenly) a first principle for the deduction of norms. Turning to the "postulates of practical reason" (such as the existence of God and the immortality of the soul), the essay presents them as implications of the highest or "uppermost good"—which for Kant consisted in the coincidence of happiness and ethical virtue. Since, even with the best intentions, this coincidence cannot be guaranteed by ideal discourse, Apel's dismissal of these postulates appears as premature.

Proceeding from a very different, even opposite vantage point, Schnädelbach's essay explores the nexus of language and rationality, and particularly the impact of the former on the latter. The basic question addressed concerns the consequences entailed by the "linguistic turn" of transcendental pragmatics for the status and meaning of reason or rationality. In large measure, the exploration revolves around the relation between rational (or normative) rules and concrete rule application. Turning to Kant's three Critiques, Schnädelbach shows that Kant, in his *Critique of Judgment*, made ample room for the complexity of rule application while simultaneously insisting, in his "transcendental doctrine of judgment," on the possibility of a specification of a priori rules governing rule application. Schnädelbach's contrary thesis is that it is precisely the linguistic turn of transcendental pragmatics which "in principle excludes the complete representability of rationality in rules" (including rules for rule application). Relying (in part) on the later Wittgenstein, the essay defines language basically as an "*impure* reason, infected by empirical concreteness and by contingency." This impurity also extends to the notion of "communicative competence" developed by both Apel and Habermas (in a variation on Chomsky's linguistic model)—since this competence or faculty cannot exhaustively regulate the range of its performative application. Pointing to the inevitable "feedback" between whole and parts, between universality and particularity, Schnädelbach presents rationality as a "complex unity of rules and rule application marked by a close interaction between its elements" or else as an "open-ended system of communicative competence not fully representable in rules." In reference to a "transformed" Kantianism what this means is that transcendental pragmatics cannot aspire to the status of "first philosophy," an aim conflicting with the linguistic turn; for one cannot simultaneously embrace the "inseparability of rule and rule application" and still adhere to a Kantain apriorism. Schnädelbach's essays ends with a defense of "historical rationality" or the "historicity of reason," a conception in which reason and historical contingency are closely correlated and where the difference between rational "foreground" and historical background can never be completely erased. With regard to communicative ethics the result is a more subdued, prudential outlook: "practical reason—furnishing the 'determining grounds of will'—is as communicative reason likewise impure."[6]

A determined shift from (pure) reasoning to practical reason as the "grounds of will" can be found in Ilting's essay which offers both a critique of transcendental pragmatics and the sketch of an alternative "justification program." According to Ilting, Apel's approach is marred by inattention to the practical life-dimension in which ethics is rooted—that is, by neglect of the fact "that a pure community of argumentation guided solely by cognitive interests is precisely exempt from those difficulties and necessities of collective life which moral norms are supposed to regulate." More specifically, the essay faults transcendental pragmatics for committing two mistakes or fallacies. The first, labeled "pragmatic fallacy," has to do with Apel's linkage of ethics with argumentative validity claims—a link which is said to obfuscate the difference between genuine truth or validity and mere "doxa" or claimed validity. The second and more grievous mistake, called "intellectualist fallacy," concerns the normative status of the inevitable (*nichthintergehbar*) premises of argumentation. As Ilting counters, participants in a purely theoretical discussion or in an effort of rational problem solving do not perform morally relevant actions; hence, "intellectualistic fallacy" denotes the attempt "to derive binding norms from the conditions of our use of reason or to uncover the validity basis of their binding character in these conditions." Ilting's counterproposal relies on the structure of morally relevant actions in a collective life-context. In his view, norms are not premises of knowledge or cognition but rather principles of human action (in Kant's sense they are "practical synthetic judgments *a priori*"). From a practical vantage point, the primary issue to be taken into account is human freedom—that is, freedom of will and of action—and the fact that normative systems are always limitations of freedom which need to be assessed in terms of their contribution to social order and their basic compatibility with freedom itself. Differently phrased: norms are justified if their acceptance by free agents can legitimately be expected (*zumutbar*). From this notion of "legitimate expectation" Ilting derives a series of metanorms undergirding the obligatory status of ethics—

especially the principle of universality and of the general acceptance of norms by all concerned. These metanorms, in turn, function as the apex of an ethical hierarchy ranging from abstract-universal to concrete-material norms and from rules to rule application (with a progressive increase of contingency). The turn from knowing to willing is intensified in Lübbe's essay on the "methodical justifiability" of norms. According to Lübbe, discussions in this area tend to be confused by the failure to distinguish between cognitive justification and actual-social validity, that is, between modes of justifying norms and procedures for their enactment or implementation. While the issue of justification is relatively unproblematic, in his view, the crux of ethical debates lies in the field of enactment and public validity—which is the field of political will and action. It is with a focus on the latter domain that Lübbe interprets Max Weber's famous thesis regarding the absence of a rational-scientific procedure for the resolution of basic value conflicts. As he points out, Weber's thesis does not challenge the possibility of methodical-cognitive justification—a task which can be undertaken with greater or lesser thoroughness—but rather the sufficiency of cognitive reasons for the adoption and enforcement of norms. Countering false hopes of scientists and academics, Weber pointed to the need for a political decision to render cognitive reasons concretely and publicly valid. The distance between cognitive and public validity, we are told, had to do less with the gulf between "is" and "ought" (emphasized by David Hume) than with "the hiatus between ought and will (*Sollen-Wollen*) familiar to us since Socrates." This hiatus corresponds to the difference between two occupational roles, those of the philosopher or scientist, on the one hand, and of the politician, on the other—a difference which can only precariously be bridged (as the example of Weber himself shows). Regarding cognitive justification—an issue not paramount in Lübbe's concerns—the essay proposes a rough schema according to which norms are justified by showing their conformity with actually or supposedly shared interests or a common will. Responding to the charge that the schema is limited to technical pursuits or strategic compromises while neglecting rational consensus, Lübbe questions the distinction between "technical" and "practical" norms, arguing that both are equally predicated on a common will.

The concluding essay by Wellmer steers a middle course between applauding the strengths and acknowledging the possible weaknesses of communicative ethics (especially in its transcendental-pragmatic form). The essay starts out by placing communicative ethics in the context of contemporary efforts to overcome the positivist fact-value dichotomy and to correct "value-neutrality" through a revival of practical cognition or practical reason. An outstanding example of this effort is Habermas's "discourse ethics" in which norms are said to be rationally validated if they are (or could be) accepted by all concerned in an unconstrained discussion. According to Wellmer, the basic maxim underlying discourse ethics is the principle of democratic legitimacy, a principle which can be traced back to the contractarian model of modern natural law (focused on the unconstrained agreement among free and equal partners) as well as to Kant's categorical ethics. As he notes the formalism of this tradition has been attacked by Hegel—but in a manner which itself remained indebted to natural law categories and thus was vulnerable to Marx's critical rejoinder. In Wellmer's account, discourse ethics seeks to move beyond Kant but in a "different direction" from that pursued by Hegel: namely, by replacing inner reflection with dialogue and by treating discourse as a purely formal procedure, in fact, by stipulating this procedure as "the only a priori intelligible content of moral consciousness." The essay next turns to two major contemporary objections to communicative or discourse ethics. The first objection proceeds from skeptical and noncognitivist assumptions (akin to Lübbe's arguments) and complains about the subordination of public decision-making processes to rational cognition or argumentation. Countering this challenge, Wellmer distinguishes between a level of "legitimation" (captured by discourse ethics) and a level of "concrete-social organization"—arguing not, however, for a strict subsumption of the latter under the former but rather for a mutual interpenetration whereby decision procedures are (as it were) embedded or submerged in "the medium of public discourses." The second objection derives from present-day hermeneutics. Taking this objection "seriously," Wellmer acknowledges that the core problem of the "idea of practical reason" is that of "its *mediation* with the concrete situation of historical agents and their society." With reference to Habermas's "ideal speech situation" and similar formulas, the problem concerns their meaningful application; for, in order to apply them sensibly, "we must always already have understood something of the concrete structure and substantive constellation of given discursive situations." Differently phrased: formal criteria can be used only "on the basis of a *substantive* preunderstanding." By way of conclusion, Wellmer rejects the construal of formal principles as "metanorms" or ideal standards and also the notion of an ultimate justification (*Letztbegründung*) of communicative ethics.

The essays collected in this volume do not offer a "final word" or a resolution of the issues under discussion. Since the essays were written, the controversy surrounding communicative or discourse ethics has gathered momentum, with contending positions being steadily intensified or sharpened in the process. One of the leading figures involved in this sharpening of issues is Albrecht Wellmer who, in some of his recent writings, has further tightened the nexus linking form and content, reason and history (to the point where formal criteria become secondary to the substantive quality of discourses). At the same time, recent debates have witnessed a resurgence and clearer formulation of neo-Aristotelian, hermeneutical, and Hegelian perspectives—a resurgence calling into question the discursive downplaying of practical judgment in favor of normative principles as well as the equation of Hegelian *Sittlichkeit* with empirical customs.[7] Seyla Benhabib's afterword reviews and critically assesses these and related theoretical developments, together with the original setting of the controversy as presented in this volume. Again, the attempt there is not to "resolve" the controversy or to suggest a definitive settlement. It may well be—and the history of the field seems to attest— that ethics is intrinsically a tensional or contested enterprise involving a "discourse" or dialogue not along uniform cognitive lines but among competing and not necessarily compatible perspectives. If the present volume is any indication, such a discourse would have to include skeptics, cognitive rationalists, and defenders of practical judgment.

Notes

1. For a discussion of some of these changes see Stanley Hauerwas and Alasdair MacIntyre, *Revisions: Changing Perspectives in Moral Philosophy* (Notre Dame: University of Notre Dame Press, 1983). The positivist privileging of "is" over "ought" was succinctly formulated by MacIntyre in these lines: "Reason is calculative: it can assess truths of fact and mathematical relations but nothing more. In the realm of practice it can speak only of means. About ends it must be silent." See Alasdair MacIntyre, *After Virtue* (Notre Dame: University of Notre Dame Press, 1981), p. 52.

2. For background readings in Anglo-American ethical theory see Paul W. Taylor *The Moral Judgment: Readings in Contemporary Meta-Ethics* (Englewood Cliffs, NJ: Prentice-Hall, 1963); William D. Hudson, *Modern Moral Philosophy* (Garden City, NY: Anchor Books, 1970); T. Henderich, ed., *Morality and Objectivity* (London: Routledge and Kegan Paul, 1985). On the recent skeptical turn compare Richard Rorty, *The Consequences of Pragmatism* (Minneapolis: University of Minnesota Press, 1982); Bernard Williams, *Ethics and the Limits of Philosophy* (Cambridge, MA; Harvard University Press, 1985); and S. Clarke and E. Simpson, eds., *The Primacy of Moral Practices* (New York: SUNY Press, 1988).

3. The reader would be well advised to read the essay in this volume in conjunction with an earlier essay by Apel, namely, "The Apriori of the Communication Community and the Foundations of Ethics" (1973) in Apel, *Towards a Transformation of Philosophy*, trans. Glyn Adey and David Frisby (London: Routledge and Kegan Paul, 1980), pp. 225–300. In the above, I restrict myself to the role of *rapporteur*. In other contexts I have critically assessed Apel's philosophical and ethical program. See "Ordinary Language and Ideal Speech" in Dallmayr, *Twilight of Subjectivity* (Amherst: University of Massachusetts Press, 1981), pp. 220–254, and "Apel's Transformation of Philosophy" in *Critical Encounters* (Notre Dame: University of Notre Dame Press, 1987), pp. 101–129.

4. See Jürgen Habermas, *Moralbewusstsein und kommunikatives Handeln* (Frankfurt-Main: Suhrkamp, 1983), pp. 53–86; trans. by Shierry Weber Nicholsen and Christian Lenhardt under the title *Moral Consciousness and Communicative Action* (Cambridge, MA: The MIT Press, 1990).

5. In the above, I have again acted as *rapporteur*. One should note, however, that the identification of *Sittlichkeit* with custom or convention sharply conflicts with Hegel's use of the term, for whom *Sittlichkeit* stood for the essence or rational idea of ethical life. For some of my earlier attempts to assess critically Habermas's work see "Transcendental Hermeneutics and Universal Pragmatics" in *Language and Politics* (Notre Dame: University of Notre Dame Press, 1984), pp. 115–147; also "Life-world and Communicative Action" in *Polis and Praxis* (Cambridge, MA: The MIT Press, 1984), pp. 224–253, reprinted in *Critical Encounters* (Notre Dame: University of Notre Dame Press, 1987), pp. 73–100.

6. In pointing to the "difference" between the foreground of rules and the background of historical rule application Schnädelbach seems to approximate poststructuralist arguments. Relying on Merleau-Ponty and Adorno (and less on Wittgenstein) I have

tried to formulate a similar critique of formal or rule-governed rationality; see "Habermas and Rationality" in *Political Theory,* vol. 16 (1988), pp. 553–579.

7. See especially Albrecht Wellmer, *Ethik und Dialog* (Frankfurt-Main: Suhrkamp, 1986), and Wolfgang Kuhlmann, ed., *Moralität und Sittlichkeit: Das Problem Hegels und die Diskursethik* (Frankfurt-Main: Suhrkamp, 1986). Compare also the Special Double Issue on "Hermeneutics in Ethics and Social Theory" (ed., Michael Kelly), in *The Philosophical Forum,* vol. 21, nos. 1–2 (Fall-Winter 1989–90), pp. iii–254; and the Special Issue on "Universalism vs. Communitarianism: Contemporary Debates in Ethics," in *Philosophy and Social Criticism,* vol. 14, nos. 3–4 (1988), pp. 237–471. The latter issue contains a very useful bibliography dealing at least in part with communicative ethics: Michael Zilles, "Universalism and Communitarianism: A Bibliography," pp. 441–471.

I

The Program of Communicative Ethics

1

Is the Ethics of the Ideal Communication Community a Utopia? On the Relationship between Ethics, Utopia, and the Critique of Utopia

Karl-Otto Apel

I Statement of the Problem

The contemporary concept of *utopia*, from which I take my departure here, is surprisingly more or less clear and well known. This stands in contrast to the extreme ambiguity and ambivalence that characterizes the concept and evaluation of utopia in the specialized literature on this theme—from the positive evaluation in the sense of Thomas More's *Utopia*[1] and the reflections upon utopia by Karl Mannheim[2] or Ernst Bloch[3] to the negative judgment of Leibniz,[4] Baumgarten,[5] the early socialists[6]—themselves later known as "utopian"—and finally of Marx and Engels.[7] Yet leaving aside this historical-hermeneutic and philosophical problematic of "utopia," there exists today a working consensus on the negative meaning "utopia" and the "utopian" that appears at first sight to be presupposed in the titular question of my contribution.

I admit that this interpretation of the question also originally stood at the forefront of my interests—that is, to a certain extent, the intention of defending a specific concept of ethics against the common attack of "utopianism."[8] Yet, the issue cannot merely be to call into question a specific conception of ethics, in the light and by the standard of an apparently unambiguous negative concept of utopia; what must also be attempted—in the light and by the standards of a rationally groundable ethics—is a clarification of the notorious ambivalence of the concept of "utopia" itself. It might indeed be the case that the contemporary critique of "utopianism" is by and large justified, but that, equally, the idea of a fictional "utopia" as representation of a hypothetical alternative world expresses an indispensable anthropological function.[9] Over and above this, it might also be the case that a rationally groundable ethics readily provides criteria for the demarcation between a dangerous and a necessary utopia: the normative standards of a "principle of responsibility" that might serve to legitimate the fictional utopia as an exploratory element in the sense of a "heuristics of hope" *and* a "heuristics of fear."[10]

The following framework for my contribution can be derived from this interpretation of the question that I have just outlined:

1. First, I wish to attempt to characterize the concept of utopia that underlies the present-day critique of "utopianism." From the outset, this takes place with the intention of rendering intelligible why it is that the contemporary critique of utopia is not related primarily to fictional-literary utopias in the narrower sense, but rather is fundamentally directed against an ethical-historical-philosophical conception that is viewed as *utopian* and thus as dangerous. From this point it will also be made clear why the critique of "utopianism" is directed against the ethics of the ideal communication community.

2. In the second section of my contribution, I wish to attempt to present this ethics in a necessarily summary form. In so doing, my intention is to demonstrate the following: that the basic form of the ethics in question can be grounded in an undisputably valid manner, independently of any historical-philosophical prognosis and of any concrete-fictional conception of a possible, better world; that, at the same time, however, it contains a quasi-historical-philosophical and quasi-utopian dimension of anticipation: a dimension of the partial justification and critique of the (anthropological function of) fictional and historically-philosophically "transcended" utopia.

3. In the third section, the conception of a "critique of utopian reason"—a conception whose necessity has already been shown in the second section with the partial ethical justification of the utopian intentions[11]—will be elucidated in exemplary

fashion by means of the "utopia" of "domination-free" communication.

II The Concept of Utopia and Motives of the Current Critique of Utopianism

The main characteristics of the concept of utopia in the contemporary critique of "utopianism" can be typified if one interprets the critique of "utopianism" as the expression of an ideological-political discussion in the "rationalized public sphere" (Kant). This provides us with the following major aspects:

1. With reference to the problematic of a reconstruction of the fictional "utopia," it should first of all be emphasized that the current critique of "utopia" does not proceed—or not immediately—from the literary paradigm established by Thomas More's *Utopia*, but rather from the extended, philosophical-anthropological concept of "utopian intention" or "form of thought" as it has been introduced by more recent exponents of a positive concept of utopia, such as Karl Mannheim or Ernst Bloch. Precisely here, in the central claim to the "transcendence of existence" or the transformation of the "condition humaine"—in the sense, broadly speaking, of Bloch's hoped for and postulated utilization of the "not yet" actualized "potential" of humanity and the corresponding "potentiality" of nature—the presumptuous and thus dangerous dimension of the "utopian intention" is to be seen. Today, with reference to this intention (just as earlier and similarly at the time of the speculative remobilization of early Christian "chiliasm" by Joachim of Fiore and the Franciscan spiritualists, leaving aside the later "fanatics"[12]) there also takes place the alliance of the orthodox theology of original sin and the *other-worldly* realm of God with the defenders of "institutions" and also with the proponents of the "constraints of the actual" and the really "do-able" who see the "condition humaine" represented in the immanently measured goals and mechanisms of the process of industrialization.[13] (Insofar as this is the case, the antiutopian alliance today also surely embraces the pragmatists of "real-existing socialism.")

2. In the concept of "utopia" adhered to by the above characterized ideological-political alliance there is, of course, seldom lacking a connotation that in fact indirectly creates the connection between the critique of "utopianism" with the literary concept of utopia. This is that the person who cannot come to terms with the "condition humaine"—or, in modern parlance, is overtaxed by the adjustment and learning constraint of the process of technical-industrial progress—hankers after a pipe dream similar to that of the literary utopia (or, indeed, after the kind of myth of the "golden age"). The dangerous aspect of the utopian problematic is thus seen to rest upon the combination of escapism and—possibly terroristic—activism; or even more precisely, upon the fact that the fantastic conception or description of a possible alternative world rests upon simplifications that follow from an underestimation of the complexity of conditions of life that are actually possible. In fact, the same is also seen to hold for the fictional-literary utopia which, however, compared with the political and social-philosophical program of utopia, appears to be relatively harmless—similar to a left-wing literary essay, compared with left-wing ideas in the political, editorial, or business section of a newspaper.

3. The concretization of the contemporary critique of utopianism refers primarily to the *utopia of socialist society*. In so doing, it assumes a tradition of utopia that reaches back through Marx and the early socialists also to Thomas More's *Utopia* (and, in the sense of a socialism of the ruling class, even to Plato as well). Beyond this, it also reaches back to the "alternative forms of life" of the monastic orders and those Christian sects that were based upon the communal property of the Christian primitive communities. Yet the present critique of utopianism does not in fact arise out of the self-understanding of the socialist and especially the official Marxist tradition with regard to "utopia." Indeed, whereas the early socialists already viewed their conceptions as *realizable* and therefore no longer "utopian" and Marx and Engels completely distanced themselves from the "utopias" of the early socialists in the name of "scientific socialism," almost the whole of the present-day Western critique of utopia sees in Marxism and neo-Marxism (and

even, indeed, beyond this, in the bureaucratic socialism of the welfare state) a contemporary representation of a dangerous social utopia.

This indicates that the *Enlightenment's idea of progress*—at least the idea of the *triadic historical dialectic* that was inspired by the ideal of perfection that anticipated a transcendence of all institutionally and class-determined division and alienation between human beings and within human beings themselves—is in no way to be understood as the transcendence of the utopian intention but rather as the realization of its possibility. At times, the secular-theological or morally oriented notion of progress of the bourgeois Enlightenment—e.g., of the Freemasons, of Lessing and Kant—is already interpreted as the beginning of a utopian questioning and ultimately dissolution of the autonomy of politics effected in "absolutism" and of the ideologically neutral state of peace thereby attained.[14] The present-day critique of utopia assumes, in any case, that the literary-fictional spatial (or island) utopia of the sixteenth and seventeenth centuries first really displayed its practically significant seductive potentiality through its transformation into a realizable temporal or future utopia.[15]

4. From the very outset, the tradition of the socialistic-communistic social utopia is viewed by the present-day Western critique of utopia in connection with the *utopia of totalitarian planning and organization*. In so doing, the conceptions of Plato, Campanella, and Marx or Lenin are set alongside one another—roughly as an alternative to the idea of the "open society" in Karl Popper's sense. Even the program of eugenic human selection that is to be found in Plato and Campanella—not to mention in National Socialism—belongs as part to this image of utopia. Constitutive for utopian thought is assumed to be a conception in which no natural diversity and contingency of individual life or the cultural spheres or subsystems of society is tolerated—for example, no separation of the public and private spheres of life. What is here taken to be the utopian intention is the outline of a socialized life in which everything is conceived in its interdependence with everything else and is rationally construed from a unified plan. Thus, for example, politics, law, the economy, work, recreation, culture, science,

and, not least, sexuality, procreation, and education are conceived as functionally integrated components of a societal reality that is made by human beings and hence also regulated by them.

5. To the extent that the *utopia of social planning and organization* rests upon rational construction and regulation, the critique of this utopia can also have recourse to the relevant outlines of a *scientific-technical utopia*: for instance, to Descartes's and Bacon's program of a "regnum hominis" by means of scientific-technical domination over nature and, above all, to the *technocratic* application of this program to society since Saint-Simon.[16]

The dimension of the current critique of utopia just indicated gains its particular significance as well as its problematic from the fact that it is directed equally against the socialism of totalitarian planning in the East as well as Western industrial capitalism and it does so on the basis of the presupposition that not only the conscious utopia or scientific utopia "transcendence" of the former but also the unconscious utopia of the latter are to the highest degree "questionable." Let us seek to elaborate this more precisely.

It is not difficult to demonstrate that the Marxist social utopia, in which human beings in the classless society no longer suffer history but *make* it in solidaristic action, is to be understood as the integration of the scientific-technological-technocratic utopia of Bacon or Saint-Simon. Indeed, the Marxist thesis of the scientific "transcendence" of utopia rests upon the utopian scientism of the "unconditional" prognosis of history.[17] But it is precisely this utopian scientism that contains the central paradox of the integration of the technocratic utopia in that of the emancipation of human beings. For the conception of the release from political domination by means of the "adminstration of things" (Saint-Simon) or the self-identification of the politician as "social engineer" (Lenin) presupposes that human beings in the "realm of freedom" will be both autonomous *subjects* and regulatable *objects* (quasi-objects) of prognoses and planning.

Yet already in the "realm of necessity"—i.e., in the development of capitalist society that belongs to "prehistory"—human beings are, as has been shown, at least the subjects of their actions to the extent that their reaction to prognoses—known to them!—of their behavior cannot be predicted (see the phenomena of the "self-fulfilling" and "self-destroying" prophecy analyzed by Merton).[18] And the nonfulfillment of Marx's long-term predictions (e.g., the immiseration of the proletariat and the disappearance of the middle classes) basically rests upon the diverse reactions of human beings to the predictions (e.g., self-organization of workers in trade unions, sociopolitical reforms and economic policy in the sense of state interventionism). Yet, on the other hand, it has become apparent that precisely the first step in the direction of the "realm of freedom" in the sense of the total planning of society—the socialization (for which read state ownership) of the means of production and the seizure of central economic and political control of the worker through the "Party" as the subject of history—has reduced the broad masses of the population largely to mere "objects" of social engineering. And since then there seems to remain open to "real existing socialism" only the way towards "technocracy," which means not the supersession of political domination by the administration of things but by the administration of human beings as quasi-objects. Such a fate for state socialism was already predicted by Max Weber and thus, very soon after the seizure of power by state socialism in Russia, the so-called negative or antiutopias were depicted—in the East, for example, in Samjatin's *Us*, in the West in Huxley's *Brave New World* and Orwell's *1984*. Precisely this development seems to be a consequence of the unseen *subject-object-dialectic* of the linear extension of the scientific-technological utopia of the domination of human beings over nature by means of the technocratic utopia of the domination of human beings over human society as quasi-nature.[19] To this extent, however, the intellectual coercion of the application of scientific-technological categories—of mathematical calculation, or universalization in the sense of exchangeable qualities and functions[20]—to human beings is also effective in Western industrial society, restrained only by the political rights to participation by individuals and their—skillful or unskillful—practice in forms of communication and interaction that cannot or may not be replaced by automatable (formulable in computer language) acts of bureaucratic administration. What is decisive for the competition between the two major types of modern industrial society seems to be the question as to whether long-term planning of the technocratic type can be replaced by a dialogical type. For a radical alternative to so-called "social technics," which rests upon the calculability of human behavior on the basis of quasi-nomological prognoses and thereby upon a tendential "reification" of human "quasi-nature" by technocrats, can only be conceived of if long-term planning were possible on the basis of the ascertaining of human behavior by the constantly renewed consultation and agreement of all mature acting human subjects.

Measured in terms of social reality, however, the above alternative to technocracy itself seems, in turn, to be utopian. In fact it oversteps precisely that concept which appears to most social policy makers in Western industrial society as a ready-to-hand alternative to totalitarian technocracy: that which Karl Popper, in his critique of the "utopian social technology" of Marxism-Leninism, has propagated as "piecemeal social engineering."[21] According to this critique, the error of "utopian social technology" (of historicist planning) lies above all in the fact that it does not match the natural scientific method precisely enough to social reality. Instead of making, on the basis of the laws of movement of history, "unconditional predictions" concerning the irreversible course of history, the social sciences, just like the natural sciences (through "initial conditions" and "laws"), should provide "conditional predictions" that enable them to be tested through social experiments and so, through "trial and error," learn from history. Aside from this, according to Popper, social policy requires an *ethical* orientation that cannot, as in a historicist Marxism, be replaced by the "ethical futurism" of pregiven scientific insight into the necessary course of history. The ethical orientation, that is, the evaluation of positive or negative consequences (and "auxiliary consequences"!) of sociotechnical measures should not be determined in a utopian manner—i.e., by a long-term goal strategy in the sense of the teleology of human happiness—but rather from case to case in the removal of social injustices in the sense of avoidance of distress.

There is no doubt that this conception, especially in its second partial aspect, approximates very closely the immanent logic of the representative democracies and their social policy and therefore can be taken as broadly accepted in modern industrial countries. Nonetheless, it is questionable whether it is in a position to bring under control the already mentioned dangers of an unconscious utopian anticipation of the future, that (also) seems to occur in the industrialization process of Western capitalism, in such a manner as is necessary in the age of ecological crisis.

In the first place, it seems to me that the first partial aspect of the Popperian conception, the recommendation of "piecemeal social engineering" on the basis of "conditional predictions," itself seems to be still imprisoned unwittingly in the subject-object-dialectic of the scientistic-technological utopia. For, as Popper himself has recognized, it is in principle impossible to predict, for instance, the process of the progress of science because each prediction enters through self-reflection into this process and transforms the preconditions of the prediction in an irreversible form. This also implies, however, that—at least with regard to all social transformations that are mediated through public discourse and thereby also through the results of science—no "conditional predictions" in the sense of replicable natural scientific experiments are possible. To this extent, too, learning from history in the sense of "trial and error" is not really possible, but rather learning in the sense of ever-renewed but never strictly replicable attempts at the critical reconstruction of unique historical processes as a process of progress, as is attempted, for instance, in the history of science and other reconstructions of processes of rationalization. Thus, something like highly problematical *predictions* can exist in the historical realm only in the form of *extrapolations of trends*, on the basis of genuine natural laws and ad hoc plausible (but not verifiable in replicable experiments) hypotheses concerning human behavior on the basis of nonfalsifiable hypotheses about principles of rationality (see, for example, the models of world development by the "Club of Rome" and *Global 2000*).

Yet if this assessment of the first partial aspect of the Popperian conception is correct and if, on the other hand, the historicist claim to unconditional historical prognoses—and that means the scientific "transcendence" of utopia through the philosophy of history—is decisively rejected by Popper, then the burden of *ethical* responsibility for the consequences and side effects of human collective actions is strengthened in a dramatic manner. This is true, for example, at the present time, for the industrialization process and its consequences for the human biosphere and for the collective life of diverse peoples and cultures in the realm of the threatened biosphere.[22] If it is not possible to gain increasing knowledge of the desirable and undesirable consequences of collective actions in replicable social experiments; if ultimately an irreversible process must be assumed in which all predictions are themselves included, then it does indeed seem highly doubtful whether the "ad hoc" identification of particular *grievances* by those affected in different countries—in practice in Western democracies by potential voters—suffices, in order to make available normative standards of critical judgment upon the irreversible industrialization process as a whole. Is not a constant normative-ethical standard for the constantly renewed attempts at reconstruction of the civilization process and the critical judgment upon its immanent goals required? Stated differently: must not the spontaneous evaluation of the consequences and side effects of social policy in diverse countries itself still be discursively justified—in the sense of a macroethics of the possible survival and collective life of diverse peoples and cultures?

6. In my opinion, the dilemma of the scientistic-technocratic subject-object-dialectic just outlined is a central motif in the deviation of Western *Neo-Marxism*—especially that of Herbert Marcuse and the Frankfurt School—from orthodox ("objectivistic") Marxism-Leninism and, over and above that, the (in Horkheimer and Adorno often very pessimistic) diagnosis of the "dialectic of Enlightenment" in modern industrial society as a whole. In terms of the philosophy of science, the deviation

of the Frankfurt School from "objectivism" found its later expression in the so-called "positivism dispute" in German sociology.[23] For in this dispute, what was at issue was not really the false and hardly decidable question as to whether Karl Popper, contrary to his own self-estimation, was to be counted as a "positivist." Rather, from the Frankfurt School side, the issue was the uncoupling of the justification, on the basis of the philosophy of science, of a "Critical Theory" of the historical-reconstructive social sciences from the scientistic program— determined by a technological interest—of nomological explanation and prediction of natural and social processes. This program had, as has been suggested, dominated orthodox Marxism and the older positivism and was continued, it seemed, by Popper and Albert under the label of a "unified methodology of the empirical sciences" (although, ironically, Popper and Lakatos, under the influence of the debate on the history of science, undertook at that time decisive steps towards the destruction of the program of a unified methodology).[24]

At that time, under the growing influence of Jürgen Habermas, "critical theory," in association with the hermeneutic tradition and the "pragmatic turn" in the analytical philosophy of language, began to consider a normative dialogical-communications theoretical foundation of the reconstructive social sciences and, what was much more difficult, the democratic organization of social practice. And in this context, the concept of an ethics of the "ideal speech situation" or the "ideal community of communication" was also developed by Habermas and the author of this study.[25]

In the context of our question as to the concept of utopia held by the contemporary critique of utopianism, however, it must be emphasized that the no-longer scientistic-technocratic neo-Marxism—primarily of Bloch and Marcuse, but also Habermas—stands much more in the center of the critique of utopianism than does orthodox Marxism. Indeed, in certain circumstances, there exists an agreement between bourgeois-conservative critics of utopia and adherents of "real existing socialism" with regard to the negative assessment of the "new utopianism," of its "lack of realism," of its failure to appreciate the ordering function of the state and institutions, and possibly its dangerous nature as a fanatical ideology that provides encouragement to terrorism.[26] How is it possible to render this phenomenon intelligible?

On the one hand, one must return to the presuppositions of the contemporary neoconservative pragmatic critique of utopia, which converge in a remarkable manner in both the West and the East. On the other hand, one must consider the distinctive background of ideal and traditional-historical motifs that have led to the revival of the utopian dimension of Marxism in the work of Bloch, Marcuse, and, finally, of Habermas.

Let me make a few comments on the first suggestion. At the present time, it is no longer the case that the conservative status quo notion is opposed in every respect to the idea of progress. Rather, there exists today in both the West and the East a status quo notion held by so-called pragmatists, which absolutizes a norm of progress that is dictated to us by the so-called "factual constraints" of what is technically and economically feasible. This quasi-automatic and system-immanent progress of modern industrial society is today in fact taken to be the *realm of what is actually possible*; and, accordingly, any person is taken to be a utopian who—for example, in the light of the ecological crisis—believes it to be possible to break out of the general direction of things, in order perhaps to express through public discourse possible goals that are not pregiven as self-evident goals by the industrialization process.

At this point, I come to the second suggestion with regard to the specific grounds for this critique. It is indeed worthy of note that in neo-Marxism—for instance, in the work of Ernst Bloch—the line of tradition of the secularization of Judeo-Christian eschatology in the sense of speculative chiliasm—from Joachim of Fiore and the Kabbala up to German philosophy of history since Lessing—at least inspires Bloch's "Principle of Hope," much as the line of tradition of the rational social utopia was once traced by Karl Kautsky from its "transcendence" in Marx through the early Socialists back to Thomas More.[27] And with this general accentuation there was associated in Bloch's work—but also in that of Horkheimer, Adorno, and Marcuse, as well as Benjamin—the acknowledgment of a messianic-utopian hope that had by no means been scientifically "transcended" by Marx.[28]

The contemporary critique of utopianism has also finally discovered in Marcuse and even Habermas the Achilles heel of the chiliastic, fanatical tradition and thereby a secularized eschatology. In what follows, I cannot go more fully into Herbert Marcuse's utopia of "liberated existence," tinged by anarchistic-erotic and depth psychology elements. I must restrict myself to the conception of Habermas, who from the beginning sought to understand the scientifically "untranscendable" eschatological-utopian "surplus" of Marx's doctrine as the "postulate of practical reason" derived from Kant.[29] In fact, with Habermas the neo-Marxist problematic of the foundation of the philosophy of history—or, more accurately, the critical reconstruction of social history from a practical standpoint—took on that turn which allowed the problem of *ethics* to step into the foreground. Accordingly, in recent times, the critique of utopianism has directed itself against a specific conception of ethics which both Habermas and I basically adhere to. I wish to term it—in my terminology, and in the sense of a formulation that is indeed provocative for the critique of utopia—the ethics of the "ideal community of communication."

With regard to Habermas, the critique of utopianism has focused above all upon the formula of "domination-free communication" in the sense of the formation of a consensus through the unconstrained constraint of argument in discourse[30]; with regard to my own contribution above all upon the claim that the ethical basic norm—in fact, the principle of the formation of a consensus concerning norms in the argumentative discourse of an ideal community of communication—proves itself to be indisputably valid (binding) in the sense of a transcendental-pragmatic ultimate justification.[31] Against both aspects of the ethics of communication there is characteristically directed not merely a specific charge of utopianism but, in association with it, the professed suspicion that the adoption of such an ethics, and even the claim for its ultimate justification, amounts in practice to a kind of Robbespierrian terror of the ideal. What is said to be ignored here is the fact that, in a pluralistic, liberal-democratic social order, the "social validity" of norms must be a matter of *institutionalized procedures of enactment*. Over and above the recognition of the results of such procedures, in a democracy the recognition of norms—that is, moral as distinct from legal norms—and equally of religion must, in contrast, be a matter of conventional traditions voluntarily adhered to or, in the last instance, of private decisions of conscience. Because of this, in a democratic social order there can and should be no demand for the intersubjectively valid, discursive-ethical *legitimation* of legal institutions and procedures for the enactment of norms. And least of all can there or should there exist the state of affairs in which one part of society—namely, (Left) intellectuals—arrogates to itself the ideological-critical questioning of the "communicative competence" of the other part of society, for instance, that of the representatives of the "military-industrial complex."

What can we reply to these objections? Stated more generally, and in the sense of our presentation of themes: How does the ethics of the discursive-consensual justification or legitimation of norms and its conception of the ideal community of communication or domination-free discourse relate to the human utopian intention and to the critique of utopianism?

III The "Ethics of the Ideal Community of Communication" as the Partial Justification of the "Utopian Intention" and the Postulate of a "Critique of Utopian Reason"

Since what follows deals with a discursive endeavor—the defense of the ethics of discourse—I wish from the outset to provisionally clarify one point that refers to the status, rights, and duties of participants in discourse (for instance, philosophers, scientists, journalists, critics of "utopianism," and defenders of the "utopian intention"). They are all—and that includes the critics of utopianism, who defend the state and its institutions against "intellectual fanatics"—representatives of the "reasoning public sphere" (Kant, Frederick the Great), and as such they can place in question and ground (justify) norms and institutions through rational arguments, without such metainstitutional critique or legitimation directly acquiring *political-legal validity (force of law)*. This does not mean, however, *that the arguments could not be intersubjectively valid or invalid*; otherwise it is evident that the arguments of antiutopian defenders of institutions must also from the outset be meaningless.

To this extent, it must be conceded from the start that there exists an (esoteric?) sense of *intersubjective validity* with regard to the justifiability of norms that neither coincides with the *legal validity* nor can be traced back to the *conventional validity* of traditions or to *private decisions of conscience*. In contrast to a decisionistic formulation, the latter have nothing at all to do with the justification of the possible validity of norms, but rather only with the observation or nonobservation of norms, about which of course it must be decided even if a discursive consensus cannot be reached on the basis of rational arguments as to their validity. However, the *conventional* validity of norms on the basis of traditions is always already placed in question in principle, once the problem of the *justification through rational arguments* is raised at all. And this cultural turning point—the philosophical enlightenment in Greece—is even necessarily presupposed for his arguments by the defender of the unquestioned validity of archaic institutional norms, as, for example, in the case of Arnold Gehlen.[32]

Now at the present time, what is the relationship of the (esoteric) *validity of rationally justifiable norms* to validity in the sense of *legal validity* (on the basis of institutionalized procedures for the justification of norms) and to the *social validity* of norms?

Hermann Lübbe, a critic of the utopian ethics of discourse, equates the latter with *legal validity* and reduces the rational justification of the validity of norms either to state-institutionalized procedures of the justification of legally binding norms or else—as is apparent in the relatively legally free realm of international politics—to the procedures for the effective negotiation of treaties concerning norms (e.g., such as whale catch quotas between interested states).[33] One readily notices that in this manner the "esoteric" question regarding the *rational justification or legitimation* of norms in the sense of a philosophical ethics is well and truly "dissolved," i.e., should be recognized as an illusory problem. More precisely, as long as harmless esoteric thinkers (or else not completely harmless utopians, who place institutionalized procedures in question on the rational and international level, and in this manner lay the foundations at least for uncertainty) do not raise the question of justification or legitimation with reference to norms, these questions are solved "in a trivial manner" by procedures that are of a purely "technical-instrumental" nature.[34] Thus, as soon as those interested in the justification of norms (such as party members in a parliament or the opposing parties to a foreign policy conflict of interests) have agreed upon a common "higher goal," "instrumental reason"—apparently unjustly criticized by the Frankfurt School as insufficient—offers rules as to which norms are appropriate and thereby rationally binding with reference to the presupposed "higher goal." How does the ethics of discourse that stands under the suspicion of esotericism and utopianism reply to this sobering analysis?

Let us begin with the institutionalized procedures for the justification of norms upon which the internal political *legal validity* of norms rests. Can the latter—in contrast to the *rational justification* of norms—be equated with *social validity*? One could answer this in the affirmative if one took the functioning legal-constitutional state for granted or self-evident, as may perhaps be the case from the West German perspective (cases of house occupations and other citizen initiatives notwithstanding). But with regard to most presently existing states, the sociologist is justified in distinguishing sharply between the positive *legally enforced* norms and *socially valid*—i.e., enforceable or accepted as valid (even though not always followed)—norms. Yet the significance of this difference in most instances may lie in the fact that it throws up the in no way trivial problem of the *legitimizability* (i.e., justifiability in the sense of capable of reaching consensus) of norms enforced by positive law (or the institutionalized procedures for justification).[35]

But here we come to the ethical problem of the *rational justification of legal norms*. Is the procedural rationality presupposed here in Lübbe's sense sufficiently explicated by the effective agreement of transacting partners—party members in parliament or representatives of states—upon a common higher goal?

It is worth considering that the procedural-rationality of consensus formation outlined above can also be followed by a mafia, where the common higher goal of the opposing parties might be the undisturbed transaction of the drugs trade. This should not be taken to mean that the successful political negotiation of agreements does not frequently follow the pattern suggested by Lübbe.[36] What must be disputed, however, is the fact that this pattern of consensus formation is already that of *ethical reasoning*. More accurately, one could say that what is at issue is a pattern of the *strategic rationality* of the successful pursuit of interests, insofar as this can be achieved not always through the struggle of competitors but often more readily through (at least partial) cooperation.[37]

Yet is not the procedure of *strategic cooperation* the sole realistic form of consensus formation? And is not any attempt to postulate a procedure of consensus formation that would exclude the outlined instance of the mafia, *utopian* in the sense of the unrealizability and potential damage to the life-interests of those concerned? I believe that this question expresses the deepest doubts of the so-called pragmatists or political realists against the ethics of the ideal community of communication. Indeed, it is no coincidence that the suggested pattern of justification of norms through the negotiation of a contract may be traced back to Hobbes's model of the justification of the legal state by the social contract of human "wolves"—to a model in which the moral rationality of "natural laws" leads back to the strategic and instrumental rationality of fully calculated self-interest.

Would not such procedures exhaust the capacity of human rationality—against Kant's supposition that reason is to be viewed as a capacity for moral legislation opposed to natural self-interest and to a certain extent transsubjective? One must concede to the political realist at least this much, that a responsible politician—and this means a person who stands for a system of self-assertion whether it be an individual, a family, a group, or a state—can hardly ever reckon with the fact that an opposing party follows Kant's "categorical imperative" and, for example, never lies. Thus, does he not at least in practice *also* have to act *strategically* and in any case may not act in the sense of that rigorous recommendation of Kant according to which it is forbidden "out of love of humanity" to deceive a possible murderer about the victim sought by him?[38]

Before we attempt to answer this question, it seems necessary to state clearly why it is that an ethics of the ideal community of communication cannot recognize as ethically satisfactory the Hobbesian or Lübbe's model of the justification of norms by the agreement of interested parties. In my opinion, there are three grounds to be mentioned, all of which indicate the distinction between *consensual-communicative discursive rationality* and *strategic rationality*:

1. The most basic reason refers to the *strategic, thoroughly calculated self-interest as motive.* Under specific situational presuppositions, but not in principle in instances of conflicts of interests, an agreement indeed recommends itself in the sense of equalization of interests. For this reason, the Hobbesian human "wolf" does indeed in general have an interest in a legal state (e.g., in the fact that all laws are followed), but cannot in principle be induced to abandon, in the conclusion of an agreement (e.g., contractual agreement), his criminal reservation that counsels him, as the opportunity arises (if no sanctions are to be feared), to dispense with adherence to the contract and thus to extract the parasitic "surplus" advantage from the functioning legal order.

2. The second reason lies in the rejection of the (strategic) *transaction* model as such. According to this model, it is indeed perfectly possible to go back to common higher goals and thereby to find a basis for an agreement on norms that lies in the interest of all participants. In so doing, however, it is not the ethical *normatively justifying principle of the argumentative universalization of interests* that is followed but rather, in the context of all strategically effective offers of negotiation (and threats with negative consequences), the reflection upon common higher goals plays an effective role. In short, what is at issue is a *strategically settled compromise of interests.*

3. The third reason refers to the *consequences of the difference between the ethical principle of the universalization of the interests of*

all those concerned and the strategic principle of the ad hoc compromise between the interests of conflicting parties. In the first case, an agreement of conflicting parties at the cost of a concerned third party (as in the case of the mafia) is strictly forbidden; in the second, on the grounds of the effectiveness of transactions, it is in fact recommended.

In my opinion, this indicates that the transaction model of ad hoc agreement concerning instrumentally expedient norms has nothing at all to do with an ethical principle of normative justification (or legitimation), since—on the grounds of self-assertion and effectiveness—it avoids having to go back to a strict *transsubjective universalization principle.* Such a principle, however, was first stated by Kant in the "categorical imperative" as a principle of ethics; and the consensual-communicative discursive ethics views the Kantian principle as the formal internalization of the principle of *universalized reciprocity* which requires that concrete norms be justified where possible by an *agreement* (informational and argumentative mediation) upon the *interests of all those concerned.*

From this confrontation of discursive ethics with the rationality of strategic transactions one thing becomes immediately clear: If the rejection of the strategic model of agreement were to be utopian, then this must hold, interestingly enough, for the specified principle of ethics as such.

In this manner, we have reached a dialectically salient point in our discussion of the relationship between *utopia* and *ethics.* For the question now arises as to whether the specified principle of ethics itself proves to be untenable because of utopianism or whether—independently of the charge of utopia, which of course itself still requires clarification as to its meaning—it can be justified as binding by rational arguments. If the latter were to be the case, then this would mean at the same time that utopia—more precisely, a specific form of the human *utopian intention*—can be justified as being unavoidable and indispensable.

Yet how is the already indicated principle of ethics—the strict transsubjective principle of the universalized reciprocity of an unlimited ideal community of communication, in which all differences of opinion are to be resolved (only) by the formation of a consensus on the basis of the unconstrained constraint of arguments—to be *justified* by rational arguments?[39] Is not the specified principle already presupposed in any serious argumentation—thus also in solitary thought, insofar as it is to be intersubjectively valid—as the normative precondition for the possibility of an ideal discourse? Yet if this is the case, then the principle can obviously not be *justified*, without itself already being presupposed in a *petitio principii*. In short, it seems as if the rational justification of the principle of ethics must founder on the fact that any rational final justification leads into a logical trilemma: either (1) into an *infinite justification regression*, insofar as each principle of justification must itself again be justified, or (2) into a *logical circle* (*petitio principii*), in that the principle that is to be justified is already presupposed in its justification, or (3) into a dogmatization of a principle (axiom) that one is not prepared to justify any further.[40] (The latter seems to happen in the case of Kant who, in the *Critique of Practical Reason* abandons as impossible the attempt at a deductive justification of the moral law [through the transcendental deduction of freedom] and characterizes "the moral law" as "a fact of pure reason, of which we are *apriori* conscious and which is apodictically certain").[41]

It is true that the principle of ethics that we have introduced is already presupposed in every serious argument; and, accordingly, it can itself not be *justified* if, as is usual, one understands by "justification" a "proof" in the sense of mathematics or of logic (*deduction* of propositions from propositions in an axiomatizable syntactical-semantic system or *induction* of general propositions from particular propositions or, more generally, of propositional predicates from sense data). In this case (i.e., in each case in which *justifying* means *deriving something from something else*) there emerges with analytical necessity the already indicated logical trilemma of final justification. Yet, in a deeper sense, this is precisely dogmatic (and rests upon a *petitio principii*): to establish in the suggested sense the concept of philosophical *justification*, and this means, to assume from the outset that each justification must result from derivation *from something else*.

In the case of the necessary presupposition of the basic principle of discursive-consensual ethics of communication by each serious argument, the *philosophical final justification* of the principle of ethics lies precisely in the (reflexive) *untranscendability* of serious argumentation (and thereby also of the normative-ethical principle of discourse) for those participating in argumentation and thus, in a certain sense, in the reflexive self-ascertainment of reason.[42] The fact that the normative principle which is necessarily presupposed in all argumentation cannot be *logically proven* without a *logical circle* (and hence not without a *petitio principii*), in this case takes on a completely new and unusual significance. It is no longer interesting merely as an indication of the failure of a logical proof but rather as an indication of the fact that the principle which is presupposed, just like the argumentation itself, is unavoidable. For the unavoidability of the logical circle in a logical proof *follows* in this case from the—not syntactical or semantic but—*transcendental-pragmatic* (i.e., reflexively observable for the subject of argumentation) necessity of the presupposition of the principle in question. In short, what is decisive in this case is not the well-known impossibility of a *noncircular final proof*, but rather the fact that the principle in question *cannot*, without the *pragmatic self-contradiction*[43] of those who are participating in arguing, be disputed as such a principle (*i.e., not without inconsistency between the act of assertion* and the asserted *propositions*, as, for instance, in the propositions expressed in "I hereby assert that I do not exist" or "I hereby assert as true [i.e., intersubjectively valid], that a consensus regarding that which I assert cannot be expected in principle" or else, "I hereby assert as true that I am not obliged *in principle* to recognize all possible members of the unlimited community of argumentation as having equal rights").

Here in fact a—constantly blocked—line of tradition of the *philosophical final justification of principles* is indicated that reaches from the *elenchi* of Socrates and Aristotle via the—apparently metaphysically-psychologically relevant—refutations of the skeptics by Augustine and Descartes down to the—still methodically-solipsistically abbreviated—insight of Kant into the necessity of the presupposition of "I think" for all objectively

valid knowledge.[44] This line of tradition of reflexive final justification reaches its explicative self-transparency only in the
transcendental-pragmatic reflection upon the indisputable
claims to validity of speech (*intelligibility* of an intersubjectively
valid meaning, *truthfulness* of speech as a subjective expression,
truth in the sense of an in principle universal propositional
content capable of consensus and *correctness* or normative justifiability or legitimizability of speech as social communicative
action). It now first becomes clear that—due to the necessity of
the unlimited sharing of linguistic meaning and truth in the
sense of intersubjective validity—the presupposition of "I
think," which is inavoidable for theoretical arguments, is not
to be separated from the ethical-practical presupposition of
recognition of the norms of an ideal community of argumentation. In short, along with the overcoming of "methodical
solipsism," final justification as the reflexive self-ascertainment
of the unity of theoretical and practical reason becomes
possible.

Yet what follows from this line of argument for the possible
justification of the human *utopian intention*? First, one might be
inclined to limit its scope from the perspective that is critical
of utopia in the following manner: The indisputable necessity
of recognition of the outlined principle of ethics, so one might
argue, refers only to a *special ethics of discourse unburdened of
action*, in which the interest of reason in the redemption of the
validity claims of speech becomes separated in an artificial
imputation from the strategic-practical human interests of self-
assertion (or the systems of self-assertion with which they are
linked). Hence, so one might infer, it would be utopian in a
questionable sense to derive an appropriate ethical obligation
with regard to the life situation of practical conflicts of interest
outside argumentative discourse from the recognition of discursive ethics. Indeed, the possible practical conflicts of interest
among discursive interlocutors that exist independently of
their interest in the redemption of validity claims, are, according to this objection, not at all affected by discursive ethics.

What seems to me to be correct in this argument is the
following: The argumentative discourse—whose constitutive
idea for philosophy and science in the West goes back to Soc-

rates who contrasted it with the rhetorical discourse of the Sophists—in fact rests upon an idealization in the sense of the separation of *consensual-argumentative and strategic rationality.* This separation is not characteristic of human forms of communication prior to and outside the introduction of argumentative discourse and itself remains, for the discourse which it constitutes as an institution, "a regulative idea to which nothing empirical can fully correspond" (Kant). Yet from this state of affairs it follows in no way that the ethics presupposed in argumentative discourse is not binding for the settling of practical life conflicts. For the following too is always already presupposed a priori by every person who seriously argues (and this means, even those who merely raise a relevant question): namely, that under the normative conditions of an ideal community of communication, discourse is not merely one possible "language game" among others but rather, as the only conceivable instance of justification and legitimation, is applicable to disputed claims to validity in all possible language games.[45]

Thus, if, in cases of dispute over normative claims to validity in the context of conflicts of interest, a *rational redemption of justified claims* is to be achieved at all (and not merely a "solution" in the way of a transaction or open conflict), then discursive ethics must also be recognized as the basis of consensus formation regarding disputed norms. (This fact, however, that not a strategic but an argumentative-consensual solution should be achieved was always already recognized by those who raised the question as to the binding nature of an ethics!)

Of course, it would be utopian in a pejorative sense, namely incompatible with an "ethics of responsibility," if those who in a real life situation are responsible for a system of self-assertion—such as the politician in particular, but virtually every person—were to overlook the distinction between life-practice and discourse unburdened of action and without further ado to assume that their opponents (who likewise are tied to systems of self-assertion) will follow without reservation the basic norm of discursive ethics. Even if two responsible politicians have fully recognized in good faith the binding nature of discursive ethics, they—as representatives of different systems of self-assertion—cannot know this with certainty of each other and thereby reckon upon it. In this fact consists the *basic paradox of political ethics* (e.g., of disarmament negotiations): it rests upon the distinction and the never fully transcendable tension between *ethical* and *strategic* reason (*rationality*).

Accordingly, ethics seems to be fundamentally distinguished from utopia in the following manner: ethics, like utopia, commences from an *ideal* that is distinguished from existing reality; but it does not anticipate the ideal through the conception of an empirically possible alternative or counterworld; rather it views the ideal merely as a *regulative idea*, whose approximation to the conditions of reality—e.g., discursive consensus formation under the conditions of strategic self-assertion—can indeed be striven for but never be completely assumed to be realizable.

Although this *disjunction* between ethics and utopia is certainly not false, yet it does not do complete justice to the internal connection between both phenomena. The ethics of the ideal community of communication can in fact not be *satisfied* with viewing its ideal as a "regulative idea" in Kant's sense. In effect, everyone who engages in serious argument—and even before that, who communicates with other people in the sense of a possible redemption of validity claims and who assumes others and themselves to be responsible[46]—must *anticipate* as an *ideal state of affairs* and assume as fulfilled in a certain manner, counterfactually, the conditions of an ideal community of communication or an ideal speech situation. (At best, this is attested to through the pragmatic self-contradiction of a speaker at a discussion who attempts with increasing eagerness to convince his public of the contrary, as through the statement, "We must in fact all concede that we are in principle not in the position of abstracting from the individual peculiarities and shortcomings of our existence.")

Such a phenomenon seems to render transparent the most basic connection between *ethics* and *utopia*—and that also means, between *reason* and *utopia*. The connection is evidently one that is embedded in the "condition humaine" as unavoidable. Human beings, as *linguistic beings* who must share *meaning and truth with fellow beings* in order to be able to think in a valid form, must at all times *anticipate counterfactually* an *ideal form of communication and hence of social interaction.* This "assumption" is constitutive for the institution of argumentative discourse; but even before this, the human being as a linguistic being can never maintain a purely strategic relationship to his fellow beings as was nonetheless presupposed, for instance, in the Hobbesian "state of nature" as a meaningful fiction. (We have already sought to show that under this fictional presupposition the transition to a functioning legal-constitutional state cannot be conceived, because of the issue of criminal mental reservation.)

In my opinion the transcendental-pragmatically justifiable necessity for the counterfactual anticipation of an ideal community of communication of argumentative consensus formation must also be seen as a central philosophical counterargument against the theological doctrine of the total depravity of humanity through original sin and therefore against a radical antiutopian position, for instance, of Protestant Christianity. For the *obligation* in the long term to transcend the contradiction between reality and ideal is established together with the intellectually necessary anticipation of the ideal, and thus a purely ethical justification of the belief in progress is supplied which imposes on the skeptic the burden of proof for evidence of the impossibility of progress.[47]

One can interpret this evidence of an inner connection between communicative reason, ethics, and utopia as justification for the indispensability and unavoidability of the *anthropological function of utopia*—i.e., the *utopian* intention in its most general sense. Yet in this case it must also be made equally clear to what extent the unavoidable utopian intention distinguishes itself from the "effusive"—to take up a term from Kant—intellectual form of utopia, which cannot be justified by means of transcendental philosophy.

It is quite correct that in arguing, that is, in serious reflection with a claim to validity, we view the communicative ideal state of affairs not merely as a "regulative idea," but over and above this must anticipate it counterfactually, and thus to a certain extent assume the formal structure of an alternative or counterworld to the existing reality. But precisely this anticipation does not refer to a "concrete utopia," whose empirical realization one could fictionally conceive of and describe, or could expect as the future emergent state of the world. For it refers only to the *normative preconditions* of ideal communication, whose empirical realization in a concrete society must indeed also be subject to additional preconditions of historical individualization—e.g., concrete institutions and conventions.

Insofar as this is the case, we must to a certain extent pay a price for the philosophical "transcendence" of the object of utopia: this "transcendence" is to be conceived of as both the preservation and negation of the utopian intention, as more and less than a *fictional utopia*. It is more insofar as it assumes not merely an alternative empirical social order but, according to the formal structure, the "ideal" of a community of communication of persons with equal rights; it is less insofar as it does not outline the pragmatic preconditions—e.g., the agreement over rules of procedure, limitations of time, limitations of themes, representation of those concerned by those who possess special role competencies, etc.—under which the empirical realization of the ideal could be conceived.

The fact that the "transcendence" of utopia just indicated is both more and less than a "concrete utopia," also indicates that, despite the counterfactual anticipation of the ideal, Kant's basic distinction between the "ideal" or the "regulative idea" and any empirically conceivable realization of the ideal remains valid. In that the normative preconditions of an ideal community of communication become realized under additional preconditions of historical individualization, these realizations in time must, at the same time and necessarily, fall below their normative ideal. The transcendental-philosophical "transcendence" of utopia escapes the *fundamental aporia of any fictional utopia* precisely through this untranscendable difference: that a further development towards the utopian realization of the ideal may not be conceived and, at the same time, must of necessity be conceived.

It seems to me that this antinomy characterizes in particular the aporia of the *utopian-chiliastic* version of Judeo-Christian *eschatology* and its secularized inheritance in the *speculative philosophy of history*, in which a temporally internal realization of the ideal is presupposed by means of a dialectical law of the course of history. Such a utopian historical teleology is, on the one hand, affirmed through the ethical transcendence of the utopian intention (as in the sense of Kant's "philosophical chiliasm")[48] and, on the other, critically negated. For neither a renunciation of the progressive realization of the ideal, nor the notion of an eschatological verification (or falsification) in time is compatible with the *ethically* justified postulate of progress. Hans Jonas has seen in this a still semitheological or Platonic-metaphysical inconsistency of Kantian philosophy of history in comparison, for instance, with the utopian philosophy of history of Hegel and Marx that he criticizes.[49] I would prefer to see in this rather a critical differentiation between (1) the *ethical* future dimension of the unconditional *ought*, (2) the *fictional-utopian* future dimension of the *hypothetical possibility*, and (3) the *speculative-historical* future dimension of *predictability* (of *causal and teleological necessity*). However, I wish to confer the priority of critical justifiability unequivocally upon *ethical-deontic teleology*. From its standpoint, the speculative and deterministic philosophy of history must be replaced by the constantly renewed attempt at a *critical* reconstruction of history with a practical intent (i.e., in the sense of its possible progressive continuability). This is the foundation of a "critical theory" of the social sciences.

At this point, it is apparent that the partial justification of the utopian intention through the transcendental-pragmatic foundation of an ethics of the ideal community of communication contains, at the same time, the postulate of a *critique of utopian reason*. In the present study, this program cannot be developed with regard to its quasi-epistemological dimension.[50] From a purely ethical-political standpoint I wish to offer by way of conclusion an exemplary elucidation in order that the challenge of the critique of utopia, sparked by Habermas's formula of "domination-free communication," does not remain unanswered.

IV The Utopia of "Domination-Free Communication" in the Light of a "Critique of Utopian Reason"

The formula of "domination-free communication" represents in a particularly striking manner the *ambivalence of the utopian intention* that we have just indicated. On the one hand, it expresses an indisputable assumption and an unrenounceable ethical postulate. On the other hand, it can signal a dangerous utopia: an anarchistic and fanatical idea, whose realization must turn into terror and ultimately into totalitarian domination. The criteria for the distinction of both dimensions of meaning supplies, first of all, the distinction that we have just introduced—but which goes back to Habermas—between "discourse unburdened of action" and those forms of communication in which, according to our interpretation, strategic action in the service of systems of self-assertion and consensual-communicative action in the sense of possible argumentative redemption of validity claims cannot be separated from one another.

The notion of "discourse unburdened of action"—which, since the Greek Enlightenment and totally since the West European Enlightenment of the modern period, has become constitutive for the institutions of philosophy, science, and the "rationalized public spheres," characterized by freedom of opinion and of the press—presupposes indisputably the notion of *domination-free communication* in the sense of the "unconstrained constraint" of arguments. As such, the institution of argumentative discourse has basically overstepped the conception of the redeemability of the validity claims of speech (meaning, veracity, truth, normative correctness) in the framework of conventional images of the world or institutions which could lay claim to a monopoly of interpretation. In this respect, it possesses postconventional and, to a certain extent like language itself, metainstitutional status (its possible function as instance of legitimation for all institutions and institutionalized norms rests upon this).

To be sure, it cannot be disputed that the quasi-institution just outlined has always presupposed for its realization the defensive and guarantor function of state or quasi-state authority. This political support of domination-free communication through functions of authority has, as it were, two sides: one side is the unequivocal task of the state to secure external defense. From this standpoint, discourse, which as such is basically related to an unlimited communication "system," must at the same time be treated as the subsystem of a state system of self-assertion that requires guarantee through authoritative power. To this extent, the political function of power—especially that of the enforceability of law—is presupposed in order to approximately implement the ideal consensus of those concerned against the actual consensus of limited interest groups. (Here, the distinctive legitimation of democratic state forms exists in the fact that the actual consensus of the majority of those concerned or their elected representatives which presupposes and results from public discourse, is considered to be a better approximation to the ideal consensus of those concerned than its anticipation through the "enlightened ruler" or an elite). However, leaving aside the support of discourse by state authority, there also exists the necessity for a quasi-political self-realization of discourse through internal self-defense. For the human participants in discourse, who do indeed also represent living systems of self-assertion, must still make the realization of domination-free communication itself dependent on a quasi-function of domination (e.g., those of a chairperson, leader of a discussion, and the like). The necessity for both these functions of defense and support renders apparent the dangerous utopianism of the anarchistic interpretation of the formula of "domination-free communication" and justifies its rejection. The regressive tendency of the anarchistic interpretation rests ultimately upon the confusion of the metainstitutional function of argumentation with the institutional authority function which makes it possible politically. In the illusory attempt to replace the latter by the former, the authoritarian power function of a charismatic leader must ultimately triumph and the revolution of the direct democracy of permanent discussion must terminate in a dictatorship.

Yet the distinction between the institutional power function, which can politically make possible domination-free discourse, and the—in this instance—metainstitutional legitimation function of discourse cannot only serve as a defense against the utopianism of an anarchistic fanatical ideology. It also releases, at the same time, the utopian—in a positive sense (of counterfactual anticipation of the ideal and its function as a regulative idea)—dimension of the metainstitution of domination-free discourse. In particular, viewed in terms of political history and legally, a revolutionary step with long-term consequences arises out of the fact that a legal-constitutional state as institution establishes a metainstitutional instance of discursive legitimation and critique and itself defends and guarantees the latter.

An important step in this direction was already carried out in the *separation of powers*. By this means, the direct authority function of the *executive* is integrated within the legitimatory institutions of the independent *legislature* (as representation of the people) and of the *judiciary*, which at least approximately embody the discursive principle. For in the democratic procedure of the institutionalized establishment and enactment of laws by majority decision there in no way lies merely a procedure of *arbitrary decision* [*Dezision*], but rather, compared with a dictatorship, at least also a procedure of the investigation and mediation of the argumentatively representable interests of all those concerned. And in the jurisdiction of a modern democracy—especially in the constitutional court—the legislature itself is once more related to an instance of legitimation and critique, an instance that in line with the *natural law tradition* already always presupposes *universal* principles of ethics (such as constitutional and human rights) in the positive law of particular constitutional states.

The relationship of reciprocal determination of the authority function and the critical or legitimatory function that is institutionalized in the separation of powers reveals its progressive possibilities, however, only in the relationship of state institutions as a whole to the metainstitution of argumentative discourse of the "rationalized public sphere." For in this metainstitution the state creates an instance of legitimation and critique that from the outset transcends and accordingly places in question the distinctiveness of the state as one system of self-assertion among others. Discourse, as it is represented in philosophy, science, and the rationalized public sphere is here always already grounded upon humanity as the substratum known to us as the unrestricted community of communication. And the state, as a distinctive system of self-assertion, has here—already in relation to the supranational church—opened the door to guaranteeing the possibility of a discursive solidarization and thus reasonable identification of individuals with humanity through its particular authority function.

The utopian dimension, in a positive sense, of this reciprocal relationship of particular institution and universal metainstitution becomes apparent in the basic aporia of Hegel's philosophy of the state. In this philosophy, it was indeed Hegel's intention that the *infinite freedom* of the person in the sense of Christian world religion and the *universality* of moral or legal principles of Stoic natural law should be once more "transcended" (following the suggestion of the Aristotelian *ethics of the polis*) in the "substantive morality" (*Sittlichkeit*) of the concrete and particular state—of a system of self-assertion subjected only to the causality of fate and thus of world history as the Last Judgment. This concept was bound to falter on the fact that the Christian freedom of conscience and the universal ethics of the postconventional age (of world religions and philosophical enlightenment) no longer permitted a total solidarization and identification of the person, as in wartime, with a merely particularistic system of self-assertion. This is not to say that war as the self-assertive function of the individual state was already superseded but rather that in this respect too the function of the state comes to require legitimation and must prove itself in the light of universalistic moral principles in the discourse of the argumentational public sphere.

The tension between the universalistic idea of the unrestricted community of discourse and any particularistic system of self-assertion becomes apparent in the tendency towards the *moralization of war*. Conservative intellectuals like to deplore the quite unavoidable transitional stages of this moralization: fanatically led religious wars and later wars between ideologies as self-declared representatives of the universalistic moral principle that stamps the particular enemy as a criminal to humanity. Yet the transcendence of these transitional stages can hardly lie in the return to the unquestioned authority of institutions (Arnold Gehlen), but rather only in the progressive realization of those regulative ideas which Kant specified in the mutually presupposed principles of the *argumentational public sphere*, of *republicanism*, and of the *legal community of world citizens*.

With these three regulative principles of a morally postulated process of progress there are, however, signified three inter-dependent dimensions of the progressive realization of the discursive principle and thereby domination-free communication as a regulative idea. In the internal state sphere of the present day, what is at issue is the not merely legal but also economic realization of freedom of communication and infor-mation mediated by the media, as well as so-called "democra-tization" and "participation"; in the supra- or interstate sphere what is at issue is the dimension of the replacement of imper-ialistic and (neo) colonial power politics by a politics of accom-modation of interests through "talks" that are similar to discourse.

In both dimensions of the possible transformation of domi-nation into domination-free communication (e.g., of techno-cratic planning into dialogical planning through advice and compromise), it cannot be a matter in this regard of rendering completely unnecessary the political function of the exercise of power. For the possible transformation of domination, in its empirically conceivable realization, is itself also still dependent upon the exercise of the functions of defense and guarantee in terms of power politics: as, for instance, the internal state democratization and realization of freedom of communication are dependent upon the functions of the constitutional state that are in a position to hold in check the informal power functions of interest groups. Similarly, the interstate realization of the accommodation of interests through "talks" is dependent upon the simultaneous balancing out of strategic equilibrium between the large and small systems of self-assertion.

From the standpoint of a political ethics of responsibility it will thus never be permitted to totally abandon the enforcea-bility of law internally and strategic self-assertion externally. This is ruled out by the difference between the interest in a possible consensus of all concerned and the factual consensus of limited interest groups at the cost of a third party. To this extent, there does indeed exist the necessity of upholding the reciprocal conditional relationship between institutions and dis-course and equally between strategic and consensual-commu-nicative action. Yet this necessity in no way contradicts the fact

Ethics, Utopia, and the Critique of Utopia

that responsible politics stands at the same time under the regulative principle of a long-term strategy of the realization of the formal preconditions for an ideal community of communication at all levels of human interaction.

Notes

1. On Thomas More, see T. Nipperdey, "Die Utopie des Thomas Morus und der Beginn der Neuzeit," in his *Reformation, Revolution, Utopie*, Göttingen 1975. See also L. Stockinger, "Überlegungen zur Funktion der utopischen Erzählung in der frühen Neuzeit," in *Utopieforschung*, Frankfurt 1985, vol. 2, pp. 229–248.

2. See K. Mannheim, *Ideology and Utopia*, London, 1936.

3. See E. Bloch, *Geist der Utopie*, 2d ed., Frankfurt 1964, further, his *Das Prinzip Hoffnung*, 2 vols., Frankfurt 1959; H. Gekle (ed.), *Abschied von der Utopie*, Frankfurt 1980.

4. See G. W. Leibniz, *Theodicy*, part I, para. 10.

5. See A. G. Baumgarten, *Meditationes Philosophie de Nonnullis ad Poema Pertinentibus*, Halle 1735, pp. 20–22 (LI–LVII). On this see H.-J. Mähl, "Der poetische Staat. Utopie und Utopiereflexion bei den Frühromantikern," in *Utopieforschung*, vol. 3, p. 273–302.

6. See T. Ramm, *Die Grossen Sozialisten als Rechts-und Staatsphilosophen*, Stuttgart 1955.

7. See especially, K. Marx and F. Engels, "Manifesto of the Communist Party" (1848), in K. Marx, *The Revolutions of 1848*, Harmondsworth 1973; "The Class Struggles in France: 1848–1850" (1850), in K. Marx, *Surveys from Exile*, Harmondsworth 1973; and F. Egels, *Die Entwicklung des Sozialismus von der Utopie zur Wissenschaft* (1882), Berlin 1955.

8. See on this topic, Study Unit 20 of the Funkkolleg, *Praktische Philosophie/Ethik*, Weinheim 1984.

9. It seems that just such an unusual extension and substantiation of the anthropological concept of the function of utopia is envisaged, for instance, in the following remarks of Lars Gustafsson (in his *Utopien*, Munich 1970, pp. 92ff.): "Utopian patterns of thought are commonly associated with political radicalism, with the revolutionary tradition. In reality, it is quite unclear as to whether such a classification exhausts the field. It is not merely our conception of what a future based upon social preconditions that are *radically* different from the present ones could look like that required utopian conceptions. In our actual action within existing Western industrial society too [. . .] there exist elements that are difficult to explain if one did not imagine an unconscious utopianism as part of their background [. . .]. Every attempt to organize the present must contain an element of prediction [. . .]. Technocratic society too has its utopia, it also presupposes a transformation towards an unknown goal [. . .]."

10. I refer here to a central motif of the book by Hans Jonas, directed against Bloch's utopian "principle of hope." See H. Jonas, *Das Prinzip Verantwortung*, Frankfurt 1979, pp. 63ff.

11. In the context of the Bielefeld colloquium on utopia, the theme of a "critique of utopian reason" constitutes my own research topic, but the elaboration of this theme was not possible in the framework of an article. The results of this research are soon to be published in book form.

12. On the history of chiliasm as a potential of time or utopia of the future, see W. Nigg, *Das ewige Reich*, Erlenbach bei Zürich 1944; further on this see S. A. Jørgensen, "Utopisches Potential in der Bibel. Mythos, Eschatologie und Säkularisation" in *Utopieforschung*, vol. 1, pp. 375–401; also, J. Mahl, *Die Idee des goldenen Zeitalters im Werk des Novalis*, Heidelberg 1965; on Joachim of Fiore see now also F. Seibt, "Utopie als Funktion des abendländischen Denkens" in *Utopieforschung*, vol. 1, pp. 254–279.

13. In West Germany, the philosophy of Arnold Gehlen must be seen as the background to all critiques of the "utopianism of left-wing intellectuals" that are oriented towards an institutional theory. See especially, *Urmensch und Spätkultur*, Bonn 1956 and, most recently, *Moral and Hypermoral*, Frankfurt 1973. On the pragmatically oriented, neoconservative critique of utopia, see especially Hermann Lübbe, "Herrschaft und Planung" in *Die Frage nach dem Menschen. Festschrift für Max Müller*, Freiburg/Munich 1966, p. 188–211; his, *Fortschritt als Orientierungsproblem*, Freiburg 1975; his *Unsere stille Revolution*, Zürich 1976; his "Flucht in die Zukunft" in *Hochschulreform und Gegenaufklärung*, Freiburg 1972, pp. 75ff; also H. Schelsky, *Die Arbeit tun die anderen. Klassenkampf und Priesterherrschaft der Intellektuellen*, Opladen 1975; his *Die Hoffnung Blochs*, Stuttgart 1979. On the distancing of the Protestant neoorthodoxy from chiliastic and utopian speculation see G. Friedrich, *Utopie und Reich Gottes*, Göttingen n.d. In terms of political ideology, such disavowal of the utopian potential of the theological tradition converges with the untiring denunciation of it by E. Topitsch. See his *Gottwerdung und Revolution*, Pullach 1973, as well as "Die entzauberte Utopie" in *Neue deutsche Hefte*, 20, no. 4, 1973, pp. 3–25.

14. See, for example, R. Kosellek, *Kritik und Krise. Eine Studie zur Pathogenese der bürgerlichen Welt*, Freiburg/Munich 1959, as well as H. Kesting, *Geschichtsphilosophie und Weltbürgerkrieg*, Heidelberg 1959.

15. See H. Kesting, *Geschichtsphilosophie und Weltbürgerkrieg*, op. cit.; and, from a completely different nondenunciatory standpoint, H. Jonas, *Das Prinzip Verantwortung*, op. cit.

16. See on this also H. Lübbe, "Zur politischen Theorie der Technokratie," in his *Praxis der Philosophie, Praktische Philosophie, Geschichtsphilosophie*, Stuttgart 1978.

17. On the critique of the "unconditional prognoses" of history, see K. R. Popper, *The Poverty of Historicism*, London 1957.

18. See R. K. Merton, *Social Theory and Social Structure*, (revised edition), New York 1957, pp. 421ff. See also K.-O. Apel, "Types of Social Science in the Light of Human Cognitive Interests" in S. C. Brown (ed.), *Philosophical Disputes in the Social Sciences*, Sussex/New Jersey 1979, pp. 3–50.

19. See K.-O. Apel, "Types of Social Science," op. cit. and *Die "Erklären-Verstehen" Kontroverse in transzendental-pragmatischer Sicht*, Frankfurt 1979, especially III, 2.

20. See on this also L. Gustafsson, "Negation als Spiegel. Utopie aus epistemologischer Sicht," in *Utopieforschung*, vol. 1, pp. 280–292.

21. See K. R. Popper, *The Poverty of Historicism*, op. cit. as well as his *The Open Society and its Enemies*, vol. 2, 5th ed., London 1966.

Ethics, Utopia, and the Critique of Utopia

22. Hans Jonas (see n. 10), primarily, takes up the issue at this point. See also K.-O. Apel, "Die Konflikte unserer Seit und das Erfordernis einer ethischpolitischen Grundorientierung," in K.-O. Apel et al. (eds.), *Praktische Philosophie/Ethik, Reader 1*, Frankfurt 1980, pp. 267–291.

23. See T. W. Adorno et al., *The Positivist Dispute in German Sociology* (trans. G. Adey and D. Frisby), London/New York 1976.

24. See, for example, K. R. Popper, "On the Theory of the Objective Mind" in his *Objective Knowledge*, Oxford 1972, pp. 153–190, and I. Lakatos, "The History of Science and its Rational Reconstructions," *Boston Studies in the Philosophy of Science*, vol. 8, Dordrecht 1971, pp. 91–136.

25. See Habermas's contributions in J. Habermas/N. Luhmann, *Theorie der Gesellschaft oder Sozialtechnologie*, Frankfurt 1971, as well as his *Legitimation Crisis*, (trans. T. McCarthy), Cambridge, MA/London 1976; additionally, K.-O. Apel, *Transformation der Philosophie*, Frankfurt 1973, vol. 2, part 2, along with the contributions of Habermas and Apel in K.-O. Apel (ed.), *Sprachpragmatik und Philosophie*, Frankfurt 1976.

26. See on this point the works by H. Lübbe and H. Schelsky cited in n. 13.

27. See K. Kautsky, *Die Vorläufer des Neueren Sozialismus*, 2 vols., Stuttgart 1896, Cologne 1968.

28. Only apparently this seems to be opposed in Adorno's work to the antiutopian "ban on images," even the avoidance of any positive formulation of a societal ideal. It expresses much more—as already in negative theology—the radical nature of the transcendence of the existent and the knowledge concerning the implicit dependency of any concretized conception of an alternative world upon the contextual implication of conception in the sense of the world that is known. On the ban on images in Adorno, see J. Habermas, "Theodor W. Adorno," *Philosophical-Political Profiles*. On the epistemological problematic of the contextual implications of utopian alternative conceptions of the world, see L. Gustafsson, "Negation als Spiegel" in *Utopieforschung*, vol. 1, pp. 280–292.

29. See J. Habermas, "Zur Philosophischen Diskussion um Marx und den Marxismus," in *Theorie und Praxis*, 2nd ed., Frankfurt 1971, pp. 387–464.

30. See on this, J. Habermas, *Knowledge and Human Interests*, (trans. J. Shapiro), Boston/London 1971, I, 3, as well as J. Habermas/N. Luhmann, *Theorie der Gesellschaft oder Sozialtechnologie?*, op. cit., especially pp. 136ff. In addition, R. Spaemann, "Die Utopie der Herrschaftsfreiheit" in his *Zur Kritik der politischen Utopien*, Stuttgart 1977, pp. 124ff., as well as the accompanying correspondence between Habermas and Spaemann, ibid., pp. 127ff.

31. See K.-O. Apel, *Towards a Transformation of Philosophy*, op. cit., pp. 262ff., as well as his "Das Problem der philosophischen Letztbegründung in Lichte einer transzendentalen Sprachpragmatik," in B. Kanitscheider (ed.), *Sprache und Erkenntnis. Festschrift für G. Frey*, Innsbruck 1976, pp. 55–82. In addition, the discussion in W. Oelmuller (ed.), *Materialien zur Normendiskussion, vol. 1: Transzendentalphilosophische Normenbegründungen*, Paderborn 1978, pp. 123ff.

32. On the reconstruction of the Greek and, in turn, the modern enlightenment thresholds of culture in the sense of the attempted transition to a postconventional jusification of norms, see Study Units 3 and 4 of the Funkkolleg, *Praktische Philosophie/ Ethik*, op. cit.

33. See H. Lübbe, "Sind Normen methodisch begründbar?", in W. Oelmüller (ed.), *Transzendentalphilosophische Normenbegründungen*, op. cit., pp. 38ff. In addition see the contributions of H. Lübbe and C. F. Gethmann in W. Oelmüller, *Materialien zur Normendiskussion*, vol. 2, op. cit.

34. H. Lübbe's thesis is to be seen in connection with his metacritique of Horkkeimer's "critique of instrumental reason" in *Fortschritt als Orientierungsproblem*, op. cit., pp. 121ff.

35. See on this point also J. Habermas, *Legitimation Crisis*, op. cit.

36. See also H. Lübbe, "Pragmatismus und die Kunst der Diskursbegrenzung" in W. Oelmüller (ed.), *Materialien zur Normendiskussion*, vol. 2, op. cit., pp. 118ff.

37. On the problem of types of rationality and their mediation in the light of a communicative ethics, see K.-O. Apel, "Die Situation des Menschen als ethisches Problem," *Akten des XII Deutschen Kongresses für Philosophie*, Innsbruck 1981.

38. See I. Kant, "Über ein vermeintes Recht aus Menschenliebe zu lügen," *Akademie-Textausgabe*, Berlin 1968, vol. 8, pp. 432ff. See also "Perpetual Peace," in I. Kant, *On History* (ed. L. W. Beck), Indianapolis/New York 1963, pp. 85–135, especially pp. 106ff., where Kant declares himself for "fiat iustitia, pereat mundus" and does not recognize the necessity for a mediation between the strategic responsibility for success in politics and morality.

39. See the author's works cited in n. 25 and n. 31 as well as more recently in W. Kuhlmann, "Reflexive Letztbegründung," *Zeitschrift für Philosophische Forschung*, 35, 1981, pp. 3–26. In the meantime, the discussion concerning the possibility or impossibility of a rational ultimate justification of ethics has taken on such a wide scope that it cannot be sufficiently taken into account in the present context. The author hopes to make good this defect on another occasion.

40. See H. Albert, *Traktat über kritische Vernunft*, Tübingen 1969, p. 13.

41. See I. Kant, *Akademie-Textausgabe*, vol. 5, op. cit., pp. 46f. Ever since G. E. Moore in analytical metaethics, the objection of the "naturalistic fallacy" has been directed at the justification of ethical norms by reference to a "fact of reason." See K.-H. Ilting, "Der naturalistische Fehlschluss bei Kant" in M. Riedel (ed.), *Rehabilitierung der praktischen Vernunft*, Freiburg 1972, vol. 1, pp. 113–132. Even if, for all that, it were possible—contrary to Kant's opinion and in the sense of speculative idealism—to demonstrate the existence of free will independently of the already presupposed binding nature of the moral law (in the sense of "You can, therefore you should"), even then in my opinion—contrary to Kant's and Fichte's presuppositions—only a *necessary* but not a *sufficient* condition of the validity of the moral law would be thereby established; for under the mere presupposition of the freedom of the self in relation to a nonself, i.e., without the presupposition of the reciprocity of claims in a communication community of ego-subjects, the meaning and the necessity of something like ethics would not even be intelligible. In my opinion, there exists here the necessity for a communicative-theoretical transformation of transcendental philosophy.

42. The argument that is constantly advanced by decisionism, that human beings must also still *decide* for or against reason, does not refer to the normative *validity* of the discursive principle of reason—for this must also already be presupposed for the correct *understanding* of "decision"—but to the practical following or nonfollowing of the norm of reason. "Decisionism" itself rests precisely upon the confusion of this problem with that of the justification of validity.

Ethics, Utopia, and the Critique of Utopia

43. It is required that, for its part, the principle of self-contradiction, which is to be avoided pragmatically, must still be justified (see, for example, S. C. F. Gethmann/R. Hegselmann, "Das Problem der Begründung zwischen Fundamentalismus und Dezisionismus," in *Zeitschrift für allgemeine Wissenschaftstheorie*, vol. 8, 1977, pp. 342–368). Yet this demand apparently rests upon the presupposition, also found in H. Albert's work, of the *deductive*—or, in the broader sense, "inferred"—concept of justification. For, by means of a reflexive return to what is irreducible, it can indeed always be demonstrated that anyone who seriously engages in argument already lays claim to the principle in question. In this evidence there lies not so much a logically circular proof of the principle as rather the demonstration that, in the sense of the transcendent pragmatic reconstruction of the preconditions for the possibility of meaningful communication, there lies in it, at all events, an additional duty of justification with reference to the above mentioned principle that it places in question.

44. This presupposition is not to be confused with that of a metaphysical-theoretical or empirical-theoretical knowledge of the self. Further, whoever rightly disputes the presuppositionless evidence of the Cartesian knowledge of the "res cogitans"—as for instance Nietzsche—must in fact acknowledge the reflexive-performative certainty of precisely this act of argumentation and its claim to validity, if argumentation is to be meaningful.

45. Without this presupposition one cannot *seriously* enter into the activity of argumentation. See on this point. K.-O. Apel, "Warum transzendentale Sprachpragmatik?," in H. M. Baumgartner (ed.), *Prinzip Freiheit*, Freiburg/Munich 1979, pp. 13–43.

46. I do indeed take this thesis of Habermas's to be correct, but in contrast to him I see in this *anthropological* truth no substitute for the *transcendental-pragmatic* ultimate justification through strict reflection upon the indisputable presuppositions of those who, for instance, question the anthropological thesis, or who view it as a mere fact as being normatively unbinding for themselves. In short, the ultimate justification of the validity of ethical norms must—in contrast to the reconstruction of its meaning constitution—commence from the methodical primacy of discourse unburdened by action, because it must always already presuppose rendering problematic the validity claims of human communication as such. See on this point, K.-O. Apel, "Sprechakttheorie und tranzendentale Sprachpragmatik zur Frage ethischer Normen" in K.-O. Apel (ed.), *Sprachpragmatik und Philosophie*, Frankfurt 1976, especially pp. 122ff.

47. On this division of the burden of proof, see also I. Kant, *Akademie-Textausgabe*, vol. 8, pp. 308f.

48. See I. Kant, "Idea for a Universal History from a Cosmopolitan Point of View," in I. Kant, *On History*, op. cit., pp. 27f.

49. See H. Jonas, *Das Prinzip Verantwortung*, op. cit., pp. 227ff.

50. See n. 11 above. In this context belong also the very interesting statements by Lars Gustafsson in his "Negation als Spiegel," op. cit., pp. 290–292.

2

Discourse Ethics: Notes on a Program of Philosophical Justification

Jürgen Habermas

I Propaedeutic Considerations

In his recent book *After Virtue,* Alasdair MacIntyre argues that the Enlightenment's project of establishing a secularized morality free of metaphysical and religious assumptions has failed. He accepts as the incontestable outcome of the Enlightenment the same thing that Max Horkheimer once pointed out with critical intent: the idea that an instrumental reason restricted to purposive rationality must let its ends be determined by blind emotional attitudes and arbitrary decisions: "Reason is calculative; it can assess truths of fact and mathematical relations but nothing more. In the realm of practice it can speak only of means. About ends it must be silent."[1] Since Kant, this conclusion has been opposed by cognitivist moral philosophies that maintain, in one sense or another, that practical questions "admit of truth."

A number of significant current theoretical approaches, notably those of Kurt Baier, Marcus Singer, John Rawls, Paul Lorenzen, Ernst Tugendhat, and Karl-Otto Apel, derive from this Kantian tradition. All share the intention of analyzing the conditions for making impartial judgments of practical questions, judgments based solely on reasons.[2] Of these theories, Apel's is not the one elaborated in the most detail; nonetheless I consider his approach, in which an ethics of discourse is recognizable in outline form, to be the most promising at present. I would like to support my assessment of the current state of the debate in ethics by presenting a program of philosophical justification of my own. In so doing, I will address other cognitivist approaches only in passing and will concentrate primarily on elaborating the shared problematic that distinguishes cognitivist theories from noncognitivist approaches.

I will begin by singling out the "ought" character [*Sollgeltung*] of norms and the claims to validity raised in norm-related (or regulative) speech acts as the phenomena a philosophical ethics must be able to explain (part I, section 1). It becomes clear (in section 2) that such familiar philosophical positions as definitional theories of the metaphysical type and intuitionist value ethics on the one hand, and noncognitivist theories like emotivism and decisionism on the other, fail from the outset to address the phenomena in need of explanation; they assimilate normative statements to a false model, either the model of descriptive statements and evaluations or that of experiential statements and imperatives. Something similar is true of prescriptivism, which uses intentional statements as its model.[3] As I will show in part II, moral phenomena can be elucidated in terms of a formal-pragmatic analysis of communicative action, a type of action in which the actors are oriented to validity claims. It will become clear why philosophical ethics, unlike, for example, epistemology, can readily assume the form of a special theory of argumentation. In part III the fundamental question of moral theory will be posed: How can the principle of universalization, which alone enables us to reach agreement through argumentation on practical questions, itself be justified? This is where Apel's transcendental-pragmatic justification of ethics on the basis of general pragmatic presuppositions of argumentation as such enters the picture. We will see, however, that this "deduction" cannot claim the status of an ultimate justification [*Letztbegründung*], and I will show why such a strong claim should not even be raised. In the form proposed by Apel, the transcendental-pragmatic argument is even too weak to counter the consistent skeptic's opposition to *any* kind of rational ethics. This problem, finally, will require us to devote at least a few brief remarks to Hegel's critique of Kantian morality, in order to provide a simple interpretation of the primacy of ethical life [*Sittlichkeit*] over morality, an interpretation that is immune to neo-Aristotelian and neo-Hegelian attempts to ideologize it.*

II The Principle of Universalization as a Rule of Argumentation

The propaedeutic comments I have just made were meant to defend the cognitivist approach in ethics against the metaethical diversionary tactics of value skepticism and to lay the groundwork for answering the question in what sense and in what way moral commands and norms can be justified. In the substantive portion of my reflections (section 3) I will begin by reviewing the role played by normative validity claims in the practice of daily life, in order to explain how the deontological claim connected with commands and norms is distinguished from the assertoric claim. I will argue that there are compelling reasons for recasting moral theory in the form of an analysis of moral argumentation. In section 4 I will introduce the principle of universalization 'U' as a bridging principle that makes agreement in moral argumentation possible. The version of the principle that I will give excludes any monological application of this rule for argumentation. Finally, in section 5 I will take up certain ideas of Ernst Tugendhat and show that moral justifications are dependent on argumentation actually being carried out, not for pragmatic reasons of an equalization of power but for internal reasons, namely that real argument makes moral insight possible.

3 Assertoric and Normative Claims to Validity in Communicative Action

The attempt to ground ethics in the form of a logic of moral argumentation has no chance of success unless we can identify a special type of validity claim connected with commands and norms and can identify it on the level on which moral dilemmas initially emerge—within the horizon of the lifeworld, where

*Part I (sections 1 and 2) and part II (section 5) have been omitted here—EDS.

Strawson had to look for moral phenomena when he marshaled the evidence of ordinary language against the skeptic. If claims to validity do not appear in the plural there, in contexts of communicative action and thus prior to any reflection, then we cannot expect a differentiation between truth and normative rightness to occur on the level of argumentation either.

I will not repeat the analysis of action oriented to reaching understanding that I have presented elsewhere,[4] but would like to review one fundamental idea. I call interactions "communicative" when the participants coordinate their plans of action consensually, with the agreement reached at any point being evaluated in terms of the intersubjective recognition of validity claims. In cases where agreement is reached through explicit linguistic processes, the actors make three different claims to validity in their speech acts as they come to an agreement with one another about something. Those claims are claims to truth, claims to rightness, and claims to truthfulness, depending on whether the speaker refers to something in the objective world (as the totality of existing states of affairs), to something in the shared social world (as the totality of the legitimately regulated interpersonal relationships of a social group), or to something in his own subjective world (as the totality of experiences to which one has privileged access). Further, I distinguish between communicative and strategic action. Whereas in strategic action one actor seeks to *influence* the behavior of another by means of the threat of sanctions or the prospect of gratifications, in order to *cause* the interaction to continue as the first actor desires, in communicative action one actor seeks to *motivate* another *rationally* by relying on the illocutionary binding/bonding effect (*Bindungseffekt*) of the offer contained in his speech act.

The fact that a speaker can rationally motivate a hearer to accept such an offer is due not to the validity of what he says but to the speaker's guarantee that he will, if necessary, make efforts to redeem the claim that the hearer has accepted. It is this guarantee that effects the coordination between speaker and hearer. In the case of claims to truth or rightness, the speaker can redeem his guarantee discursively, that is, by adducing reasons; in the case of claims to truthfulness he does so through consistent behavior. (One can convince someone that he means what he says only through his actions, not by giving reasons.) As soon as the hearer accepts the guarantee offered by the speaker, obligations are assumed that have consequences for the interaction, obligations that are contained in the meaning of what was said. In the case of orders and directives, for instance, the obligations to act hold primarily for the hearer; in the case of promises and announcements, they hold for the speaker; in the case of agreements and contracts, they are symmetrical, holding for both parties; and in the case of substantive normative recommendations and warnings, they hold asymmetrically for both parties.

Unlike these regulative speech acts, the meaning of a constative speech act gives rise to obligations only insofar as the speaker and the hearer agree to base their actions on situational definitions that do not contradict the propositions they accept as true at any given point. Obligations to act flow directly from the meaning of an expressive speech act in that the speaker specifies what it is that his behavior does not contradict now and will not contradict in the future. Owing to the fact that communication oriented to reaching understanding has a validity basis, a speaker can persuade a hearer to accept a speech-act offer by guaranteeing that he will redeem a criticizable validity claim. In so doing he creates a binding/bonding effect between speaker and hearer that makes the continuation of their interaction possible.

The two *discursively redeemable* claims to validity which are of particular interest to us, i.e., claims to propositional truth and claims to normative rightness, however, play their roles as coordinators of action in different ways. A number of asymmetries between them suggest that they occupy different "loci" (*Sitz*) in the communicative practice of everyday life.

On the face of it, *assertoric statements* used in *constative speech acts* appear to be related to *facts* in a similar way as *normative statements* used in *regulative speech acts* are related to *legitimately ordered interpersonal relations*. The *truth* of propositions seems to signify the *existence* of states of affairs in much the same way as the *rightness* of actions signifies the *observance* of norms. If we look at the matter more closely, however, we notice some interesting differences. The relation of speech acts to norms is not the same as the relation of speech acts to facts. Let us look at the case of moral norms that can be formulated in terms of universal "ought" sentences or commandments, e.g.,

(a) 'One ought not to kill anybody.'

(a') 'It is commanded not to kill anybody.'

We make reference to norms of action of the above kind in regulative speech acts, and we do so in a variety of ways: by giving orders, making contracts, opening meetings, issuing warnings, granting exceptions, giving advice, etc. A moral norm, however, lays claim to meaning and validity regardless of whether it is promulgated or made use of in a specific way. A norm may be formulated in a statement like (a), but this act of formulating it, i.e., the writing of a sentence, *need not* itself be conceived of as a speech act, that is, as something other than the impersonal expression of the norm. Statements such as (a) are commands that we can address *secondarily,* in one way or another, through speech acts. This has no equivalent in the domain of facts. There are no assertoric propositions that have an existence independent of speech acts, as norms do. If such assertoric statements are to have pragmatic meaning at all, they *must* be used in a speech act. Unlike sentences (a) and (a'), descriptive statements such as

(b) 'Iron is magnetic', or

(b') 'It is the case that iron is magnetic'

cannot be expressed or used independently of the illocutionary role of a certain type of speech act if they are to retain their assertoric power.

We can account for this asymmetry by saying that claims to truth reside *only* in speech acts, whereas the locus of normative claims to validity is primarily in norms and only derivatively in speech acts.[5] To use an ontological mode of expression, we might say that this asymmetry is due to the fact that the orders of society, which we either conform to or deviate from, are not constituted *independently of validity,* as are the orders of nature, toward which we can assume an objectivating attitude. The social reality which we address in our regulative speech acts has by its very nature an *intrinsic* link to normative validity claims. Claims to truth, on the other hand, have no such intrinsic link to entities; they are inherently related only to the constative speech acts with which we refer to entities when we use fact-stating locutions to represent states of affairs.

Owing to the fact that normative validity claims are built into the universe of norms, the latter reveals a peculiar kind of objectivity vis-à-vis regulative speech acts, an objectivity that the universe of facts does not possess vis-à-vis constative speech acts. 'Objectivity' in this connection, to be sure, refers only to the independence of 'objective spirit'. For, of course, entities and facts are independent in a completely different sense than is everything we consider part of the social world when we take a norm-conformative attitude. For example, norms are dependent upon the continual reestablishment of legitimately ordered interpersonal relationships. They would assume a "utopian" character in the negative sense and lose their very meaning if we did not *complement* them, at least in our minds, by actors who might follow them and by actions which might fulfill them. States of affairs, for their part, must be assumed to exist independently of whether we formulate them by means of true propositions or not.

Normative claims to validity, then, *mediate* a *mutual dependence* of language and the social world that does not exist for the relation of language to the objective world. This interlocking of claims to validity that reside in norms and claims to validity raised in regulative speech acts is also connected with the *ambiguous nature* of *normative validity.* While there is an unequivocal relation between existing states of affairs and true propositions about them, the 'existence' or social currency of norms says nothing about whether the norms are valid. We must distinguish between the social fact that a norm is intersubjectively recognized and its worthiness to be recognized. There may be good reasons to consider the validity claim raised in a socially accepted norm to be unjustified. Conversely, a norm whose claim to validity is in fact redeemable does not necessarily meet with actual recognition or approval. Gaining acceptance on the part of a norm is encoded in a twofold fashion because our motives for recognizing normative claims to validity are rooted both in convictions and in sanctions, or derive from a complex mixture of rational insight and force. Typically, rationally motivated assent will be combined with empirical *acquiescence,* effected by weapons or goods, to form a belief in legitimacy whose component parts are difficult to isolate. Such alloys, however, are interesting in that they indicate that a positivistic enactment of norms is not sufficient to secure their *lasting* social acceptance. Enduring acceptance of a norm is *also* dependent on whether, in a given context of tradition, reasons for obedience can be mobilized, reasons that suffice to make the corresponding validity claim at least appear justified in the eyes of those concerned. Applied to modern societies, this means: no mass loyalty without legitimacy.[6]

But if in the long run the social currency of a norm depends on its being accepted as valid in the group to which it is addressed, and if this recognition is based in turn on the expectation that the corresponding claim to validity can be redeemed with reasons, then it follows that there is a connection between the 'existence' of norms on the one hand and the anticipated justifiability of the corresponding "ought" statements on the other, a connection for which there is no parallel in the ontic sphere. There is, certainly, an internal connection between the existence of states of affairs and the truth of assertoric statements, but there is no inner connection between the existence of states of affairs and the *expectation,* held by a certain group of people, that such statements can be justified. This difference may also explain why it is that when we ask what makes valid moral judgments possible we are compelled to proceed *directly* to a logic of practical discourse, whereas the question of the conditions for the validity of empirical judgments requires analysis in terms of epistemology and the philosophy of science, analysis that is, at least initially, independent of a logic of theoretical discourse.

4 The Moral Principle or the Criterion of Generalizing Maxims of Action

Following Toulmin,[7] I have recently set forth the outlines of a theory of argumentation.[8] I shall not discuss that here. In what follows, I presuppose that a theory of argumentation must take the form of an 'informal logic', because it is impossible to *force* agreement on theoretical and moral-practical issues either by means of deduction or on the basis of empirical evidence. To the degree to which arguments are deductively valid, i.e., compelling in terms of logical inference, they reveal nothing substantively new. To the degree to which arguments do have substantive content, they are based on experiences and needs/wants that are open to various interpretations in the light of changing theories using changing systems of description. Such experiences and needs/wants thus fail to offer an *ultimate* basis for argumentation.

In theoretical discourse the gap between particular observations and general hypotheses is bridged by some canon or other of induction. An analogous bridging principle is needed for practical discourse.[9] Accordingly, all studies of the logic of moral argumentation end up having to introduce a moral principle as a rule of argumentation that has a function equivalent to the principle of induction in the discourse of the empirical sciences.

Interestingly enough, in trying to identify such a moral principle, philosophers of diverse backgrounds always come up with principles whose basic idea is the same. *All* variants of cognitivist ethics take their bearings from the basic intuition contained in Kant's categorical imperative. What I am concerned with here is not the diversity of Kantian formulations but their underlying idea, which is designed to take into account the impersonal or general character of valid universal commands.[10] The moral principle is so conceived as to exclude as invalid any norm that could not meet with the qualified assent of all who are, or might be, affected by it. This bridging principle, which makes consensus possible, is to ensure that only those norms are accepted as valid which express a *general will*. As Kant noted time and time again, moral norms must be suitable for expression as "universal laws." The categorical imperative can be understood as a principle that requires the universalizability of *modes of action* and *maxims,* or of the *interests* furthered by them (that is, embodied in the norms of action). Kant wants to eliminate as invalid all those norms that "contradict" this requirement. He focuses on "that inner contradiction which promptly arises for an agent's maxim when his behavior can lead to its desired goal only upon the condition that it is not universally followed."[11] Admittedly, this and similar versions of the bridging principle imply a requirement of consistency which has led to *formalistic misunderstandings* and *selective interpretations.*

The principle of universalization is by no means exhausted by the requirement that moral norms must take the *form* of unconditionally universal "ought" statements. The *grammatical form* of normative statements alone, which does not permit such sentences to refer to or be addressed to particular groups or individuals, is not a sufficient condition for valid moral commands, for we could give such universal form to commands that are plainly immoral. What is more, in some respects the requirement of formal universality may well be too restrictive; it may make sense to submit nonmoral norms of action, whose range of jurisdiction is socially and spatio-temporally limited, to a practical discourse (restricted in this case to those concerned, and hence relative), and to test them for generalizability.

Other philosophers subscribe to a less formalistic view of the consistency required by the principle of universality. Their aim is to avoid the contradictions that occur when equal cases are treated unequally and unequal ones equally. R. M. Hare has given this requirement the form of a semantic postulate. As we do when we attribute descriptive predicates (". . . is red"), so we should attribute normative predicates (". . . is of value", ". . . is good", ". . . is right") in *conformity with a rule,* using the same linguistic expression in all cases that are the same in the respects relevant to the particular case. Applied to moral norms, Hare's consistency postulate comes to this: Every individual, before making a particular norm the basis for his moral judgment, should test if he can will the adoption of this norm by every other individual in a comparable situation. However, this, or another similar postulate is suitable to serve as a moral principle only if it is conceived as a warrant of impartiality in the process of judging. But one can hardly derive the meaning of impartiality from the notion of consistent language use.

Kurt Baier[12] and Bernard Gert[13] come closer to this meaning of the principle of universalization when they argue that valid moral norms must be generally teachable and publicly defendable. The same is true of Marcus Singer[14] when he proposes the requirement that norms are valid only if they ensure equality of treatment. Just as, however, an empirical check to see that allowance for disagreement has been made does not guarantee an impartial process of judging, so a norm cannot be considered the expression of the common interest of all who might be affected simply because it seems acceptable to some of them under the condition that it be applied in a nondiscriminatory fashion. The intuition expressed in the idea of the generalizability of maxims intends something more than this—namely, that valid norms must *deserve* recognition by *all* concerned. It is not sufficient, therefore, for *one person* to test

• whether he can will the adoption of a contested norm in consideration of the consequences and the indirect effects that would occur if all persons followed that norm; or

• whether every other person in an identical position could will the adoption of such a norm.

In both cases the process of judging is relative to the vantage point and perspective of *some* and not *all* concerned. True impartiality pertains only to that standpoint from which precisely those norms are generalizable that can count on universal assent because they perceptibly embody an interest common to all concerned. It is these norms that deserve intersubjective recognition. Thus the impartiality of judgment is expressed in a principle that constrains *all* concerned to adopt the perspectives of *all others* in the balancing of interests. The principle of universalization is intended to compel the *universal exchange of roles* that G. H. Mead called "ideal role-taking" or "universal discourse."[15] Thus every valid norm has to fulfill the condition that *all* concerned can accept the consequences and the side effects its *universal* observance can be anticipated to have for the satisfaction of *everyone's* interests (and that these consequences are preferred to those of known alternative possibilities for regulation).[16]

We should not, however, mistake this principle of universalization for a principle already containing the distinctive idea of an ethics of discourse. According to discourse ethics, a norm may claim validity only if all who might be affected by it reach (or would reach), *as participants in a practical discourse,* agreement that this norm is valid. This principle of discourse ethics (D), to which I will return after offering my justification for the principle of universalization (U), already *presupposes* that we *can* justify our choice of a norm. At this point in my argument that presupposition is what is at issue. I have introduced 'U' as a rule of argumentation which makes agreement in practical discourses possible whenever matters of concern to all are open to regulation in the equal interest of everyone. Once this bridging principle has been justified, we will be able to make the transition to discourse ethics. I have, however, formulated 'U' in a way that precludes a monological application of this principle: 'U' regulates only argumentation among a plurality of participants; it even suggests the perspective of real-life argumentations in which all concerned are admitted as participants. In this respect, our universalization principle differs from the one John Rawls proposes.

Rawls wants to ensure impartial consideration of all affected interests by putting the moral judge into a fictitious 'original position' where differences of power are eliminated, equal freedoms for all are guaranteed, and the individual is left in a condition of ignorance with regard to the position he might occupy in a future social order. Like Kant, Rawls operationalizes the standpoint of impartiality in such a way that every individual can undertake to justify basic norms on his own. The same holds for the moral philosopher himself. It is only logical, therefore, that Rawls views the substantive parts of his study (e.g., the principle of average utility), not as the *contribution* of a participant in argumentation to a process of discursive will-formation regarding the basic institutions of late capitalist society, but as the outcome of a 'theory of justice' which he, as an expert, is qualified to construct.

If we keep in mind the action-coordinating function that normative validity claims play in the communicative practice of everyday life, we see why the problems to be resolved in moral argumentation cannot be handled monologically but require a cooperative effort. By entering into a process of moral argumentation, the participants continue their communicative action in a reflexive attitude, with the aim of restoring a consensus that has been disrupted. Moral argumentation thus serves to settle conflicts of action by consensual means. Conflicts in the domain of norm-guided interaction can be traced directly to some disruption of a normative consensus. Repairing a disrupted consensus can mean one of two things: restoring intersubjective recognition to a validity claim after it has become controversial, or assuring intersubjective recognition for a new claim to validity which is a substitute for the old one. Agreement of this kind expresses a *common will*. If moral argumentation is to produce this kind of agreement, however, it is not enough for the individual to reflect on whether he can assent to a norm. It is not even enough for *all* individuals, each one on his own, to reflect in this way and then to register their votes. What is needed is a "real" process of argumentation in which the individuals concerned cooperate. Only an intersubjective process of reaching understanding can produce an agreement that is reflexive in nature; only it can give the participants the knowledge that they have collectively become convinced of something.

From this viewpoint, the categorical imperative needs to be reformulated as follows:

Rather than ascribing as valid to all others any maxim that I can will to be a universal law, I must submit my maxim to all others for purposes of discursively testing its claim to universality. The emphasis shifts from what each can will without contradiction to be a general law, to what all can will in agreement to be a universal norm.[17]

This version of the universality principle does in fact entail the idea of a cooperative process of argumentation. For one thing, nothing prevents the perspectively conditioned distortion of one's own interests by others better than his actual participation. It is in this pragmatic sense that the individual is the last court of appeal for judging what is in his best interest. On the other hand, the descriptive terms in which each individual perceives his interests must be open to criticism by others. Needs and wants are interpreted in the light of cultural values. Since cultural values are always components of traditions we share intersubjectively, the revision of the values used to interpret needs and wants cannot be a matter for individuals to handle monologically.[18]

III Discourse Ethics and Its Bases in Action Theory

With the introduction of the principle of universalization, the first step in the justification of a discourse ethics has been accomplished. We can review the systematic content of the argument in the form of an imaginary debate between an advocate of ethical cognitivism and an advocate of moral skepticism.

In the opening round it was a question of opening the die-hard skeptic's eyes to the domain of *moral phenomena*. In the second round the issue was whether practical questions *admit of truth*. We saw that as an ethical subjectivist the skeptic could score some points against the ethical objectivist. The cognitivist could salvage his position by asserting that for normative statements a claim to validity is only *analogous to a truth claim*. The third round opened with the skeptic's realistic observation that it is often impossible to reach a consensus on questions of moral principle, despite the best intentions of all concerned. Faced with the fact of a *pluralism of ultimate value orientations,* which seems to support the skeptic's position, the cognitivist has to try to demonstrate the existence of a bridging principle that makes consensus possible. A moral principle having been proposed, the question of cultural relativism occupies the next round of the argumentation. The skeptic voices the objection that 'U' represents a hasty generalization of moral intuitions peculiar to our own Western culture, a challenge to which the cognitivist will respond with a transcendental justification of his moral principle. In round five the skeptic brings in further objections to a *strategy of transcendental justification,* and the cognitivist meets them with a more cautious version of Apel's argument. In the sixth round, in the face of this promising justification of a discourse ethics, the skeptic can take *refuge in a refusal of discourse.* But as we shall see, by doing so he has maneuvered himself into a hopeless position. The theme of the seventh and last round of the debate is the skeptic's revival of the objections to ethical formalism that Hegel brought up in his criticism of Kant. On this issue the astute cognitivist will not hesitate to meet the well-considered reservations of his opponent halfway.

The external form of my presentation does not coincide precisely with the ideal course of the seven-round debate I have just sketched. To counter the deeply ingrained reductionist concept of rationality characteristic of empiricism and the reinterpretation of basic moral experiences that corresponds to it, I stressed (in section 1) the web of moral feelings and attitudes that is interwoven with the practice of everyday life. I turned next (in section 2) to metaethical arguments denying that practical questions admit of truth. These proved to be irrelevant, because we abandoned the false identification of normative and assertoric claims to validity and showed (in section 3) that propositional truth and normative rightness play different pragmatic roles in everyday communication. The skeptic was not impressed by this argument and restated his doubts that even the specific claims to validity associated with commands and norms could be justified. This objection fails if one adopts the principle of universalization (introduced in section 4) and can demonstrate (as in section 5) that this moral principle is a rule of argumentation comparable to the principle of induction and not a principle of participation in disguise.

This is where the debate stands now. Next, the skeptic will demand a justification for this bridging principle. I will meet the charge of having committed the ethnocentric fallacy with (in section 6) Apel's proposal for a transcendental-pragmatic justification of ethics. I will modify Apel's argument (in section 7) so as to give up any claim to "ultimate justification," without damage to the argument. In section 8, I will defend the principle of discourse ethics against the skeptic's renewed objections by showing that moral arguments are embedded in contexts of communicative action. This internal connection between morality and ethical life does not impose limits on the universality of moral claims of validity, but it does subject practical discourses to constraints to which theoretical discourses are not subject in the same way.

6 Is a Justification of the Moral Principle Necessary and Possible?

The demand for a justification of the moral principle is hardly unreasonable when one recalls that the Kantian categorical imperative, as well as the many variations of the universalization principle put forward by ethical cognitivists following in his footsteps, expresses a moral intuition whose scope is questionable. Certainly, only such norms of action as embody generalizable interests correspond to *our* conceptions of justice. But this "moral point of view" might be only the expression of the particular moral ideas of our Western culture. Paul Taylor's objection to Kurt Baier's proposal can be extended to all versions of the universalization principle. In view of the anthropological data available, we cannot but concede that the moral code expounded by Kantian moral theories is indeed only one among many:

However deeply our own conscience and moral outlook may have been shaped by it, we must recognize that other societies in the history of the world have been able to function on the basis of other codes. . . . To claim a person who is a member of those societies and who knows its moral code, nevertheless does not have true moral convictions is, it seems to me, fundamentally correct. But such a claim cannot be justified on the ground of our concept of the moral point of view, for that is to assume that the moral code of liberal Western society is the only genuine morality.[19]

There are, then, grounds for suspecting that the claim to universality raised by ethical cognitivists on behalf of the moral principle they happen to favor is based on an 'ethnocentric fallacy'. Cognitivists cannot evade the skeptic's demand that it be justified.

Where he does not simply appeal to a 'fact of reason', Kant bases his justification of the categorical imperative on the substantive normative concepts of autonomy and free will; by doing so he makes himself vulnerable to the objection that he has committed a *petitio principii*. In any case, the justification of the categorical imperative is so closely intertwined with the overall design of Kant's system that it would not be easy to defend it if the premises were changed. Contemporary moral theorists do not even offer a justification of the moral principle but content themselves with reconstructing pretheoretical knowledge. A case in point is John Rawls's concept of reflective equilibrium.[20] Another example is the constructivist proposal to erect a language of moral argumentation on a systematic basis; the introduction of a moral principle that regulates language is convincing only because it conceptually explicates *extant* intuitions.[21]

I am not dramatizing the situation when I say that cognitivists, faced with the demand for a justification of the universal validity of the principle of universalization, are in trouble.[22] The skeptic feels emboldened to recast his *doubts* about the possibility of justifying a universalist morality as an *assertion* that it is impossible to justify such a morality. Hans Albert took this tack with his *Treatise on Critical Reason*[23] by applying Popper's model of critical testing, which was developed for the philosophy of science and intended to take the place of traditional foundationalist and justification models, to the domain of practical philosophy. The attempts to justify moral principles with universal validity, according to Albert, ensnares the cognitivist in a "Münchhausen trilemma" in which he must choose between three equally unacceptable alternatives: putting up with an infinite regress, arbitrarily breaking off the chain of deduction, or making a circular argument. The status of this trilemma, however, is problematic. It arises only if one presupposes a *semantic concept of justification* that is oriented to a deductive relationship between statements and based solely on the concept of logical inference. This deductive concept of justification is obviously too narrow for the exposition of the pragmatic relations between argumentative speech acts. Principles of induction and universalization are introduced as rules of argumentation for the sole purpose of bridging the logical gap in *nondeductive* relations. These bridging principles, accordingly, are not susceptible of deductive justification, which is the only form of justification allowed by the Münchhausen trilemma.

Carrying on this line of argument, Karl-Otto Apel has subjected fallibilism to an illuminating metacritique and refuted the objection of the Münchhausen trilemma.[24] There is no need to go into the details of his argument. More important in the context of our problematic is that Apel has succeeded in revealing the buried dimension of the nondeductive justification of basic ethical norms. He revives the transcendental mode of justification using the tools of a pragmatics of language. One of the key elements of Apel's transcendental-pragmatic line of argumentation is the notion of a *performative contradiction*. A performative contradiction occurs when a constative speech act 'kp' rests on noncontingent presuppositions whose propositional content contradicts the asserted proposition 'p'. Following a suggestion by Jaakko Hintikka, Apel illustrates the significance of performative contradictions for understanding the classical arguments of the philosophy of consciousness. The example he chooses is the 'cogito ergo sum'. Descartes' argument can be reconstructed in terms of a performative contradiction by giving the judgment of an imaginary opponent the form of the speech act "I hereby doubt that I exist." The speaker raises a truth claim for the following proposition:

(a) "I do not exist (here and now)"

At the same time, by uttering statement (a), he ineluctably makes an existential assumption, the propositional content of which may be summed up in the expression

(b) "I exist (here and now),"

where the personal pronoun in both statements refers to one and the same person.[25]

Similarly, Apel uncovers a performative contradiction in the objection raised by the 'consistent fallibilist', who in his role as ethical skeptic denies the possibility of grounding moral principles and presents the above mentioned trilemma. Apel characterized the argument as follows: the proponent asserts the universal validity of the principle of universalization; he is contradicted by an opponent relying on the Münchhausen trilemma (t); based on (t), the opponent concludes that attempts to ground the universal validity of principles are meaningless. This the opponent calls the principle of fallibilism (f). But the opponent will have involved himself in a performative contradiction if the proponent can show that in making his argument he has to make assumptions that are inevitable in *any* argumentation game aiming at critical examination, and that the propositional content of those assumptions contradicts the principle (f). This is in fact the case, since the opponent, in putting forward his objection, necessarily assumes the validity of at least those logical rules that are irreplaceable if we are to understand his argument as a refutation. Even the consistent fallibilist has, in taking part in a process of reasoning, already accepted as valid a minimum number of unavoidable rules of criticism. This state of affairs, however, is incompatible with (f).

This debate about a 'minimal logic'[26] which is currently being carried out among critical rationalists is of interest to Apel insofar as it refutes the skeptic's claim that it is impossible to ground moral principles. But it does not thereby relieve the ethical cognitivist of the burden of proof. This controversy has also drawn attention to the fact that the injunction to avoid performative contradictions applies not only to individual speech acts and arguments but to argumentative speech in general. In "argumentation as such" Apel has gained a reference point that is as fundamental for the analysis of unavoidable rules as the "I think" or "consciousness as such" is for the philosophy of reflection. Just as someone who is interested in a theory of knowledge cannot adopt a standpoint outside his own cognitive acts (and thus remains caught in the self-referentiality of the subject of cognition), so too a person engaged in developing a theory of moral argumentation cannot adopt a standpoint outside the situation that is defined by the fact that he is taking part in a process of argumentation (e.g., with a skeptic who is following his every move like a shadow). For him, the situation of argumentation is just as inescapable as the process of cognition is for the transcendental philosopher. The theorist of argumentation becomes aware of the self-referentiality of his arguments, as the epistemologist becomes aware of the self-referentiality of his knowledge. Such awareness means giving up futile attempts at a deductive grounding of 'ultimate' principles and returning to the explication of 'unavoidable', i.e., universal and necessary, presuppositions. At this point the moral theorist will assume the role of the skeptic experimentally, in order to determine whether the skeptic's rejection of a specific moral principle involves him in a performative contradiction with the inescapable presuppositions of moral argumentation as such. In this indirect way, the cognitivist can demonstrate to the skeptic that in involving himself in a specific argument with the goal of refuting ethical cognitivism the skeptic must inevitably subscribe to certain tacit presuppositions of argumentation that are incompatible with the propositional content of his objection. Apel turns this form of performative refutation of the skeptic into a mode of justification, which he describes as follows:

If, on the one hand, a presupposition cannot be challenged in argumentation without actual performative self-contradiction, and if, on the other hand, it cannot be deductively grounded without formal-logical *petitio principii*, then it belongs to those transcendental-pragmatic presuppositions of argumentation that one must always (already) have accepted, if the language game of argumentation is to be meaningful.[27]

Thus the necessary justification of the proposed moral principle could take the following form: Every argumentation, regardless of the context in which it occurs, rests on pragmatic presuppositions from whose propositional content the principle of universalization 'U' can be derived.

7 Structure and Status of the Transcendental-Pragmatic Argument

Having established that a transcendental-pragmatic justification of the moral principle is in fact possible, I shall now present the argument itself. (a) I will begin by enumerating certain conditions that all transcendental-pragmatic arguments must satisfy. I will then use these criteria to assess two of the best-known proposals of this kind, namely, those of R. S. Peters and K.-O. Apel. (b) Second, I will present a version of the transcendental-pragmatic argument that can stand up to the familiar objections against it. (c) Finally, I will show that this justification of discourse ethics cannot have the status of an ultimate justification, and why there is no need to claim this status for it.

(a) Following Collingwood, a type of philosophical analysis has gained credence in England that corresponds quite closely to the procedure Apel terms 'transcendental pragmatics'. A. J. Watt calls it 'analysis of the presuppositions of a mode of discourse'. Watt characterizes the structure of this approach as follows:

> The strategy of this form of argument is to accept the skeptical conclusion that these principles are not open to any proof, being presuppositions of reasoning rather than conclusions from it, but to go on to argue that commitment to them is rationally inescapable because they must, logically, be assumed if one is to engage in a mode of thought essential to any rational human life. The claim is not exactly that the principles are *true*, but that their adoption is not a result of mere social convention or free personal decision: that a mistake is involved in repudiating them while continuing to use the form of thought and discourse in questions.[28]

Collingwood's influence shows up in the application of presuppositional analysis to the way specific *questions* are posed and dealt with: "A presuppositional justification would show that one was committed to certain principles by raising and considering a certain range of *questions*."[29] The purpose of such arguments is to prove that certain discourses entail inescapable presuppositions; moral principles would have to be derivable from the propositional content of such presuppositions. The significance of these arguments is proportional to the degree of generality of the discourses which are found to entail substantive normative presuppositions. Strictly speaking, arguments cannot be called 'transcendental' unless they deal with discourses, or the corresponding competences, so general that it is impossible to replace them by functional equivalents; they must be so constituted that they can be replaced only by discourses or competences of the same kind. Accordingly, it is of the utmost importance to specify the precise object domain to which the procedure of presuppositional analysis is to be applied.

Yet the delineation of an object domain must not already prejudge the normative content of its presuppositions, or one will be guilty of a *petitio principii* that could have been avoided. R. S. Peters tries to avoid both pitfalls. He limits himself to practical discourses, i.e., to processes of reaching understanding designed to answer practical questions of the form "what ought I/we to do?" In restricting himself to these issues, Peters hopes to single out an order of discourses for which there are no substitutes and at the same time to avoid normative prejudgments in the demarcation of practical discourses:

It is always possible to produce *ad hominem* arguments pointing out what any individual must actually presuppose in saying what he actually says. But these are bound to be very contingent, depending upon private idiosyncrasies, and would obviously be of little use in developing a general ethical theory. Of far more importance are arguments pointing to what any individual *must* presuppose in so far as he uses a public form of discourse in seriously discussing with others or with himself what he ought to do. In a similar way one might inquire into the presuppositions of using scientific discourse. These arguments would be concerned not with prying into individual idiosyncrasies but with probing public presuppositions.[30]

Only these *public* presuppositions are comparable to the transcendental preconditions on which the Kantian analysis was focused. Only of them can one say that they are inescapable presuppositions of irreplaceable discourses and in that sense universal.[31]

Peters proceeds to derive certain basic norms from the presuppositions of practical discourses: first, a fairness principle ("all people's claims should be equally considered"), and then more concrete principles like freedom of thought and expression. Instead, however, of identifying the relevant presuppositions of practical discourses one by one and subjecting their content to systematic analysis, Peters merely offers some ad hoc reflections. In my view, Peters's analyses are by no means without merit, but in the form he gives them they are open to two objections.

The first objection is a variant of the charge of a *petitio principii*, to the effect that in the presuppositions of discourse Peters finds only the normative substance he had previously put into his implicit definition of practical discourse. This objection could be raised against Peters's semantic deduction of the principle of equal treatment, for example.[32]

Apel tries to meet this objection by extending presuppositional analysis to the preconditions of argumentative speech *as such*, rather than restricting it to *moral* argumentation. He wants to show that any subject capable of speech and action necessarily makes substantive normative presuppositions as soon as he engages in any discourse with the intention of critically examining a hypothetical claim to validity. With this argumentative strategy Apel reaches even the skeptic who insists on a metaethical treatment of questions of moral theory and consequently refuses to be drawn into *moral* argumentation. Apel wants to make this kind of skeptic aware that no sooner does he object (and defend his objection) than he commits himself to an 'argumentation game' and thus to presuppositions that entangle him in a performative contradiction. Peters also makes occasional use of this more radical version of presuppositional analysis, as for example when grounding the principle of freedom of opinion:

The argument need not be based simply on the manifest interest of anyone who seriously asks the question "what ought I to do?". For the principle of liberty, at least in the sphere of opinion, is also surely a (general presupposition of this form of) discourse into which any rational being is initiated when he laboriously learns to reason. In matters where reason is paramount it is argument rather than force or inner illumination that is decisive. The conditions of argument include letting any rational being contribute to a public discussion . . .[33]

Admittedly, a second objection can be raised against such arguments, one that is not so easily refuted. True as it may be that freedom of opinion in the sense of freedom from external interference in the process of opinion formation is one of the inescapable pragmatic presuppositions of every argumentation, the fact remains that what the skeptic is now forced to accept is no more than the notion that as a *participant* in a process of *argumentation* he has implicitly recognized a 'principle of freedom of opinion'. This argument does not go far enough to convince him in his capacity as an *actor* as well. The validity of a norm of action, as for example a publicly guaranteed constitutional right to freedom of expression, cannot be justified in this fashion. It is by no means self-evident that rules which are unavoidable *within* discourses can also claim to be valid for regulating action *outside* of discourses. Even if participants in an argumentation are forced to make substantive normative presuppositions (e.g., to respect one another as competent subjects; to treat one another as equal partners; to assume one another's truthfulness; and to cooperate with one another),[34] they could still shake off this transcendental-pragmatic compulsion when they leave the field of argumentation. The necessity of making such presuppositions is not transferred directly from discourse to action. In any case, a separate justification would be required to explain why the normative content discovered in the pragmatic presuppositions of *argumentation* should have the power to *regulate action*.[35]

One cannot demonstrate a transfer of this kind as Apel and Peters try to do, namely by deriving basic ethical norms *directly* from the presuppositions of argumentation. Basic norms of law and morality fall outside the jurisdiction of moral theory; they must be viewed as substantive principles to be justified in practical discourses. Since historical circumstances change, every epoch sheds its own light upon fundamental moral-practical ideas. Nevertheless, in such practical discourses we always already make use of substantive normative rules of argumentation. It is *these rules* alone which transcendental pragmatics is in a position to derive.

(b) We must, then, return to the justification of the principle of universalization. We are now in a position to specify the role that the transcendental-pragmatic argument can play in this process. Its function is to help to show that the principle of universalization, which acts as a rule of argumentation, is implied by the presuppositions of argumentation in general. This requirement is met if it can be shown that

• every person who accepts the universal and necessary communicative presuppositions of argumentative speech, and who knows what it means to justify a norm of action, implicitly presupposes as valid the principle of universalization (whether in the form I gave it above or in an equivalent form).

It makes sense to distinguish three levels of presuppositions of argumentation, along the lines suggested by Aristotle: those at the logical level of products, those at the dialectical level of procedures, and those at the rhetorical level of processes.[36] First, reasoning or argumentation is designed to *produce* intrinsically cogent arguments with which we can redeem or repudiate claims to validity. This is the level on which I would situate the rules of a 'minimal logic' currently being discussed by the Popperians, for example, or the consistency requirements proposed by Hare and others. For simplicity's sake, I will follow the catalogue of presuppositions of argumentation drawn up by R. Alexy.[37] For the logical-semantic level, the following rules[38] can serve as *examples*:

(1.1) No speaker may contradict himself.

(1.2) Every speaker who applies predicate F to object A must be prepared to apply F to all other objects resembling A in all relevant aspects.

(1.3) Different speakers may not use the same expression with different meanings.

The presuppositions of argumentation at this level are logical and semantic rules that have no ethical content. They are not a suitable point of departure for a transcendental-pragmatic argument.

In *procedural* terms, arguments are processes of reaching understanding that are ordered in such a way that proponents and opponents, having assumed a hypothetical attitude and being relieved of the pressures of action and experience, can test validity claims that have become problematic. At this level are located the pragmatic presuppositions of a special form of interaction, namely, everything necessary for a search for truth organized in the form of a competition. Examples would include recognition of the accountability and truthfulness of all participants in the search. At this level we also situate general rules of jurisdiction and relevance that regulate themes for discussion, contributions to the argument, etc.[39] Again, I shall cite a few examples from Alexy's catalogue of rules:

(2.1) Every speaker may assert only what he really believes.

(2.2) A person who disputes a proposition or norm not under discussion must provide a reason for wanting to do so.

Some of these rules obviously have an ethical import. At this level, presuppositions come to the fore that are common to both discourses and action oriented to reaching understanding as such, e.g., presuppositions about relations of mutual recognition.

But to fall back directly here on argumentation's basis in action theory would be to put the cart before the horse. The presuppositions of an unrestrained competition for better arguments are, however, relevant to our purpose in that they are irreconcilable with traditional ethical philosophies which have to protect a dogmatic core of fundamental convictions from all criticism.

Finally, in *process* terms, argumentative speech is a process of communication which, given its goal of reaching a rationally motivated agreement, must satisfy improbable conditions. In argumentative speech we see the structures of a speech situation that is immune to repression and inequality in a particular way: it presents itself as a form of communication that adequately approximates ideal conditions. This is why I tried at one time to describe the presuppositions of argumentation as the defining characteristics of an ideal speech situation.[40] I cannot undertake here the elaboration, revision, and clarification that my earlier analysis would require, and accordingly the present essay is rightly characterized as a "sketch" or a "proposal." The intention of my earlier analysis still seems correct to me, namely, the reconstruction of the general symmetry conditions that every competent speaker who believes he is engaging in an argumentation must presuppose as adequately fulfilled. The presupposition of something like an "unrestricted communication community," an idea that Apel developed following Peirce and Mead, can be demonstrated through systematic analysis of performative contradictions. Participants in argumentation cannot avoid the presupposition that the structure of their communication, owing to certain characteristics that require formal description, rules out all external or internal coercion other than the force of the better argument, and thereby also neutralizes all motives other than that of the cooperative search for truth. Following my analysis, R. Alexy has suggested the following rules of discourse for this level:[41]

(3.1) Every subject with the competence to speak and act is allowed to take part in a discourse.

(3.2) a. Everyone is allowed to question any assertion whatever.

b. Everyone is allowed to introduce any assertion whatever into the discourse.

c. Everyone is allowed to express his attitudes, desires, and needs.[42]

(3.3) No speaker may, by internal or external coercion, be prevented from exercising his rights as laid down in (3.1) and (3.2).

A few explanations are in order here. Rule (3.1) defines the set of potential participants. It includes all subjects without exception who have the capacity to take part in argumentation. Rule (3.2) guarantees all participants equal opportunity to contribute to the argumentation and to put forth their own arguments. Rule (3.3) sets down conditions under which the right to universal access and the right to equal participation can be enjoyed equally by all, that is, without the possibility of repression, be it ever so subtle or covert.

If these considerations are to amount to something more than a definition favoring an ideal form of communication and

Discourse Ethics: Notes on Philosophical Justification

thus prejudging everything else, we must show that our rules of discourse are not mere *conventions* but inescapable presuppositions.

The presuppositions themselves are identified by convincing* a person who contests the hypothetical reconstructions offered that he is caught up in performative contradictions. In this process, I must appeal to the intuitive preunderstanding which every subject competent in speech and action brings to a process of argumentation. At this point I shall be content to discuss a few examples, indicating what such an analysis might actually look like.

(1) "Using good reasons, I finally convinced H that p" can be read as someone's report on the outcome of a discourse. In this discourse the speaker, by using reasons, motivated the hearer to accept the truth claim connected with the assertion 'p', that is, to consider 'p' true. Central to the meaning of the word 'convince' is the notion that a subject other than the speaker adopts a view on the basis of good reasons.

Which is why the statement

(1)+ "Using lies, I finally convinced H that p" is nonsensical. It can be revised to state:

(2) "Using lies, I finally talked H into believing that p."

I can refer someone to a dictionary to look up the meaning of the verb 'to convince'. But that will not explain *why* statement (1)+ is a semantic paradox that can be resolved by statement (2). To explain that, I can start with the internal connection between the expressions 'to convince someone of something' and 'to come to a reasoned agreement about something.' In the *final* analysis, convictions rest on a consensus that has been attained discursively. Now, statement (1)+ implies that H has formed his conviction under conditions which simply do not permit the formation of convictions. Such conditions contradict

*In what follows, Habermas contrasts *überzeugen* and *überreden*, here translated as "convince" vs. "talk into." The contrast is more emphatic in German than in English; *überzeugen* implies the use of argument, while "to cause to believe by argument" is one but not the only meaning of "convince."—TRANS.

the pragmatic presuppositions of argumentation as such (in this case rule 2.1). This presupposition holds not only for particular instances but inevitably for every process of argumentation. I can prove this, furthermore, by making a proponent who defends the truth of statement (1)+ aware that he thereby gets himself into a performative contradiction. For as soon as he cites a reason for the truth of (1)+, he enters a process of argumentation and has thereby accepted the presupposition, among others, that he can never *convince* an opponent of something by resorting to lies: at most, he can talk him into believing something to be true. But then the content of the assertion to be justified contradicts one of the presuppositions the proponent must operate with if his statement is to be regarded as a justification.

Similarly, performative contradictions can be demonstrated in the statements of a proponent who tries to justify the following sentence:

(3)+ "Having excluded persons A, B, C . . . from the discussion by silencing them or by foisting our interpretation on them, we were able to convince ourselves that N is justified."

Here A, B, C . . . shall be assumed to be (a) among the persons who would be affected by putting norm N into effect, and (b) are indistinguishable in their capacity as *participants in argumentation* in all relevant respects from the other participants. In any attempt to justify statement (3)+, a proponent would necessarily put himself in contradiction with the presuppositions set out in rules (3.1) to (3.3).

In giving these presuppositions the form of rules, Alexy may well be promoting the misconception that all actual discourses must conform to these rules. In many cases this is clearly not so, and in all cases we have to be content with approximations. This misconception may have something to do with the ambiguity of the word 'rule'. 'Rules of discourse', in Alexy's sense, are not *constitutive* of discourses in the sense in which chess rules are constitutive of real chess games. Whereas chess rules *determine* the playing of actual chess games, discourse rules are merely the *form* in which we present the implicitly adopted and intuitively known pragmatic presuppositions of a special type of speech, presuppositions that are adopted implicitly and known intuitively. If one wanted to make a serious comparison between argumentation and playing chess, one would find that the closest equivalents to the rules of chess are the rules pertaining to the construction and exchange of arguments. It is these rules that must be followed in *actual fact* if error-free argumentation is to take place in real life. By contrast, the discourse rules (3.1) to (3.3) state only that participants in argumentation must assume these conditions to be approximately realized, or realized in an approximation adequate enough for the purpose of argumentation, regardless of whether and to what extent these assumptions are counterfactual in a given case or not.

Discourses take place in particular social contexts and are subject to the limitations of time and space. Their participants are not Kantian intelligible characters but real human beings driven by other motives in addition to the one permissible motive of the search for truth. Topics and contributions have to be organized. The opening, adjournment, and resumption of discussions must be arranged. Given all this, institutional measures are needed to neutralize empirical limitations and avoidable internal and external interference sufficiently that the idealized conditions always already presupposed by participants in argumentation can at least be adequately approximated. The need to *institutionalize discourses*, trivial though it may be, does not contradict the partly counterfactual content of the presuppositions of discourse. To the contrary, attempts at institutionalization are subject in turn to normative conceptions of their goal, which spring *spontaneously* from our intuitive grasp of what argumentation is. This assertion can be verified empirically by studying the authorizations, exemptions, and procedural rules that have been used to institutionalize theoretical discourse in science or practical discourse in parliamentary activity.[43] To avoid the fallacy of misplaced concreteness, one must differentiate carefully between rules of discourse and conventions serving the institutionalization of discourses, conventions, that is, which help to actualize the ideal content of the presuppositions of argumentation under empirical conditions.

If, after these cursory remarks and pending a more detailed analysis, we accept the rules tentatively set down by Alexy, we have at our disposal, in conjunction with a weak idea of normative justification (i.e., one that does not prejudge the matter) premises that are strong enough for the derivation of the universalization principle 'U'.

If every person entering a process of argumentation must, among other things, make presuppositions whose content can be expressed in rules (3.1) to (3.3), and if, further, we understand what it means to discuss hypothetically whether norms of action ought to be adopted, then everyone who seriously tries to redeem normative claims to validity in a *discursive* way intuitively accepts procedural conditions which amount to an implicit acknowledgment of 'U'. It follows from the aforementioned rules of discourse that a contested norm cannot meet with the consent of the participants in a practical discourse unless 'U' holds true, that is,

• unless the consequences and the side effects which the *general* observance of a controversial norm can be expected to have for the satisfaction of the interests of *each individual* can be *freely* accepted by all.

But once it has been shown that 'U' can be grounded upon the presuppositions of argumentation through a transcendental-pragmatic derivation, discourse ethics itself can be formulated in terms of the economical principle 'D', which stipulates

• that only those norms can claim to be valid that meet (or could meet) with the approval of all concerned in their capacity as participants in a practical discourse.[44]

The justification of discourse ethics outlined here avoids confusions in the use of the term 'moral principle'. The only moral principle here is the universalization principle given above, which is conceived as a rule of argumentation and is part of the logic of practical discourses. 'U' must be carefully distinguished from

- substantive principles or basic norms, which can only be the *subject-matter* of moral argumentation;
- the normative content of the presuppositions of argumentation, which can be expressed in terms of rules (as in 3.1 to 3.3);
- 'D', the principle of discourse ethics, which stipulates the basic idea of a moral theory but does not form part of a logic of argumentation.

Previous attempts to ground discourse ethics were flawed because they tended to collapse *rules, contents,* and *presuppositions* of argumentation and in addition confused all of these with 'moral principles' in the sense of principles of philosophical ethics. 'D' is the assertion that the philosopher as moral theorist finally seeks to justify. The program of justification I have outlined in this essay describes what I regard as the most promising *road* to that goal. This road is the transcendental-pragmatic justification of a rule of argumentation with normative content. This rule is selective, to be sure, but it is also formal. It is not compatible with all substantive legal and moral principles, but it does not prejudge substantive regulations, as it is a rule of argumentation only. All contents, no matter how fundamental the action norm involved may be, must be made dependent on real discourses (or advocatory discourses conducted as substitutes for them). The moral theorist may take part in one of them as one of 'those concerned', perhaps even as an expert, but he may not conduct such discourses by *himself alone.* To the extent to which a moral theory touches on substantive areas—as Rawls's theory of justice does, for example—it must be understood as a contribution to a discourse among citizens.

(c) F. Kambartel has characterized the transcendental-pragmatic justification of discourse ethics as a procedure whereby a proponent tries to convince an opponent "who asks for justification of a rational principle put forth by someone else that his intention in asking the question, rightly understood, already involves an acceptance of that same principle."[45] The question arises as to what status this kind of justification may claim for itself. There are two schools of thought on the subject. The *first* refuses to speak of justification at all, since, as G. F. Gethmann points out, the recognition of something that is presupposed, in contradistinction to the recognition of something that is justified, is always hypothetical in the sense of being dependent on the prior acceptance of some end. The transcendental pragmatist counters this by pointing out that the necessity of accepting as valid the propositional content of inescapable presuppositions is all the less hypothetical the more general the discourses and competences are to which the presuppositional analysis of transcendental pragmatics is applied. The 'end' of argumentation, the argument continues, is not something we can treat quite so arbitrarily as the contingent ends of action. The former is so intimately interwoven with the intersubjective form of life to which subjects competent in speech and action belong that there is no way we can either posit or bypass it.

The *second* school of thought saddles transcendental pragmatics with a far-reaching claim to 'ultimate justification'. Ultimate justification is, as W. Kuhlmann emphasizes, supposed to create an absolutely secure basis of unerring knowledge, a basis that is immune to the fallibilism of all experiential knowledge:

> What I cannot meaningfully dispute (i.e., without contradicting myself) because it is necessarily presupposed in a process of meaningful argumentation, and what for the same reason I cannot meaningfully justify by deriving it deductively (except at the price of a *petitio principii*), is therefore a secure, *unshakable basis*. As participants in a process of argumentation, we have necessarily always already accepted the propositions and rules that belong to these presuppositions. We are unable to question them skeptically, either to dispute their validity or to adduce reasons for their validity.[46]

In other words, the type of argument that H. Lenk calls *petitio tollendi* serves only to demonstrate the inevitability of certain conditions and rules. It can be used only to show an opponent that he makes performative use of a *tollendum*, that is, of the very thing he wants to negate.

Demonstrating the existence of performative contradictions helps to identify the rules without which no argumentation game works; if one is to argue at all, there are no substitutes.

The fact that there are *no alternatives to these rules of argumentation is what is being proved; the rules themselves are not being justified.* True, the participants must have accepted them as a 'fact of reason' in setting out to argue. But this kind of argument cannot accomplish a transcendental deduction in the Kantian sense. The same thing holds for Apel's transcendental-pragmatic analysis of the presuppositions of argumentation as for Strawson's transcendental-semantic analysis of the presuppositions of judgments of experience. As G. Schönrich puts it,

the conceptual system underlying our experience owes its necessity to its being without alternatives. It is proved by showing that any attempt to develop an alternative system of concepts fails because it makes use of structural elements of the system it seeks to replace. . . . As long as Strawson's method remains confined to immanent conceptual relationships of implication, it is impossible for him to justify a conceptual system a priori, since it is in principle an open question whether the subjects of cognition will change their way of thinking about the world at some point or not.[47]

Schönrich warns provocatively against overburdening this *weak form of transcendental analysis*: "The acceptance of certain conceptual relationships of implication wrung from the skeptic through cunning can have no more than quasi-empirical validity."[48]

The explanation for Apel's stubborn retention of transcendental pragmatics' claim to ultimate justification lies, I believe, in his inconsistent recourse to motifs of thought that he himself discredited in the paradigm shift from the philosophy of consciousness to the philosophy of language, a shift which he promoted vigorously. In his interesting essay "The A priori of the Communication Community and the Foundations of Ethics," Apel refers, not coincidentally, to Fichte, who sought to "dissolve the fact of reason in its mere facticity" through "coenactment and re-enactment informed by insight" (*einsichtigen Mit- und Nachvollzug*).[49] Although Apel speaks of Fichte's "residual metaphysical dogmatism," he bases, if I understand him correctly, the transcendental-pragmatic claim to ultimate justification on the equation of propositional truth with the experience of certitude—an equation which can be made only in the reflective reenactment of something previously done intuitively, that is, only under the conditions of a philosophy of consciousness. Once we are on the analytic level of the pragmatics of language, it becomes impossible to make the above equation. This becomes clear when we isolate the steps in the justification, as outlined above, and present them one by one. My programmatic justification of discourse ethics requires

1. a definition of a universalization principle that functions as a rule of argumentation;

2. the identification of pragmatic presuppositions of argumentation that are inescapable and have a normative content;

3. the explicit statement of that normative content (e.g., in the form of discourse rules);

4. proof that a relation of material implication holds between steps 3 and 1 in connection with the idea of the justification of norms.

Step (2) in the analysis, for which the search for performative contradictions provides a guide, relies upon a maieutic method which services

2a. to make the skeptic who presents an objection aware of presuppositions he knows intuitively;

2b. to cast this pretheoretical knowledge in an explicit form, enabling the skeptic to recognize his intuitions in this description; and

2c. to corroborate, through counterexamples, the proponent's assertion that there are no alternatives to the presuppositions he has made explicit.

Substeps 2b and 2c contain unmistakable hypothetical elements. The description we employ to pass from 'know how' to 'know that' is a hypothetical reconstruction that can provide a more or less correct rendering of intuitions. It needs maieutic confirmation. Similarly, the assertion that there is no alternative to a given presupposition, that it is one of the inescapable, i.e., necessary and general presuppositions, has the status of an assumption. Like a lawlike hypothesis (*Gesetzeshypothese*), it must be checked against individual cases. To be sure, the intuitive knowledge of rules that subjects capable of speech and action must use if they are to be able to participate in argumentations is in a certain sense not fallible. But this is not true of *our reconstruction* of this pretheoretical knowledge and the claim to universality we connect with it. The *certainty* with which we put our knowledge of rules into practice does not extend to the *truth* of proposed reconstructions of presuppositions hypothesized to be general, for we have to put our reconstructions up for discussion in the same way the logician, for example, or the linguist presents his theoretical descriptions.

No harm is done, however, if we deny that the transcendental-pragmatic justification constitutes an ultimate justification. Rather, discourse ethics then takes its place among the reconstructive sciences concerned with the rational bases of knowing, speaking, and acting. If we cease striving for the foundationalism of traditional transcendental philosophy, we acquire new corroborative possibilities for discouse ethics. In competition with other ethical approaches, it can be used to describe empirically existing moral and legal ideas. It can be built into theories of the development of moral and legal consciousness at both the sociocultural and the ontogenetic levels and in this way can be made susceptible to indirect corroboration.

Nor need moral philosophy maintain the claim to ultimate justification because of its presumed relevance for the life-world. The *moral* intuitions of everyday life are not in need of clarification by the philosopher. In this case, the therapeutic self-understanding of philosophy, as initiated by Wittgenstein, is for once, I think, appropriate. Moral philosophy does have an enlightening or clarifying role to play vis-à-vis the confusions it has created in the minds of the educated, that is, to the extent to which value skepticism and legal positivism have established themselves as professional ideologies and have infiltrated everyday consciousness by way of the educational system. Together, skepticism and positivism have misinterpreted and thus neutralized the intuitions people acquire in a quasi-natural manner through socialization. Under extreme conditions they can further the moral disarmament of academic strata in the grip of a cultivated skepticism.[50]

8 Morality and Ethical Life (*Sittlichkeit*)

The dispute between the cognitivist and the skeptic has not yet
been definitively settled. The skeptic is not satisfied with the
surrender of the claim to ultimate justification and the prospect
of indirect confirmation of the theory of discourse. First, he
can (a) question the soundness of the transcendental-pragmatic
derivation of the moral principle. And even if he has to grant
that discourse ethics can be justified in this way, he still has
enough ammunition for one parting shot: he can (b) join the
ranks (revived for political reasons) of the neo-Aristotelians
and neo-Hegelians, who point out that discourse ethics does
not represent much of a gain for the real concern of philosophical ethics, since discourse ethics offers at best an empty
formalism whose practical consequences would even be disas-
trous. I will respond to these "final" two skeptical objections
only to the extent necessary to clarify the action-theoretical
bases of discourse ethics. Because morality is always embedded
in what Hegel called *Sittlichkeit* ('ethical life'), discourse ethics
is always subject to limitations—not, however, limitations that
could devalue its critical function or strengthen the skeptic in
his role as counterenlightener.

(a) The fact that the transcendental-pragmatic strategy of
justification is dependent on the objections of a skeptic is not
wholly to its advantage. Such arguments are telling only with
an opponent who does his proponent the favor of entering
into an argumentation. A skeptic who sees in advance that he
is to be caught in performative contradictions will reject the
game of wits from the outset. The *consistent skeptic* will deprive
the transcendental pragmatist of a basis for his argument. He
may, for example, take the attitude of an ethnologist vis-à-vis
his own culture, shaking his head over philosophical argumentation as though he were witnessing the unintelligible rites of
a strange tribe. Nietzsche perfected this way of looking at
philosophical matters, and Foucault has now rehabilitated it.
When this happens, the debate suddenly changes. If the cognitivist persists in his analysis, he will now be talking only *about*
the skeptic, not *with* him. At this point the cognitivist usually
throws up his arms, confessing he has no further remedy

against this dropout posture on the part of the skeptic. He will say that a willingness to argue and to think about one's actions really must be presupposed if the whole concern of moral theory is not to become pointless. There may be, he will continue, a residue of decisionism which cannot be disproved by argumentation—this, he will grant, is where the volitional moment comes into its own.

It seems to me that the moral theorist ought not to leave it at that. A skeptic who could wrest the topic from the cognitivist's grip by his mere behavior might not have the last word, but he would be in the right performatively, so to speak—he would assert his position mutely and impressively.

At this juncture in the discussion, if we can still call it that, it helps to keep in mind that through his behavior the skeptic voluntarily terminates his membership in the community of beings who argue—no less, but also no more. By refusing to argue, for instance, he cannot, even indirectly, deny that he moves in a shared sociocultural form of life, that he grew up in a web of communicative action, and that he reproduces his life in that web. In a word, the skeptic may reject morality but he cannot reject the ethical substance (*Sittlichkeit*) of the life circumstances in which he spends his waking hours, not unless he is willing to take refuge in suicide or serious mental illness. He cannot extricate himself, in other words, from the communicative practice of everyday life in which he is continually forced to take a position by giving a "yes" or a "no" response. As long as he is alive *at all*, a Robinson Crusoe existence through which the skeptic could demonstrate mutely and impressively that he has dropped out of communicative action is inconceivable, even as a thought experiment.

As we have seen, in reaching understanding about something in the world, subjects engaged in communicative action orient themselves to validity claims, including assertoric and normative validity claims. This is why there is no form of sociocultural life that is not at least implicitly geared to maintaining communicative action by means of argument—be the actual form of argumentation ever so rudimentary and be the institutionalization of discursive, consensus-building processes ever so inchoate. Once argumentation is conceived as a special form of rule-governed interaction, it reveals itself to be a reflective form of action oriented to reaching understanding. Argumentation derives the pragmatic presuppositions we found on the procedural level from the presuppositions of communicative action. The reciprocities undergirding the mutual recognition of competent subjects are already built into the action oriented to reaching understanding in which argumentation is *rooted*. That is why the radical skeptic's refusal to argue is an empty gesture. No mater how consistent a dropout may be, he cannot drop out of the communicative practice of everyday life, to the presuppositions of which he remains bound. And these in turn are, at least partly, identical with the presuppositions of argumentation as such.

Of course one would need to see in detail what normative content a presuppositional analysis of action oriented to reaching understanding can uncover. Alan Gewirth, for example, tries to derive basic ethical norms from the structures and general pragmatic presuppositions of goal-directed action.[51] He applies presuppositional analysis to the concept of the capacity to act spontaneously and teleologically, in order to show that every rational actor is forced to view the latitude he has to act, or more generally all resources for the realization of his ends, as goods. Interestingly, however, the teleological concept of action is inadequate to provide a transcendental-pragmatic justification of the notion of a *right* to such 'necessary goods,' as opposed to the idea of the goods themselves.[52] If the concept of communicative action is chosen as a basis instead, one gets, via the same methodological route, a concept of rationality strong enough to *extend* the transcendental-pragmatic derivation of the moral principle into the validity basis of action oriented to reaching understanding.[53] I cannot develop this idea farther here.[54]

If the concept of teleological action is replaced by the more comprehensive concept of action oriented to reaching understanding and the latter is made the basis of a transcendental-pragmatic analysis, then the skeptic will return to the scene with the argument that a concept of social action that has a built-in normative content necessarily prejudges the moral theory to be developed.[55] Assuming that action oriented to success and action oriented to reaching understanding are mutually exclusive types of action, opting for a move from communicative to strategic action seems to give the skeptic a new opportunity. He might insist not only on not arguing but also on not acting communicatively, thereby for the *second time* knocking the ground out from under a presuppositional analysis that traces discourse back to action.

In order to meet this new objection, the cognitivist has to be able to show that contexts of communicative action represent an order for which there is no substitute. I will dispense with conceptual arguments here and content myself with a factual observation intended to make the centrality of communicative action clear. The possibility of *choosing* between communicative and strategic action exists only abstractly; it exists only for someone who takes the contingent perspective of an individual actor. From the perspective of the lifeworld to which the actor belongs, these modes of action are not matters of free choice. The symbolic structures of every lifeworld are reproduced through three processes: cultural tradition, social integration, and socialization. As I have shown elsewhere,[56] these processes operate only in the medium of action oriented to reaching understanding. There is no other, equivalent medium in which these functions could be fulfilled. Now, individuals acquire and sustain their identity by appropriating traditions, by belonging to social groups, and by taking part in socializing interactions. That is why they, as individuals, have a choice between communicative and strategic action only in an abstract sense, i.e., in individual cases. They do not have the option of a long-term absence from contexts of action oriented to reaching understanding. That would mean regression to the monadic isolation of strategic action—or schizophrenia and suicide. In the long run such absence is self-destructive.

(b) If the skeptic has followed the argumentation that has gone on in his presence and has seen that his demonstrative exit from argumentation and action oriented to reaching understanding leads to an existential dead end, he may finally be ready to accept the justification of the moral principle we have proposed and the principle of discourse ethics we have introduced. He does so, however, only to now draw upon the remaining possibilities for argumentation; he calls into question the meaning of a formalistic ethics of this kind. Rooting the practice of argumentation in the lifeworld contexts of communicative action has called to mind Hegel's critique of Kant, which he will now bring to bear against the cognitivist.

Albrecht Wellmer has formulated this objection as follows:

> In the idea of a 'discourse free from domination' we only seem to have gained an objective criterion for 'assessing' the practical rationality of individuals or societies. In reality it would be an illusion to believe that we could emancipate ourselves from the normatively charged facticity of our historical situation with its traditional values and criteria of rationality and see history as a whole, and our position in it, 'from the sidelines,' so to speak. An attempt in this direction would end only in theoretical arbitrariness and practical terror.[57]

There is no need for me to reiterate the counterarguments Wellmer develops in his brilliant study. What I will do instead is to briefly review those aspects of the critique of formalism that deserve consideration.

i. The principle of discourse ethics makes reference to a *procedure*, namely, the discursive redemption of normative claims to validity. To that extent, discourse ethics can properly be characterized as *formal*, for it provides no substantive guidelines but only a procedure: practical discourse. Practical discourse is not a procedure for generating justified norms but a procedure for testing the validity of norms that are being proposed and hypothetically considered for adoption. This means that practical discourses depend on content brought to them from outside. It would be utterly pointless to engage in a practical discourse without a horizon provided by the lifeworld of a specific social group and without real conflicts in a concrete situation in which the actors considered it incumbent upon them to reach a consensual means of regulating some controversial social matter. Practical discourses are always related to the concrete point of departure of a disturbed normative agreement. These antecedent disruptions determine the topics that are "up" for discussion. This procedure, then, is not formal in the sense that it abstracts from content. Quite the contrary is true. In its openness, practical discourse is dependent upon contingent content being "fed" into it from outside. In discourse this content is subjected to a process in which particular values are ultimately discarded as being not susceptible to consensus. The question now arises whether this very selectivity might not make the procedure unsuitable for resolving practical questions.

ii. If we define practical issues as issues of the 'good life,' which invariably deal with the totality of a particular form of life or with the totality of an individual life history, then ethical formalism is incisive in the literal sense: the universalization principle acts like a knife that makes razor-sharp cuts between evaluative statements and strictly normative ones, between 'the good' and 'the just.' While cultural values may imply a claim to intersubjective acceptance, they are so inextricably inter-twined with the totality of a particular form of life that they cannot be said to claim normative validity in the strict sense. By their very nature, cultural values are at best *candidates* for embodiment in norms that are designed to express a general interest.

Participants can distance themselves only from norms and normative systems that have been set off from the totality of social life to the extent necessary to assume a hypothetical attitude toward them. Individuals who have been socialized cannot take a hypothetical attitude toward the form of life and the personal life history that have shaped their own identity. We are now in a position to define the scope of application of a deontological ethics: it covers only practical questions that can be debated rationally, i.e., those that hold out the prospect of consensus. It deals not with value preferences but with the normative validity of norms of action.

iii. It remains for us to deal with the hermeneutic objection that the discourse-ethical procedure for justifying norms is based on an extravagant idea whose practical consequences may even be dangerous. The principle of discourse ethics, like other principles, cannot regulate problems concerning its own application. The application of rules requires a practical pru-dence that is *prior to* the practical reason that discourse ethics explicates. Prudence itself is not subject to rules of discourse. If that is so, then the principle of discourse ethics can be effective only if it makes use of a faculty that links it with the local conventions of a hermeneutic point of departure and draws it back within the provincialism of a particular historical horizon.

This objection cannot be disputed as long as problems of application are viewed from a *third-person perspective*. The hermeneuticist's reflective insight, however, does not undercut the claim of the principle of discourse ethics to transcend all local conventions. No participant in argumentation can escape this claim as long as he takes a *performative attitude*, confronts normative claims to validity seriously, and does not objectify norms as social facts, i.e., avoids reducing them to something that is simply found in the world. The transcending force of validity claims that are dealt with in a straightforward manner has an empirical impact as well, and the hermeneuticist's reflective insight cannot catch up with it. The history of human rights in the modern constitutional states offers a wealth of examples showing that the application of principles, once they have been recognized, does not fluctuate wildly from one situation to another but tends to have a *stable direction*. The universal content of these norms itself makes those concerned aware, through the reflecting mirror of different interest positions, of the partiality and selectivity of applications. Applications can distort the meaning of the norm itself; we can operate in a more or less biased way in the dimension of prudent application. *Learning processes* are possible in this dimension, too.[58]

iv. In the face of foundationalist programs, one must stress the fact that practical discourses are in fact subject to limitations. What these are has been shown with consummate clarity by Albrecht Wellmer in an unpublished manuscript on "Reason and the Limits of Rational Discourse."

First, practical discourses—which must address, among other things, the question of how adequately needs are interpreted—are intimately linked with two other forms of argumentation: aesthetic and therapeutic criticism. These two forms of argumentation are not subject to the premise we posit for strict discourses, namely that *in principle* a rationally motivated agreement must always be reachable, where the phrase 'in principle' signifies the counterfactual reservation: if argumentation were conducted openly and continued long enough. But if in the last analysis forms of argumentation make up a system and cannot be isolated from one another, the fact that the practical (along with the theoretical and explicative) discourse, with its stricter claim, is related to forms of argumentation with more lenient criteria represents a liability for the former, a liability that originates in the sociohistorical situatedness of reason.

Second, practical discourses cannot be relieved of the burden of social conflicts to the degree that theoretical and explicative discourses can. They are less "free of the burdens of action," because contested norms tend to upset the balance of relations of intersubjective recognition. Even if it is conducted with discursive means, a dispute about norms is still rooted in the 'struggle for recognition.'

Third, like all argumentations, practical discourses resemble islands threatened with inundation in a sea of practice where the pattern of consensual conflict resolution is by no means the dominant one. The means of reaching agreement are repeatedly thrust aside by the instruments of force. Hence action that is oriented to ethical principles has to accommodate itself to imperatives that flow not from principles but from strategic necessities. On the one hand, the problem posed by an ethics of responsibility that is mindful of the temporal dimension is in essence trivial, since the perspective that an ethics of responsibility would use for a future-oriented assessment of the indirect effects of collective action can be derived from discourse ethics itself. On the other hand, these problems do give rise to questions of a political ethics, which deals with the aporias of a political practice whose goal is radical emancipation and which must take up those themes that were once part of Marxian revolutionary theory.

These limitations of practical discourses testify to the power history has over the transcending claims and interests of reason. The skeptic for his part tends to give an overdrawn account of these limits. The key to understanding the problem is that moral judgments, which provide "demotivated" answers to "decontextualized" questions require offsetting *compensation*. If we are clear about the feats of abstraction to which universalistic moralities owe their superiority to conventional ones, the old problem of the relationship between morality and ethical life appears in a different, rather trivial light.

For the hypothesis-testing participant in a discourse, the relevance of the experiential context of his lifeworld tends to pale. To him, the normativity of existing institutions seems just as open to question as the objectivity of things and events. In a discursive framework we perceive the lived world of the communicative practice of everyday life from an artificial, retrospective point of view: as we hypothetically consider claims of validity, the world of institutionally ordered relations becomes *moralized*, just as the world of existing states of affairs becomes *theoretized*. Facts and norms that had previously gone unquestioned can now be true or false, valid or invalid. In the realm of subjectivity, furthermore, modern art inaugurated a comparable thrust toward problematization. The world of lived experiences is aestheticized, that is, freed of the routines of *everyday perception* and the conventions of everyday action. For this reason, we would do well to look at the relationship of morality and ethical life as part of a more complex whole.

According to Max Weber, one of the features of Western rationalism is the creation in Europe of expert cultures that deal with cultural traditions in a reflective attitude and in so doing isolate the cognitive, aesthetic-expressive, and moral-practical components from one another. These cultures specialize in questions of truth or questions of taste or questions of justice. With the internal differentiation into what Weber calls 'spheres of value' (i.e., scientific production, art/art criticism, and law/morality), *the* elements that make up an almost indissoluble syndrome in the lifeworld are dissociated at the cultural level. It is only with these value spheres that reflective perspectives emerge, perspectives from which the lifeworld appears as 'practice' with which theory is to be mediated; as 'life' with which art is to be reconciled (in line with the surrealist credo), or even as 'ethical life' to which morality must be related.

From the viewpoint of a participant in moral argumentation, the lifeworld that he has put at a distance, a world in which unproblematic cultural givens of moral, cognitive, or expressive origin are interwoven with one another, appears as the sphere of ethical life. In this sphere, duties are so inextricably tied to concrete habitual behavior that they derive their self-evident quality from background convictions. In the sphere of ethical life, questions of justice are posed only within the horizon of questions concerning the good life, questions which have *always already* been *answered*. Under the unrelenting moralizing gaze of the participant in discourse this totality has lost its quality of naive acceptance, and the normative power of the factual has weakened. Familiar institutions can be transformed into so many instances of problematic justice. Under this gaze the store of traditional norms has disintegrated into those norms that can be jusified in terms of principles and those that are operative only de facto. The fusion of validity and social acceptance that characterizes the lifeworld has disintegrated. With this, the practice of everyday life separates into norms and values, into the component of the practical, which can be subjected to the demands of strict moral justification, and another component that cannot be moralized, a component that comprises the particular value orientations integrated to form individual and collective modes of life.

To be sure, cultural values too transcend de facto behavior. They congeal into historical and biographical syndromes of value orientations through which subjects can distinguish the 'good life' from the reproduction of 'mere life.' But ideas of the good life are not something we hold before us as an abstract 'ought.' Rather, they shape the identities of groups and individuals in such a way that they form an intrinsic part of culture or personality. Thus the development of the moral point of view goes hand in hand with a differentiation within the practical into *moral questions* and *evaluative questions*. Moral questions can in principle be decided rationally, i.e., in terms of *justice* or the generalizability of interests. Evaluative questions present themselves, at the most general level, as issues of the *good life* (or of self-realization); they are accessible to rational discussion only *within* the unproblematic horizon of a concrete historical form of life or the conduct of an individual life.

If we consider the abstraction achieved by morality, two things become clear: the increase in rationality achieved when we isolate issues of justice, and the problems of mediating morality and ethical life that arise therefrom. Within the horizon of the lifeworld, practical judgments derive both their concreteness and their power to motivate action from their inner connection to unquestioningly accepted ideas of the good life, in short, to ethical life and its institutions. Under these conditions, 'problematization' can never be so profound as to risk all the assets of the existing ethical substance. But the abstractive achievements required by the moral point of view do precisely that. This is why Kohlberg speaks of a transition to the *postconventional* stage of moral consciousness. At this stage moral judgment becomes dissociated from the local conventions and historical coloration of a particular form of life. It can no longer appeal to the naive validity of the context of the lifeworld. Moral answers retain only the rationally motivating force of insights. With the naive self-certainty of their lifeworld background they lose the thrust and efficacy of empirical motives for action. To become effective in practice, every universalistic morality has to make up for this loss of concrete ethical substance, which is initially accepted because of the cognitive advantages attending it. Universalistic moralities are dependent on forms of life that are 'rationalized' in that they make possible the prudent application of universal moral insights and they support motivations for translating insights into moral action. Only those forms of life that 'meet' universalistic moralities 'halfway' in this sense fulfill the conditions necessary to reverse the abstractive achievements of decontextualization and demotivation.

Notes

1. A. MacIntyre, *After Virtue* (London, 1981), p. 52; M. Horkheimer, *Eclipse of Reason* (New York, 1974), ch. 1, pp. 3–57.

2. R. Wimmer, *Universalisierung in der Ethik* (Frankfurt, 1980).

3. W. K. Frankena, *Ethics* (Englewood Cliffs, N.J., 1973), ch. 6.

4. J. Habermas, *Theory of Communicative Action*, vol. 1 (Boston, 1984), ch. 3, "Social Action, Purposive Activity, and Communication," p. 273ff.

5. At most we could compare theories, as higher-level systems of propositions, with norms. But it is debatable whether theories can be said to be true or false in the same

Discourse Ethics: Notes on Philosophical Justification

sense as the descriptions, predictions, and explanations we derive from them, whereas norms for their part are right or wrong in the same sense as the actions that satisfy them.

6. J. Habermas, "Legitimation Problems in the Modern State," in Habermas, *Communication and the Evolution of Society* (Boston, 1979), pp. 178ff. On the relation between the justification of norms, their being put into effect, and their being accepted, see also W. Kuhlmann, "Ist eine philosophische Letztbegründung von Normen möglich?" in *Funkkolleg Ethik*, Studienbegleitbrief 8, (Weinheim, 1981), p. 32.

7. *The Uses of Argument* (Cambridge, 1958).

8. J. Habermas, "Wahrheitstheorien," in H. Fahrenbach, ed., *Festschrift für W. Schulz* (Pfullingen, 1973), pp. 211ff; J. Habermas, *The Theory of Communicative Action*, vol. 1 (Boston, 1984), pp. 22ff.

9. On the logic of practical discourse, see T. McCarthy, *The Critical Theory of Jürgen Habermas* (Cambridge, MA, 1978), pp. 310ff.

10. Wimmer (1980), pp. 174ff.

11. G. Patzig, *Tatsachen, Normen, Sätze* (Stuttgart, 1980), p. 162.

12. K. Baier, *The Moral Point of View* (London, 1958).

13. B. Gert, *Moral Rules* (New York, 1976).

14. M. Singer, *Generalization in Ethics* (New York, 1961).

15. G. H. Mead, "Fragments on Ethics," in *Mind, Self, and Society* (Chicago, 1934), pp. 379ff. See also H. Joas, *G. H. Mead: A Contemporary Reexamination of His Thought* (Cambridge, MA, 1985); J. Habermas, *The Theory of Communicative Action*, vol. 2 (Boston, 1987), pp. 92ff.

16. With reference to B. Gert's *Moral Rules*, p. 72, G. Nunner-Winkler has raised the objection that 'U' is unable to single out from among the norms that fulfill the stated conditions those that are moral in the narrow sense and to exclude others (e.g., "you ought to smile when you say hello to people"). This objection is met when one proposes to call moral only those norms that are strictly universalizable, i.e., those that are invariable over historical time and across social groups. This usage of the moral theorist does not of course coincide with that of the sociologist or historian who tends to describe epoch-specific and culture-specific rules as moral rules, if they are accepted as such by the members of the group under study.

17. T. McCarthy (1978), p. 326.

18. S. Benhabib, "The Methodological Illusions of Modern Political Theory: The Case of Rawls and Habermas," in *Neue Hefte für Philosophie* 21, 1982, pp. 47ff.

19. P. Taylor, "The Ethnocentric Fallacy," in *The Monist* 1963, p. 570.

20. J. Rawls, *A Theory of Justice* (Cambridge, MA, 1971), pp. 20ff. and 40ff.

21. P. Lorenzen and O. Schwemmer, *Konstruktive Logik, Ethik und Wissenschaftstheorie* (Mannheim, 1973), pp. 107ff.

22. Wimmer (1980), pp. 358f.

23. H. Albert, *Treatise on Critical Reason* (New York, 1985).

24. K.-O. Apel, "The A priori of the Communication Community and the Foundations of Ethics," in Apel, *Towards a Transformation of Philosophy* (London, 1980), pp. 225ff.

25. K.-O. Apel, "The Problem of Philosophical Fundamental Grounding in Light of a Transcendental Pragmatics of Language," in K. Baynes, J. Bohman, T. McCarthy, eds., *After Philosophy* (Cambridge, MA, 1987), pp. 250–290.

26. H. Lenk, "Philosophische Logikbegründung und rationaler Kritizismus," in *Zeitschrift für Philosophische Forschung* 24, 1970, pp. 183ff.

27. Apel (1987), p. 277.

28. A. J. Watt, "Transcendental Arguments and Moral Principles," in *Philosophical Quarterly* 25, 1975, p. 40.

29. Ibid., p. 41.

30. R. S. Peters, *Ethics and Education* (London, 1974), pp. 114f.

31. Peters himself points this out: "If it could be shown that certain principles are necessary for a form of discourse to have meaning, to be applied or to have point, then this would be a very strong argument for the justification of the principles in question. They would show what anyone must be committed to who uses it seriously. Of course, it would be open for anyone to say that he is not so committed because he does not use this form of discourse or because he will give it up now that he realizes its presuppositions. This would be quite a feasible position to adopt in relation, for instance, to the discourse of witchcraft or astrology; for individuals are not necessarily initiated into it in our society, and they can exercise their discretion about whether they think and talk in this way or not. Many have, perhaps mistakenly, given up using religious language, for instance, because they have been brought to see that its use commits them to, e.g., saying things which purport to be true for which the truth conditions can never be produced. But it would be a very difficult position to adopt in relation to moral discourse. For it would entail a resolute refusal to talk or think about what ought to be done." Peters (1974), pp. 115f.

32. Ibid., p. 121.

33. Ibid., p. 181.

34. Kuhlmann (1981), pp. 64ff.

35. This constitutes a revision of assertions I made earlier. See J. Habermas and N. Luhmann, *Theorie der Gesellschaft oder Sozialtechnologie* (Frankfurt, 1971), pp. 136ff. Compare also Apel (1980), pp. 276ff.

36. B. R. Burleson, "On the Foundation of Rationality," in *Journal of the American Forensic Association* 1979, pp. 112ff.

37. R. Alexy, "Eine Theorie des praktischen Diskurses," in W. Oelmüller, ed., *Normenbegründung, Normendurchsetzung* (Paderborn, 1978); in this volume, pp. 151–190.

38. Ibid., p. 37. The numbering has been changed.

Discourse Ethics: Notes on Philosophical Justification

39. To the degree to which these are of a special kind and cannot be distilled from the general meaning of a competition for better arguments, they are *institutional* mechanisms that belong to a *different* level of analysis (see below).

40. Habermas, "Wahrheitstheorien" (1973), pp. 211ff.

41. Alexy (1978), p. 40; in this volume, pp. 166–167.

42. This presupposition is obviously irrelevant for theoretical discourses since they only test assertoric validity claims. All the same, it is one of the pragmatic presuppositions of argumentation as such.

43. See Habermas, "Die Utopie des guten Herrschers," in Habermas, *Kleine Politische Schriften I–IV* (Frankfurt, 1981), pp. 318ff.

44. A somewhat different formulation of the same principle can be found in F. Kambartel, "Moralisches Argumentieren," in Kambartel, ed., *Praktische Philosophie und konstruktive Wissenschaftstheorie* (Frankfurt, 1974), pp. 54ff. According to Kambartel, those norms for which the consent of all concerned can be obtained through 'rational dialogue' are justified. Justification is based on "a rational dialogue (or the sketch of such a dialogue) leading to an agreement by all participants that the orientation which is being questioned can be agreed to by all concerned in an imaginary situation of undistorted communication" (p. 68).

45. F. Kambartel, "Wie ist praktische Philosophie konstruktiv möglich?," in Kambartel (1974), p. 11.

46. Kuhlmann (1981), p. 57.

47. G. Schönrich, *Kategorien und Transzendentale Argumentation* (Frankfurt, 1981), pp. 196f.

48. Ibid., p. 200.

49. Apel (1980), p. 273 (translation altered). The quote by Fichte goes as follows: "Our method almost always is (a) to do something, whereby we are doubtless guided by a law of reason working in us.—In this case, what we are . . . is still a facticity.—Then we set about (b) to study and discover the law that guided our mechanically determined doing. What we at first apprehended immediately we now apprehend mediately through the principle and ground of its thusness, that is, we grasp the genesis of its determinacy. We thus progress from the factual analysis of parts to their genetic analysis. The genetic can also be factual but in a different way. Which is why we are forced to go beyond it to examine its genesis, and so on, until we reach absolute genesis, the genesis of the science of knowledge." J. G. Fichte, *Werke*, ed. F. Medicus (Leipzig, 1910), vol. 4, p. 206.

50. Things are different when we talk about the political relevance of an ethics of discourse, to the degree to which it affects the moral-practical basis of the legal system or any political aspect transcending the private sphere of morality. In this regard, that is, in regard to providing guidance for an emancipatory praxis, discourse ethics can acquire a significance for orienting action. It does so, however, not as an ethics, that is, not prescriptively in the direct sense, but indirectly, by becoming part of a critical social theory that can be used to interpret situations, as for example when it is used to differentiate between particular and universalizable interests.

51. A. Gewirth, *Reason and Morality* (Chicago, 1978).

52. A. MacIntyre has shown this to be the case: "Gewirth argues that anyone who holds that the prerequisites for his exercise of rational agency are necessary goods is logically committed to holding also that he has a right to these goods. But quite clearly the introduction of the concept of a right needs justification both because it is at this point a concept quite new to Gewirth's argument *and* because of the special character of the concept of right. It is first of all clear that the claim that I have a right to do or to have something is a quite different type of claim from the claim that I need or want or will be benefited by something. From the first—if it is the only relevant considera-tion—it follows that others ought not to interfere with my attempts to do or have whatever it is, whether it is for my own good or not. From the second it does not. And it makes no difference what kind of good or benefit is at issue." MacIntyre (1981), pp. 64f.

53. Habermas (1984), vol. 1, chs. 1 and 3. See also Stephen K. White, "On the Normative Structure of Action," in *Review of Politics* 44, 1982, pp. 282ff.

54. R. S. Peters has propagated this sort of analytical strategy in another context: "To say . . . that men ought to rely more on their reason, that they ought to be more concerned with first-hand justification, is to claim that they are systematically falling down on a job on which they are already engaged. It is not to commit some version of the naturalistic fallacy by basing a demand for a type of life on features of human life which make it distinctively human. For this would be to repeat the errors of the old Greek doctrine of function. Rather it is to say that human life already bears witness to the demands of reason. Without some acceptance by men of such demands their life would be unintelligible. But given the acceptance of such demands they are proceeding in a way which is inappropriate to satisfying them. Concern for truth is written into human life." R. S. Peters, *Education and the Education of Teachers* (London, 1977), pp. 104ff.

55. This question is sharply posed by T. McCarthy in W. Oelmüller, ed., *Transzenden-talphilosophische Normenbegründungen*, 1978, pp. 134ff.

56. Habermas (1987), vol. 2, pp. 140ff.

57. A. Wellmer, *Praktische Philosophie und Theorie der Gesellschaft* (Konstanz, 1979), pp. 40f.

58. I am referring to Tugendhat's concept of 'normative learning', as presented in G. Frankenberg and U. Rödel, *Von der Volkssouveränität zum Minderheitenschutz* (Frankfurt, 1981).

3

Transcendental Pragmatics and Critical Morality: On the Possibility and Moral Significance of a Self-Enlightenment of Reason

Dietrich Böhler

A motto to reflect upon—Socrates' redeemable rational inheritance:

I have always had the habit that I listen to nothing else in myself other than *logos* which for me, through reflection, has been shown to be the best.

What Plato puts in the mouth of Socrates in this statement, which I wish to characterize as the *principle of logos or discourse,* and what he elsewhere indicates through his critical-dialogical life-practice, we can elucidate and elaborate further in this manner: Socrates advances the claim that only those modes of action can be truly good and only that injunction or norm holds as binding which can be rationally defended in practical discourses and which prove in such critical testing to be well-justified, to be carried by the best argument. Socrates advances this claim exclusively in practical contexts. But this limitation is unfounded. For regardless of whether a person argues theoretically or practically, they always assume, through their argumentation or assertions, that what they assert can be held on the basis of good grounds, so that through testing it is shown to be a sound argument which, under ideal conditions of knowledge and speech, would also be recognized by all rational persons. In addition, the communicative action of argumentation *succeeds* as argumentation only if it is borne by the willingness *not to accept anything as valid other than that which also, and precisely in such discourses—which take place under ideal condi-*

tions (freedom of speech and equal rights of partners, of time, of competent participation)—can be defended through arguments.

The Socratic *logos*-principle contains at least three necessary preconditions for meaningful argumentation: Whoever asserts or follows this maxim has first of all committed themselves *to recognizing no other authority than that of the better argument* and (in *actu argumentationis*) to following no institution other than that of the language game of argumentation itself. This means, however, that the *logos*-principle implies an *autonomous rule of argumentation* and makes possible a critical, that is, meta-conventional, ethics which elevates the procedure of argu-mentative discourse into a principle, into a standard of validity. In addition, those who assert the *logos*-principle im-plicitly accept the community of meaningful participants in argumentation as the tribunal for testing the validity of norms. In this way, the *logos*-principle contains the *idea of an unlimited community of argumentation* and the obligation to anti-cipate it. Finally, it contains the *dialogical obligation* to recognize the other participants in argumentation as partners with equal rights and to respect them as critics, hence with reference to one's own assertions to justify them to the other participants in argumentation.

But what kind of normative-logical status does this prin-ciple of discourse and its moral implications concerning the be-havior of human beings toward others themselves possess? Does it merely have the status of a decision or does the prin-ciple show itself to be universally valid and its normative content to be unconditionally binding and thus ultimately justified?

The transcendental pragmatics initiated by Karl-Otto Apel seeks to achieve such an ultimate justification (*Letztbegründung*) and thereby answer the crucial question that is unavoidably raised primarily in philosophy, as the discipline of reflexive discourse, but is also raised in the second instance in democracy as the institution of the practical discourse of interested parties and in the critique of society as the testing ground of demo-cratic practice: How do you relate to the validity, to the re-deemability of your claim to reason?

I The Transcendental-Pragmatic Reconstruction of Pure Reason as the Ideal Basis of the Validity of Argumentation

The tradition of reflexive philosophizing whose greatest thinkers are Plato and Kant points out that a self-justification of philosophy and thereby the redemption of its claim to validity is only possible if pure reason establishes itself as the origin of nontrivial universal statements that are true without being gained from experience and if it proves fruitful for the self-enlightenment of human beings. For Plato, these are the statements, conceptual analyses, or discursive investigations which raise questions of the type, "What is . . . (virtue)?" and thereby look for universal definitions that would provide the "essence" or the "basis of existence" (*to aition to onti*), and thus the "idea" of the object of the question.

Kant's *Critique of Pure Reason* showed that this claim to pure reason should be raised in strictly normative-logical terms and without mixing questions of validity with speculation about existence, or logic with ontological metaphysics. It reformulated the philosophical claim to reason as the transcendental-logic claim to "a priori synthetic judgments."

1 The Discursive-Reflexive Critique of Meaning or Transcendental-Pragmatic *Elenchos*

The philosophical claim to reason, however, has been heavily contested from Plato to the present day. It has been most heavily disputed from relativistic positions that can be traced from the Sophists to historicism and its variants in the philosophy of science. Yet precisely in the method of refutation of such fundamental criticisms do we find the distinctive philosophical method of justification and that methodical approach which alone makes ultimate justification possible. This is the approach of a *strict reflection upon argumentation* that entails that the concept of justification is not restricted, as for instance in "Critical Rationalism," to the special case of deduction.[1] This approach rather upholds the method of a nondeductive but *discursive-reflexive justification* of evidence that, without self-contradiction (in the sense of pragmatic inconsistency), cannot be doubted and, on the other hand, cannot be inferred (i.e., deduced) without *petitio principii*. It has its model in the *Socratic elenchos* and in the *Aristotelian* insight that the basic principles of logic, such as the maxim of avoidable contradiction, are for their part not justifiable by means of logical inference (*apodeixis*) but only elenctically. They are justified in such a way that those who place in question the validity of such principles or require a deductive proof for them, will experience their validity in dialogue—elenctically—through the refutation of their thesis.[2]

The historistic-relativistic denial of pure reason serves as an example: "All philosophical (including those of the human sciences) statements are historically conditioned and are therefore only valid in a restricted manner." As a counter to this, the Platonic general suspicion is raised: "The criticism is untenable because the denial of ideas would destroy the possibility of *dialegesthai*." This suspicion must allow itself to be proven by an *elenchos*. I wish to show in three steps that an elenctical demonstration of the cogency of this suspicion is possible and how it proceeds:

(1.1) Justification for why it is that the *elenchos* takes its methodical starting point in the pragmatic element of an argument, namely, in the performative act of assertion;

(1.2) Interpretation of the scheme of a transcendental-pragmatic *elenchos* as discursive-reflexive critique of meaning;

(1.3) Elucidation of this critique of meaning as a function of pure reason.

1.1 The counterfactual anticipation of an ideal community of argumentation through the assertional act of an argument.
The starting point of the performative act of an argument, the activity of assertion, is essential and crucial for the justification of the philosophical claim to reason, because in this way and only in this way can the basis of the validity of thought be conceived, a basis that is both the precondition for the possibility of the self-consciousness of the thinking subject *and* for the validity of what is thought as an intersubjective meaning content that is worthy of recognition. Put more simply and concretely: Only the performative act, "I assert," makes it pos-

sible for a thinker to grasp (and *uno actu* to represent) his or her thought both as his or her *own* opinion or thesis and as an appropriate opinion or correct thesis, i.e., as *intersubjectively shareable*. In the act of assertion, one says both "*I*," in that one identifies a meaning content as one's own, and one relates to *others*, in that one asserts the meaning content as a true proportion (against possible criticisms by others). The self-reference of the thinking subject which, from Augustine via Descartes, Kant, and Fichte to Husserl, was treated solipsistically as an unmediated "I think," is realized only in the performative attitude. This means that only by means of the virtual reference to others, which is regularly produced by the communicative *role* of a language game (for instance that of the argumentative language game of asserting something) without a human subject having to *intend* this social reference, is a self-reference and reflexive identity of the human subject possible.[3]

The starting point of "I assert" is thus—and this is decisive— not methodically solipsistic but rather methodically related to communication. And indeed what is at issue here is a counterfactual universal, i.e., an ideal relation to communication.[4] But to what extent is this the case and why? As an argumentative language game, i.e., as a rule-following and thus intersubjectively available act of argumentation, an assertion raises the *validity claim* to truth and thereby refers to an ideal community of argumentation. In the light of this claim, the act of assertion may be reconstructed as follows: "I hereby assert over against you or me and ultimately over against all possible participants in the argument that the content of that which I am now saying is valid."

An assertion's claim to validity implies that what is asserted is not solely recognized as valid by the fortuitous listeners who are present, indeed not even solely by an expert contemporary public but that it is so constituted that it could also be recognized by an ideal community of argumentation. The meaning of the claim to validity raised by assertions is as follows:

I assert over against the unlimited community of argumentation that the statement which I will now make is so constituted and so justified or can be so justified that it withstands the test of all skeptics who comply with the rules of argumentation and who have both understood and considered all justifications, and therefore would be recognized as valid in an unlimited community of argumentation that fulfilled the ideal preconditions (of time, speech, and competence).

For any kind of restrictions with regard to the circle of those over against whom the claim to validity is raised would amount to restrictions of the claim to validity and would contradict the meaning of an assertion as an argumentative act.[5] The validity claim of a meaningful argument is thus necessarily the claim that *all* consistent participants in argumentation, under ideal preconditions of understanding, competence and speech, would recognize the argument as valid so that *à la longue a true consensus* is to be expected *in the unlimited community of argumentation;* i.e., a consensus which, if all the grounds or all relevant grounds that support the argument are understood and considered by all the participants, would arise in the process of argumentation.

1.2 The model of a discursive-reflexive critique of meaning exemplified in the historicism thesis.

The thesis raised earlier of a historistic skepticism with regard to the philosophical claim to reason may be reconstructed in the following way as an act of assertion with a claim to validity (A) and as a proposition (p):

I assert < I claim validity/truth for my (following) statement < I assert that my following statement is valid, in fact is true < I assert that my statement is valid, independently of its factual historical conditions of emergence, with regard to its justification, so that it also withstands the test by means of an unlimited community of possible participants in argumentation who abide by the rules of argumentation and are competent and would be recognized as valid by this ideal community of argumentation,

    that all philosophical statements (including those of the human sciences) are historically conditioned and therefore only valid to a limited extent,

    < *that no philosophical (etc.) statement* can be *valid* independently of its historical conditions of emergence so that a universal validity claim (A) would be incorrectly raised for such a statement.

What about p? If p holds then the thesis of historical relativity ("No philosophical etc., statement is . . . valid") is, for its part, historically conditioned and therefore not valid. Yet how is a meaningful argument, a *dialegesthai*, then possible with reference to p? p denies A. How is it possible to assert p, and that means to advance it as an argument, if p holds? The possibility of *dialegesthai*, of argumentation of a speaker with him or herself and with others is destroyed if the speaker

(a) does not recognize that through his act of assertion he enters into or anticipates the (simultaneously) ideal level of universal validity (A)

(b) does not limit the number of his possible assertions (p) to that portion of which it holds that their elements do not contradict A.

There then exists in fact a *pragmatic inconsistency,* i.e., a contradiction in the activity of argumentation (A and p). A necessary precondition for a meaningful—Austin says "felicitous," successful—activity of argumentation is the consistency between A and p, the *"pragmatic consistency."*

1.3 The critique of meaning as a function of pure reason.
If we pause and look at the argument just introduced, then we arrive at the following results or elucidations:

(a) Historistic skepticism cannot refute philosophical propositions' claim to universal validity but rather is itself refuted and is removed as a serious candidate from scientific or philosophical discussion.

(b) The claim for the universal validity of philosophical propositions is an instance of the claim to truth which every act of assertion necessarily contains as part of an activity of argumentation.

(c) The demonstration of this claim to truth and its counterfactual anticipation of true consensus in an unlimited community of argumentation as the ideal basis of validity of arguments redeems, in an exemplary manner, the *particular* claim to universal validity of philosophical propositions. Indeed, it indicates that the possibility of pure reason can be established by strict reflection upon the necessary preconditions of argumentation. For such a reflection leads to *nontheoretical* propositions, independent from experience, which are universally valid results of reflection and fulfill the two main tasks of pure reason postulated by the philosophical tradition.

These are

• first, to specify the preconditions under which assertions can and should be taken seriously as meaningful and hence worthy of discussion (preconditions for meaning),

• second, to specify the preconditions under which propositions asserted can and should be recognized as true (preconditions for truth).[6]

Of course, what is involved in the reflection carried out here is merely an exemplary redemption of the claim to pure reason, especially since the preconditions for truth in this context are referred to only under a single standpoint, that of the true consensus with regard to given preconditions. In addition, our reflection has not really developed the testing of truth but rather its unavoidable preliminary stage, the purgatory of the linguistic-pragmatic *critique of meaning* which only as a result of the "transformation of philosophy"—dealt with and basically coproduced by Apel—can be recognized and established as an elementary function of pure reason.[7]

(d) The *criterion of meaning of pragmatic consistency* is the transcendental-pragmatic touchstone for the discussion-worthiness of a thesis or a position *as* a principle. It particularly recommends itself for application to "isms," such as skepticism, historicism (including historical materialism), empiricism, naturalism, and solipsism, but also absolute fallibilism. For they are thereby demonstrated to be contradictory acts of argumentation and thus meaningless. In such cases, the transcendental-pragmatically developed test of meaning makes a test of the truth of the given grounds on the proportional level superfluous since it already reveals an inconsistency between the claim of the performative act and the content of the proposition.

That pragmatic inconsistency is to be distinguished from *logical* inconsistency since what is at issue in the latter is an error in the deductive sequence of propositions from higher propositions that is recognized by means of a technical rule—i.e., the formal-logical basic principle of the need to avoid contradiction. This recognition of an error in a system of propositions is theoretically monological; concentrated upon the syntactic-semantic dimension, it methodically abstracts from the pragmatic dimension.[8] And rightly so, for this knowledge of error requires no awareness of the relationship of the author of the propositions to other persons. An interpersonal and thus *social* relationship plays no role here. Yet this role is important in the genesis and recognition of a *pragmatic inconsistency*. Here, what is at issue is the contradiction within an act of argumentation that as such is situated in the communicative and recognitional relationship of *persons* (as participants in argumentation). For this reason, this contradiction is the destruction of an expectation on the part of other persons and can be compared with breaking a promise.

For, with the act of assertion, the person engaged in argument raises a claim to validity over against (himself and) others. He thereby awakens the *expectation* that he himself is prepared and capable of redeeming this claim in communal discourse. In addition, he thereby recognizes the others as representatives of the community of testing claims into which he himself, as someone asserting something, has entered. This means that he confers upon the others the right to criticism and judgment; he himself is *obliged* to advance propositions worthy of discussion and testing and to participate seriously in their testing. The dialogical relationship of a community of argumentation sketched here is a relationship of reciprocal recognition and obligation. This social relationship becomes disturbed if the person arguing withdraws in the proposition the validity claim of the performative act (and thereby the recognition of others as well as his own obligation).

"I" can only recognize such a disturbance if "I" make myself reflexive through the role taking of the other or if others make me aware of what the *communal relation* of argumentation as communicative action requires of me. This means that "I" must make clear to myself, must reflexively acquire a knowledge of what "I" in my communicative role as a person arguing *owe* to the others as representatives of the community of argumentation. Then and only then can my acts of argumentation (not only fortuitously but regularly) succeed.

Hence, the demand for pragmatic consistency may not be traced back to a technical rule (for the avoidance of a mere error). Rather, it is a kind of social norm whose observance is at the same time the precondition of success for a particular kind of social practice (more precisely, metapractice), namely, for argumentation. However, argumentation is the language game of reason. Therefore, the concept of pragmatic inconsistency belongs to the answer to the transcendental-pragmatic question of meaning that is the elementary part of the question as to *pure reason,* namely, the question as to the preconditions that an assertion must fulfill in order that it may be successful as an act of argumentation. The answer to this question refers to the following norm of the language game of reason: an assertion, which is to be admitted as valid and worthy of discussion, must fulfill the precondition of *pragmatic consistency.*

2 Transcendental Pragmatics as Strict Reflection upon Validity

To what extent, however, is the reflection upon validity just commenced and outlined "transcendental-pragmatic" and how is it distinguished from traditional transcendental philosophy? Karl-Otto Apel has suggested "transcendental pragmatics" as the name for a reflection upon validity that, in contrast to the Platonic-Cartesian-Kantian tradition, investigates the *pragmatic dimension of reason,* namely, the communicative mediation and communicative anticipation of possible validity and the performative (and that means action) character of the claim to validity. For it asks about the necessary preconditions under which argumentation can succeed and also whether an obligation belongs to these necessary preconditions; stated more precisely, whether *norms* belong to them that are not disputable through meaningful arguments because we, as persons engaged in argument, as coplayers in the metainstitution of argumentation, have already and necessarily invoked and implicitly recognized them—regardless of whether we subjectively know and bear this in mind, whether we concede or dispute it.

2.1 The transcendental-pragmatic epoché.

This problematic raises the transcendental claim to obtain *ultimately justified* assertions and thereby apodictic evidence concerning the preconditions of possible validity.[9] In order to make such ultimate validity and certainty possible, everything that is sensibly questionable must be methodically left out of account: all possible statements of a theoretical knowledge of objects—including theoretical assertions concerning the objects "human language," "human speech," "human communication" *as* subject-free or irreflexively thematizable objects of research—must be bracketed. This must be done for three reasons: first, because such statements are in principle fallible; second, because the objectifying *intentio recta,* the theoretical attitude, abstracts precisely from the action and virtual knowledge of action that the theoretician himself completes *in actu:* from argumentation and from the necessarily presupposed intuitive knowledge of what meaningful and consistent argumentation means, and finally, too, because no valid normative propositions can be derived solely from statements concerning facts ("naturalistic fallacy"). Because transcendental pragmatics is primarily reflection upon validity, the *epoché* of the meaningfully questionable and, in accordance with this, the change from the theoretical to the strict reflexive attitude, form its characteristic opening move.

Herein lies a *Husserlian* inheritance. In contrast to Edmund Husserl's Cartesian-Platonic approach, transcendental pragmatics treats the "sphere" of possible ultimate justification not at the same time as ontologically fundamental, as the "absolute region of being,"[10] but rather only as logically fundamental, as the unavoidable medium of any meaningful substantive thought. Strict reflection upon validity is not a "philosophy of origins" (in Adorno's sense). Just as little does transcendental pragmatics define this sphere of evidence, along with Husserl, as the realm of "transcendental subjectivity" and thus make methodical solipsism into a starting point[11]; rather, it commences from the dual a priori of communication that is both normative-logical and constitutive of meaning.[12]

2.2 Is there a problem of the transition from reflection on validity to moral philosophy?

The transcendental-pragmatic *epoché* leaves intact only the core realm of the rational and thereby the realm of what is *argumentatively unavoidable,* whose reflexive scrutiny alone has the status of ultimate justification.

If this point is not recognized as such or the strict argumentationally reflexive approach of ultimate justification is underestimated, then the objection of circularity emerges. This objection, which Otfried Höffe for instance has often advanced, in this volume too,[13] commences from two false presuppositions which are nonetheless in accord with common sense and hence quite resistant to criticism. The *first* of these presuppositions refers to the character of transcendental pragmatics. Without recognizing post-Kantian self-understanding as strict reflection (or testing it and, if necessary, rejecting it as inappropriate), Höffe and several critics, above all Hans Albert, interpret transcendental pragmatics as a theory. They thereby find themselves in accord with the theoreticism (still) characteristic of scientized civilization, at whose foundation lies an objectivating *intentio recta.* Commencing from this standpoint, the complementary line of thought of an explicative strict reflection must be misunderstood, because from the outset it is subsumed under the preunderstanding of "theory."

It is characteristic of a theory that it approaches its object from the outside with expectations (in the form of hypotheses) and criteria (in the form of methodical standards, among others). If one assumes that strict reflection—once misunderstood as theory—proceeds in the same way, then one can raise against it the objection of *logical circularity*: "The theories of ideal discourse find themselves . . . in a logical circle." For as theories they must provide from outside a standard— to be more precise, a substantive standard—for the validity of the "moral principles" (namely consensual communication in ideal discourse) of its object ("morality" or "moral principles"). In fact they draw this standard from the realm of their object ("consensual communication is the paradigmatic instance of morality," "the obligation towards such communication is a moral principle"), although they raise the claim to ground or justify the standard for that which may be valid as a true "moral principle."[14]

Quite apart from the fact that the whole theoreticist view of transcendental pragmatics is erroneous, as has been shown elsewhere,[15] the objection of circularity is already invalid because transcendental-pragmatic reflection in no way requires a standard for "true morality" that is drawn from outside. For in fact it mobilizes precisely that standard which can be gained *solely through reflection* upon the scientific or philosophical "subject" as *subject of a serious argumentation* (which counts, or which should be valid) and that can be shown to be the rationally unavoidable (because indisputable through meaningful arguments and therefore logically necessary) *standard for the validity of an argumentation.* This is the whole secret of the transcendental-pragmatic ultimate justification as the simultaneous justification of a morally relevant standard; and, *in nuce,* this is the answer to the question as to the transition from the transcendental pragmatics of language to the transcendental ethics of communication or the discursive communicative ethics of reason. Everything rests upon the thesis *that the standard* of the pure capability of an argument to achieve a discursive consensus as such—hence also a practical argument that, for instance, advances a moral principle—*is rationally unavoidable.* Transcendental pragmatics, and also its relevance for moral philosophy, stands and falls upon this thesis. This is the heart of the matter to which criticism must be directed if it is not to offer mere shadow fencing. What could be more characteristic of the oblivion of reflection in parts of contemporary philosophy—Kant spoke of the shallowness of popular philosophy—than that one must first show and explain to philosophical opponents the genuine philosophical battleground, the problem of reflection?

My polemic, borrowed from Kant, is directed against an oblivion of reflection that is partly hidden behind the label "Kantian skepticism." For with this reference to Kant, Höffe lowers his moral philosophy to a precritical, in fact neo-Aristotelian level. Yet at this level—and here we come to the critique of Höffe's second presupposition—an adequate understanding of the qualitatively new mode of argumentation and of the new legitimation level of a critical ethics[16] in (and after) Kant is not possible at all. The *second* presupposition of Höffe's criticism of circularity feeds upon Aristotelianism, brought to life especially in the modern period by Catholic natural law and by the practical philosophy of the Enlightenment, and refers primarily to the concept and task of ethics and, secondly, to the concept of "reflection": "ethics" becomes defined in a neo-Aristotelian manner through a substantive concept of "moral goodness" as "the perfect good" that is the result of a "genuine ethical reflection."[17] In another context, Höffe has characterized this reflection as the "reflection upon principles" that Aristotle had already achieved in his pragmatics by distinguishing happiness as the *telos* of all human activity; for there exists no distinction between the mode of argumentation or type of reflection of a teleological ethics of happiness and a deontological normative ethics.[18]

In the context of the foundation of ethics, to which the question of the moral significance of the transcendental-pragmatic reflection upon validity belongs, it is crucial that this pre-Kantian, even anti-Kantian approach commences from a substantive, teleological understanding of ethics, which treats ethics as the sum of substantive, moral maxims or standards for the truly good and correct life (and hence for the well-understood happiness). In contrast, transcendental pragmatics, as the reflection upon validity, makes use of a formally normative and thus criteriological deontological concept of ethics, thereby raising itself to the level of a foundation of ethics achieved by Kant from which the whole classical tradition of ethics (and its actualization) is rejected as aporetical and ultimately lacking in criteria.

Höffe fuses the two mutually exclusive concepts of ethics and hence interprets the critical Kant as once more precritical. Certainly, in the precritical period, roughly in the prize essay of 1764, Kant had argued in a manner such as Höffe still ascribes to him in his critical moral philosophy: In the sense of (Wolffian) Aristotelianism, Kant commenced with a "genuine ethical reflection"—more precisely with a definition of the ethical as that which is as perfect as possible and which accords with God's will—and from this point defined an ostensibly "specifically moral sense of obligation" (Höffe)[19]: "Act in the most perfect manner possible for you—this is the first formal principle of all obligation to act."[20] But two decades later Kant had completed the paradigm change: In his major writings on moral philosophy (1785 and 1788) he only recognized the "form of universality, which reason requires as a precondition," because only it makes possible intersubjective validity and thereby obligation, as the morally "determining ground of the will."[21] Only in this way did he make obligation into the final standard and definition of the practically good: "That is practically good which determines the will by means of representations of reason and hence . . . objectively, i.e., on grounds valid for every rational being as such."[22] Transcendental pragmatics continues this insofar as it makes the possibility of intersubjective validity in the form of the pure argumentative capability of achieving consensus (under ideal preconditions of a community of reason) into the highest maxim of any argumentation and hence also of ethics (as argumentation).[23] Nevertheless, practical popular philosophy insists upon the objection of circularity according to which "the 'transition' from the pragmatics of language to ethics [is] . . . the basic ethical problem of a transcendental pragmatics of language."

At first sight, this thesis of the surreptitious transition appears plausible. It does so, however, only as long as one first has a substantive pre-Kantian concept of ethics, that is itself sited in the *intentio recta* and, in accord with this propositional approach, refers directly to the object of what is ethical; whereas transcendental pragmatics adopts a reflexive approach that is related to performance. Transcendental pragmatics is moral philosophy *as* reflection upon validity and as a model for the discursive application of the criterion of validity of pure argumentative capability of achieving consensus to ethical arguments that, as activities of assertion, contain the claim to intersubjective validity. Second, the assertion of the surreptitious transition is plausible only as long as one does not see that the basic thesis of the irreducibility of argumentation as the situation of thinkers—developed in a reflexive approach—

and the normative-logical thesis derived from it of the indisputability of the criterion of pure argumentative capability of achieving consensus already contains the sufficient (of course, possible and intelligible only in the reflexive approach) answer to the question as to the sought after transition from transcendental pragmatics to ethics. To what extent is this the case? It is not a transition—*intentione recta,* in the observing attitude of natural consciousness or of objectivating theoretical consciousness "representable"—from one theoretical field to another theoretical field. It is a recognition of the *interwoven nature of argumentation and ethics* on the basis of a reflection upon the necessary preconditions of argumentation, regardless of the field. Argumentation and ethics reciprocally presuppose one another. *Argumentation,* which wishes to be successful, *presupposes ethics* in a certain manner; and in particular, it presupposes the basic norm of discursive consensus formation (under the regulative principle of the ideal community of argumentation). This basic norm is, at the same time, the principle of logical validity of all argumentations including ethical ones—and is therefore unavoidable. This point is also decisive for the question of the foundation of ethics.

Ethics is dependent upon consistent argumentation, to the extent that, as an orientation to action, it stands and falls with the claim to valid and hence binding standardization. By raising this validity claim, an ethics—stated more precisely, one who espouses an ethics—has already entered into the language game of argumentation as the sole medium of raising and resolving claims to validity and in fact is subject to the constitutive rules of this language game. It would be otherwise only in the case of someone who does not wish to seriously espouse an ethics, but rather merely pretends to do so and thereby deceives him or herself as well as the others; or someone who does not know what it means to argue correctly and thus consistently; such a person can also not successfully espouse an ethics. Whoever seriously (and not for the purpose of deception or in self-contradiction) espouses an ethics in fact argues. Yet whoever argues has thereby—in that *nolens volens,* with or without awareness of this, the person has taken on the *role* of one who argues—also entered into the rules of argumentation.

These rules contain ultimate standards of validity for all possible, including ethical, arguments *as* arguments.

II The Ethical-Philosophical and Moral Significance of the Transcendental-Pragmatic Self-enlightenment of Reason

Transcendental pragmatics is the reflexive explication of standards of validity and not a doctrine of morality or a substantive ethics. As a reflection upon validity, it is significant for any ethics and for the solution to ethical questions because it responds to the issue of the (logical) validity of arguments and hence of the unconditional binding nature of ethical arguments. Insofar as it asserts to develop an ultimate, sensibly indubitable standard for the binding nature of ethical arguments, transcendental-pragmatic reflection upon validity also claims to have answered this question: How can one "justify what argumentation bound to language, what consensual communication as such has to do with ethics?" One can only justify this by demonstrating to the questioner by means of a transcendental-pragmatically grounded critique of meaning the following: No thesis about ethics or morality can be made consistently operable and be valid that has not assumed in the performative act (of assertion) the basic norm of discursive consensus formation (under the regulative principle of an ideal community of argumentation and communication) as the constitutive rule of argumentation that the agent is able and prepared to follow. The application of such a critique of meaning to unreflected or half-reflected ethical positions—such as moral solipsism, neo-Aristotelianism, and utilitarianism, including both contractual and discursive utilitarianism[24]—indicates the *criteriological, moral* significance of transcendental pragmatics. This significance lies in the fact that the argumentative unavoidability of a criterion for the validity and thereby for the obligatory binding nature of ethical argumentation is critically demonstrated and is applied in practical philosophical discourses proceeding along the lines of a critical semantics. Thus, the transition from the pragmatics of language to ethics does not exist in a substantive definition or stipulation that defines consensual communication as morality. This would be a regression behind the level achieved by Kant of a normative ethics of principles that makes the criterion of intersubjective validity, namely, "the form of universality which reason requires as a precondition,"[25] itself into the highest ethical maxim, and thereby introduces the "moral law" as a metanorm by means of which candidates for moral norms (or for "maxims") can be tested. In this respect, Kant's ethics possess a discursive structure.[26] This structure is revealed and developed by transcendental pragmatics and it is justified by the fact that "the objective reality of the moral law"[27]—conceived with Kant against Kant and his skepticism—is shown in a post-Kantian sense to be transcendentally philosophically "deduced,"[28] namely, argumentational-reflexively as the constitutive rule of argumentation. The transition from the transcendental-pragmatic reflection upon validity to a philosophical ethics consists in nothing other than the application of the universal criterion of validity—of pure argumentative capability of achieving consensus under ideal conditions—to practical judgments. Such an application produces the following ethical criterion of obligations:

An ethical statement or a practical judgment must be so constituted that the mode of action/call for action or norm or maxim (of personal formation of the will and judgment)—with reference to warranted (i.e., for their part, ideally capable of achieving consensus) practical claims, e.g., life-interests of all possible participants—is capable argumentatively of achieving a consensus, and this under ideal preconditions.

The inclusion of all possible participants[29] construed as virtual partners in discourse with equal rights is no moral *petitio principii*, but rather a consequence of the unlimitable nature of the circle of addressees to whom the claim to validity raised in the assertive act of an argument is directed. To this extent, this definition—which is decisive for the moral content of the criterion of obligation—is merely an explication of the universalistic meaning of the general norm of argumentation of universal discursive consensus-formation that is revealed by reflection upon the preconditions of all, including theoretical, discourses.[30] I will return to this later.

1 Morally Significant Constitutive Rules of Argumentation, i.e., of the Language Game of Reason

A transcendental pragmatics claims that the ethical criterion of obligation just provided and the underlying universal criterion of validity may be demonstrated by reflection upon the language game of reason, of argumentation. This reflection, already commenced earlier (I 1.), is now continued in a perspective that concentrates upon its moral-philosophical aspects. Does not the preunderstanding of "morality" or "ethics" contained within this perspective in the end bring with it problems of circularity? This is not the case. First, this thematic concentration of reflection upon argumentation brings into play nothing but the purely general preunderstanding according to which ethics or morality refers to the normative orientation of human behavior. In so doing, one type of ethics is indeed distinguished above others, namely, the normative type. Yet this distinction is unproblematical because it is philosophically unavoidable and also in no way estranged from the life-world, but rather emphasizes an essential element of any possible prescientific interpretation of ethics in conceivable life-worlds. For insofar as ethics has anything at all to do with orientations towards action—and to dispute this would be meaningless—it implies norms as binding guideposts of orientation and standards for the judgment of actions. Philosophically, the preference for the normative type of ethics is therefore both unavoidable and justified because any ethics that is to be valid as an argument must fulfill the claim to an intersubjectively *binding nature*. Yet this it cannot do for instance with value-judgments of the form "X is good," from which alone no imperative ("You should do X") can be derived, because it can give no ground for obligation but rather merely a recommendation.[31] For these reasons, the key question as to the morally significant rules of the language game of argumentation, which always and unconditionally bind us, can be stated impartially.

1.1 The autonomy rule of argumentation.
Whoever argues has in so doing always already entered into a discourse in which he or she plays the language game of ar-

gumentation. Thereby he or she has recognized the rule of this game, chiefly the highest norm of all games that commands: "When you play, you should only follow the rules of the game and not, for instance, other rules that are alien to the game." Carried over into the language game of argumentation this means: "When you argue, you should only accept arguments and no authorities that are alien to argumentation." Among such authorities belong social institutions and the concrete norms embedded in them, together with assumptions about the nature of human beings or the teleological determination of their nature in the sense of a speculative natural law. Neither the authority that emanates from the normative power of the factual (an institution, for instance), nor the claimed immemorial nature of a putative natural order or the claimed holiness of an order of creation, but rather solely the authority of rational argument is of significance for those who play the language game of argumentation and do not, for instance, arbitrarily terminate it. Whoever argues is, as participant in an argument, only bound by the rules of a single institution, namely, by the rules of the metainstitution of the language game of argumentation itself. This "rule of autonomy" both sets free argumentation and binds it. It constitutes the communicative freedom of argumentation. In connection with the rule of pragmatic consistency introduced earlier, it shows itself to be significant for moral philosophy in the critique of all types of "argumentative heteronomy" that is characteristic of institutionalism and decisionism or the natural law of the Aristotelian-Thomist tradition.

1.1.1 Argumentative heteronomy in natural law-type ecological ethics. The contemporary crisis of rationality that manifests itself—against the background of the problem of ecological survival—in the trenchant critique of the predominant instrumental concept of rationality, seems increasingly to be tackled by a leap into the irrational. In the hurry to satisfy the need for ethical orientation, one easily overlooks the untenable nature of argumentation for the nonrational, which always possesses the form of argumentative heteronomy. A prominent contemporary example of argumentative heteronomy is Robert Spaemann's natural-law justification of the principle of life or the principle of "respect for life" on the basis of a "religious relationship to nature." Spaemann argues in the Thomistic tradition for an "ethics of the triple respect for that which is above us, which is our equal and which is below us" and emphasizes that such a respect "requires other foundations than argumentative ones."[32] Here one is confronted with a pragmatic inconsistency. For through his argumentation, in the form of a published monograph and hence at the performative level, the author claims intersubjective validity and obligatoriness for his thesis of a "principle of respect for life." Yet, at the propositional level, namely, in his statements about this principle, he disputes its argumentative demonstrability and appeals to an instance that is alien to argumentation. If one asserts "respect for life" as a principle of the ethical realm, then one *has* however already argued and raised a claim to intersubjective obligation which one should be able to redeem in philosophical discourses. Yet this redemption is unsuccessful. For, as teleological, substantive ethical maxims, the principle of life and the principle of "respect for life" contain no grounds for intersubjective validity and hence for the obligatory character which a philosophical ethics claims. Therefore, they are not suited to ethical justification. They can in fact lapse into a "utilitarianism of life" (Skirbekk),[33] or a moral rigorism with dogmatic-moralistic casuistics—one thinks of Spaemann's derivation of the ban on abortions with the exception of medical grounds—the illusion of justification.[34]

It is necessary, both for the purpose of a foundation of ethics and also for the facilitation of a rational test of individual moral norms that are inferred from substantive principles, to subordinate each substantive ethical principle to the formal basic norm of argumentation, the norm of discursive consensus-formation under the regulative dual principle of an ideal community of argumentation and communication. For the concrete justification of norms this means: normative statements cannot be sufficiently justified by inference from substantive principles—such as that of respect for life—but rather only through testing in discourses that proceed according to the maxim of not recognizing as valid anything other than that which, against all possible claims capable of being universalized, and in fact ultimately under the counter-factual preconditions of an ideal community of argumentation and communication, would be justifiable and accountable.

It is interesting that Robert Spaemann too, at the decisive point, does not merely argue from the principle of life or "respect for life" but assumes the universal principle of responsibility. Hence it is difficult to understand what he means when he says: "Respect for life lies at the foundation of all discursive ethics and, at the same time, it extends further than such ethics." If "respect for life" is to have an intersubjectively binding and a rationally justifiable meaning, then in my opinion this formulation can mean no more than "recognition of all claims to life, that can also be rendered intelligible, justified and recognized in an ideal community of communication and argumentation." Albert Schweitzer's formulation that, in his case, stands by no means in a merely teleological and natural theological context but also in the context of the ethics of reason, can in this way be reconstrued as a communicative-discursive maxim that is demonstrable by reflection upon the preconditions of meaning and validity of argumentation.

1.2 The duty to anticipate the ideal community of argumentation.
We have only laid the ground for such a demonstration in our previous discussion, but have already claimed it in our critique. The rule of autonomy already referred to, and the pragmatic rule of consistency, are obviously inadequate because they only provide the procedural framework for testing validity. They do not provide a standard of validity itself, nor a not merely critical but also positive metanorm that is capable of orientating us. At this point, we can advance a step further if we take into account the reconstruction of the act of assertion of an argument elaborated above (I 1.1). The results of this earlier reconstruction were: The claim to validity, which the act of assertion of a serious, and that means a real, argument contains, is necessarily the claim that *all* possible consistent participants in argumentation under ideal conditions would recognize as valid the procedure of argument, so that *a consensus in an unlimited,* i.e., excluding no argument without suffi-

cient justification, *community of argumentation* is to be expected. Insofar as the validity claim of a real argument necessarily anticipates an ideal community of argumentation, the latent knowledge of participants in argumentation contains a normative-logical distinction (in the form of virtual awareness of a tension)—a distinction that is to be made conscious reconstructively—between the performative anticipated ideality or infinite nature of the propositional content together with its capacity for recognition, on the one hand, and the finite nature and contingency possibly merely represented by the propositional content, on the other. It is the distinction between a *real argumentation,* which takes place with the state of knowledge and on the basis of numerous, untested presuppositions (merely assumed to be valid) within the limits of an already given real community of argumentation, and the *ideal argumentation,* which would take place on the basis of the best possible procedures and tested presuppositions in the unlimited public sphere of all possible consistent participants in argumentation.

In addition, the validity claim of an argument presupposes the readiness to adopt a commitment to concern oneself with and bring about such a consensus that would also stand firm under ideal conditions. At the same time, this commitment is a self-critical one with regard to one's own argument and with regard to *bringing about the best possible public sphere of participants in argumentation.* For the validity claim of an assertion to be true or binding, and that means capable of achieving a consensus under ideal conditions, can only then be raised in a pragmatically consistent manner and hence truthfully as a move in the language game of argumentation (and not as the trick of a mere deception); moreover, it can be tested and redeemed solely to the extent to which the conditions for the demonstration of this capacity for consensus (at least long term and approximately) are produced. Accordingly, the following can be specified as the formal communicative basic norm of argumentation: "*Always engage in arguments that would also be capable of achieving consensus in an ideal community of argumentation and endeavor to bring about such circumstances as approximate more closely to the structures and conditions of an ideal community of argumentation."*

1.3 The dialogical reciprocity of validity and the duty to recognize the other as a partner in argumentation with equal rights.

The communicative action of argumentation is only successful if the validity claim raised with an argument is borne by the preparedness for dialogical conduct in discourses. Whoever raises a validity claim through his or her argumentation and thereby requires that others respond to his or her speech in that they test an assertion, thereby *recognizes the others* at least implicitly as possible competent testers and as critical questioners to which he or she has to reply. For a person can only play the language game of argumentation if they are themselves prepared to justify their assertion with reasons and to recognize as such the good grounds of others.

In the act of assertion there is included both the claim to validity (truth) for p *and* the recognition of the competence to test claims of the actual or possible partner in discourse. This recognition implies that the person making assertions is prepared for the serious critical testing of their proposition; this means, however, that he or she admit their own finitude and thereby capacity for error. The admission of possible error is bound up with the claim to truth. Both are preconditions for the meaning of asserting something and reciprocally presuppose one another.

The recognition of others and their arguments by "myself," when I assert something, lies in the fact that "I" comply with the expectations which "I" have awakened in others through my statement of an assertion. Only if "I" do not disappoint these expectations, thus only if "I" also assume the role of the other and thus bring the other or others into play, can the language game of argumentation be implemented and "my" activity of argumentation be successful. If one fails to achieve this *dialogical-reciprocity of validity,* then the argumentation at once breaks off after one has opened it; but then one has not really argued, but rather only acted as if . . . Then one would have contradicted one's own claim.

An act of argumentation can only succeed if the person arguing treats the others, as long as they adhere to the rules of the language game of argumentation, as equal, insofar as the person guarantees to them the same right "to assume the roles of dialogue and to execute speech acts."[35] In accordance with this, the norm that is internal to discourse can be formulated as follows: *"Regard and treat each other person, who follows the rules of the language game of argumentation, as a partner in argumentation possessing equal rights, responsibility, and truthfulness."*

This norm of reciprocity contains requirements for consensual-communicative behavior such as

• not to deceive, to trick, or merely treat strategically (see the third maxim of the "categorical imperative") others and oneself,

• not to avoid argumentation and thereby accountability,

• not to be dogmatic, but rather to accept good arguments self-critically.

Viewed in isolation, the norm of dialogical recognition is morally inadequate because, as a norm internal to discourse, it only relates to those who are participants in a discourse. But in connection with the communicative basic norm of argumentation it also includes *those who do not participate.* For by virtue of the fact that this basic norm binds us to ideal argumentation capable of achieving consensus, it also thereby obliges us to advance the arguments of nonparticipants *and* to take account of them in one's own argumentation. Even actual nonparticipants are members with equal rights of the unlimited community of argumentation and, as such, are to be taken into account. Hence, the dialogical reciprocity of validity is not only an empirical-dialogical standard but also, at the same time and in addition, a *universal* dialogical-regulative principle. From this there arises, for instance, the consensual-comunicative obligation to recognize all others (including children and the mentally ill) as *potential* partners in argumentation possessing equal rights, i.e., to take them seriously as persons who (on their own behalf or—e.g., in the case of minors—represented by a third party) may step forward as critics or persons demanding justification and may register and justify validity claims or claims to life (needs).

1.4 Ultimate justification or explication of the theoretical role in discourse?

Looking back, we can ask whether our reflection has achieved its goal of giving an *ultimate justification* of critical morality by uncovering unavoidable norms of argumentation.[36] For an important skeptical objection has not yet been removed: the objection that that which binds unconditionally—the unavoidable norms of argumentation—is exclusively valid for those who raise truth claims through assertions, hence only for the participants in theoretical discourse. If that were the case, then it would again be doubtful whether something exists at all that was *unconditionally* valid for the discussion of practical questions and for the relationship of acts of argumentation to life-practice and political practice.[37] A theoretical discourse is no mere internal-scientific exercise but rather the enterprise of every person who thinks and speaks, insofar as in so doing they seek to answer correctly questions of the kind: "Is it true (in the sense of, is it really the case) that $X \in p$?" A person *must* raise such questions, independently of the topic upon which he or she reflects and speaks. Such questions also belong essentially to practical discourses because practical questions of the type "What should we do?" cannot be addressed without resolving the theoretical question as to what is the case ("Is the description of the situation $D\text{-}S_1$ correct?"). Often—and not only in the case of disarmament negotiations—the descriptions of the situation are the decisive (or dead) point in practical discourses. Contemporary examples from the crisis of civilization are provided by the ecological and peace movements in that they place in doubt the truth claims of governments' situational descriptions that legitimate action and orientation—for instance, through contrary ecological reports or through strategic information and testing the truth of strategic assertions: "Is it true that the nuclear balance will be destroyed by the installation of 300 SS20 missiles?"—"Is it true that the stationing of 108 Pershing II missiles in West Germany and of 464 Cruise missiles in

Western Europe represents an effort to 'catch up' militarily?" "In view of the effective removal of the early warning time by this weapons system (with a flight time of only ten minutes) and in view of their deadly accuracy and thereby their capacity to wipe out the nuclear potential of the Soviet Union in a first strike, can we still speak of reciprocal security (on the basis of deterrence) and balance?"[38]

The duty to achieve an argumentative consensus, which would be upheld under ideal conditions, is valid too for essentially practical discourses. For they are, first, substantively dependent upon and necessarily include theoretical discourses. Second, theoretical discourses depend upon the dialogical realization of practical discourses because life-practical viewpoints can either play a role as orientations in theoretical discourses or even act as criteria for deciding the *planning* of theoretical discourses. The latter is the case, for instance, where it is a matter of deciding which problem (in the form of which project) is to be researched with what resources (money, time, etc.), and that means, to what extent (and in what manner) which theoretical discourse is to be realized. Third, both theoretical and practical discourses are, in terms of logical validity, dependent upon an explicative *agreement concerning the meaning* of the interests or needs or life-forms, cultural traditions, and norms that are presented in situational descriptions.

1.5 The duty to anticipate the ideal community of communication and to foster a universal reciprocity of agreement.
The precondition for the realization of such a consensus is, however, a worldwide public sphere, in which all people would participate who are prepared to take part in the interpretation of their needs, which can be advanced as life-interests, as well as in the clarification of meaning and change in meaning of life-practical concepts and moral or legal norms. To this extent, there emerges the demand for the anticipation and approximate realization of an *ideal community of communication* through the establishment of a worldwide public sphere as the hermeneutical-practical extension of the postulate regarding the anticipation and approximation to the conditions of an ideal community of argumentation.

The justification of such a regulative principle of the best possible worldwide public sphere is of a *transcendental-hermeneutic* nature. The primarily performatively orientated transcendental pragmatics is here enlarged by a transcendental-hermeneutic reflection upon the preconditions for the possibility and validity of propositional discourse. Each argument is internally grounded, that is, with reference to its propositional content, upon predicative understanding. Through predicative understanding we experience not only identifiable objects "always already *as* something (in order to)," but also characterize needs, intentions, actions, and expressions "*as* something definite." This hermeneutic "as-structure" of understanding always possesses the form of a "prestructure": The understanding of something in the world is made possible by an anticipatory characterizing relationship of what is to be understood to that which we already know—thus by *preunderstanding*. Preunderstanding is the precondition for the possibility of meaning and hence of understanding in an unspecific sense. The specific sense of "understanding" is actually the normative aspect of correct understanding. But preunderstanding makes false and correct understanding possible; as an anticipatory characterizing relationship to background knowledge it can also distort and falsify. For instance, if we anticipate something specific as "something of the kind A that is known to us" or as "deviation from the kind A," we can completely misunderstand its specific meaning. Hence, preunderstanding is a precondition *and* possible limit of the validity of understanding. Without preunderstanding we could not understand at all, yet only by the critical use of preunderstanding can we understand correctly.

The instance of correction and critique for the use of preunderstanding is ultimately the *interpretandum* itself, but this means in discourses: the others whose expressions or needs must be correctly understood in order that their theses or life-interests can be made into a theme of discourse, or can be taken into account in discourse as that which they really are. Because every argumentation includes understanding, it cannot redeem its validity claim without orientation towards the regulative principle of an agreement in the ideal community of communication. For, in the case of the absence of such a critical principle, it would be immune neither against the solipsistic dogmatism of an absolutization of the perspective of the individual subject, nor against the pragmatic-hemeneutic dogmatism of an absolutization of the authority of a contingently real community or tradition.

Practical *solipsistic* dogmatism consists in the fact that the arguing subject would surreptitiously place his or her *own understanding of the needs of others* and his or her own usage of life-practical concepts and norms as the correct understanding and would make it into an uncriticized standard. Whereas solipsistic dogmatism absolutizes the preunderstanding of the individual subject, because it does not distinguish between this preunderstanding and an adequate understanding and hence does not take seriously the normative sense of understanding as correct understanding, *pragmatic-hermeneutic* dogmatism leads to the absolutization of an institutionalized, contingent intersubjectivity: it commences from a constitutive superiority of the meaning and interpretive horizon of a *tradition* or *actual community* over the interpreting and arguing human subjects. It thereby removes the ground from both the critique of handed-down and established meaning as well as the possible advance in the understanding of handed-down meaning (through explicatory interpretation and critical appropriation). For the critique of and advance in understanding are only possible to the extent to which the arguing subjects overstep the pregiven horizon of their prevailing actual community of communication, by anticipating the standpoint of an ideal community of communication and thereby extending the boundaries of their actual community of communication in the direction of an ideal one. The introduction of the regulative principle of an ideal community of communication (for the clarification of intended meaning and thereby for rendering possible a reciprocity of agreement, which would not merely exist in a contingent and specific community but in the universal human community) leads to a critique of Hans-Georg Gadamer's philosophical hermeneutics and to the foundation of a critical hermeneutic method.[39]

Within transcendental pragmatics, the introduction of this principle entails that the normative transcendental-pragmatic concept of an a priori of the ideal community of argumentation is enlarged by the normative transcendental-hermeneutic concept of an a priori of the ideal community of communication. The practical consequence of this enlargement is the duty *to be conscious of the doubly finite boundaries of understanding* as the basis of argumentation—namely, the dependency of the propositional content upon subjective perspectives and upon the particularity or contingency of actual communities—*in order to overstep these finite boundaries* self-critically and social-critically as well. In this sense, the transcendental-hermeneutic norm of argumentation can be formulated thus: "*Engage in communication for the critique and enlargement of the horizon of understanding of your arguments,* and *endeavor to bring about such preconditions for agreement that approximate towards the realization of a best possible worldwide public sphere.*"

2 Critical Ethics as a Standpoint and as the Self-reflection of Practical Reason

Transcendental-hermeneutic reflection is of importance both for a logic of validity of discourse in general and of practical discourse in particular, as well as for a critique of the ethical significance of transcendental pragmatics. It makes concrete the universal criterion of validity and of practical obligation through the communicative principle of universal reciprocity of agreement or *the public sphere.* In addition, it leads to the critical inference that a rational justification of *substantive* norms that is to be intersubjectively valid, is only possible by means of agreement in actual discourses or (anticipatory and hence hypothetical) discourses among representatives.

2.1 The principle of the universal public sphere and unrestricted communication as a principle immanent to discourse.
The principle established by transcendental-hermeneutic reflection is both a regulative and constitutive principle of practical reason.

(a) It possesses a *constitutive* function for the *attitude* of practical argumentation. Transcendental-hermeneutic reflection demonstrates that moral philosophy and practical argumentation both in relation to itself and with regard to its objects of judgment must adopt a communicative-discursive attitude if it wishes to redeem its validity claim and not lapse into pragmatic inconsistency. On the basis of transcendental pragmatics, transcendental-hermeneutic reflection on validity determines the standpoint of critical ethics, on the one hand, by supplying a communicative validity principle for practical arguments and, on the other, by making possible a critique of dogmatic moral philosophy. In fact, it dismisses the latter's exaggerated claims as self-contradictory and as theoretical illusion—namely, the claims to be able to think and realize both "the standpoint of morality" or the ultimate standard for morality (and law), as well as its application for testing norms and maxims according to the model of a basically solitary thought experiment. This is the attitude of methodical or "transcendental *solipsism*" (Husserl) that also predominates in contemporary moral philosophy.[40] The methodically solipsistic perspective can at most make *those affected* by the consequences of a grounded norm into the object of a solitary thought experiment and deal with them only in a theoretical expertocratic manner.

In contrast, the linking of transcendental-pragmatic with transcendental-hermeneutic reflection upon validity leads to the thesis that it is necessary, in terms of the logic of validity, to include those possibly affected as communications partners and partners in discourse in the process of the justification of norms. For the transcendental-*pragmatic* reflection shows that the *validity claim* of an argument can only be redeemed if it can also be defended against those kinds of arguments which can be advanced for the claims of all those possibly affected. The transcendental-*hermeneutic* reflection, however, leads to the conclusion that the real *meaning* of the claims of those possibly affected cannot be established monologically theoretically but rather only communicatively or quasi-communicatively (by self-critical hermeneutic procedures). Accordingly, the transcendental-hermeneutic norm of argumentation extends in principle beyond the circle of participants in discourse and hence beyond the framework of an ethical expertocracy. It starts out from the fact that those practically engaged in argumentation are obliged to both ascertain and to advance via arguments the possible claims of all those who could be affected by the norm or by its consequences—including all future generations. From this is derived the following validity principle for practical discourse as a regulative touchstone of practical reason: *"If they were made aware of the norm N, could outsiders or future generations affected by it defend themselves with arguments capable of achieving consensus?"* The normative-logical standpoint of critical morality thus consists in the counterfactual anticipation of an ideal public sphere of argumentation, whereas the traditional standpoint of morality already regards the formal-logical principle of universalizability as a sufficient criterion of validity.[41]

(b) The principle of the universal public sphere and unrestricted communication is also *constitutive* for the *procedure* and *concept* of practical argumentation: concept and procedure of argumentation must correspond to it. The community of argumentation may not be merely postulated as the validating instance sufficiently anticipatable by any conscientious persons or moral experts, but rather it must also be *realized* as a community of agreement and as a community of discourse or validity testing. Practical argumentation can only proceed in a *communicative-discursive* manner. This means that it proceeds either in real agreement and consensual discourse (e.g., in the form of public communicative planning procedures with participation of those affected), or in hermeneutic anticipation of a free formation of consensus, with which, however, only the level of an anticipation of discussion is achieved. In a certain way, (practical) argumentation is a communicative practice that, in contrast to life-practice, is unburdened by action, decision, and relative pressure of time.

In contrast, the *solipsistic* concept of practical argumentation—as instanced by the monological applicability of the principle of universalization to historical and life-practical situations already assumed by Kant—proves to be self-contradictory and dogmatic. For the assumption of the self-sufficiency of the rational will in precommunicative isolation includes the assumption that one person alone in each case knows the situation to which the principle of universalization is to be applied. Yet, fundamentally, the intended objectives (and hence the needs) of others belong to the situation, objectives which they would wish to advance over against the solitary moralist—if he would only give them a hearing. But the solitary moralist who would understand them solely from his own perspective, hence in terms of his preunderstanding, would himself determine what the intended objectives and needs of others should be. The solitary ego and his supposed knowledge of others then becomes the—uncriticized and untested, and hence dogmatic—standard; and indeed the standard for both the understanding of something as an intended objective and need of others (that can be adversely affected by my action) as well as for the judgment and evaluation of these needs (or a part of these needs) as valid claims which "I" must take into account in my actions insofar as "I" wish to act morally. It is precisely in this that the pragmatic self-contradiction or pragmatic inconsistency of the solitary moralist lies. For he does indeed claim to behave morally, that is, in a manner that he would be able to justify in the unrestricted community of rational beings (the "realm of ends"); this means that he claims that he makes the unrestricted community of argumentation into his ultimate standard. In reality, however, he makes his private or group-specific preunderstanding into the standard.

From this the conclusion may be drawn that the justification or testing of a normative statement is dependent upon both the actual agreement and consultation with those potentially affected, as well as having to be able to be measured against the general criterion of validity, the standard of an ideal argumentation in the unlimited public sphere of knowledgeable participants in argumentation. Thus, two elements of dialogical reciprocity must always exist:

• a real reciprocity of agreement realized or simulated through consultation between "myself" and those actually affected,

• a nonfactual but rather transcendental reciprocity of validity actionable by critique in discourses between "my" validity claim and the ideal community of argumentation as the final instance for the validity of an argument in general, and for the binding nature of a practical argument in particular.

For the procedure of practical argumentation or more precisely for the procedure for justifying moral norms the preceding entails that ultimately justified norms of argumentation may not be directly applied to the moral problems of actual practice that are dealt with in philosophical-practical discourses. It follows, positively, that communication for the establishment of concrete meaning and a consultation for testing the validity of the *claims* of those potentially affected must be carried out (in principle) with the latter themselves. Yet because no strict discursive test of validity can be expected from actual consultations, which, for their part, are subject to the contingent marginal conditions of empirical behavior such as pressure of time, strategies of enforcement (the "power of perseverance"), and possible modalities of voting, a philosophical metalegitimation through strict practical discourses is required. The latter serve, as it were, as the methodical conscience of real consultations; more accurately, as the approximating instance of practical reason. In accordance with this, the critical-moral procedure for the justification of norms contains three main levels:

1. Ultimate justification of norms of argumentation by transcendental-pragmatic and transcendental-hermeneutic reflection upon validity,

2. real agreement upon, and real consultation with, the claims of those affected,

3. testing the validity of the norms recommended in (2) in practical discourses that follow strictly the norms of argumentation of (1) and obey the critical-moral standard of validity for practical argumentation.

(c) Both the contingent limitations that apply to real consultations, as well as the "approximating" instance of practical reason—the safeguard applied to the characterization of philosophical-practical discourse—demonstrate that the principle of ideal consensus-formation always remains a *regulative principle*.

A realization of the ideal community of communication and argumentation *per definitionem* is not possible. The difference between the real and ideal community of discourse is untranscendable. Indeed, it remains always operative as critical tension. No realizable argumentation can ever completely correspond to the postulate of an ideal agreement and discursive consensus-formation: it remains the regulative guiding idea of argumentation that as such first makes possible criticism of specific results and procedures of discourse, a criticism which is constantly kept alive.

2.2 The principle of the universal public sphere and unlimited communication as a discursive political principle.
Evidently, the ideal principle of communication and the public sphere is not only a principle internal to argumentation but, at the same time, a discursive political principle. As such a principle, it has both a regulative as well as an anticipatory constitutive status.

(a) From a *discursive*-political standpoint, it possesses an anticipatory-constitutive significance for the applicability of the basic norm of argumentation and of the principle of universalization contained within it. This holds in any case for practical argumentation: The moral principle of universalization can only then be implemented if agreement upon meaning and consensus-formation on the basis of universal communicative freedom are really possible, so that all have access to the same social possibilities for the representation of their claims. This fact, however, does not deprive the principle of its function as a regulative principle. For here too the difference, and hence also the critical tension cannot be removed between that which, in one's life-role as actual member of a contingent, real system of communication and action, one follows as norms recognized by the majority and as positive duties, and that which, in the rational role of participant in the unlimited community of argumentation and communication, one necessarily recognizes as norms of argumentation and should follow as critical moral duties.[42]

(b) From a discursive-*political* standpoint, the principle of the best possible and universal agreement as well as consensus-formation possesses a distinctive dialectical status. As a *regulative* principle, it is at the same time *constitutive* for the claim to reason and hence for the legitimation of democratic constitutional states. Democratic constitutional states have raised a claim to reason by virtue of the fact that they have recognized human rights as universal claims to reason and have committed themselves to their realization. In so doing, they have placed themselves on the level of judgment of a post-conventional critical morality. They have submitted their system of norms to a metalegitimation before the unlimited global instance of practical reason. For this reason, the *third level* of the justificatory scheme of critical morality mentioned above can also be grounded by a reconstruction of the normative foundations of democratic constitutional states. The latter belongs within the ethics of democratic pluralism, as long as the politically and sociologically construed concept of pluralism is reformulated normatively in Kant's sense—namely, differentiated antithetically from "practical egoism" and affirmatively related to the concept of the citizen of the world.[43] The ideal principle of communication and consensus-formation has a constitutive significance also for the idea of the democratic procedure for the justification of norms that is not solely related to human rights as rational rights but also to unlimited free public discussion.

At the present time, this principle has acquired a new weight through the planetary and unlimited future dimension of the effects of the technical means of political action. The crisis of military politics and the ecological crisis or, stated less euphemistically, the almost apocalyptical possibilities of a military and ecological catastrophe, indicate the point at which politics can only be legitimated now upon a strictly universalistic level. The moral demands of the situation upon the citizen extend to civil courage which he or she must mobilize in order to impel self-assertive political systems towards a politics that is capable of being universally justified. The moral demand upon the statesman refers to practicing a politics in terms of the indivisibility of responsibility for one's own nation and for humanity. We must thank Karl-Otto Apel for the outline of a communicative-discursive ethics of responsibility that is appropriate to this new situation of mankind.[44]

Transcendental Pragmatics and Critical Morality

Notes

1. On this see K.-O. Apel, "Das Problem der philosophischen Letztbegründung im Lichte einer transzendentalen Sprachpragmatik. Versuch einer Metakritik des 'Kritischen Rationalismus'," in B. Kanitscheider (ed.), *Sprache und Erkenntnis. Feschrift für G. Frey*, Innsbruck 1976, pp. 55–82.

2. Aristotle, *Metaphysics*, 1006a.

3. The traditional methodical solipsistic approach is aporetical because it cannot show how the transition from "my certainty," that is expressed in the first person singular, to the required validity, which must be capable of being expressed in the first person plural, is at all possible.

4. On this, see J. Habermas, "Vorbereitende Bemerkungen zu einer Theorie der kommunikativen Kompetenz," in J. Habermas/N. Luhmann, *Theorie der Gesellschaft oder Sozialtechnologie?*, Frankfurt 1971.

5. See W. Kuhlmann, "Ethik der Kommunikation" in K.-O. Apel, D. Böhler, et al. (eds.), *Praktische Philosophie/Ethik. Aktuelle Materialien*, vol. 1, Frankfurt 1980, pp. 292ff.

6. On this, see U. Anacker, "Vernunft," in H. Krings et al. (eds.), *Handbuch philosophischer Grundbegriffe*, Munich 1974, especially pp. 1607ff.; J. Habermas, "Wahrheitstheorien," in *Wirklichkeit und Reflexion: W. Schulz zum 60. Geburtstag*, Pfullingen 1973, pp. 211ff.; K.-O. Apel, "C. S. Peirce and the Post-Tarskian Problem of an Adequate Explication of the Meaning of Truth," *The Monist*, 63, 3.

7. K.-O. Apel, *Towards a Transformation of Philosophy* (trans. G. Adey and D. Frisby), London/Boston 1980; K.-O. Apel, "Einführung" to C. S. Peirce, *Schriften I*, Frankfurt 1967, especially pp. 53–147 and C. S. Peirce, *Schriften II*, Frankfurt 1970, esp. pp. 100–152.

8. See D. Böhler, "Philosophische Meta-Normenbegründung durch Argumentationsreflexion" (chs. 1 and 2.2), in *Akten des XII Deutschen Kongresses für Philosophie*, Innsbruck 1982.

9. The sought-after sphere of evidence can be characterized first of all along with Husserl as the "sphere of self-evidence of such a nature that any attempt to inquire behind it would be absurd." (*The Crisis of European Sciences and Transcendental Phenomenology*, (trans. D. Carr), Evanston 1970, p. 188). Yet whereas Husserl defined the sphere of evidence once more in the sense of Platonic metaphysics as an "absolute region of existence" and justified it through "*the absolute unimaginableness* (inconceivability) of . . . *non-being*" (*Cartesian Meditations* (trans. D. Cairns), Hague 1960, para. 6, p. 16; see also n. 10 below), this is gained in transcendental pragmatics through strict reflection upon the preconditions of the meaning of doubt or problematization *as* argumentation: what is at issue are the certainties "which problematizing first of all makes possible" because it is due to them "that the person rendering something problematic understands his action as real problematizing," and can thus trust in this so that it is a meaningful doubt; thus, W. Kuhlmann in *Funkkolleg Praktische Philosophie/Ethik*, Weinheim/Basel, 14 issues, 1980 and 1981, "Studienbegleitbrief" and W. Kuhlmann, "Reflexive Letztbegründung," *Zeitschrift für philosophische Forschung*, 35, 1, pp. 3ff., especially p. 11f.

10. E. Husserl, *Ideas: General Introduction to Pure Phenomenology*, (trans. W. R. Boyce Gibson), London 1931; E. Husserl, *The Idea of Phenomenology*, (trans. W. Alston and G.

Nakhnikian), Hague 1964; see R. Boehm, *Vom Gesichtspunkt der Phänomenologie*, Hague 1968, pp. 7ff., 72ff.; E. Husserl, *Cartesian Meditations*, op. cit., para. 64, see also paras. 12, 62.

11. E. Husserl, *Cartesian Meditations*, op. cit., para. 11. From a transcendental-pragmatic viewpoint, in contrast to Husserl's self-understanding, his discussion of intersubjectivity and of "others" as "constituted in myself" (para. 62, see para. 42 ff.), as well as his characterization of transcendental solipsism as the "philosophical subordinate stage" (para. 13) are also and especially proofs of his methodical solipsism. See also *The Crisis of European Sciences*, op. cit.

12. See K.-O. Apel, *Transformation der Philosophie*, Frankfurt 1973, vol. 2, pp. 311ff., 330ff., and *Towards a Transformation of Philosophy*, op. cit., pp. 225ff. See the confrontation concerning methodical solipsism and the instance of the dual a prioris of communication in *Funkkolleg*, op. cit., "Studienbegleitbrief" 4, pp. 39–47; 5, pp. 37–41 and pp. 48ff.; 7, p. 59; 8, p. 61 and pp. 85f.; 11, pp. 55ff.; 13, pp. 9–12. See W. Kuhlmann's contribution in W. Kuhlmann and D. Böhler (eds.), *Kommunikation und Reflexion*, Frankfurt 1982.

13. O. Höffe, *Ethik und Politik*, Frankfurt 1979, pp. 247 ff.; and his contribution to this volume. See the discussions and clarifications in W. Oelmüller (ed.), *Transzendentalphilosophische Normenbegründung*, Paderborn 1978, especially pp. 15–26, 143, 153ff., 197f., 209, 210; *Funkkolleg*, op. cit., "Studienbegleitbrief" 2, pp. 73f.; 4, pp. 39ff; 5, pp. 20ff; 7, pp. 18ff., 28ff., and above all 8, pp. 46f., as well as 13, pp. 12f., 18ff.

14. See O. Höffe in this volume; earlier in *Funkkolleg*, op. cit., 7, p. 58: "In the theories concerning discourse, however, a part of these normative maxims is already presupposed as valid, namely, that part which corresponds to the preconditions and structural feature of ideal discourse. Yet this means: normative moral elements, for which a standard has first of all to be sought after, already enter into the definition of precisely this standard."

15. *Funkkolleg*, op. cit., 5, pp. 20f.; 8, pp. 54f.; 13, pp. 12f. and 18.

16. On the characterization of this new level of legitimitation and the new mode of rational-reflexive argumentation in Kant's moral philosophy, see the contributions of Apel, Böhler, and Kuhlmann to *Funkkolleg*, op. cit., 2, pp. 62ff. and 77ff.; 5, pp. 121ff. and 7, pp. 27ff.; already earlier J. Habermas, "Legitimation Problems in the Modern State" in *Communication and the Evolution of Society*, op. cit., pp. 178ff.

17. O. Höffe, in this volume.

18. In *Funkkolleg*, op. cit., 12, pp. 94ff., see pp. 50ff. On p. 94 it is stated: The "distinction between a eudaemonistic ethics and an imperative ethics rests . . . upon the object level of moral philosophy (the type of moral obligations), it does not rest upon the meta-level (the kind of philosophical argumentation)."

19. Thus, in various places in *Funkkolleg* and in this volume.

20. I. Kant, "Untersuchung über die Deutlichkeit der Grundsätze der natürlichen Theologie und der Moral," *Akademie-Ausgabe*, p. 96.

21. I. Kant, *Critique of Practical Reason*, (trans. L. W. Beck), Indianapolis/New York 1956, pp. 59ff.; I. Kant, *Ethical Philosophy* (trans. J. W. Ellington), Indianapolis/Cambridge 1983, "Grounding for the Metaphysics of Morals," pp. 2, 24, 39f., 42 *passim*.

22. I. Kant, *Ethical Philosophy*, op. cit., p. 24.

23. See the transcendental-pragmatic explications and critique of Kant by Apel, Kuhlmann, and Böhler in *Funkkolleg*, op. cit., 2, pp. 62ff.; 5, pp. 121ff., 88, 26; 7, pp. 27ff.; 8, pp. 82ff. and 11, pp. 52ff., 60ff.

24. One thinks here of the discourse-utilitarianism developed by P. Lorenzen and O. Schwemmer, also espoused in a practical manner by H. Lübbe in his consultative model, but also of that of the critique-of-ideology criterion of legitimation that Habermas recommended in 1971: Neither in the former nor the latter is the level of *moral* argumentation reached, because merely the perspective of *participants* in dialogue, who wish to resolve a conflict of interests or correctly interpret their needs, is reckoned with without the perspective of those outside, whose interests or needs could be affected by the result of an internal dialogical "elimination of conflict" or an internal "unconstrained formation of the will," having been expressly taken into account. See P. Lorenzen and O. Schwemmer, *Konstruktive Logik, Ethik und Wissenschaftstheorie*, Mannheim/Vienna/Zurich 1973, pp. 107ff.; as well as O. Schwemmer, "Grundlagen einer normativen Ethik" in F. Kambartel (ed.), *Praktische Philosophie und Konstruktive Wissenschaftstheorie*, Frankfurt, 1974, pp. 73ff. In contrast, F. Kambartel has introduced as the characteristic of "moral argumentations," justification vis-à-vis all (and the virtual agreement on the part of all) those affected: ibid., pp. 54ff., especially pp. 65ff. See also the discussion in *Funkkolleg*, op. cit., 8. pp. 16, 26–29; and 11, pp. 50f. See Habermas's contribution in J. Habermas/N. Luhmann (eds.), *Theorie der Gesellschaft oder Sozialtechnologie?* op. cit., pp. 164f. Recently, however, with reference to Mead, Habermas has similarly defined the universality of a moral norm by recourse to the justified "communal wills of all affected": see J. Habermas, *Theorie des kommunikativen Handelns*, vol. 2, Frankfurt 1981, p. 143.

25. See I. Kant, *Critique of Practical Reason*, op. cit., p. 63.

26. See my pertinent construction or explication of the "Grounding for the Metaphysics of Morals" in *Funkkolleg Praktische Philosophie/Ethik*, op. cit., 5, pp. 121ff.; further in D. Böhler, *Rekonstruktive Pragmatik und Hermeneutik*, Frankfurt 1983, ch. 5.

27. See *Critique of Practical Reason*, op. cit., pp. 83f.

28. See *Critique of Pure Reason*, op. cit., pp. 120ff., and *Critique of Practical Reason*, op. cit., pp. 82f.

29. As far as I am aware, F. Kambartel (1974) was the first to use the term, whereas the thereby postulated explication of the universalistic meaning of the "apriori of argumentation" was already provided earlier by Apel (*Towards a Transformation of Philosophy*, op. cit., pp. 276f.).

30. If my line of argument is correct, then the principle of universalization, contained in the particular criterion of discursive-ethical obligation, is therefore not merely, as Habermas evidently assumes, a part of "the logic of practical discourse," but rather *the logic of the validity of discourse as such*—hence also that of *theoretical* discourse. This is the point, because the possibility of justifying categorical imperatives and not merely hypothetical (dependent upon ends and therefore decisions) imperatives depends upon this.

31. See the elaborate justification by W. Kuhlmann in *Funkkolleg*, op. cit. 7, pp. 18ff.

32. R. Spaemann, "Technische Eingriffe in die Natur als Problem der politischen Ethik," in *Scheidewege*, 4, 1979, p. 491.

Dietrich Böhler

33. Thus Skirbekk in his contribution to the 15th teaching unit (Radio transmission) of the *Funkkolleg*, op. cit., which was broadcast under the title, "Die technologische und ökologische Krisenerfahrung als Herausforderung an die praktische Vernunft." See Böhler in K.-O. Apel et al. (eds.), *Praktische Philosophie/Ethik, Aktuelle Materialien, 1*, op. cit., pp. 147ff.

34. See R. Spaemann, *Funkkolleg*, op. cit., 6, especially pp. 62ff. and the dispute in 13, pp. 15ff.

35. J. Habermas in J. Habermas and N. Luhmann, *Theorie der Gesellschaft oder Sozialtechnologie*, op. cit., p. 139, see pp. 109ff., and J. Habermas, "What is Universal Pragmatics?" in *Communication and the Evolution of Society*, (trans. T. McCarthy), Cambridge, MA/London 1979, pp. 1–68.

36. Norms are ultimately justified when, on the one hand, their validity cannot be disputed and, as a result, their recognition cannot be avoided without lapsing into a pragmatic inconsistency and thereby withdrawing from the language game of argumentation; on the other hand, however, if their validity cannot be justified by inference without lapsing into the error of the *petitio principii*. See K.-O. Apel, "Das Problem der philosophischen Letztbegründung im Lichte einer tranzendentalen Sprachpragmatik," in B. Kanitscheider (ed.), *Sprache und Erkenntnis. Festschrift für G. Frey*, Innsbruck 1979, pp. 55ff.

37. See the thorough treatment of this question by W. Kuhlmann in *Funkkolleg*, op. cit. 8, pp. 66ff.

38. See G. Bastian, "Notwendige Anmerkungen zum NATO Doppelbeschluss," in A. Mechtersheimer (ed.), *Nachrüsten?*, Reinbek 1981, pp. 68ff.; G. Bastian, "Warum die 'Nachrüstung' den nuklearen Krieg in Europa möglich macht," in H. A. Pestalozzi et al. (eds.), *Frieden in Deutschland*, Munich 1982, pp. 53ff.

39. H.-G. Gadamer, *Truth and Method*, London 1975; K.-O. Apel, *Transformation der Philosophie*, 1, op. cit., pp. 22–68; J. Habermas, "Zu Gadamers Wahrheit und Methode," in K.-O. Apel et al., *Hermeneutik und Ideologiekritik*, Frankfurt 1971, pp. 45ff.; J. Habermas, *A Theory of Communicative Action*, 1, (trans. T. McCarthy), Cambridge, MA/Oxford 1985, especially pp. 102–141; D. Böhler, "Philosophie, Hermeneutik und hermeneutische Methode," in H. Hartung et al. (eds.), *Fruchtblätter: Freundesgabe für Alfred Kelletat*, Pädagogische Hochschule Berlin 1977, pp. 15–43; also in M. Führmann et al. (eds.), *Text und Applikation: Poetik und Hermeneutik, IX*, Munich 1981, pp. 483–511.

40. See J. Rawls, *A Theory of Justice*, Cambridge, MA 1971. (On this see the corresponding critique by J. Habermas: "Diskursethik—Notizen zu einem Begründungsprogramm," in *Moralbewusstsein und kommunikatives Handeln*, Frankfurt 1983, pp. 53–126.)

41. See the relevant controversy in *Funkkolleg*, op. cit., between Apel, Böhler, Höffe, and Riedel.

42. Compare Apel, Böhler, Fetscher, and Lübbe in *Funkkolleg*, op. cit., "Studienbegleitbrief" 11, especially pp. 42–54 and 65–82.

43. See Kant, "Anthropologie in pragmatischer Hinsicht," *Werke*, ed. Weischedel, Frankfurt, vol. 12, p. 411.

44. Apel, "Ist die philosophische Letztbegründung moralischer Normen auf die reale Praxis anwendbar?," in *Funkkolleg*, op. cit., "Studienbegleitbrief" 8, pp. 72ff.

4

A Theory of Practical Discourse

Robert Alexy

1 On the Problem of the Justification of Normative Statements

Whoever expresses a value judgment or an obligational judgment[1] such as "It is unjust if citizens in a state are discriminated against because of the color of their skin" or "You should help your friend who has got into difficulty," raises the claim that it is justifiable and hence correct or true.[2] This is evident already from a preliminary glance at actual linguistic practice. Contradictorily formulated statements of this type are interpreted as mutually incompatible theses.[3] Whoever utters a value judgment or an obligational judgment is as a rule prepared to advance grounds for it upon request. It will be resented if he does not do so, without at least advancing grounds for the avoidance of grounds. What can occur in discussions concerning value judgments and obligational judgments is at least not completely arbitrary. Thus, one cannot advance a statement as the ground for a value judgment that contradicts the latter and one cannot advance a statement against a value judgment that implies the latter.

There are strong grounds, therefore, for not viewing judgments of value and obligation, as is the case in emotivist theories,[4] as mere expressions and/or descriptions of feelings and/or attitudes and/or as means to their production. Different descriptions or expressions of feelings or attitudes as well as contrary means of psychological influence would not be interpreted as incompatible theses that can be disputed with reasons in a discussion.[5] Hence, one should start off from the fact that, as Patzig formulates it, by means of the "claim to justifiability which moral value-judgments always raise according to their meaning ... the sense of judgment of such statements [becomes] first of all intelligible."[6]

The fact that a claim to justifiability is raised with value judgments and obligational judgments does not yet signify that this claim is also redeemable. The latter follows just as little from the former as the former follows from the latter. There do exist close relationships, however, between the two. Thus, in the case of the truth of an assertion concerning the redeemability of the claim to justifiability, one will be more readily prepared to accept the assertion concerning the existence of this claim than one would be prepared to do so in the case of its falsity. Therefore, the question of the redeemability of the claim to justifiability is not only connected directly with the question as to the existence of this claim: it is, over and above this, also of no little significance for the answer to this question.

There exist two metaethical positions according to which the question of the justifiability of normative statements may be answered relatively simply in the positive sense: those of naturalism and intuitionism.

Those theories are characterized as "naturalistic" here, following Moore, in which it is taken as a starting point that normative expressions such as "good" and "should" can be defined by descriptive expressions.[7] If this were possible, the normative expressions which are to be found in normative statements could be replaced by descriptive expressions. Each normative statement would thereby become a descriptive statement. As such it would be testable according to the procedures of the natural and empirical social sciences. The task of ethics would be limited to the translation of normative expressions into descriptive ones.

Those theories are characterized as "intuitionistic" for which expressions such as "good" and "should" stand for some kind of qualities or relations of a nonempirical kind.[8] These nonempirical entities are not recognized through the five senses but on the basis of a further capacity. For some authors, this further capacity is something like a sixth sense, for others it is something like the ability of a priori insight, for yet others it is a mixture of both. Despite many differences in detail, which refer above all to the question as to what entities can be recognized in the manner indicated, the intuitionistic theories have this in common: the enterprise of the justification of normative statements is basically accomplished through evidences of some kind or other.

Countless arguments have been advanced against both naturalism[9] and intuitionism.[10] A central argument against naturalistic theories consists in the fact that, in the reduction of moral discourse into an empirical discourse, essential qualities of normative language are lost sight of. The function of normative language is not limited to the description of the world.[11] This is indicated, for instance, in the fact that two persons, A and B, who dispute the correctness or truth of "x is good," do not have to abandon their conflict if A defines "good" by "G_1" and B "good" by "G_2" and both assert in agreement that "x is G_1" is true and "x is G_2" is false. Against intuitionism it can above all be objected that, in the light of the fact that different people experience different evidence, it supplies no criterion for correct and false, genuine and nongenuine evidence.[12] In terms of results, therefore, intuitionism amounts to the same as subjectivism.[13] These hints should suffice here. Perhaps the arguments advanced against naturalism and intuitionism are not appropriate to demonstrate as untenable the theories typified by these expressions in all their variations and in all aspects. This may be the case especially for neonaturalistic[14] and more recent intuitionist theories.[15] Yet, nonetheless, the critique of these theories has so strongly shaken their plausibility, that sufficient grounds exist to search for further possibilities for the justification of normative statements.

Whoever states a ground such as "A had lied" (G) for a normative statement such as "A has acted badly" (N), presupposes a rule such as "lying is bad" (R), from which in association with G, N logically follows. As Hare has emphasized, "the notion of a reason, as always, . . ." includes "the notion of a rule which lays down that something is a reason for something else."[16] Hence, in the case just stated, N can be characterized as "justifiable by G and R." Whoever wishes to question the justification of N by G and R, can attack either G or R. If he attacks R, it is necessary to justify the rule expressible by "Lying is bad."

On this second level of justification a statement such as "Lying causes avoidable suffering" (G′) can be introduced as a justification. In so doing, a rule such as "What causes avoidable suffering is bad" (R′) is in turn presupposed. If, further, one wishes to also justify R′ in this manner, then a further rule (R″) is necessary, and so on. An infinite regress only seems to be avoidable if justification is terminated and replaced by a decision that is no longer to be justified. Yet this would have the result that one would be able to speak of the correctness or truth of the statement to be justified (N) only in a very limited sense. The arbitrariness of this decision is carried over to the whole justification depending on it. Therefore, the attempt to endlessly justify further normative statements in this manner leads either to an infinite regress or, at best, to a psychologically or sociologically explicable decision, but one that is no longer justified. Both could only be avoided by a logical circle, a hardly acceptable solution.

2 The Basic Idea of the Theory of Discourse

Nonetheless, this situation, characterized by Albert as the "Münchhausen trilemma",[17] is not a hopeless one. It can be avoided if the demand for yet further justification of each statement by another statement is replaced by a series of demands upon the activity of justification. These demands may be formulated as rules and forms of rational discussion. The rules of rational discourse relate not merely, as those of logic, to statements but, over and above this, to the behavior of the speakers. To this extent, they can be characterized as "pragmatic rules." It is the task of a theory of rational practical discourse to lay down such a system of rules and forms,[18] to justify it, and to test it with regard to its consistency and efficiency.

Quite different types of systems of rules may be distinguished. From the viewpoint of the system to be recommended here, extreme cases are, for example, those systems for which such strong rules or conditions[19] are formulated that the decisions made according to these rules and under these conditions are thereby determined. Rawls, for instance, speaks in this sense of the fact that the choice of his principles of justice is "the only choice consistent with the full description of the original position."[20] This means that the choice in the original position can be undertaken "from the standpoint of one person selected at random."[21] Theories such as those of Rawls are therefore not theories of rational discourse but theories of decision. Hence, Rawls's remark that "all have the same rights in the procedure for choosing principles; each can make proposals, submit reasons for their acceptance, and so on"[22] contains no essential description of the original position for his theory.

Theories such as those recommended by Rawls promise indisputable advantages. The moral geometry[23] which Rawls strives for, if it were possible to an appreciable extent, and owing to the security which it guarantees, would indeed be a considerable triumph for moral philosophy. In fact, these advantages do seem to be circumscribed. Thus Rawls's justification of the two principles of justice presupposes, inter alia, his theory of basic goods,[24] his definition of the least advantaged,[25] and his decision-making maxim of the minimization of risk.[26] In addition, there is the fact that, in the application of Rawls's principles in the four-stage sequence[27] recommended by him, so many additional considerations become necessary that Rawls himself speaks of an "indeterminacy in the theory of justice."[28] In so doing, the advantages of the decision theory approach become relativized.

These remarks are not meant as criticism of Rawls's theory. This would not at all be possible in such a brief space. Their purpose is limited to contrasting the type of theory developed by Rawls from the one recommended and to indicating the grounds that exist for the development of a theory of this latter kind. In so doing, a convergence of both theories is not ruled out; this would be a topic in its own right.

Extreme cases of another sort are theories which dispense totally or very largely with the provision of fixed rules and forms of practical argumentation. Instances of theories of this type are the perspectives developed in legal topics.[29] Viehweg's statement, "Discussion manifestly remains the sole controlling instance,"[30] is typical. The question as to how discussion is to be checked is not answered by such a statement. The provision of rules and forms in addition to this is necessary whose observance guarantees the rationality of discussion.

The degree of checking rises with the strength of rules and forms. A system of rules and forms S_1 is in a simple sense stronger than a system S_2, if S_1 equally excludes all speech acts which S_2 excludes and in addition excludes at least one act which S_2 does not exclude. The dilemma of any theory of practical discourse lies in the fact that, to the extent that its strength does indeed raise its significance for decision and thereby its usefulness, yet its chance of being generally accepted fails. Whoever, for instance, only demands the observation of the rules of logic, the truth of applied empirical premises, and perhaps also the taking into account of consequences, can quickly find broad agreement for these demands, but must pay for this with the weakness of the criteria offered.

3 The Justification of Rules of Discourse

Hence the problem presents itself as to how rules of discourse can be justified. At first glance, this problem seems to be hardly soluble. The rules of rational practical discourse are norms for the justification of norms. Therefore, are not norms of a third level necessary for their justification, so that the difficulties which arose with the justification of norms of the first level merely repeat themselves? Before an answer is sought to this question, the possibilities of justification of individual rules of discourse as well as of systems of such rules should first of all be examined. In so doing, the concept of justification will be very broadly interpreted. It permits, crudely, four modes of justification.

3.1 Technical Justification

The first mode consists in justifying rules of discourse through the specification of ends which should be achieved by their fulfillment. Lorenzen and Schwemmer, for instance, do this when they attempt to make their rules of rational practical discussion intelligible by the provision of the goal of conflict resolution free from force,[31] as does H. P. Grice who attempts to formulate his postulate of conversation in such a way that its observance serves the goals of "giving and receiving information, influencing and being influenced by others."[32] In these instances, technical rules, i.e., rules which prescribe the means for particular ends, underlie the rules of discourse.[33] Therefore, this mode of justification can be termed *technical*.

Two objections in particular can be raised against the technical mode of justification. First, the end itself must be justified once more. The technical mode of justification can achieve this only to a limited extent. The hierarchy of ends has a limit. Second, an end that could justify all rules of discourse and thus the system of rules of discourse may be either so general that incompatible norms can be recommended for it as means—this is the case, for instance, of ends such as happiness or human dignity—or, however, the state of affairs stipulated as the end is already defined by the observance of these norms. The latter may be the case, for instance, if, by the goal of resolution of conflict free from force one understands not, as Lorenzen and Schwemmer also deny,[34] a state of social pacification but a state in which conflicts can be resolved rationally.

This does not mean that the technical mode of justification is without value. It is certainly not suitable for the complete justification of all rules; yet it appears to be not merely thoroughly appropriate but to be indispensable for the justification of concrete rules by limited ends that are in turn to be justified by other modes of justification.[35]

3.2 Empirical Justification

A second possibility consists in demonstrating that specific rules are in fact binding, and hence are in fact observed, or that individual results producible according to particular rules correspond to our actually prevailing normative convictions. This mode of justification can be termed *empirical*.[36]

The main problem in the empirical mode of justification lies in the transition from the ascertainment that a rule is factually binding or corresponds to factually existing convictions to the claim that its observance leads to correct or true results, that it is thus, in this sense, rational. In this connection, what is at issue is a special case of inference from an is to an ought statement. This inference would then only be permissible if one accepted the premise that existing practices or the actually prevailing convictions are rational.

This premise is certainly not completely incorrect. At least the existence of an existing practice demonstrates that it is at all possible. One cannot be certain of it by the recommendation of not yet tested methods. The existence of an extant practice such as the presence of specific normative convictions shows, furthermore, that so far no convincing grounds have been stated against them so that all participants in the practice or carriers of the convictions would have been induced to abandon them. If one considers that the possibility of critique existed not always but certainly often, then one will not be able to deny a limited reasonableness to them at least to the extent to which they have withstood criticisms. Furthermore, a considerable advantage of the empirical mode of justification consists in the fact that within its framework it is possible to point out contradictions in an existing practice and between factually normative convictions. Thereby, the partner in justification can be prompted to abandon particular rules of specific convictions in order to adhere to others that contradict them but that appear more important to him. Finally, the existing practice and existing convictions are also of heuristic interest. It can hardly be assumed that individual theorists of discourse are in a position to construct in a presuppositionless manner the whole diversity of possible forms and rules. It seems sensible, therefore, to first of all analyze the existing practice and existing convictions and to provisionally commence from them.[37]

On the other hand, the history of the sciences and of procedural law, for instance, shows that the practice prevailing at a specific point of time is not the only one possible but also that it does not have to be the best one. Therefore, a statement such as Hegel's, "What is rational is real; and what is real is rational,"[38] at least cannot be taken literally. In the sense indicated, an empirical justification is therefore always only provisional with regard to corrections by other modes of justification.

3.3 Definitional Justification

One way which often overlaps with other modes of justification is that which analyzes and presents a system of rules (including the principles underlying such a system of rules) defining an actually existing or merely possible or continued practice, and recommends its acceptance. What is important for this mode of justification is solely that the presentation of the system of rules defining a practice is deemed to be motivating a decision for acceptance. Of course it is not ruled out here that yet further modes of justification will be used alongside this one, such as, for instance, by reference to the fact that the recommended rules are already ("have always been") in fact followed and should merely be consciously affirmed once more, or that following them has definite consequences. The only thing that is important is that the presentation of a system of rules is viewed as the ground or motive for its acceptance, independently of the provision of further grounds. This mode of justification will be termed *definitional*.[39]

The definitional mode of justification suffers from a weakness that makes it doubtful whether one is dealing in this case with a mode of justification at all. No further grounds at all are introduced for the system of rules that are to be justified; it is merely explicated and presented. This is to suffice as motive or ground. Thus, the definitional mode of justification includes a certain measure of decision or arbitrariness. Nonetheless, one cannot dismiss it as meaningless. It does make a difference as to whether one decides in favor of an explicitly formulated and fully presented system of rules, or whether one chooses something or other without this conceptual-analytical arrenal. From yet another viewpoint, the definitional mode of justification can be advantageous: it allows the construction of completely new systems of rules.

3.4 Universal-Pragmatic Justification

Finally, a fourth way consists in showing that the validity of specific rules is the precondition for the possibility of linguistic communication. According to Apel, the validity of such rules can be demonstrated from "the transcendental-pragmatic reflective perspective" and only "conclusively demonstrated"[40] from this perspective. In this manner, norms of communication are to be justified which we "can indeed violate but not negate as norms on the basis of our private decision, without abandoning a precondition for the possibility of communication as such and thereby for agreement with ourselves."[41] Habermas, however, hesitates with regard to the application of the term associated with Kant: "transcendental." He introduces two reasons here: (1) in the case of the rules of discourse what is at issue is not as in Kant the constitution of experience, but rather the production of arguments,[42] and (2) in the elaboration of these rules one cannot sharply distinguish between logical and empirical analysis.[43] Therefore, he recommends for the "reconstruction of general and unavoidable presuppositions of possible processes of understanding"[44] the expression "universal pragmatics." Since this expression, unlike the term "transcendental pragmatics," awakens fewer associations that could create misunderstandings and would be quite appropriate for characterizing Apel's approach too (the different types of universal pragmatics would then have to be distinguished), it is to be preferred. The fourth mode of justification can therefore be termed *universal-pragmatic.*

A weaker variant of this mode of justification consists in showing that (1) the validity of specific rules is constitutive for the possibility of specific speech acts,[45] and that (2) we cannot dispense with these speech acts without abandoning forms of behavior which we view as specifically human.[46]

The variants of the universal-pragmatic mode of justification just indicated present a great many problems. They raise not merely the questions as to which rules befit the character of "general and unavoidable presuppositions of possible processes of understanding," which rules are constitutive for which speech acts, what are specifically human forms of behavior and which speech acts are necessary to them, but, over and above this, the question as to the scientific-theoretical possibility of such justificatory procedures as such. We do not wish to enter here into this dispute which can be viewed as a new variant of the old controversy between logico-empirical and transcendental-philosophical positions.[47] It should merely be noted that the battle lines in this conflict are in no way clear any more. Nonetheless it can be maintained, if one can show that specific rules are generally and necessarily presupposed in linguistic communication or are constitutive for specifically human forms of behavior, that one can then definitely speak of a justification of these rules. Such a justification, however, may only be possible for relatively few fundamental rules.

3.5 The Discourse of Discourse Theory

The presentation of these four modes of justification raises no claim to completeness. It is quite conceivable that there exist still other methods, certainly other classifications are possible and in any case further differentiations can be made within the individual modes of justification. The observations already made certainly indicate clearly enough that no modes of justification are to be found which lack weaknesses. In the case of the technical justification, nonjustified ends must be presupposed. Moreover, there exists the danger that the ends are too abstract or that they contain already the rules to be justified. The empirical method makes existing practice or existing convictions into the standard of reason; the definitional method is ultimately arbitrary and the universal-pragmatic approach is suitable at best for the justification of less fundamental rules.

On the other hand, one would not wish to dispense entirely with any of these modes of justification. Each method seems to contain an important aspect. The rules which can be justified in a universal-pragmatic manner can be seen as a valuable foundation. The factually valid rules have the advantage that one knows that compliance with them is possible. To the extent to which critique of them was possible, they can be viewed as holding good; in the end, the theorist of discourse himself must allow himself to be guided by them at least initially in his justifications. Furthermore, empirically discovered rules can be examined with regard to their appropriateness and can be confronted with systems of rules built up in accordance with other functions. Through the construction of new systems of rules, the definitional model opens up the way to new modes of procedure.

These findings make it clear that a discourse about the rules of discourse is also meaningful. Such a discourse can be characterized as *discourse-theoretical discourse*. How the four possible modes of justification of discourse-theoretical discourse just outlined are to be applied, must be left to the participants in discourse. In the discussion within the framework of these four modes of justification some rules will already be followed. In the case of these rules, what is at issue are in part factually valid rules among speakers, in part provisionally justified rules. The fact that one does not proceed only according to justified rules is not unreasonable. Since this is not possible and since it is rational to begin above all with discussion, it is also rational first of all to commence on the basis of rules that have not been justified.

Discourse-theoretical discourses can proceed in very different ways. Hitherto discussions predominate in which, mostly in relation to linguistic theories, the question of the justifiability of rules of discourse is debated in general terms. A further possibility is the investigation of individual rules or forms. Here, another approach will be followed. An attempt will be made to explicitly formulate as completely as possible a system of rules and forms. In so doing, reference will be made not only to contemporary discussions in linguistics and transcendental philosophy but also to discussions in the area of analytical moral philosophy. The explicit formulation of such a system promises to have the advantage of elucidating the problems of a theory of discourse to their full extent, to make possible checks for consistency, and to facilitate if not to assure the testing of the utilizability of theories of discourse. The price of such an attempt, which consists in the fact that the problems associated with any rule and form can at best be mentioned, is thereby accepted. The explicit formulation has the goal not least of allowing deficiencies to clearly stand out. Such deficiencies can relate to the content of rules, to the incompleteness of specification, to the superfluous character of individual rules and forms as well as to their insufficiently precise formulation. If these deficiencies can be overcome, then it may be possible one day to produce something like a statute book of practical reason. Such a statute book would be the summary and explicit formulation of the rules and forms of rational practical argumentation, in part intimated in so many writings, in part only sporadically analyzed.

4 The Rules and Forms of Practical Discourse

The rules defining rational practical discourse are of a very varied kind. There are rules that are only valid in practical discourses and rules that are also valid in other language games. There exist commands, prohibitions, and permissions. Some rules require being strictly followed, others contain demands which can only be fulfilled in an approximate manner. Further, there are rules that standardize conduct within practical discourse, and rules that meet the arrangements for the transition into other forms of discourse. Finally, the forms of argument are to be distinguished from the rules of discourse.

In what follows, the different rules and forms will be condensed into their respective groups.

4.1 Basic Rules

The validity of the first group of rules is the precondition for the possibility of any linguistic communication in which what is in question is correctness or truth:

(1.1) No speaker may contradict him or herself.

(1.2) Each speaker may only assert what he himself believes.

(1.3) Each speaker who applies a predicate F to an object a, must also be prepared to apply F to any other object which is similar to a in all relevant respects.

(1.4) Different speakers may not use the same expression with different meanings.

(1.1) refers to the rules of logic. These rules will be presupposed here. Nonetheless, two points should be noticed. First, it will be presupposed that the rules of logic are also applicable to normative statements.[49] Second, the reference to the rules of logic expressed in (1.1) relates not merely to classical logic but also and above all to deontic logic.[50] The ban on contradicting oneself therefore also extends to deontic incompatibilities.

(1.2) secures the sincerity of discussion. (1.2) is constitutive for all linguistic communication.[51] Without (1.2) not even lying would be possible for if no rule is presupposed that demands sincerity then deception is inconceivable. (1.2) does not exclude the utterance of conjectures, it requires merely that they can be characterized as such. (1.3) refers to the use of expressions by a speaker, (1.4) to the use of expressions by different speakers. (1.3) is more strongly formulated to the extent that it demands the preparedness for consistent application. Yet this is not a basic distinction for one could strengthen (1.4) by saying that only that person may use an expression who is prepared to apply it, if it is applicable. On this precondition, one could unite (1.3) and (1.4) together into a rule that demands that all speakers must use all expressions with the same meaning. That this does not occur here lies in the fact that (1.3) and (1.4) contain totally diverse aspects of this general rule that are well worth distinguishing.

(1.3) refers to the consistency of the speaker. Applied to evaluative expressions, (1.3) takes on the following form:

(1.3′) Any speaker may only assert such value and obligational judgments as he would equally assert in all situations which are the same in all relevant respects to the situation in which he or she makes the assertion.

(1.3′) is a formulation of Hare's principle of universalizability.[52]

(1.4) requires the communality of linguistic usage. How this communality can be created and secured is disputed. Exponents of the Erlangen School demand that, to this end, every expression must be standardized ortholinguistically. Toward this end, everyday language may only subsidiarily be applied.[53]

The question as to whether this program can be implemented can remain open here.[54] At all events, it seems to suffice to first of all commence from everyday language and to make stipulations concerning the usage of words only when obscurities and misunderstandings crop up.

The discussions carried out for the purposes of clarifying problems of understanding may be seen as discourses of a distinctive type. They may be called language-analytical discourses. Alongside the creation of a common linguistic usage, what is also at issue in language-analytical discourse is securing clear and meaningful speech. (1.4) might be amplified in this sense.

4.2 The Rules of Reason

The fact that the claim to correctness or truth is raised with value judgments and obligational judgments means that value judgments and obligational judgments are to be interpreted as genuine assertions.[55] In practical discourses, what is at issue is the justification of such assertions.[56] In the discussion of these assertions, further assertions are advanced and so on. Assertions are also necessary in order to refute something, in order to reply to questions, and in order to justify recommendations. A practical discourse without assertion is impossible.

Whoever asserts something will not only express the fact that he or she believes something; over and above this, the person asserts that that which they state is also justifiable, that it is true and correct. This holds equally for normative as well as for non-normative statements.

The content of the claim to justifiability is not that the speaker is in a position to provide a justification. It suffices that the speaker refers to the justificatory competency of specific or specifiable persons. Reference to the justificatory competence of others is discussable like any other argument. Thus, it can be asked whether the authority invoked by the speaker actually guarantees the correctness of his or her thesis. In this connection, it is possible and, as a rule, necessary to consider the substantive correctness of his or her assertion. The recourse to the justificatory competence of specific or specifiable others can thus also be viewed as justification. Yet it does not suffice that the speaker—without being able to give grounds for this—merely holds the view that at some time or other some person or other will be in a position to justify his or her statement.

Furthermore, the claim to justifiability does not imply that the speaker must justify every assertion vis-à-vis every other person. The speaker must only do this on request.[57] If he or she avoids a justification, however, it is necessary that he or she can provide grounds which justify such an avoidance.

Hence, the following rule is valid for the speech act of asserting something:

(2) Every speaker must justify what he or she asserts upon request, unless he or she can provide grounds which justify avoiding giving a justification.[58]

This rule can be termed the *general rule of justification.*

Whoever justifies something at least pretends, at least with regard to the justification, to accept the other person as equal partner in justification and neither to exercise constraint nor to support constraint exercised by others. Further, he claims to be able to justify his assertion not only to the discussion partner but, over and above this, to anyone. Language games which do not at least pretend to fulfill these demands cannot be viewed as justifications.[59] The demands for equality, universality, and lack of constraint can be formulated as three rules. These rules correspond to the conditions stimulated by Habermas for the "ideal speech situation."[60] The first rule refers to participation in discourses. It contains the following:

(2.1) Anyone who can speak may take part in discourse.
The second rule standardizes the freedom of discussion. It may be subdivided into three demands:

(2.2) (a) Anyone may render any assertion problematic.
(b) Anyone may introduce any assertion into the discourse.
(c) Anyone may express his/her opinions, wishes and needs.

A Theory of Practical Discourse

(c) is especially important in practical discourses. Finally, the third rule has the aim of protecting discourses from constraints. It states:

(2.3) No speaker may be prevented by constraint within or outside the discourse from making use of his/her rights established in (2.1) and (2.2).

It can be questioned as to whether (2.3) is a rule of discourse at all. One could also view it as a precondition for the fulfillment of (2.1) and (2.2). Nonetheless, it must suffice here to indicate its special status.

The problems associated with these rules are easy to see. It is precluded on factual grounds that all persons utilize their rights standardized in (2.1) and (2.2) and it can be questioned as to whether the absence of constraint demanded by (2.3) can ever be achieved. Here we wish merely to draw attention to these problems; they will be discussed below in a detailed look at the usefulness of discourse theory. (2) as well as (2.1)–(2.3) define the most typical preconditions for discourse theory's concept of rationality. Therefore, they may be termed "rules of reason."

4.3 The Rules of the Burden of Argumentation

The rules of reason permit anyone to problematize any assertion without restrictions. Any speaker can thereby force each speaker into a corner like a child who mechanically asks more and more "why" questions. Further, it is possible to make out everything to be questionable at once. In so doing, the question arises as to the distribution and extent of the burdens of argumentation and justification.[61] This problem arises in very diverse contexts. Thus, according to Singer, the principle of generalizability requires that he who wants to treat one person differently from another person must provide a reason for this.[62] In Lorenzen's dialogical logic, for instance, the person who asserts that all x possess the quality F ([x] Fx) has the duty to show of every a that a is an F (Fa).[63] Perelman's principle of inertia[64] requires that an interpretation or practice that is once accepted may not be given up again without reason.[65] The distribution of the burden of argumentation demanded by Singer results from the principle of universalizability (1.3′) together with the rule of justification (2). Whoever wishes to treat A differently from B asserts (insofar as he presupposes (1.3′) that a relevant difference exists. He must justify this assertion. The following rule thus applies:

(3.1) Whoever wishes to treat a person A differently from a person B is obliged to justify this.[66]

A further justification of (3.1) consists in the fact that, according to the rules of reason, all are equal and therefore reasons must be advanced in order to justify a deviation from this state of affairs. The rules of reason establish a presumption for equality.[67]

The justification of a dialogical construction of logic cannot be discussed here. Therefore, attention is only drawn to the self-evident fact that the rules of logic impose the strictest argumentative obligations. Whoever asserts "p → q" must, if his partner in discussion advances "¬ q", either accept "¬ p" or refute "¬ q" or abandon "p → q".

Perelman's principle of inertia is of considerable importance. If a speaker asserts something, then his partners in discussion have the right according to (2) to demand a justification. In contrast, a statement or a norm which in fact is presupposed to be true or valid in a speech community without being expressly asserted or discussed may, according to this principle, only be doubted by the specification of a reason. In order that something is the object of discourse, it must thus either be asserted or called into question by the specification of reasons.

(3.2) Whoever attacks a statement or norm that is not the object of discussion must provide a reason for doing so.

Further, no speaker has the right to demand more and more reasons from his partner.[68] The partner's reasons would quickly be exhausted. If the partner has provided a reason, to which the rule of justification has obliged him, then he is only still obliged to react to counterarguments. Of course, he also remains justified to reply to mere doubts:

(3.3) Whoever has put forward an argument is only committed to further arguments in the case of a counterargument.

(2.2.b) and (2.2.c) allow any speaker at any time to introduce into the discourse any number of assertions as well as statements concerning his opinions, wishes, and needs. Anyone at any time, without a connection existing with the problem discussed, can utter assertions concerning the weather, for instance, as well as statements about how he finds it. It is not necessary to exclude such statements completely. If they only occur occasionally they need not damage the discussion. When they should be excluded must be left to the discretion of the participants in the discourse. It is also not appropriate to exclude them by the demand of only expressing what is relevant,[69] in the sense that it is stated in the theory of discourse what is relevant. To pass judgment on this is equally a matter for participants in argumentation. Hence, the following rule suggests itself:

(3.4) Whoever introduces an assertion or a statement concerning his opinions, wishes, or needs into the discourse, which as argument is not related to a previous statement, has to justify upon request why he/she has introduced this assertion or this statement.

4.4 The Forms of Argument

Before we enter into further rules of discourse, it is first of all meaningful to look at the forms of argument[70] typical of practical discourses.

The immediate object of practical discourse is *singular normative statements* (N). There are two basic types of their justification. In the first type, reference is made to a rule (R) that is presupposed as valid, in the second attention is drawn to the consequences (F) of following the imperative[71] implied by N.[72]

There exists an important structural affinity between these two types. Whoever has recourse to a rule in a justification presupposes at least that the preconditions for the application of this rule are fulfilled. In the case of these preconditions for application, the qualities of a person, an action, or an object, the existence of a specific state of affairs, or the occurrence of a specific event can be at issue. This means that the person who states a rule as a reason presupposes a statement (T) describing such qualities, states of affairs, or events as true.

On the other hand, the person who states an assertion about the consequences as a reason for N presupposes a rule of the content that bringing about these consequences is important or good. This is the case because of the general statement that "the notion of a reason, as always, brings with it the notion of a rule which lays down that something is a reason for something else."[73]

In this way, the following forms of argument may be distinguished:

(4.1) T
       R
       —
       N
(4.2) F
       R
       —
       N

(4.1) and (4.2) are subordinate forms of the more general form:

(4) G
     R˙
     —
     N˙[74]

A theoretical discourse can be carried on concerning the truth of T as well as whether F is actually a result of the action that is in question.[75] The requirement of being able at all times to open such a discourse needs to be stated in a further rule still to be introduced below.

Here we are interested above all in the dispute over R. There are different possibilities of defending R. R can be justified by reference to the state of affairs which prevails if R is valid (Z_R), or by reference to a future state of affairs that is brought about if R is followed (Z_F). Z_R and Z_F can be distinguished by the fact that for the description of Z_R alongside the reference to results that are describable independent of R, a reference to R is necessary. If one bears these distinctions in mind, it is nonetheless justified on grounds of simplicity to speak of *following the rule* $R(F_R)$ equally in the case of Z_R as in the case of Z_F.

In the case of the justification of R by F_R, too, the principle obtains that the provision of a reason for an assertion presupposes a rule which states that that which is introduced as a reason is a reason for this assertion. Therefore, a second-order rule (R') is necessary. Alongside the reference to F_R, reference to a further rule R' is possible which requires R under a condition T' that is not to be classified as a result of R. For instance, T' can be the by no means morally irrelevant reference to the fact that a specific rule was adopted in a specific manner.

Two forms of argument of the second order are thus provided:

(4.3) F_R
      R'
      —
      R

(4.4) T'
      R'
      —
      R

In the case of (4.3) and (4.4), too, we are dealing with subordinate forms of the basic form (4).[76]

In (4.2)–(4.4) in each case the application of a *single* rule leads to a *single* result. Yet different rules in justifications of the same form or in justifications of different forms can lead to mutually incompatible results. In these cases it must be decided which justification has precedence. The rules that are referred to for the justification of such decisions are called *rules of precedence*.[77]

There are rules of precedence which prescribe that some rules take precedence over others under all conditions; but there also exist rules of precedence which prescribe that specific rules take precedence over others only under specific conditions (C). "P" shall stand for a preferential relation between two rules. The rules of precedence can then have two forms:

(4.5) R; P R_k or R'; P R'_k

(4.6) (R_iP R_k)C or (R'_iP R'_k)C

The rules of precedence can in turn be justified according to (4.3) and (4.4).[78] If a conflict between rules of precedence exists, second-order rules of precedence are to be applied.

Within the different forms, a plurality of further differentiations is possible. Thus, for instance, the reference to negative consequences represents a particularly important variant of (4.2) and (4.3). Perhaps even more forms can also be found. Yet for the theory of rational practical discourse outlined in this investigation, the analysis carried out so far is sufficient.

Above all, it shows one thing: the different forms of argument (except for limitations resulting from the two-stage nature of justification) can be combined and reiterated at will. The different connections of forms of argument result in a structure of argument.[79] Here a distinction is to be made between a regressive and an additive structure of argument.[80] Justifications can be associated with investigations, investigations lead to justifications.[81] The structures of argument resulting in this manner are always finite. All rules can never be justified, some must indeed be recognized if the activity of justification is to be at all possible.[82] The demand for rationality does not mean that all rules are to be justified at once but rather only that each rule can be the object of justification.

4.5 The Rules of Justification

Only *forms* of argument utilizable in practical discourses are provided with (4.1)–(4.6). It is indeed already a gain in rationality if argumentation takes place at all in these forms and attempts are not made to bully others through the substitution of persuasive means.[83] On the other hand, many normative statements and rules can be justified in these forms. We should therefore search further for rules for justifications undertaken in these forms.

A first important group of rules is formed by the different variants of the principle of universalizability.[84] Hence, three versions of the demand for universalizability are to be distinguished: those of Hare, Habermas, and Baier.[85]

Hare's principle of universalizability has already been formulated as a rule (1.3′). From this principle, together with the principle of prescriptivity, Hare obtains a demand such as the following:[86]

(5.1.1) Everyone must be able to accept the consequences[87] of the rule—presupposed in his normative statements—regarding the satisfaction of the interests of each individual person even for the hypothetical case in which he finds himself in the situation of this person.[88]

In short, each person must be able to agree to the consequences of the rules for everyone that are presupposed or asserted by that person.

Habermas's principle of universalizability derives directly from the structure of discourse determined by the rules of reason ([2.1]–[2.3]). If all persons have equal rights to deliberate about practical questions, then only such normative statements and rules can find universal agreement which each person can accept. In (5.1.1) we commenced from the normative conceptions of the *individual* speaker. Habermas's principle of universalizability refers to the *communal* interpretations to be produced in discourse. It can be formulated in the following way:

(5.1.2) The consequences of every rule for the satisfaction of the interests of each and every individual must be capable of being accepted by all.[89]

In short, every person must be able to agree to every rule. (5.1.2) shares the ideal character of the rules of reason.

Baier's principle may be justified from the demands for openness and honesty operative in discourse. One could interpret it as a concretization of (1.2). It directly excludes a series of rules as unjustifiable:[90]

(5.1.3) Every rule must be openly and universally teachable.

(5.1.1)–(5.1.3), too, do not yet offer something like the guarantee of a rational *agreement*. (5.1.1) allows us to commence from the diverse, factually available normative convictions of the respective speaker, (5.1.2) shares the ideal character of the rules of reason, and (5.1.3) excludes only relatively few moral rules.

Yet it is not possible to provide a procedure which leads in every case to a rational agreement. But much would already have been gained if a procedure did exist which at least raised the probability of the transformation of factually prevailing irreconcilable conceptions in the direction of a rational agreement. Such a procedure is recommended by Habermas[91] as well as by Lorenzen and Schwemmer[92]—in a form worked out in full detail—in their program of critical genesis. In such a genesis, the development of the moral system of rules is replicated by the participants in discourse. It can thus be discovered at the different stages of development how far the conditions of rational discourse were realized. Correspondingly, the rules can be criticized that emerged in this developmental process and that now determine our practical argumentation. Hence, the following additional rule of discourse can be formulated:

(5.2.1) The moral rules that form the basis of the moral conceptions of the speakers must be able to withstand scrutiny in a critical, historical genesis. A moral rule does not withstand such a scrutiny.

(a) if it was indeed originally justifiable rationally but in the meantime has lost its justification, or

(b) if it was already originally not justifiable rationally and if no sufficient new reasons for it can be found.

The investigation of the historical-social emergence of norms proposed by Lorenzen and Schwemmer can be extended by an investigation of the individual emergence of normative conceptions:

(5.2.2) The moral rules that form the basis of the moral conceptions of the speakers must be able to withstand the scrutiny of their individual history of emergence. A moral rule does not withstand such a scrutiny if it is only accepted on the basis of conditions of socialization that are not justifiable.

At this point, it must remain open what "conditions of socialization that are not justifiable" are. Here it can only be pointed out that the conditions of socialization are in any case unjustifiable if they lead to the situation in which the person concerned is not prepared or not in a position to participate in discourses.

A final rule in this group arises out of the fact that practical discourses are carried on for the purpose of solving actually existing practical questions. This means that it must be possible to translate the result of a discourse into action. To be sure, one can also organize discourses for pleasure but this possibility, compared to the former aim, is parasitical. It follows from this that practical discourses must lead to results that can also be implemented:

(5.3) The factually given limits of realizability are to be observed.[93]

This application of (5.3) presupposes substantial empirical knowledge. (5.1)–(5.3) directly decide about the content of the statements and rules that are to be justified. Therefore they may be called *rules of justification*.

4.6 Rules of Transition

It has already been mentioned that in practical discourses problems often arise which cannot be solved by means of practical argumentation. In this context, the issue can be questions of fact, especially the prediction of consequences, linguistic problems, especially problems of understanding, and questions that relate to practical discussion itself. In these cases, it must also be possible to switch to other forms of discourse. This possibility is secured by the following rules:

(6.1) It is possible at all times for any speaker to switch to a theoretical (empirical) discourse.

(6.2) It is possible at all times for any speaker to move to a linguistic-analytical discourse.

(6.3) It is possible at all times for any speaker to move to a discourse on discourse theory.

(6.1)–(6.3) may be termed *rules of transition*. (6.1) is of special significance. It is often the case that speakers agree on the normative premises but are in dispute concerning the facts. Often the necessary empirical knowledge cannot be obtained with the certainty that is wished for. In this situation, rules of rational conjecture are necessary.

5 The Usefulness of Discourse Theory

The rules and forms we have introduced offer neither a guarantee for the prospect that agreement can be reached in each practical question nor for the fact that an agreement reached is final and irrevocable. The reason for this is that the rules of reason (2.1)–(2.3) especially are only realizable incompletely, that not all the steps in argumentation are laid down, and also that each discourse must be connected to historically pregiven and changeable normative conceptions. Hence the question arises as to the usefulness of the system of rules presented here.

This question has different meanings and can be asked from different presuppositions. The strongest presupposition would be that a theory of discourse is only to be viewed as useful if it leads in each case to a secure result. The latter would then be possible if the rules of discourse were to be so strongly formulated that they contained the solution to each individual case (in a sense that cannot be made more precise here). This might only be achievable through a situation in which the rules of procedure were enlarged by substantive rules, which would amount to a codification of a morality. The disadvantage is easy to see. Such a codification of a morality could hardly hope for universal agreement. The greater certainty of results must be paid for by a greater uncertainty with regard to presuppositions. In addition, such a codification, as experience with legal codifications teaches us, would not always lead to secure results.

The uncertainty would only be reduced but not eliminated.

Since no other procedure for justification is in sight that guarantees the certainty of results on the basis of a high acceptability of presuppositions, the person who insists strongly on the certainty of results would have to renounce rules of justification altogether. What remains for him is mere decision. Yet such an all or nothing standpoint is neither necessary nor meaningful. Even the modes of procedure of the empirical sciences do not guarantee ultimate certainty in all questions.

5.1 Discursive Necessity, Impossibility, and Possibility

It would be a mistake to conclude from the fact that the rules of discourse do not guarantee certainty in every case that anything is compatible with them. There are some results that are absolutely demanded or absolutely excluded by them. This is true, for instance, of norms which completely exclude some people from discursive will-formation, by assigning to them the legal status of a slave. In this sense, one may speak of "discursive impossibility" or "discursive necessity."

In those cases in which, without violating rules of discourse,[94] two mutually incompatible normative statements can be justified, one can speak of "discursive possibility." Although the scope for discursive possibilities is great, nonetheless by no means everything is possible. The scope is further circumscribed by the fact that much of what would be possible solely according to the rules of discourse, and thus presupposing randomly constituted individuals, is not possible according to the rules of discourse together with the actual characteristics of participants in discourse. Insofar as the theory of discourse in this sense leaves much to the discussants, it starts out from the fact that the latter are sufficiently rational in order to arrive at rational results under the conditions of discourse.

5.2 The Function of Discourse Theory as an Instrument of Critique

The judgment of the usefulness of discourse theory has to take place with reference to four functions that it can fulfill. A first function is that of an *instrument of critique*. Thus, in answer to individual normative statements, it can be shown that the person who asserts them could not adhere to them in a discussion that takes place according to the rules of discourse. This is the case, for instance, if it becomes apparent that the normative statement which is asserted leads to contradictions (1.1), that it cannot withstand a scrutiny in the forms of argument (4.1)–(4.6), that the speaker would not accept it if he had to bear the consequences implicit in it himself (5.1.1) or if he would clearly perceive on the basis of which conditions of socialization he arrived at these convictions (5.2.2), etc. Furthermore, argumentations can be criticized, for instance, on the grounds that a confrontation with the arguments of potential speakers does not take place, in contravention of the rules of reason (2.1) and (2.2).

5.3 The Function of Discourse Theory as a Hypothetical Criterion

Related to the function of an instrument of critique is the function of providing a *negative* or *positive hypothetical criterion* for the correctness or truth of normative statements. The function of rules as a negative hypothetical criterion is relatively unproblematical. It is easy to produce normative statements about which one can say that no agreement would be reached concerning them in a discussion carried out according to the rules of discourse. Stated crudely, this includes all those normative statements that are in fact not impossible discursively but which nonetheless imply such a considerable disregard of the interests of one group in favor of another that the disadvantaged would refuse to agree to them in a discourse. Hence, the application of the rules of discourse as a negative criterion is thus relatively unproblematical because no consensus but rather only a dissensus must be predicted.

In contrast, an anticipation of a consensus is necessary for the application of rules of discourse as a positive hypothetical criterion. Spaemann has quite rightly emphasized that no operationalizable criterion exists for this.[95] It is factually impossible to predict with certainty the behavior of everyone in discussion. The empirical knowledge necessary for this would hardly be achievable. Nonetheless, this does not yet make the criterion meaningless. Well-grounded predictions can be distinguished from arbitrary ones. What is important is solely that the character of these prognoses as conjectures, as hypotheses corrigible at all times, remains intact. Whoever bases his actions upon such conjectures carries the responsibility for them. The weakness of the standard is thus on its own no decisive argument against its application. As long as no stronger criterion is specified, it is better to put up with a weak one than to do totally without criteria.

5.4 The Function of Discourse Theory as Explication

The function of the system of rules as a means to *explicate the claim to correctness or truth* is not directly related to practical usefulness. Nonetheless, there is an indirect relation to practical significance. Whoever realizes what he claims with the expression of a value or obligational judgment will incline towards a cautious, fallibilistic attitude. His personal responsibility for actions based upon such judgments will be perfectly obvious to him. The preparedness for tolerance may also be increased. Further, the recommended explication of the claim to correctness and truth makes clear that totally different, concrete, normative conceptions can be derived from or be compatible with the same system of rules. The differences can be explained by different factual assumptions and different initial normative conceptions. From this angle, preparedness for discussion is closely linked with tolerance. The interpretations which associate "potentially totalitarian consequences" with the theory of discourse[96] must therefore be resolutely rejected. The consequences for individuals observed here are rather those of a fallibilistic attitude, tolerance, and readiness for discussion.

5.5 The Function of Discourse Theory as the Definition of an Ideal

The function of the rules of discourse as the *definition of an ideal* refers to the question of the factual realizability or institutionalizability of discourses. Despite manifold connections, this question is to be distinguished from that of the role of rules of discourse in the analysis and critique of the justifications of normative statements.[97]

5.6 Possibilities and Limits of the Institutionalization of Discourses

Numerous arguments against the possibility of the institutionalization of discourses rest upon the unrealizability of ideal conditions. On factual grounds, it is impossible that everyone discuss everything without restriction; time is short.[98] The problems that must be resolved in a modern society are too numerous and too complex for them all to be thoroughly discussed.[99] In order to fulfill the decision-making requirements of a society, discourses must be broken off at the right moment. How should this happen according to the rules provided here? Some authors, therefore, are worried about the termination of discourses.[100] Thus, Weinrich fears that every group is put in the position of persisting in debate for so long until it obtains an advantage: the "dictatorship of perseverance."[101]

The ideal of freedom from domination, closely associated with discourse, has also been objected to. On the one hand, it is argued that structurally determined features of domination also emerge in systems of discussion. The influence of the skillful talker is greater than that of the unskillful.[102] On the other hand, it is emphasized that constraint cannot be replaced by discourse. "It can only be demanded of someone to voluntarily remain within the limits laid down for him if he possesses the security that all others will also do the same with regard to him . . . But he can only have this security if the obedience of all can be enforced in case of need."[103] The promised freedom from domination, so it is constantly feared, leads to the unchecked domination of the self-styled enlightener.

Regarding these objections, it should be pointed out first of all that the recommendation of rules of discourse does not imply a model for the organization of discourses or for decision-making processes or for society as a whole. Closest to the model implicit in rules of discourse is the moral-philosophical discussion conducted in the context of the institution of science without pressure of decision and in principle without restriction as to participants over generations. Even for the organization of a seminar discussion the system of rules does not suffice. What is needed is the introduction of further rules concerning, for instance, the leadership of the discussion, permitted deviations from the theme, etc. The necessity for such subsystems of rules increases in the case of discussions meant to lead to decisions. Thus, no parliament gets along without majority principles, rules for the formation of executive committees, or principles of representation, in short, without rules determining its constitution and its standing orders.[104] Hardly a system of discussion committed to decision-making will today be able to dispense further with rules for the intervention of expert competence but also for its control. In this manner, systems of discussion are able through organization to increase their capacity to accomplish their tasks. It can at least not be taken for granted that an organization of decision-making processes oriented towards the requirements of discourse necessarily has worse consequences than does the renunciation of such an orientation. It should be mentioned here that it is quite compatible with such an orientation in a society to withdraw individual areas of decision-making from the mandate of discursive regulation. An example of such an area for which this would be advisable may be that of the choice of partners. A discourse can be held anew concerning the rules regulating discourse and thus limiting the freedom of discussants, as well as concerning the question as to areas in which decisions are to be made by organized discourse. Those limitations are justified which, compared with others or even with no limitations at all, offer a greater chance that a result emerges which would also emerge under ideal conditions. In a certain sense, however, this is merely a postponement of the problem. Such additional systems of rules also affect interests; agreement cannot always be expected.[105] The introduction of a system of rules, such as that of parliamentarianism, rests not merely upon good arguments but also upon political action. Yet the fact that carrying out something depends upon political action does not mean that it is of no consequence whether good grounds exist for it. This would be a variation of the all-or-nothing standpoint outlined above. In any case, the fact that something is carried out not merely on the basis of good reasons means that there is sufficient ground for openness to criticism and for tolerance.

The idea of discourse is not only compatible with an organization of discourses limiting the freedom of discussion. It also does not exclude the exercise of constraint. Thus, it cannot be ruled out that in a discourse an agreement is reached concerning a rule of communal life which sets certain limits to the pursuit of individual interests but that this rule is then not adhered to by all. Following a rule under these circumstances can be demanded of no one. Therefore, constraint to adhere to the rule is already necessary to ensure that discourse does not remain without results. Given the possibility of deviation from rules established discursively, the notion of discourse already implies that of a legal order. A legal order is also necessary for a series of further reasons. Thus, in view of the extent of the need for decisions in a modern society, it is not possible to decide every emerging practical question on the basis of a newly organized discussion. Rules for the deciding of cases must be formed and adhered to rigorously. In this way, legal rules make an important contribution to the unburdening of practical discourse.[106] Furthermore, it must be emphasized that legal rules have the additional important function to secure factually the by no means self-evident possibility of holding discourses.[107] Of course, the fact that legal rules are able to secure the possibility of holding discourses does not mean that they are not amenable to, and in need of, discursive justification.

Agreement may perhaps be achieved concerning the fundamental possibility of institutionalizing discourses in the sense indicated. What will be disputed is, above all, the extent to which practical questions can be subjected to discursive will-formation and the amount of freedom and directness of this will-formation. The answer to these questions rests, not least, upon how optimistic or how pessimistic is the explicitly or implicitly held anthropology of the person involved. In that case the dispute may be largely undecidable.

A conclusion derived from this, namely, that one can do nothing for the institutionalization of discourses and hence of reason, and that one cannot for instance consciously cultivate in schools the capacity for rational practical discussion,[108] nonetheless rightly deserves the unattractive name of "pessimistic fallacy."

Notes

The present reflections are a summary and extension of some of the ideas contained in the author's work, *Theorie der juristischen Argumentation. Die Theorie des rationalen Diskurses als Theorie der juristischen Begründung*, Frankfurt, Suhrkamp, 1978, new edition 1983.

1. By "obligational judgment" is understood here all those normative statements that can be formulated with the help of deontic basic terms "should," "forbidden," or "allowed"; "value judgment" refers to all other normative statements.

2. No opinion is given here on the question as to the truth-status of normative statements responded to by the formulation "true or false." This question cannot be discussed in the framework of a theory of practical discourse but rather only in the context of an investigation of theories of truth. Nonetheless, a theory of practical discourse can supply important arguments for such a discussion. Those outlined here offer largely positive ones. For a summary of arguments for the truth-status of normative statements, see A. R. White, *Truth*, London/Basingstoke 1970, pp. 57–65.

3. See G. Patzig, "Relativismus und Objektivität moralischer Normen," in his *Ethik ohne Metaphysik*, Göttingen 1971, p. 71.

4. See, for instance, C. L. Stevenson, *Ethics and Language*, New Haven/London 1944; A. J. Ayer, *Language, Truth and Logic*, London 1936, new edition Harmondsworth 1971, pp. 26–29, 136–151; R. Carnap, *Philosophy and Logical Syntax*, London 1935, pp. 22–26.

5. On further features of moral language which support the view that moral judgments are genuine assertions, see P. Glassen, "The Cognitivity of Moral Judgments," in *Mind*, 68, 1959, pp. 57ff.

6. G. Patzig, op. cit., p. 75. See further, W. K. Frankena, *Ethics*, Englewood Cliffs, N.J. 1963, pp. 91f.; J. Habermas, "Wahrheitstheorien," in H. Fahrenbach (ed.), *Wirklichkeit und Reflexion, Festschrift für W. Schulz*, Pfullingen 1973, p. 220.

7. See G. E. Moore, *Principia Ethica*, Cambridge 1903, p. 40. Moore characterizes as "naturalistic" both theories which define normative expressions by empirical expressions as well as those which in addition use metaphysical expressions. Here only the first alternative is considered. For a critique of Moore's terminology, see W. K. Frankena, "The Naturalistic Fallacy," in P. Foot (ed.), *Theories of Ethics*, Oxford 1967, pp. 57ff.

8. See, for instance, G. E. Moore, op. cit., p. 7; M. Scheler, *Formalism in Ethics and Non-Formal Ethics of Values* (trans. M. S. Frings and R. L. Funk), Evanston 1973, pp. 111ff.; W. D. Ross, *The Right and the Good*, Oxford 1930, pp. 12ff., 91ff.

Robert Alexy

9. See on this, above all, the discussion which takes up Moore's open-question argument (G. E. Moore, op. cit., pp. 15ff.): R. Brandt, *Ethical Theory*, Englewood Cliffs, N.J. 1959, p. 165; G. C. Kerner, *The Revolution in Ethical Theory*, Oxford 1966, pp. 19f.; N. Hoerster, "Zum Problem der Ableitung eines Sollens aus einem Sein in der analytischen Moralphilosophie," in *Archiv für Rechts- und Sozialphilosophie*, 55, 1969, pp. 20ff.; K. Nielsen, "Covert and Overt Synonymetry. Brandt and Moore and the 'Naturalistic Fallacy'," in *Philosophical Studies*, 25, 1974, pp. 53f.

10. See on this, for instance, P. H. Nowell-Smith, *Ethics*, Harmondsworth 1954, pp. 36–47; P. Edwards, *The Logic of Moral Discourse*, New York/London 1955, pp. 94–103; S. E. Toulmin, *The Place of Reason in Ethics*, Cambridge 1950, pp. 10–28; E. V. Savigny, *Die Philosophie der normalen Sprache*, Frankfurt 1969, pp. 196–199.

11. See, instead of many others, R. M. Hare, *The Language of Morals*, London/Oxford/ New York, 1952, p. 91.

12. P. Strawson, "Ethical Intuitionism," in *Philosophy*, 24, 1949, p. 27.

13. G. C. Kerner, op. cit., p. 33.

14. See G. J. Warnock, *Contemporary Moral Philosophy*, London/Basingstoke 1967, pp. 62–77; P. Foot, "Moral Argument," in *Mind*, 67, 1958, pp. 502ff.; P. Foot, "Moral Beliefs," in P. Foot (ed.), *Theories of Ethics*, Oxford 1967, pp. 83ff.

15. See, for instance, E. V. Savigny, *Die Überprüfbarkeit der Strafrechtssätze*, Freiburg 1967.

16. R. M. Hare, *Freedom and Reason*, Oxford 1963, p. 21; see further, S. E. Toulmin, *The Uses of Argument*, Cambridge 1958, p. 97.

17. See H. Albert, *Traktat über kritische Vernunft*, Tübingen 1968, p. 13, as well as K. R. Popper, *The Logic of Scientific Discovery*, London 1968, p. 71.

18. The distinction between rules and forms is made clear in detail in its formulation below. Here it should merely be remarked that forms may be reformulated in rules, namely, in rules which require that in particular situations of argumentation one can make use of particular forms and only particular forms of arguments. Therefore, one speaks more often only of rules.

19. It should be assumed here that preconditions (e.g., that of lack of knowledge of one's own situation) may indeed by reformulated in rules (e.g., that of not stating any arguments which one would not state if one found oneself in another situation). If this assumption does not hold, then for this reason alone significant distinctions emerge between theories which only produce rules and theories which also formulate preconditions.

20. J. Rawls, *A Theory of Justice*, Cambridge, MA 1971, p. 121.

21. Ibid., p. 139.

22. Ibid., p. 19.

23. Ibid., p. 121.

24. Ibid., pp. 95ff.

25. Ibid., pp. 92f.

26. Ibid., pp. 152ff.

27. Ibid., pp. 195ff.

28. Ibid., p. 201.

29. See, for instance, T. Viehweg, *Topik und Jurisprudenz*, 5th edition, Munich 1974; G. Struck, *Topische Jurisprudenz*, Frankfurt 1971.

30. T. Viehweg, op. cit., p. 43.

31. P. Lorenzen and O. Schwemmer, *Konstruktive Logik, Ethik und Wissenschaftstheorie*, Mannheim/Vienna/Zurich 1973, p. 109; O. Schwemmer, *Philosophie der Praxis*, Frankfurt 1971, p. 106; O. Schwemmer, "Grundlagen einer normativen Ethik" in F. Kambartel (ed.), *Philosophie und konstruktive Wissenschaftstheorie*, Frankfurt 1974, p. 77.

32. H. P. Grice, *Logic and Conversations*, MS 1968, p. 38.

33. See on this, G. H. v. Wright, *Norm and Action*, London 1963, pp. 9ff. For an attempt at formalizing Grice's conversational postulate as a technical rule, see S. Kanngiesser, "Sprachliche Universalien und diachrone Prozesse" in K.-O. Apel (ed.), *Sprachpragmatik und Philosophie*, Frankfurt 1976, p. 301.

34. P. Lorenzen and O. Schwemmer, op. cit., p. 109.

35. Arne Naess's six main rules can perhaps be viewed as such concrete rules. See A. Naess, *Kommunikation und Argumentation*, Kronbert 1975, pp. 160ff.

36. The characterization "empirical" should not imply that totally general facts can be advanced in the framework of this mode of justification. Only those arguments count which make reference to a definite class of facts, namely, to the factual validity of rules and the factual existence of normative convictions.

37. Kriele's request is directed towards this point, that the theory "must (gain) its standards for judging practice from the observation of practice, i.e., it must learn from the experience of practice itself what good and bad practice is." (M. Kriele, *Theorie der Rechtsgewinnung*, 2nd edition, Berlin 1976, p. 22). In this connection, theory should of course not be limited to the mere description and analysis of practice. In order to discover whether a specific practice is a good one, it must ask whether good grounds or reasons speak for this practice (Kriele, op. cit., p. 288). What good grounds are can hardly be inferred once more from the practice.

38. G. W. F. Hegel, *Philosophy of Right*, (trans. T. M. Knox) Oxford 1942, p. 10.

39. Popper's line of argument goes in this direction, which attempts "to define empirical science by methodological rules." He characterizes these methodological rules as "conventions" which must correspond to the highest rule "that a falsification . . . will not be hindered" (K. R. Popper, *The Logic of Scientific Discovery*, London 1968, pp. 41ff.) The highest rule expresses the "rationalist attitude," which one can only adopt through decision. "That is to say, a rationalist attitude must be first adopted if any argument or experience is to be effective, and it cannot therefore be based upon argument or experience" (K. R. Popper, *The Open Society and its Enemies*, vol. 2, 5th edition, Princeton, N.J. 1966, p. 230). One can indeed indicate the consequences of such a decision, yet this cannot determine the decision (K. R. Popper, op. cit., p. 233).

At a certain critical point, Albert speaks of the "rationalism of criticism" as of the "outline of a way of life," whose acceptance entails a moral decision (H. Albert, op. cit., pp. 40f.).

40. K.-O. Apel, "Sprechakttheorie und transzendentale Sprachpragmatik zur Frage ethischer Normen" in K.-O. Apel (ed.), *Sprachpragmatik und Philosophie*, Frankfurt 1976, p. 117.

41. Ibid., p. 11.

42. J. Habermas, "What is Universal Pragmatics?" in J. Habermas, *Communication and the Evolution of Society* (trans. T. McCarthy), Cambridge, MA/London 1979, pp. 22ff.

43. Ibid., pp. 24f.

44. Ibid., p. 21. On the procedure of such a reconstruction see *passim*, pp. 8ff.

45. On this concept see J. R. Searle, *Speech Acts*, Cambridge 1969, pp. 33ff.

46. See ibid., p. 186, note 1.

47. See on this the articles by Apel, Habermas, Kanngiesser, Schnelle, and Wunderlich in the collection cited above in n. 40.

48. For a thorough discussion see R. Alexy, *Theorie der juristischen Argumentation*, Frankfurt 1978, 5.53ff.

49. On this problem see, on the one hand, J. Jørgensen, "Imperatives and Logic" in *Erkenntnis*, 7, 1937/38, pp. 288ff.; on the other hand, A. Ross, "Imperatives and Logic," *Theoria*, 7, 1941, pp. 55f.; A. Ross, *Directives and Norms*, London 1968, pp. 139ff.; R. M. Hare, *The Language of Morals*, op. cit., pp. 20ff.

50. On deontic logic see the collections R. Hilpinen (ed.), *Deontic Logic: Introductory and Systematic Readings*, Dordrecht 1971; H. Lenk (ed.), *Normenlogik*, Pullach 1974.

51. On the precondition of sincerity see, for instance, J. L. Austin, "Other Minds," in his *Philosophical Papers* (ed. J. O. Urmson and G. J. Warnock), 2nd edition, London/Oxford/New York 1970, p. 85, 115; J. L. Austin, *How to do Things with Words*, London/Oxford/New York 1962, p. 15; J. R. Searle, *Speech Acts*, op. cit., p. 65; H. P. Grice, *Logic and Conversation*, op. cit., p. 34.

52. See R. M. Hare, *Freedom and Reason*, op. cit., pp. 10ff.

53. See, for instance, P. Lorenzen and O. Schwemmer, *Konstruktive Logik, Ethik und Wissenschaftstheorie*, op. cit., pp. 10ff.

54. On the same doubts see R. Alexy, *Theorie der juristischen Argumentation*, op. cit., p. 174.

55. See, for instance, G. Patzig, "Relativismus und Objektivität moralischer Normen," op. cit., p. 75.

56. On the possibility of speaking of the speech act of assertion also with reference to normative statements, see R. Alexy, op. cit., p. 75.

57. See on this F. Kambartel, "Was ist und soll Philosophie?" in his *Theorie und Begründung*, Frankfurt 1975, p. 14.

A Theory of Practical Discourse

58. On a rule of this type, see D. Wunderlich, "Zur Konventionalität von Sprechhandlungen," in D. Wunderlich (ed.), *Linguistische Pragmatik,* Frankfurt 1972, p. 21; J. R. Searle, *Speech Acts,* op. cit., pp. 65f.; H. Schnelle, *Sprachphilosophie und Linguistik,* Reinbek bei Hamburg 1973, pp. 42f. The status of such a rule is disputed. Some take it to be constitutive for the speech act of assertion (on the concept of constitutive rule see J. R. Searle, op. cit., pp. 33ff.). Thus, Wunderlich maintains: "Since one can in fact obviously not assert something and, at the same time, deny the fact that one possesses some kind of evidence for this, then this already belongs analytically to the concept of assertion *qua* speech act" (D. Wunderlich, "Über die Konsequenzen von Sprachhandlungen" in K.-O. Apel (ed.), *Sprachpragmatik und Philosophie,* op. cit., p. 452). In contrast, Schnelle is of the opinion that the concept of assertion unlike that of a promise is not associated with that of such an obligation. Therefore, a rule such as the stated rule of justification should only be seen as a general conversational postulate (H. Schnelle, op. cit., pp. 42f. On the concept of the conversational postulate see H. P. Grice, *Logic and Conversation,* op. cit., pp. 32ff.). There is something to be said for the view that if one associates the claim to truth or correctness with the concept of the assertion, one must then also view the rule of justification as constitutive for the assertion.

59. See on this R. Alexy, op. cit., pp. 157f.

60. J. Habermas "Wahrheitstheorien," op. cit., pp. 255f. For a discussion of Habermas's theory see R. Alexy, op. cit., pp. 149ff.

61. In this investigation, these expressions should be applied synonymously. A differentiation that is not necessary here is to be found in A. Poldech, *Gehalt und Funktionen des allgemeinen verfassungsrechtlichen Gleichheitssatzes,* Berlin 1971, pp. 87f.

62. M. G. Singer, *Generalization in Ethics,* New York 1961, p. 31.

63. P. Lorenzen and O. Schwemmer, *Konstruktive Logik, Ethik und Wissenschaftstheorie,* op. cit., p. 46.

64. See on this R. Alexy, op. cit., pp. 206ff.

65. C. Perelman and L. Olbrechts-Tyteca, *La nouvelle rhétorique. Traité de l'argumentation,* Paris 1958, 2nd edition Brussels 1970, p. 142.

66. For a very similar interpretation of the "pragmatic content" of the constitutional statement of equality see A. Poldech, op. cit., p. 89.

67. See on this J. Rawls, "Justice as Fairness" in *The Philosophical Review,* 67, 1958, p. 166: "There is a presumption against the distinctions and classifications made by legal systems and other practices to the extent that they infringe on the original and equal liberty of the persons participating in them."

68. See J. L. Austin, "Other Minds" in *Philosophical Papers,* op. cit., p. 84: "If you say, 'That's not enough', then you must have in mind some more or less definite lack . . . If there is no definite lack, which you are at least prepared to specify on being pressed, then it's silly (outrageous) just to go on saying 'That's not enough'."

69. For a demand of this kind see H. P. Grice, op. cit., p. 34. ·

70. It must be emphasized that here only the forms of argument specific to general practical discourse are dealt with. In addition, there are a large number of forms of

Robert Alexy

argument that crop up both in general practical discourses as well as in other discourses.

71. On the implication of imperatives by normative statements (value judgments and obligational judgments) see R. M. Hare, *The Language of Morals,* op. cit., p. 171.

72. On these two types of justification see S. E. Toulmin, *The Place of Reason in Ethics,* op. cit., p. 132.

73. R. M. Hare, *Freedom and Reason,* op. cit., p. 21.

74. "R'," in contrast to "R" and to the equally utilizable "R'," should be a rule of the optional level; "N'," in contrast to "N," should be an optional (and not merely a singular) normative statement. The introduction of "R'" and "N'" is necessary in order to be able to express the universality of (4).

75. It should be emphasized that in many discourses the reply to this question is the decisive problem. Much disagreement concerning practical questions could be decided immediately if enough secure empirical knowledge were available. To conclude from this that all practical problems are soluble solely through the supply of empirical information would nonetheless be a mistake.

76. On the fact that the four forms of justification ([4.1])–[4.4]) correspond to four forms of testing as well as the fact that as forms of justification compared to their formulation as forms of testing the former have priority, see R. Alexy, op. cit., pp. 236f.

77. On the concept of the rule of precedence see K. Baier, *The Moral Point of View,* Ithaca/London 1958, pp. 99ff.

78. (4.5) and (4.6) are themselves not forms of argument but forms of rules. But the insertion of (4.5) or (4.6) for R in (4.3) or (4.4) supplies four further forms of argument or, more precisely, two subordinate forms for (4.3) and (4.4) respectively. Since (4.3) and (4.4) are subordinate forms of (4) one can also say that there are two groups of subordinate forms of (4) characterized by (4.5) and (4.6) as a conclusion.

79. On the concept of the structure of argument see R. Alexy, op. cit., p. 110.

80. An additive structure of argument is produced if a statement or rule is justified by different arguments that are independent of one another. Here one could also speak of several justifications. In a regressive structure, one argument serves to support that of others.

81. R. Alexy, op. cit., p. 237.

82. See, for instance, S. E. Toulmin, *The Uses of Arguments,* op. cit., pp. 100, 106.

83. See on this C. L. Stevenson, *Ethics and Language,* pp. 139ff., 206ff.

84. These rules may be basically justified by rules already stated. This could be advanced as a reason for not including them in the canon of rules. Nonetheless, considerations of expediency at least support such an inclusion.

85. Not considered here is Singer's argument of generalizability: it can readily be reduced to the rules and forms elaborated above. See R. Alexy, op. cit., pp. 239ff.

86. R. M. Hare, *Freedom and Reason*, op. cit., pp. 86ff.

87. Under "consequences" should be understood here both the actual results of following a rule as well as the limitations which derive directly from following the imperative implied by the rule.

88. On the problems associated with (5.1.1), especially with regard to its limited capacity, see R. Alexy, "R. M. Hares Regeln des moralischen Argumentierens und L. Nelsons Abwägungsgesetz," in P. Schröder (ed.), *Vernunft Erkenntnis Sittlichkeit, Internationales philosophisches Symposion aus Anlass des 50. Todestages von Leonard Nelson*, Hamburg 1979, pp. 95ff.

89. On the question of the compatibility of (5.1.1) with (5.1.2) see R. Alexy, *Theorie der juristischen Argumentation*, p. 140.

90. See on this K. Baier, op. cit., pp. 195ff.

91. J. Habermas, *Legitimation Crisis*, (trans. T. McCarthy), Boston/London 1976, p. 113.

92. P. Lorenzen and O. Schwemmer, *Konstruktive Logik, Ethik und Wissenschaftstheorie*, op. cit., pp. 190ff.

93. (5.3) requires both that the realizability of a norm be logically possible at all as well as that it lies in the realm of actual possibilities. On the first requirement see F. v. Kutschera, *Einführung in die Logik der Normen, Werte und Entscheidungen*, Freiburg/Munich 1973, pp. 69f. On the concept of realizability see further S. Kanngiesser, "Sprachliche Universalien und diachrone Prozesse," op. cit., pp. 32ff.

94. The concept of the violation of the rule of discourse should be defined differently because of the different character of different rules. In the case of nonideal rules such as (1.1) (freedom from contradiction), (1.3′) (universalizability), and (5.3) (realizability), it is indeed basically ascertainable whether a violation exists or not. In contrast, the ideal rules such as (2.1) (universality of participation) and (5.2.1) (universality of agreement) can only be fulfilled approximately. Therefore, one would in fact speak of a fulfillment if the rule is complied with to an optimal extent in the given situation. In any case, the latter is more the formulation of a problem than its solution.

95. R. Spaemann, "Die Utopie der Herrschaftsfreiheit," *Merkur*, 26, 1972, p. 751.

96. See, for instance, F. Loos, "Zur Legitimität gerichteicher Entscheidungen," Ms. Göttingen 1977, p. 17.

97. On such a distinction, see J. Habermas, "Die Utopie des guten Herrschers. Eine Antwort auf R. Spaemann," in J. Habermas, *Kultur und Kritik*, Frankfurt 1973, p. 382.

98. R. Spaemann, "Die Utopie der Herrschaftsfreiheit," op. cit., p. 750; N. Luhmann, "Systemtheoretische Argumentationen: Eine Entgegnung auf Jürgen Habermas," in J. Habermas and N. Luhmann, *Theorie der Gesellschaft oder Sozialtechnologie*, Frankfurt 1972, p. 336.

99. N. Luhmann, op. cit., pp. 327f.; H. Weinrich, "System, Diskurs und die Diktatur des Sitzfleisches," in *Merkur*, 26, 1972, p. 809.

100. H. Weinrich, op. cit., p. 808; N. Luhmann, op. cit., p. 337.

101. H. Weinrich, op. cit., p. 809.

Robert Alexy

102. N. Luhmann, op. cit., p. 332.

103. R. Spaemann, op. cit., pp. 735f.

104. See J. Habermas, "Die Utopie des guten Herrschers," op. cit., pp. 384ff.

105. See R. Spaemann, "Die Utopie des guten Herrschers. Eine Diskussion zwischen Jürgen Habermas und Robert Spaemann," in *Merkur*, 26, 1972, pp. 1273ff.

106. On the consequences for legal argumentation that follow from this see R. Alexy, *Theorie der juristischen Argumentation*, pp. 247ff.

107. On the necessity for such a safeguard see W. Wieland, "Praxis und Urteilskraft," in *Zeitschrift für philosophische Forschung*, 28, 1974, pp. 40ff.

108. See on this, for instance, O. Ludwig and W. Menzel, "Diskutieren als Gegenstand und Methode des Deutschunterrichts," in *Praxis Deutsch*, no. 14, 1976, pp. 16ff., as well as the eight teaching models recommended in this issue.

II

The Controversy

5

Kantian Skepticism toward Transcendental Ethics of Communication

Otfried Höffe

In recent discussion, transcendental philosophy has acquired an unexpected significance. Alongside a number of historical and systemic interpretations (with regard to Kant especially, but also Fichte, Schelling, and Husserl), and independent of systematic attempts to develop classical transcendental philosophy further for the present day, a wide-ranging discussion is taking place in analytical philosophy today under the rubric of "transcendental arguments," while a large number of philosophers and social scientists are resuscitating Husserl's transcendental phenomenology.

Within the framework of this newly awakened interest in transcendental philosophy, the reflections of Karl-Otto Apel assume a prominent place. His attempt to correlate Continental and Anglo-American philosophizing and thereby to engage in dialogue such diverse traditions as American pragmatism, analytical philosophy, hermeneutics, and transcendental philosophy, quite rightly finds increasing recognition far beyond the confines of the German-speaking area.

Transcendental pragmatics, as Apel terms his mediating position, is presented as the mode of "First Philosophy" appropriate to present-day problematics. For although Apel avoids using this expression, the claim of his philosophy is no less than to develop, in a contemporary manner, a *fundamental philosophy.*

Among the most important of the "Second Philosophies," into which Apel's transcendental pragmatics extends, there belongs his ethics which, as a result of the *Practical Philosophy/*

Ethics course offered by the German radio corporations during 1980/81, has become extremely well known under the label "communicative ethics" far beyond the sphere of professional philosophy.[1]

The transcendental ethics of communication or, more precisely, the transcendental-pragmatically grounded ethics of discourse presents itself as the transformation of traditional philosophy and, especially of Kant's philosophy. In agreement with Kant, and in opposition to a reduction of human action to merely technical or strategic action, it seeks to open up a genuine ethical dimension. Furthermore, it is in agreement with Kant when it defines ethics not in terms of the concepts of enlightened self-interest but of those of autonomy. It also corresponds to the intention of Kantian philosophy in searching for ultimate principles. It argues against Kant, however, that his "ethical problematic is still developed from the standpoint of the isolated individual, whose basic concern is whether his will—i.e., his inner sentiment—could be judged to be good by a suprahuman, all-knowing judge. Thus, Kant takes the reciprocity of interhuman relations specifically into account only at the level of law (of action 'according to duty'), and not—as a transcendental ethics of communication must demand—also at the level of the factually isolated decision of conscience ... Viewed in this way, Kant represents the step from the *heteronomous ethics of command* to the *autonomous ethics of conviction,* but not yet the still remaining step to the *ethics of responsibility.* In terms of this still remaining step, a standpoint is conceivable upon which the individual understands his fundamental moral duty basically from the *reciprocity of the claims of responsibility in a community of communication of rational creatures.*" (*SBB2,* p. 49f.)

According to Apel, the transcendental ethics of communication that goes beyond Kant has two different consequences:

On the one hand, the moral duty of the individual, that is expressed in the 'categorical imperative', should already be viewed as the reflexive internalization of the universalized duties of reciprocity in an anticipated *ideal community of communication.* The individual's standard of conviction, internalized in the categorical imperative, would thus always only be a *monological substitute* for the demand for a real agreement concerning the reciprocal claims (and thereby the expressed interests or needs), that form the *principle of dialogical morality* ... On the other hand, some of those presuppositions of morality would be removed which Kant still expressed in his postulates of practical reason: for instance, the postulate regarding the existence of an omniscient God who judges the inner conviction of human beings. (ibid.)

A further point in which Apel seeks to advance beyond Kant relates to the ultimate justification of the principle of morality, since according to Apel, Kant founders here (*SBB2*, pp. 71–74).

I wish to advance several doubts, articulated in what follows in a provisional form, as to whether Apel's attempt to transform Kant's position into an ethics that is appropriate to the contemporary problematics of philosophy and the life-world is actually successful.[2]

1 Two Preliminary Remarks

1.1 Apel's thesis that the reciprocity of interhuman relationships is only to be found in Kant at the legal level, may already be countered by the fact that, according to Kant, all legal duties are also moral duties (duties of virtue). As a result, the legally required reciprocity is also always a moral requirement. Furthermore, among the obligations specific to morality, that is, those obligations that are not also required by law, there are to be found two groups: alongside the duties of human beings toward themselves are the duties with regard to others, so that Kantian ethics, in an essential part, is a social ethics. For the rest, the question deserves serious discussion as to whether, alongside the moral duties to others, there are not also duties to oneself—even if, in a period of the overvaluation of society and the undervaluation of the person, such a consideration is all too quickly dismissed as not being worthy of closer discussion.

1.2 Without hesitation, Apel terms his ethics of communication transcendental. Apel wishes to indicate by means of the qualification "transcendental" that his ethics owes basic impulses to Kant. At the same time Apel assumes, at least implicitly, that Kant's foundation of ethics is basically transcendental. Yet this is in no way established.

First of all, Kant formulated the transcendental-philosophical program in the *Critique of Pure Reason* from the outset with reference to epistemology and the theory of the object (B 25/A 11f.) and expressly disputed a transcendental knowledge in the sphere of ethics (B 28f./A 15). Of course, in contrast to Kant, several reasons support the notion of developing the transcendental-philosophical program also with regard to the justification of morality. But even then the Kantian justification of ethics is not thoroughly transcendental. Quite the contrary, only a relatively small part, namely, the reduction of the moral law to the autonomy of the will, possesses a transcendental character. A larger part, including the conceptual determination of the moral law, which leads to form as the sole determining ground of the will, taken by itself, has the character of a problematic of conceptual analysis. At the same time, this part is absolutely necessary for the preparation of transcendental reflection; for freedom as autonomy is the determinate negation of heteronomy, of a concept that is formed in the analytical-problematical part. Over and above this, the theoretical portion characterized by the label "fact of reason" possesses a still looser connection to a transcendental ethics. In short; Kantian ethics cannot be reduced to a transcendental ethics. A communicative ethics likewise must consider how far it contains transcendental elements at all; further, how far it may be limited to transcendental elements.

1.3 If Apel's insistence on the transcendental status of his claim draws less from Kant's ethics than from the *Critique of Pure Reason,* other considerations come into play. Even when transcendental pragmatics is meant to be transcendental, it contains—to mention only the first objection—nonetheless a noticeable impoverishment of the program of critical reason. Perhaps with the principle of the ideal communication community it takes up the theme of the transcendental apperception. Yet this facet of Kant's teaching constitutes only a small part of the *Critique of Pure Reason;* reflections which correspond to the transcendental Aesthetic, the Analytic of Principles, and the transcendental Dialectic are missing in Apel.

It can furthermore be said against Apel that he relies upon Kant's conception of the transcendental but does not take up his two-part definition of it. According to this definition transcendental conceptions are (1) valid before all experience but (2) still are necessary for the constitution of experience itself. Instead of this Apel considers the ideal communication community transcendental because it is "unavoidable" (*unhintergehbar*). The idea of unavoidability contains two meanings which build upon each other. According to the weaker sense of the term, Apel means that one cannot do without it, that it cannot be renounced: the anticipation of the ideal communication community is necessary. According to the stronger sense of the term, he means that it is the last resort, that one cannot go beyond the ideal communication community. It has the status of a final foundation.

In understanding unavoidability in this fashion, Apel distorts the nature of Kant's transcendental program in one respect. He skips over the first part of the definition of "transcendental," namely, the proof of a strict validity which relies on no empirical evidence. There are, for example, physiological conditions without which one can neither talk nor hear and which are only valid empirically. Similarly, the conception of unavoidability in the sense of a final foundation risks distorting Kant's transcendental program; the pure concepts of space and time are for Kant both independent of experience as well as essential for experience. They are of transcendental significance but despite this they do not constitute "the highest point of transcendental philosophy," which alone lies in the transcendental apperception.

Even when one compares Apel's vision of the ideal communication community only with Kant's conception of transcendental apperception, a third objection comes to the fore. The transcendental apperception has its place in the transcendental deduction of pure concepts of reason. Regardless of all the interpretative problems and controversies on this issue, we can claim that the deduction contains two important steps. First, the categories are presented as the precondition for all objective experience, and second, transcendental self-consciousness is shown to be the origin of every (categorical) synthesis. In contrast, Apel wants to reach his goals a bit faster. He begins with language (respectively, the understanding) and moves directly to "the highest point," thus avoiding the "detour" via the pure concepts of reason or an analogous theoretical construction. But without the categories, the objectivity of transcendental synthetic unity (*Einheitsstiftung*) cannot be established. What appears to be a "detour" is in reality a necessary element of a transcendental justification for knowledge or language.

Furthermore, it is doubtful that the anticipation of an ideal communication community has its systematic place in a transcendental Analytic instead of in a transcendental Dialectic. Due to the ideal nature of the communication community, it likely has the significance of a regulative Idea of Reason rather than that of a constitutive moment of the understanding.

2 A Logical Circle?

The "existential place" of philosophical ethics is the situation of unclarity, uncertainty, and lack of agreement of human beings concerning morally good and correct action. In this situation, philosophical ethics undertakes the task of justifying in a methodical way the foundations and standards of personal and sociopolitical morality. Philosophy does not first of all ask which concrete deed or action is morally good and correct; it does not even investigate primarily the principles, the rules of norms, the basic attitudes or institutions that are appropriate to the claim of morality. It searches for the highest and ultimate standard of all moral action, against which even the principles are tested with regard to their morality. Since, for their part, the ethical principles supply the standard for concrete moral action, a standard for moral standards is to be justified, a second-order standard that may also be termed a metastandard, metacriterion, metanorm, or basic norm.

With the aid of the highest standard, the colorful multifariousness of moral action can be grasped as that of a world of morality. Above all, however, with the aid of the ultimate ethical criterion, obscurities in reflection and decision can be eliminated, moral conflicts can be settled, and what is ethically commanded or permitted can be distinguished from what is ethically forbidden.

Apel asserts discourse or communication to be the highest standard of morality. This assertion comes very close to Kant's categorical imperative or to the contemporary principle of universalization. For a ground that allows itself to be universalized does not depend upon this or that personal interest; it is valid for any human being, indeed for any rational creature. But then this ground must find agreement among those who are in fact rational. As a result, it is only plausible to assume as the standard of morality the strictly general or universal agreement in a discourse.

Of course, the principle of morality does not lie in the factually given or denied agreement of a certain circle of persons in a specific situation. For, first of all, shortage of time and fundamental diversities of opinion could prevent an agreement. Further, each consensus depends upon the intellectual and emotional marginal conditions, and also upon deep structures, which could be obstructive to reason and could disadvantage some of the participants or nonparticipants. Hence it is justified that Apel does not elevate historical-factual discourse into an ethical principle. Such a discourse is, at best, the attempt to apply approximately the principle of universalization also in those situations in which—and this holds for all occasions—one is threatened as an individual or as a group by intellectual and emotional delusions.

On the other hand, communication and discourse already presuppose that the participants do not reciprocally destroy one another, do not lie; in general that they recognize one another as having equal rights. In the reciprocal recognition and its manifestation in nondestruction, not lying, etc., we encounter not possible results but rather preconditions or presupposed structural features of a successful discourse. At the same time, the genuine ethical principles lie hidden in the preconditions.

Because of the obvious difficulties of historical-factual discourse, Apel asserts as the basic norm not an arbitrary but rather an ideal discourse. Not every arbitrary conversation, not every naturally arrived at agreement is valid as the highest standard. Only a discourse is recognized as the basic norm which takes place under ideal conditions.

By means of the preconditions or structural features which define the ideal discourse, fundamental normative principles are designated which the discourse must fulfill if it is to be suitable as a moral criterion. The preconditions thus possess a normative significance and in fact not just some, perhaps even strategic-normative, significance; they have an ethical-normative significance. True discourses are differentiated from false discourses out of the wealth of possible discourses; only true discourses, those which fulfill the ideal preconditions, can lay claim to be the highest standard of morality.

Because it is not the historical-factual discourse but the ideal discourse which provides the moral principle and because the ideal discourse possesses ethical-normative presuppositions, Apel falls into a methodical difficulty. His ethics of discourse presupposes certain ethical principles as self-evidently valid, although the discourse in fact should be that instance through which the ethical principles are first of all justified. Theories of ideal discourse thus find themselves in a logical circle. For it is the task of the highest moral criterion to test *all* principles with regard to their ethical validity or nonvalidity. In the case of the ethics of discourse, however, a part of these principles is already presupposed as valid, namely, that part which encompasses the preconditions and structural features of the ideal discourse. This means, however, that normative (ethical) elements, for which a standard is still first of all to be sought, already enter into the definition of precisely this standard.

Indeed, the criticism must be made more pointedly: the normative elements which define the ideal nature of discourse correspond to those fundamental or simply valid obligations which, as normative *basic* principles, are the major object of a highest moral criterion. For the explicit or implicit presuppositions of ideal discourse consist of the fact that the body and life of the participants in discourse are inviolable; that consciously and voluntarily, hence without reciprocal constraint, one seeks an agreement; that, in so doing, one does not lie to or deceive one another. Then, however, the first task of a philosophical justification of morality is not a discourse under certain ideal conditions but rather the standard for justifying precisely these conditions as ideal conditions.

Since discourse can only be valid under specific normative conditions as the highest moral criterion, since these conditions are no longer the object but rather the presuppositions of discourse, a discourse-theoretical justification of morality is a philosophically insufficient procedure.

But Apel has objected that the criticism of circularity does not clearly distinguish between the different levels of justification or of application (*SBB*8, 86f.). There exists complete agreement concerning the thesis that the first task of a philosophical-moral justification is not a discourse under certain ideal conditions but rather the standard for the justification of precisely these conditions as the ideal preconditions. For this reason, he argues, the ethics of discourse begins with the transcendental-pragmatic final justification of the basic norm of consensual communication. What a self-reflection of argumentative discourse reveals is, on the one hand, the irreducibility of argumentation bound up with language and, on the other, the fact that in argumentation bound up with language we always already recognize certain norms. To be sure, argumentationally reflexive discourse does not lead to the categorical imperative or to the principle of universalization, but rather to consensual communication as the basic norm. In addition, Apel notes, the transcendental-pragmatic final justification is not precommunicative. Even if it is in fact completed in solitary thought, yet what is involved is not *in principle* solitary thought that can go behind the norm of the consensual requirement of argumentation; the irreducibility of argumentation bound up with language and the basic norm that is always already recognized in it imply the repudiation of methodical solipsism.

The counterargument against the accusation of circularity correctly points attention to two levels in the transcendental-pragmatic justification of norms. More precisely, Apel's ethics contains three levels: (1) the reflexive grounding of the ideal communication community as the "highest point," as the last and irreducible standard of judgment for all ethical obligations; this level, which leads to the principle of morality, Apel considers to be transcendental; (2) the reflexive explication of the ethical obligations implied in the ideal communication community—for example, the command to be truthful or the prohibition on killing, without the recognition of which the ideal communication community loses its ideal character; this level is not transcendental, at least not in the same sense as the first level; (3) the "application" of the ideal communication community, that is, its grounding of concrete obligations on the basis of interpersonal communication under ideal conditions. The ideal communication community has a threefold significance appropriate to this tripartite structure. First, it is valid as the ultimate precondition for the possibility of argumentation; it is *the* principle of morality. Second, within it there are middle level principles, namely, acknowledged basic ethical obligations. Third, it is the point at which concrete ethical obligations are grounded and at which questions of concrete practice are decided. The transcendental ethics of communication does not maintain, as the claim that it is circular suggests, that all ethical obligations need to be tested in the ideal communication community. Instead it maintains that the ideal communication community is the final precondition of all communication and that this precondition always brings with it "always already" acknowledged ethical obligations.

After the charge of circularity is countered, a new problem nonetheless becomes apparent. This problem concerns the transition from a general First Philosophy, transcendental pragmatics, to a specific discipline of "Second Philosophy," ethics. This problem is implicit in a double claim at the second level of justification. On the one hand, obligations are explicated at the second level which are contained in the idea of the ideal communication community. On the other hand, it is said of these obligations that they are of an ethical nature. This claim presupposes that the ideal communication community is not only concerned with the theory of language or communication, but that it also has an ethical significance: that it is a case, even a paradigmatic case, of ethics. This presupposition could hold true if it could be demonstrated; Apel, however, fails to do this.

The problem of transition emphasized here is a problem of identification: something is identified as something else, the ideal communication community as the (outstanding) case of ethics. In order to justify this identification one needs a conception—or at least a presupposition—of ethics. But Apel does not develop this. Apel's transcendental pragmatics already presupposes genuine ethical or metaethical reflection, although it itself claims the status of an ultimate justification.

3 On the "Fact of Reason"

Yet, according to Apel, it is not transcendental pragmatics but rather Kant who founders in the final justification of ethics: "The fact, however, that the moral law is 'given' as a 'fact of pure reason' and a conscious 'a priori' (that is, prior to all experience) and apodictically certain' (that is, indubitable)—this assertion of Kant's, in the light of contemporary philosophy, must either appear as a dogmatic break with the attempt at rational justification or, however, as a 'naturalistic fallacy', that is, as a contravention of the principle recognized by him, to derive no *norm* from a *fact*, no *ought* from an *is*" (*SBB*2, 73).

It is correct that because of its casual treatment, Kant's teaching of the "fact of reason" has not found a perfectly convincing interpretation. But one can still argue that Apel's critique is based on a misunderstanding. Certainly, the "fact of reason" reveals the paradoxical situation of Kantian—and perhaps of any—ethics: that which is reflected upon is already given in moral consciousness (or moral discourse, etc.), in other words, one reflects upon a fact, upon what *is*, but in spite of this, such reflection should lead us to a moral principle—the basis and standard of the *ought*. But this paradox appears less stark when one looks at the peculiarity of this "fact." It is not something empirically given, but is instead a fact of practical reason, a fact which derives its "oughtness" not from principle, but from the finite nature of national creatures.

In the *Critique of Practical Reason*, Kant clearly characterizes as a fact of reason not the moral law itself but rather the consciousness of the moral law: "the consciousness of this fundamental law (i.e., of pure practical reason) may be called a fact of reason" (*Critique of Practical Reason,* para.7, p. 31).

Kant speaks of a fact because he holds the consciousness of the moral law to be a fact, hence to be something real, not something fictional or merely assumed; morality is no mere unrealistic ought but rather something that we always already recognize. And indeed what is at issue is the—according to Kant indubitable (apodictically certain)—fact of moral consciousness as the consciousness of an unconditional duty. At the same time, this consciousness does not have the character of an empirical fact; and in addition the fact of reason has no justificatory function for it serves neither to support the inference of the basic norm, of the categorical imperative, nor to justify the autonomy of the will. The fact of reason should only demonstrate the *reality* of the object of ethical justifications, so that the reproach which contemporary discussion occasionally advances somewhat hastily, namely, that of the naturalistic fallacy, is inapplicable.

Furthermore, according to Kant, the fact of reason constitutes the sole fact of reason (not merely for the practical realm) by which the latter "proclaims itself as originating law (*sic volo, sic iubeo*)" (ibid.). In the light of the ever-renewed pragmatic, scientific and philosophical-principled doubts as to the possibility of morality and because of the fundamental significance of morality for human life just as much as for ethics, what is at issue in the problem raised by Kant is not a merely academic question, nor merely a question for Kantian philology. In the theoretical section on the "fact of reason" as the reality of moral experience, Kant wishes to substantiate the fact that ethics speaks about something real and not about an illusion. Only because moral experience actually exists is it no longer an intellectual game of billiards but rather meaningful in terms of the life-world to search for the criterion and principle of morality; only because moral consciousness is no mere self-delusion does philosophical ethics lose the character of a shrewd but unreal intellectual construction and thereby contributes to making human existence intelligible.

Kant justifies the assertion that the fact of reason is undeniable with the statement: "one need only analyze the judgment which human beings pronounce concerning the lawfulness of their actions" (ibid.). Thus, the fact of reason is documented for Kant in specific judgments, and specifically in those judgments in which, independently of a potential competing inclination (ultimately of one's own happiness), the lawful (morally correct) action is expressed. An example of such a judgment can be formulated in connection with the last part of the annotation to paragraph six. There Kant asks whether someone who is called upon under threat of immediate death penalty—thus a radical threat to one's own happiness—to present false testimony against an honest man, nonetheless holds it to be possible, despite the greatest possible love for life, to overcome this inclination and refuse the false testimony. Without doubt, the answer to this is in the affirmative. While Kant seeks to show by this that human beings consider it possible to decide against even an enormous inclination, what is at issue, from the perspective of the fact of reason, is that a deliberately false testimony against an honest man may be intelligible under the special circumstances of the threat of death, that one perhaps even expects the false testimony in this situation, because each reckons with a preponderance of self-love for himself over his fellow human beings, but that nevertheless each person takes the false testimony to be morally illegitimate. In order to be able to understand such a judgment regarding what is morally legitimate and illegitimate about actions, one must have recourse to the concept of the moral law or the categorical imperative as an unconditional and, also against the competing inclination of self-love, valid legislation. Yet since in fact we pass judgment in this way and take the deliberately false testimony to be illegitimate, moral consciousness (not the actual moral life!) demonstrates itself to be real.

Apel's transcendental-pragmatic ethics of discourse also exhibits a functionally analogous problem to Kant's fact of reason. The argumentational situation, to which Apel has recourse, may in fact be irreducible; it may anticipate an ideal community of communication and in this manner document the fact that we "always already" recognize certain moral obligations. But in so doing, the argumental situation does not thereby lose the character of a fact. Certainly it is no natural fact, so that perhaps the problem of the naturalistic fallacy does not arise, although for Apel, in contrast to Kant's fact of reason, the argumentational situation indeed has a justifying function. In any event, for Apel the argumentational situation is a fact that should demonstrate our factual recognition of morality. Insofar as we speak, argue, and thereby act in the horizon of consensual communication, we move within the horizon of morality—on the presupposition that consensual communication is an instance of morality.

Apel has an unsolved problem with this presupposition that is solved in Kant's ethics. The assertion that argumentation (language, communication) is not merely language and a manifestation of thought but in fact stands for morality, presupposes that one has a concept of morality and then identifies the argumentation according to the standard of the concept of morality as a (possibly exemplary) instance of morality.

4 A Deficiency in Conceptual Development (Metaethics)

Whoever seeks something must already have a conception of that which they seek; whoever wishes to justify the basic norms of all morality also requires, aside from a conception of a "basic norm," a knowledge of that which is termed morality. Hence, the justification of morality must commence at a stage more radical than the ethics of discourse justified on transcendental-pragmatic grounds. It must develop a concept of morality in order subsequently to regard consensual communication as an "instance of" morality or to repudiate it as such. Kant was aware of this necessity. And although he did not yet know the contemporary concept of metaethics, his justification of ethics nonetheless commenced with a metaethical assertion: the *Groundwork for the Metaphysics of Morals* begins—implicitly of course—with the metaethical thesis that the morally good is the unlimited good or the good *per se,* and the *Critique of Practical Reason* defines the morally good as pure practical reason or as the practical law. An important task of the extension ("transformation") of Kant's ethics would be to explicate this implicitly metaethical starting point, to further elaborate upon it, to justify it and to define more closely its methodical status.

Kant develops the concept of the categorical imperative out of the concept of the unlimited good or the practical law. Hence, the categorical imperative has first of all a metaethical significance; it defines the specifically moral sense of obligation—with regard to those creatures for whom philosophical ethics not merely has a contemplative import but also a significance for life practice—that is, for persons who not automatically and of necessity act morally, namely, for finite rational creatures, that is, human beings. (1) As a consequence of the concept of the unlimited good, moral obligations are not valid on the basis of subjective intentions which originate from discretion or self-interest; since their validity is independent of subjective intentions, moral obligations are autonomous or unlimited, thus objectively or categorically valid.

(2) Since a human being as a creature with needs does not indeed solely and necessarily act morally, since he also acts strategically and can orient his whole way of life toward the totality of the fulfillment of his needs, toward his own welfare of happiness, morality possesses for human beings the character of a claim which they can also ignore, a demand to which they can close their ears; it possesses an imperative character.

Both aspects taken together, that of the character of a demand and that of unlimited validity, give to the categorical imperative its metaethical significance; they define the concept of morality for conditions of finite rational creatures.

When Kant speaks of imperatives, he means more than any old exhortation. The arbitrary order of a superior power he eliminates from the very beginning. In response to the basic practical question for humanity—"What should I do?"—imperatives do not respond with inner or outer coercive power, but instead with rational reasons, with reasons, for that matter, which the actor does not necessarily acknowledge (*Grundlegung zur Metaphysik der Sitten, Akademieausgabe,* vol. 4, p. 413). Even nonethical imperatives are practical necessities—that is to say, practical obligations which are valid for everyone and which are distinct from pleasurable ones based only in subjective sensations. Kant shows that the basic question—what should I do?—can be understood in three different ways. Thus there are three different classes of answers which contain the same number of types of rational grounds. According to Kant, the teaching of practical argumentation sought after today has three parts. These three parts do not simply stand next to each other; they build upon one another. They signify three levels of practical reason—one could say, of the rationality of action. And the three levels of rationality indeed do not differ according to their strictness, but according to their scope. In the case of the first two levels of hypothetical imperatives, strict necessity, which is due all rationality, is bound to a nonnecessary presupposition. On the third level of the categorical or moral imperative, all limiting presuppositions are eliminated. There is nothing irrational about the categorical imperative and morality. In contrast, only here does the idea of practical reason or of the rationality of action find its fundamental conclusion.

Within the framework of metaethics, a descriptive-metaethical investigation ("how do we in fact apply the concept of morality?") may be distinguished from a normative-metaethical discussion ("how should we apply the concept of morality?"). One could understand the metaethical side of Kant's categorical imperative in both respects and assert, on the one hand, that we do in fact apply the concept of morality in this way and, on the other, that we should apply the concept in this way. The descriptive-metaethical interpretation would only lead the justification of morality back to a fact, and one could speak of a naturalistic fallacy, or more exactly of the fallacy of deriving an "ought" from an "is," of the derivation of a standard of morality from a fact, namely, the factual application of the concept of morality. The other interpretation is more meaningful, according to which, through the concept of the moral good as the good in itself or unlimited good, attention is called to a sense of goodness by means of which the concept of the good "can be thought through to its conclusion"; only through the concept of the good in itself is the possibility of responsibility fully plumbed, is the responsibility of human action understood radically. Therefore, what is involved in the concept of the moral good as the good in itself is first a possible and second a necessary concept, insofar as by necessity is meant the full plumbing of the conceptual field of responsibility.

Both of these diverse aspects in Kant's categorical imperative are implicitly recognized but not explicitly justified by the ethics of discourse that is grounded transcendental-pragmatically. Therefore, we encounter here a sensitive deficit in justification and, at the same time, a regression behind the level reached by Kant.

(1) Consensual communication or ideal discourse possesses the character of a demand; we do not recognize it always and of necessity since we also have the possibility of acting technically, strategically, or pragmatically, and often enough pursue these possibilities; nevertheless, we *ought* not merely to act technically, strategically, or pragmatically, but rather also and above all recognize the basic norm of consensual communication.

(2) The demand for recognition is not only valid whenever we have a natural desire for it or promise ourselves an advantage from it; this would mean placing strategic or pragmatic action above consensual communication; in contrast, the demand for consensual communication is valid unconditionally.

The unrestricted validity is also not adversely affected by the fact that, according to Apel, an ethics of responsibility is necessary which occasionally makes room for strategic action. For *either* strategic action would suspend consensual communication, which would mean that consensual communication no longer represents the basic norm of Apel's ethics; the basic norm would then be termed "solidary responsibility" (certainly a still imprecise concept), and to solidary responsibility the dual metaethical determination of the categorical imperative would apply: first, that we should observe it, even when we do not do so automatically and of necessity and, second, that the demand for the observation of solidary responsibility is valid unconditionally. *Or* one asserts that consensual communication is not relativized as a basic norm by an occasionally necessary strategic action; strategic action being rather something like an infrastructural element in the framework of consensual communication. In this case, the basic norm is in fact termed consensual communication for Apel and it holds for the latter that we are unrestrictedly required to factually recognize it in our acts and deeds so that the categorical imperative in its metaethical significance is once more the standard with whose help Apel's basic norm too is to be judged as moral.

The identification of a metaethical deficit in the transcendental communication ethics does not aim to question the view that the transcendental-pragmatic argument is of a reflexive nature. The person who carries on ethics argues and willy-nilly follows the rules of argumentation. Argumentation and ethics are woven together. Nor does this argument mean to deny that the ideal communication community is the precondition for the possibility of argumentation; Böhler's criticisms do not apply.[3] Still, attention needs to be paid to the fact that it is not simply obvious that argumentation and its presupposition, the ideal communication community, are to be considered an ethical phenomenon and hence that an ethical meaning can be attributed to transcendental pragmatics.

Transcendental pragmatics deems the ideal communication community irreducible. This statement permits both weak and strong interpretations. According to the weak interpretation, the ideal communication community is a necessary grounding for ethics, while according to the stronger interpretation it is plain and simple the final justification and standard for ethics. The strong view does not hold true. Even if the ideal communication community represents the necessary presupposition of all communication, this fails to demonstrate that it is the highest principle of ethics. This principle lies much more so in that standard by which the ideal communication community proves itself to be ethical; that is Kant's categorical imperative in its metaethical significance.

5 Normative Ethics: Categorical Imperative or Consensual Communication?

A supporter of the ethics of discourse could object that he of course recognizes these two metaethical elements of the categorical imperative, but that still further elements are contained in the categorical imperative—elements which he disputes. In fact, still further conceptual elements are hidden in the categorical imperative. But, first, although the supporter of discursive ethics may, of course, have recognized the two first elements, nonetheless he has not justified them. Second, it remains to be seen whether, upon closer observation, the other conceptual elements are not also presupposed by a discursive ethics.

Kant derives his normative ethical principle from the categorical imperative in its metaethical components, the definition of the morally good as an unlimited valid obligation, as follows: Because that which is unlimited (unconditionally) valid is universally valid and indeed simply without exception and necessarily universally valid, it can be asserted that those principles are of a moral nature which can be conceived of or are intended as universal law. The transcendental-pragmatically justified ethics of discourse also recognizes this normative-ethical side of the categorical imperative—but in opposition to its own self-understanding. For, in its assertion that the basic norm is consensual communication, the ethics of discourse presupposes that consensual communication can be intended not merely by this or that human subject on the basis of his more or less arbitrary opinion, hence basically only as a particular rule; the ethics of discourse implicitly asserts that consensual communication must be intended by all and in principle, hence as a universal law.

A further constitutive element of Kant's categorical imperative is the concept of maxims. Kant understands by maxims rules of action that are not imposed externally but rather are determined by actors themselves and represent the factually ultimate mainsprings of their intentions. Since human action is played out in a natural and intersubjectively determined field of forces that is not solely constituted by the wills of the acting human subjects, not even fully surveyed by them as empirical human subjects, the naked result of action, the objective outcome, can itself not be a yardstick of morality. Hence, Kant quite rightly asserted that morality is inherent not in the action as such but rather only in the quality of the will that lies behind it, and an ethics of discourse too may not evade this insight.

At the same time, one must object to Apel's intention to develop Kant's ethics of conviction into an ethics of responsibility that for Kant "willing" is not a mere wish ("I would like" or "I would like to do"). Kant is in no way a supporter of the ethics of conviction in the sense that his principle of morality, of the good will, would characterize a world of actionless inwardness that remains without any expression in the political, social, and personal world. The will is no "other world" to the reality of human life, but rather the determining ground—insofar as it lies in the acting subject himself.

Certainly, because of physical, spiritual, economic, and other imperfections, the expression of the will can fail to match that which is wanted. Assistance, for example, can come, without cause, too late or be too weak to be helpful. Still, humanity can never avoid this danger. Human action plays itself out in a power-field dependent upon natural and social conditions which the will of the agent alone cannot determine and which is never fully transparent. Ethics only refers to the agent's field of responsibility, it is here that considerations (of an "ethics of responsibility" type) belong about whether—because of a noticeable lack of power and capacities—one should obtain the help of others. Because ethics only concerns that which is possible, the naked result, the objective observable success of actions, can never be the standard of measurement for ethics. The ultimate goodness of a person cannot be determined by his or her actions as such, but only by the will which lies at the basis of all action. An alternative to a "mere ethics of conscience" which sees in the actual success of an action a standard for evaluating the morality of an action, holds human beings to be responsible for that which they cannot be responsible for. In obfuscating the nature of the human situation, such an alternative represents no improvement. Instead, in a fundamental sense, it is inhumane.

6 Heteronomy or Solipsism?

Apel's ethics of discourse wishes to recognize Kant's principle of autonomy and, at the same time, overcome Kant's (presumed) solipsism, since "Kant's ethical problematic is still developed from the standpoint of solitary individuals" (*SSB2*, p. 69). In so doing, the ethics of responsibility, going beyond Kant's ethics of conviction, has recourse to the concept of internationalization. Each individual is exhorted to internalize the obligations of dialogical morality, such as the duty to solidary responsibility (ibid., p. 70). Yet it must be asked here, is the principle of autonomy actually recognized with an internationalization of communicative obligations and, over and above this, is the principle of autonomy sufficiently comprehended?

An internalization of communicative obligations does not exclude the fact that one ultimately behaves strategically or submits to social constraints. The demand for the internalization of communicative obligations does not prevent the fact that—in accordance with the goal of friendly human adaptation, "to be a good guy"—one seeks as many (naturally, superficial) social contacts as possible, that, in accordance with the motto "make friends, not enemies," one nowhere seeks to attract attention and is perhaps—because one does not know any different—even incapable of ever being alone. Or, expressed more seriously and philosophically, the internalization of communicative obligations can take place for reasons of social adaptation or for the purpose of having a good reputation and being taken for a respected fellow human being. Yet it can also result from "conviction," from a recognition of fellow human beings as human beings of equal esteem and with equal rights. Thus, Kant's distinction between legality and morality also retains its correctness with respect to the internalization of communicative obligations. Provided the communicative obligations are also the genuinely moral obligations, one can act in agreement with them, one can even make the agreement into a routine habit insofar as one internalizes it—and yet ultimately act on the basis of social constraints or strategically, namely, for the sake of one's personal welfare. However, only that person who recognizes communicative obligations as such, who thus, in Kant's language, acts not only dutifully (legally) but also from duty, lives morally (in a morally good manner and not merely a morally correct manner). Since autonomy is the principle of morality and not also that of legality, and since the category of internalization also permits nonmoral, namely, legal forms of human action, Kant's principle of morality remains an "empty assurance" in the transcendental-pragmatic ethics of discourse. Once more Apel does not go beyond Kant but rather falls back behind his problematic.

The critique of the psychologizing mode of expression of internalization can also be formulated from the angle of communication. For talk of internalization presupposes that, on the one side, there exists an independent exterior, the communicative obligations and, on the other side, an already constituted human subject that is different from the exterior and has the choice (and moral task) of appropriating the exterior into itself. But in this case talk of internalization is associated with the notion that the constitution of the human subject occurred prior to and independently of communication. The human subject called upon to internalize communicative obligations is an autonomous individual; contrary to his basic intent, Apel's ethics of discourse thus contains solipsistic elements.

Communicative obligations commence with the obligation *to* communication, namely, the obligation to lead a fundamentally communicative and not a strategic existence. However, understood correctly, communication does not take place before or beyond the human subject but in a self-opening of human subjects for one another, in a reciprocal recognition and, conversely, truly communicative human subjects are only those who first constitute themselves in the reciprocal self-opening and recognition as persons, so that the recognition of communication and the constitution of the person becomes one and the same process.

Thus, both from the standpoint of autonomy and from that of communication, the category of internalization is suggested to be counterproductive.

7 Does the Ethics of Communication Make Kant's Doctrine of the Postulates Superfluous?

According to Apel, in the framework of an ethics of communication, several presuppositions of morality disappear which Kant expressed in his "Postulates of Practical Reason":

"For example, the one that an omniscient God exists who judges the inner conviction of human beings, who has created the world as an arena for the moral testing of human beings, and thereby ultimately himself, as the real ruler of world history, retains the responsibility for that which occurs. Instead of this, the human community of interaction and communication would itself assume the charge—and thereby also the duty—of a *solidary responsibility* for all the possible results of their activities. And this duty also would have to be internalized by the individual who stands as representative for the community in a responsible position" (*SBB*, 2, p. 70).

Even to those favorably disposed interpreters of Kant, the postulate of an omniscient and omnipotent God seems to be a survival of dogmatic metaphysics that one would do better to bypass in order not to have to put the great thinker to shame. The rejection of metaphysical postulates is all the more necessary since an ethics which seeks universal recognition in an industrial society that is neutral among competing worldviews cannot be based upon religious foundations which for all too many contemporaries have become problematical. Yet before Apel's ethics can boast to have dispensed with the problematic, it is worth asking what the aim of Kant's doctrine of postulates is and whether the community of interaction and communication could in fact take over this task.

Kant seeks to solve the "dialectic of pure reason in the determination of the concept of the highest good" through the postulates of pure, practical reason. What is at issue in this dialectic of pure reason are not the "presuppositions of morality" as Apel assumes (ibid.). Kant's justification of the categorical imperative, of the moral law and of the autonomy of the will is in no way dependent upon the existence of God and—according to a further postulate of pure, practical reason—on the immortality of the soul. Quite the contrary, it is one of Kant's main theses that a theological justification of morality, a grounding of morality in God's will is just another material ground of determination, and hence is heteronomous and nonmoral like a grounding in education, in the civil constitution, in physical or moral feeling, or in perfection (*Critique of Practical Reason*, para. 8, Remark II, pp. 41f.). Like the immortality of the soul, the existence of God is no presupposition of morality but rather a presupposition of the higher good.

By the highest good, Kant understands more than the uppermost good. The highest good is not the dominant end that surpasses and determines all other ends. The highest good is the complete good in the sense of the unconditional totality: the inclusive end, which unifies within itself all other ends, thus not the (unconditional) pinnacle of a rising series but rather the totality of the series.

The complete good, for Kant, lies in the congruence of happiness with morality (virtue) as the worthiness for happiness; happiness (*eudaimonia*) should thus be strictly distributed according to the standard of mortality; each should be happy precisely to the degree to which they live a good and righteous life. Yet this is not the case in a world in which there are villains for whom things nonetheless go well and righteous people for whom things go badly. Even though it may be true that one can not really be happy without morality, the person acting morally, the righteous person in no way must be happy in every respect. The disproportionality of morality and happiness is indicated paradigmatically in the fate of Job and countless others after him, who sought to lead a moral life without as a result having things always go well for them.

The ethics of communication cannot overcome the fact that happiness is not (always) "distributed" strictly proportionally to the worthiness for happiness, to morality. Even if the community of interaction and communication were to take over the "solidary responsibility" for all possible results of its activity, the following still holds for it too: First, action takes place in a natural and social field of forces, which the particular actors cannot completely control, which they do not even manage fully to survey; second, the results and secondary consequences develop their own dynamic which one cannot always anticipate; third, one should not overlook the fateful character of human life, of being at the mercy of external fate: whoever is terminally ill or permanently injured, whoever's best friend or life partner dies, whoever—like millions upon millions in our century—has lost possessions and a home; such a person, by virtue of his moral convictions, may remain protected from despair, yet his well-being will be painfully impaired. The community of communication and interaction might be able to prevent many such sad fates if it did indeed always act from solidaristic responsibility. But the community of communication and interaction is not all-powerful in the sense that it could either banish all sorrow from the world or else distribute sorrow according to moral merit or demerit. The community of communication and interaction may use legal and social sanctions which punish the evil and reward the good and hence create a certain balance. But human sorrow derives not only from the punishments by fellow human beings, and human well-being derives only in part from the reward which one receives from society for one's good deeds.

In short, if one does not wish to impute an extravagant omnipotence to the community of communication and interaction, then one cannot believe that the solidaristic community of interaction and communication guarantees the proportionality between happiness and worthiness of happiness. In addition, we do not lead our lives under the conditions of an ideal community of interaction and communication but rather in association with individuals, groups, and institutions that often enough lack solidary responsibility. Indeed, therein lies the character of norms as moral "demands" which the communicative ethics cannot deny; we may be called to solidarity and yet often enough prefer to follow self-interest. But then even that amount of proportionality between happiness and being worthy of happiness vanishes which would be provided in a community of communication and interaction acting in solidarity—so that skepticism is strengthened: Despite the best will, the community of communication cannot fulfill that task which Kant has expressed in the formula of the "dialectic of pure reason in determination of the concept the highest good."

Today, not only in the sciences, the themes of language and communication are experiencing a boom. Among the very varied reasons for this fact there certainly belongs the self-evident manner in which—at least "in principle"—we recognize democracy as a political institutional reality. On the other hand, some things are only vehemently defended when their existence is threatened. Without doubt, this is true of language and communication; for we should not minimize the dangers of the impoverishment of language and even of speechlessness; the increase of television, advertising, and comics, the advance of technical languages and would-be technical languages, the profusion of stimuli, self-imposed obligations, and functional imperatives of the industrial "culture" threaten linguistic capacity as well as the readiness to enter into intensive personal relationships and nonfunctional conversations.

In this situation, it is meaningful, along with Apel, to draw attention to the fundamental and comprehensive significance of language and communication. It is also right to argue against an individualistic and in support of a communicative understanding of freedom; for true freedom manifests itself in the recognition of others as free and equally entitled persons. In view of the diverse needs and interests of human beings, communicative freedom includes the readiness to respect fellow human beings in their diversity. Thus, concrete norms of action are not the result of a monological and ahistorical process of subsumption; still less are they the result of pure power and pure decision. Rather, they arise out of historical processes of communication. For instance, it is the task of the legal order to make possible institutionally discursive will-formation in the framework of the communicative process.[4] Yet the endorsement of language, communication, and argumentation is no sufficient reason for basing a philosophical ethics solely upon a transcendental pragmatics of language.

Notes

1. See especially *Funkkolleg, Praktische Philosophie/Ethik*, Studienbegleitbrief (*SBB* in the text), Weinheim and Basel, 1980–81, I, pp. 29–31; *SBB* 2, pp. 68–74; *SBB* 8, pp. 77–100. Apel's standpoint is also supported in the *Funkkolleg* by D. Böhler (see especially *SBB* 5, pp. 11–51; *SBB* 11, pp. 48–83) and W. Kuhlmann (*SBB* 8, pp. 59—68). An early development of Apel's ethics is found in "The Apriori of the Communication Community and Foundation of Ethics" in his *Towards a Transformation of Philosophy* (trans. G. Adey and D. Frisby), London/Boston, 1980, pp. 225–300. On the thesis of the irreducibility of the argumentational situation see also W. Kuhlmann, "Reflexive Letztbegründung," *Zeitschrift für philosophische Forschung*, 35, 1981, pp. 3–26.

2. Preparatory work on the following reflections: O. Höffe, *Ethik und Politik*, Frankfurt 1979, chs. 8–9; *Sittlich-politische Diskurse*, Frankfurt 1981, ch. 3; *SBB* 7, pp. 56–59; *SBB*

12, pp. 55f.; "Transzendentale oder vernunftkritische Ethik (Kant)?," *Dialectica*, 35, 1981, pp. 195–221.

3. "Transzendentalpragmatik und Kritische Moral," in W. Kuhlmann and D. Böhler, eds., *Kommunikation und Reflexion. Zur Diskussion der Transzendental-Pragmatik*, Frankfurt 1982, pp. 83–123; English translation in this volume. See also D. Böhler, *I. Kant. Leben, Werk, Wirkung*, Munich 1983, ch. 9, and *Introduction à la philosophie pratique de Kant. La Morale, le Droit et la Religion*, Albeuve, Switzerland, 1985, chs. 2–6.

4. Hence the second, constructive part of my *Strategien der Humanität. Zur Ethik öffentlicher Entscheidungsprozesse*, Freiburg/Munich 1975, is called, "Bausteine zu einer kommunikativen Entscheidungstheorie" (building blocks for a communicative theory of decision).

6

The Basis of the Validity of Moral Norms

Karl-Heinz Ilting

One may characterize the attempt to derive binding norms from the nature of things or human beings as a "naturalistic fallacy." This attempt must fail because "ought" is no more a "real predicate" (Kant) than "is." The naturalistic fallacy is thus the deontological analogue to the ontological proof of God. Indeed, I wish to characterize the attempt to derive binding norms from the conditions of our use of reason or to detect the basis of the validity of its binding nature in these conditions as an "intellectualistic fallacy." Such an attempt also rests, in my view, upon a fallacy and does so because it confuses the rules which we must follow in order to gain knowledge with those norms the recognition of which is expected of us if we wish to live with one another in morally and legally ordered relationships. If, as I wish to show, such rules are in no way binding in the same ways as are moral norms, then any attempt to justify the binding nature of norms[1] by recourse to the rules for the use of our reason must fail.

My objection to the intellectualistic fallacy is directed against my old friend Karl-Otto Apel and his efforts at justifying an ethics through a theory of communication. Apel himself speaks of an "obligation for argumentation."[2] But even if one does not care to follow such linguistic usage, then one will not wish to deny, in this case too, the justification of recourse to the argument, "*Amicus Plato, magis amica veritas.*" At all events, I do not intend to make my objection, based upon the argument of the intellectualistic fallacy, into the central theme of this essay, but rather I wish to take my rejection of the justification of ethics by means of a theory of communication as the occasion for answering the question as to the basis of the validity of moral norms and then to develop this answer to the extent to which it is possible within the parameters of an article.

First of all I will present Apel's justification program through a theory of communication with specific reference to the question of the ground for the validity of moral norms and seek to establish that this implies the intellectualistic fallacy. Then, I will criticize this justification project by showing exactly where the fallacy that I have just characterized lies. Subsequently, I will put forward my own attempt at justification. It starts out from the fact that a universally binding ethics and doctrine of law has the task of formulating the conditions for a well-ordered collective life on the basis of the claim to self-determination, and that this task can be solved with reference to the universal and "legitimate expectability" (*Zumutbarkeit*) of the recognition of norms.* A system of metanorms is produced via an analysis of this expectability. This in turn defines the conditions which must be fulfilled in order for norms to be viewed as universally binding at all. At a second stage of this endeavor, the basic norms of a universally binding and therefore rational ethics are then justified on the basis of these metanorms. At a third stage, and in association with hypotheses concerning universal human needs and interests as well as types of specifically human interaction, these formal basic norms can then be developed further into *prima facie* universal, binding substantive norms. Since, however, these substantive norms as well do not suffice to define the normative conditions of a well-ordered communal life, the task at the fourth stage will consist in specifying the conditions for the concretization and the applicability of binding norms. Then, finally, at the fifth stage, the origin of different types of systems of binding norms, such as are

---

*Ilting's concept of *Zumutbarkeit* is hard to render accurately in English. It refers in this context to the legitimate or plausible nature of an expectation or imputation. Ilting emphasizes that any recognition of norms, since it is ultimately dependent upon the will of moral agents, is a demand, an expectation that something will be done. These normative demands and expectations, however, can be plausible, legitimate, and likely to be fulfilled. In his view, moral theory must elaborate the conditions under which fulfillment of these expectations is plausible rather than presumptuous.—Eds.

encountered in a developed society, can be reconstructed. Only at this point may the question of the ground of validity of binding norms be considered to have been answered.

I

Since he wrote his article, "The A priori of the Communication Community and the Foundations of Ethics" (1973; English 1980), the solution which Apel offers for grounding ethics has remained basically the same. It exists for him in the justification of the thesis "that the *rational argumentation* that is presupposed . . . in every discussion of a problem, in itself presupposes the validity of universal, ethical norms" (*Towards a Transformation;* p. 257). Fully in the same vein, in his article "Why a Transcendental Pragmatics of Language?",[3] he views his task as lying in an "ultimate justification of ethical norms through reflection upon the performatively evident normative preconditions of communication in argumentative discourse." Herein lies, first of all, the thesis that the rules that must be observed in any argumentation, if argumentation is not to be without purpose, are *moral* norms. Since it can thus be assumed that anyone who argues has recognized the validity of these rules of argumentation, one can conclude from this that they should recognize the moral norms of those who argue. With the proof of the recognition of moral norms by those who argue, the task of an ultimate justification of ethical norms can then be taken to be already solved, since in fact no one could without contradiction dispute the validity of moral norms, if indeed, in addition, they were in a position to do so merely as a participant in argument. Apel seeks to counter the objection that this all could at best mean that the recognition of moral norms would be established for individuals ready to engage in discussion but that in any case their binding nature would still not be secured for all others. He responds with the claim that a refusal to discuss would amount to self-exclusion from the community of rational beings and therefore could not be consistently maintained.[4]

In explicit dependency upon Kant's categorical imperative, Apel finds a moral basis presupposed in all rational argumentation, in the fact that "in the community of argumentation . . . all the members mutually recognize each other as participants with equal rights in the discussion" (Apel, 1980, p. 259). More recently, however, he has clarified these reflections, explaining that this "ethical basic norm" represents merely a "metanorm of consensus formation concerning norms, in the sense of the establishment and mediation of the interests of all those affected under the preconditions of discourse in an ideal communication community."[5] It is now valid for him above all as a "procedural norm for the justification of norms in general by consensual communication"[6]; this, in turn, makes possible the justification of institutional norms. In this way, the "demand for a substantive mediation of all human interests as possible claims in a future institution of universal and repression-free mutual consultation" is to be realized.[7] Apel believes he has taken account of the criticism which Hegel had made of the formalism of Kantian ethics by the "interposition of the discursive formation of consensus in a two-stage procedure of justification of norms," and is thus able to overcome the one-sidedness of both Kant and Hegel.[8]

Certainly, there are numerous theses requiring examination in this line of thought and their logical interconnections need closer investigation. However, with reference to the "ultimate justification of ethical norms," Apel's attempt to justify the validity of universal moral norms by reflection upon the presuppositions of rational argumentation seems to be especially problematical. For it is surely evident that moral norms have the task of ordering human relations as a whole; in contrast, in an ideal communication community the normal conditions of human collective existence themselves are transcended. The ideal nature of a community of argumentation and communication may indeed, on the one hand, evoke the ideal of an untainted moral perfection; on the other hand, however, it cannot allow us to forget that, in a pure community of argumentation orientated towards cognitive interests, precisely those difficulties and necessities of collective life have been transcended which, among other things, should have been regulated by moral norms. The fact that a community of argumentation of all things should be suitable as a model of morally ordered human relations, at least *prima facie,* appears to be not very plausible and in fact this point has aroused considerable astonishment. For this reason alone it should be made the object of a closer investigation.

In his key 1973 article, Apel gave his argument the following structure[9]:

(1) In every discussion of a problem what is at issue is the validity of arguments.

(2) The validity of arguments can only be tested in a community of thinkers.

(3) The validity of arguments is in principle dependent upon the justification of linguistic statements in an actual community of argumentation.

(4a) A lie would make the dialogue of those engaged in argument impossible.

(4b) An avoidance of critical understanding or of the explication and justification of arguments would make the dialogue of those engaged in argument impossible.

(5) In the community of argumentation, the reciprocal recognition of all members as partners in discussion with equal rights is presupposed.

(6) In (5), the recognition of all human beings as persons is implied, since all linguistic expressions and, over and above this, all the meaningful actions and bodily expressions of human beings (insofar as they are verbalized) can be interpreted as virtual arguments.

(7) In the intersubjective agreement concerning the meaning and validity of statements an ethics is already presupposed.

One can interpret propositions (1)–(3) of this argumentation as the minor and proposition (5) as the major of a syllogism.

(I) In every discussion of a problem, an actual community of argumentation is presupposed.

(II) In the community of argumentation, the basic norm of reciprocal recognition of the partner in discussion is presupposed.

It follows from this that:

(III) In every discussion of a problem, the reciprocal recognition of the partner in discussion is presupposed.

Propositions (4a) and (4b) are clearly auxiliary propositions for the justification of (5). Now the conclusion (III) in proposition (6) is extended to all meaningful actions:

(IV) All meaningful actions . . . can be interpreted as virtual arguments.

(V) Therefore (II) is valid for all meaningful actions.

(VI) As a result, in all meaningful action the reciprocal recognition of partners is presupposed (partners who reciprocally recognize one another are called persons).

Finally, in that it is assumed that all human beings can be partners in meaningful action, the following results:

(VII) In any meaningful action all human beings are recognized as persons.

This result (VII) is obviously equivalent to proposition (7).

If one now surveys my reconstruction of Apel's argumentation, then one notices first of all that it is less their logical structure than the individual propositions and the basic concepts or presuppositions utilized in them that are open to attack. Let us look closely, for instance, at propositions (2) and (3): Here there is a transition from the testability of the validity of arguments in a community of argumentation to the dependency of the validity of an argument upon the existing (!) community of argumentation. In (4a) it is clearly assumed that the inadmissibility of lies in a rational argumentation can and must be *morally* justified. In (4b) it is obviously thought that anyone who enters into an argumentation is *morally obliged* to concern themselves with critical understanding and with the *unlimited* explication and justification of arguments. The reciprocal recognition of members of the community of argumentation that is spoken of in (5) refers not merely to their capacity to participate in a rational discussion of problems, but also to their status as morally accountable persons, so that any discussion of problems *as such* already presupposes the reciprocal recognition of all participants as morally responsible acting persons. At the same time, it is clearly implicit that they should all possess equal rights not only as discussion partners who are to be taken seriously and as responsible actors but also in their contributions to discussion and hence with regard to their arguments—indeed, the recognition of the equal rights of all arguments is almost a moral duty. Naturally the thesis (see proposition (6)) that "all linguistic expressions and, over and above this, all meaningful actions and bodily expressions of human beings (insofar as they can be verbalized) can be interpreted as virtual arguments" is also problematical in that it implies that bodily expressions of animals are to be interpreted as virtual arguments and therefore to be taken into account in an ethical discussion among those possessing equal rights. More generally, it is striking that in this attempt at a grounding of ethics attention is directed above all toward the problem of "recognition,"[10] while the question of the concept of the moral (i.e., the question of the distinction between moral and nonmoral norms) is not raised at all.

It follows then that the basis for a critical test of Apel's argumentation is to be found in the syllogism (I)–(III), since this syllogism purports to demonstrate the thesis "that already the . . . argumentation presupposed in every discussion of a problem presupposes the validity of universal ethical norms." This demonstration basically consists in the fact that the intermediate concept of "preconditions for a community of argumentation" is interposed between the concepts "discussion of a problem" or "rational argumentation" and "the validity of ethical norms." If anyone who merely asserts or disputes something can only meaningfully do this if he has recognized the preconditions for a community of argumentation and if, furthermore, the recognition of moral norms belongs to the preconditions for a community of argumentation, then the binding nature of moral norms is already recognized in every act of assertion or disputation. One should also test whether, in this context, the concept of "the preconditions for a community of argumentation" can really assume the function which Apel has imputed to it. I dispute this for the first as much as the second premise of the syllogism (I)–(III) with the claim that (I) implies a pragmatic fallacy and (II) an intellectualistic fallacy.[11] In view of the problematic at stake in this article, I will concentrate upon the intellectualistic fallacy.

II

In my opinion, propositions (1) and (2) are unproblematical, but proposition (3) is not, at least if one speaks differently about "validity" than in the normal sense of the term. In a somewhat unusual sense, the "validity" of an argument is of course dependent upon its justification in an actual community of argumentation: namely, in the sense in which one speaks of "valid law." In this sense, "validity" means as much as *validitas*," or the enactment of norms of positive law, which, if necessary, can be upheld by the use of state power. At the same time, it is implied that the norms of positive law are binding, and that they should be obeyed, even without the use of state power. But two totally different circumstances are implied by the actual *operation* and the *binding* nature of positive law, and this ambiguity is merely hidden in the concept of *validitas*. In an analogous manner, one can indeed also speak of the "validity" of an argument in the double sense that it both finds general agreement and is sound; but, in this case too, there exists a basic distinction between the fact that the argument is generally *held to be* valid and the assumption that it actually *is* valid. This becomes perfectly clear if—instead of arguments—one speaks of the validity (i.e., of the truth) of a judgment p and the "validity" of the assertion contained in this judgment (i.e., its being held to be true). The assertion is a speech act in which someone makes a validity (truth) claim for a judgment p and volunteers to redeem this claim. Whereas a judgment can only be true or false, the validity claim of a judgment is either redeemable or not; and in this case the judgment is either verifiably false or undemonstrably true.

When Apel asserts in (3) that the validity of an argument is dependent in principle upon its justification in the current community of argumentation, then he undoubtedly does not mean "validity" in the sense of a mere claim to validity but validity in the sense of truth or soundness. Thus, he makes the validity of an argument dependent upon the redeemability of a corresponding claim to validity, i.e., he falls victim to the pragmatic fallacy.[12] For, as has been shown, nothing at all has been decided concerning the validity of a judgment or an argument by the nonredeemability of a corresponding claim to validity. In my opinion, neither Wittgenstein's private-language argument[13] nor Peirce's idea of a *community of investigators* is capable of disproving the categorical distinction which exists between *validity* and the *claim to validity*. Therefore, a critical analysis of the concept of a community of argumentation must generate doubts about any attempt to demonstrate the binding nature of moral norms by recourse to the implicit preconditions of any rational argumentation.

But even if (I) were sufficiently sound in its full range within the context of the type of justification sought for here, the grounding of an ethics through communications theory would have to founder on the untenability of (II). In order to demonstrate this, first of all I wish to test propositions (4a), (4b), and (5) individually.

The proposition that, according to (4a), a lie would make arguing impossible and that the binding nature of the moral norm that prevents lying is thus already presupposed by all participants in argumentation seems *prima facie* irrefutable. Nonetheless, the impression that in the discussion of a given problem lying could benefit someone should strike us as curious. Since this impression is not useful as an argument, an analysis may perhaps help here.

One can define what a lie is without much difficulty: an action in which someone intentionally speaks untruth. The fact that such an act is not permitted is already a prejudice which is supported by the Ten Commandments. This is immediately clear if one brings to mind instances in which lies are obviously allowed or even demanded in some way. For instance:

(a) Someone makes an April Fool of another person.

(b) Someone insists, contrary to the facts, that he or she is not at home.

(c) A sick person does not know what his/her condition is.

(d) Someone refuses to disclose the innocence of an accused person.

In (a) we are dealing with a joke to which no one normally has anything to object. In the case of (b), circumstances permitting, one could openly say to an unwelcome visitor or caller that one has no time. But it would hurt the person to make clear to them that their visit or call is felt to be disturbing; the person is spared this unpleasant experience by a lie out of politeness and their sensitivity is preserved. In (c) the truth about the person's state is perhaps no longer to be demanded of the sick person, so that, circumstances permitting, the lie is an act of humanity. In (d) we are dealing with a famous case, unfortunately insufficiently discussed by Kant, in which the lie is forbidden in positive legal terms[14] but certainly not in any other sense, since otherwise one would have to assume that someone could in some sense be obliged to assist in the pursuit of innocent persons.

Hence, if it is clear that lying is not totally forbidden or reprehensible but rather only under specific circumstances or in a specific sense, then one might take the view that a lie is always forbidden on *moral* grounds if it is avowedly inadmissible. That this too is an error can be made clear from the following cases:

(e) In a question game (e.g., "What am I?"), someone gives a false answer.

(f) In the analysis of an adjourned game in chess, someone falsely asserts that they have already tried out a particular variation.

(g) A married man declares to a girl that he is unmarried.

(h) Someone puts the blame on another person in court by false testimony.

In the case of (e), the correctness of the replies belongs among the rules of the game. Whoever gives a false answer—perhaps in order to mislead the others as a joke—thereby thwarts the game, and the remaining participants have every reason to accuse him of being a spoilsport; but this is no moral accusation since the spoilsport, in contrast, for instance, to the cheat at a card game, does not deceive others with a view to his own self-interest. On the contrary, in certain games, it is part of the rules of the game that someone lies, e.g., if the identity of the lier is to be elicited from questions in such instances, then that person would be a spoilsport who, instead of lying, stated the truth.[15] In contrast, the analysis of an adjourned game of chess in case (f) is a relatively serious matter, comparable for instance with the attempt to solve a mathematical exercise collectively: the commonly sought goal of action here consists in the discovery of a strategy for winning or avoiding losses through maximizing success by means of the accumulation and testing of recommended solutions. Out of this goal and the pregiven marginal preconditions (state of the game, number and competence of participants, available time, etc.) are to be derived the rules to be observed in the debate (e.g., orderly procedure, objectivity, consideration for the interests or sensitivities of those taking part), and naturally, above all, the reununciation of actions which are appropriate for foiling the collectively sought goal—for instance, false information. Since the participants wish to achieve a goal of action collectively, it is not at all easy to conceive of an instance in which one of them deliberately thwarts the common effort, since he would have to knowingly act contrary to his own interests. In this case, one could only accuse him of having deceived the others under the illusion of willing cooperation; although, with reference to the communal goal of action, a lie would be inadmissible, but insofar as it was it could not be *morally* condemned. Only in (g) is lying not allowed morally. This is not because it would be inadmissible with reference to a common goal, but rather because a self-interested goal of action directed against the interests of another is to be achieved by exploiting through deception the other's trust in one's own worthiness. Here the sense in which and the conditions under which a lie is morally reprehensible become clear: when the apparently justified trust of another is misused and exploited to carry out self-interested goals or even malevolent ones. Such a case is also to be found in (h)—it is intended above all in the Fourth Commandment—

except that now, in addition, the legal culpability of the deliberately false statement enters into the equation.

If one now looks back at proposition (4a), then it is apparent that in a community of argumentation the recognition and adherence to a morally basic norm, namely, the ban on lying, is unfounded. Just as in instance (f), in a community of argumentation a deliberately false statement is taken to be inadmissible *only* in reference to the collectively sought goal of action; in other words, what is also at issue here is a hypothetical-problematical imperative in the sense of Kant's well-known distinction in the "Groundwork of the Metaphysic of Morals." This is also endorsed by Apel when he states: "Lying, for instance, would obviously make the dialogue of people engaged in argument impossible" (*Transformation of Philosophy,* p. 259). It is precisely because Apel justifies the inadmissibility of lying with reference to a commonly striven-for goal of action that we are concerned here not with a morally binding norm but with a hypothetical-problematical imperative. (This hypothetical imperative is problematical because one can strive after the goal of action in question but one does not have to; and even if one had to strive after it—which is not the case—then an assertorical-hypothetical imperative would merely emerge out of the problematical imperative.)[16]

Therefore, proposition (4b) is also unfounded. It is true that the avoidance of a critical understanding and of the explication and justification of arguments can be inadmissible in reference to the common goal of action; but, insofar as this is the case, it is not morally reprehensible *precisely because of this.* Still less can the corresponding preparedness be morally incumbent upon agents since no one can be unconditionally committed to critical understanding or to the explication and justification of arguments, for participation in a communal effort is always only conditional, that is, dependent upon following other interests and upon the fulfillment of other duties. Since the word "duty" is commonly used only with reference to some kind of binding norms, it is furthermore mistaken to speak of a "duty towards argumentation."

As a result, thesis (5), "In the community of argumentation, the reciprocal recognition of all members as equal partners in discussion is presupposed," is also unfounded—not only because this is to be understood as the recognition of *moral* basic norms, but because it would even be incompatible with the communal goals of action of a community of communication. Along with the problematical-hypothetical imperatives that can be derived from the mutual goals of a community of argumentation and other pregiven marginal preconditions, there also exists the rule that the specific competence of individual members justifies an order of precedence. One can only speak of "equality of rights" in this situation insofar as arguments must indeed be evaluated according to their pertinent relevance and "without regard to the person"; but as long as what is primarily at issue is achieving the communal goal of action as securely and quickly as possible, the special competence of some individuals must have precedence over the personal interests of the members of a community of argumentation—for instance, over the equal consideration of all in discussion. In fact, the existing sensitivities and animosities of some individuals are only to be taken into account with reference to the common goal of action as far as their nonconsideration would disturb or thwart the communal effort. But such considerations also have nothing to do with the recognition of members as responsible acting persons and their claim to human respect. In their capacity as participants in a communal effort they all have to subordinate their claims to the realization of the communal goal of action; as soon as they register claims as acting persons, then they already enter upon the scene as individuals with their own justified interests.

The discussion until now has proceeded strictly from that particular presupposition which Apel places at the basis of his reflections, namely, that what is at issue are purely objective arguments that, where possible, are to be rationally discussed and not, for instance, arguments within a context of action which is terminated by a decision—whether it be that of an arbitrator or by the casting of votes by those entitled to do so. If a temporally circumscribed discussion is terminated by a decision then the contributions to discussion take on the character of an advertisement for individual interpretations and explanations; the claim to equal consideration in the distribution of chances of codiscussion for this reason is significant. This is particularly the case if participants have an interest in which decision is reached at the end; in this case, however, the objectivity of the discussion is also still preserved if personal attacks are disapproved of. Nonetheless, escalations are always possible with growing interest in the facilitation or obstruction of specific decisions and only thus does the orientation of individuals in conversation with one another—in the meantime, to speak of a "community of argumentation" is not permissible—toward moral norms gain significance. A similar development away from the objectivity of a rational argumentation and toward the predominance of personal interests is also to be expected if the chances of an unambiguous solution to a problem disappears and the discussion threatens to become an endless process. This is obviously the case (also dealt with by Apel) of a discussion concerning the justification and compatibility of divergent interests, especially if it is directly led by the interested parties. It is difficult to conceive how such a discussion can achieve the rationality of a strictly objective argumentation. It must unite the equal distribution of chances for discussion with the precedence of factual competence to the satisfaction of all participants.

In a community of argumentation orientated toward problem solving, participants have not recognized one another as discussion partners *with equal rights* but indeed merely as participants. Contrary to the view which lies behind proposition (5), however, they have also not recognized one another as responsible (i.e., morally responsible) acting individuals. One does not have to reflect on the fact that, under certain circumstances, a computer could be a member of a community of argumentation in order to convince oneself that the participants in a common effort towards the rational solution of a problem as such perform no morally responsible actions. Just as a computer—falsely programmed or falsely constructed—can fail, so too can discussion partners make mistakes. For instance, when they reach agreement for clarifying linguistic usage and for shortening their discussion, what is at issue is not, for example, a one-sided morally binding promise but rather, with reference to the common effort, an appropriate convention whose observance is necessary from the point of view of the goal of the discussion, and thus, once more, a hypothetical-problematical imperative. In the case of a one-sided or reciprocal promise, a behavioral expectation is justified which, under certain circumstances, can also be made valid against the interests of those who have bound themselves to it; in the case of a linguistic convention within a community of argumentation, its contravention impairs the common effort, even if it remains unnoticed, so that those affected knowingly or unknowingly themselves place obstacles in its path. Thus, it is incorrect for Apel to declare that the "normative preconditions for the possibility of a promise [must] . . . be presupposed for any possible discussion as unavoidable."[17] Under certain circumstances, in the case of divergent goals of action, a promise requires a person to do what he or she (no longer) wishes to do; a linguistic convention, with reference to the unchanged communal goal of action, can be changed, since in this case divergent interests are not in play. As soon as someone had occasion to require a participant in moral discussions to abide by linguistic conventions, then the objectivity of a common effort at problem solving would long have disappeared. Whoever deliberately damages linguistic conventions in objective argumentations does not act morally reprehensibly but rather behaves like someone who, when driving a car, purposely puts their foot simultaneously on the gas pedal and the brake. With this we can see that my original impression that this argument is absurd is confirmed and explained: Whoever unknowingly and unintentionally damages the rules of purposive rational action acts *irrationally;* whoever does this deliberately acts *absurdly.* However, whoever damages a binding norm, whether proceeding in a purposive-rational manner or not, acts reprehensibly.[18]

The implicit presuppositions of a rational argumentation are justified in the effort to achieve a common goal of action; consequently, they contain no morally binding norms but rather merely purposive-rationally conditioned, problematical-hypothetical imperatives. Something completely different, namely, obligation, first comes into play when the importance of the goal of action itself and the participation in the common effort in individuals' life-context is questioned. If, for instance, they have undertaken the tasks of a solution to a problem on the basis of a labor contract, and one of them, whether it be out of indolence or indifference, fails to comply with or insufficiently complies with the (problematical-hypothetical) imperatives justified in the task, then he too can in fact be morally reproached. But thereupon the reproach does not rest upon the inappropriate nature of his behavior but rather upon the fact that he has made himself morally and legally bound by his participation.

The thesis "that in any discussion of a problem presupposing *rational argumentation* the validity of universal ethical norms is already presupposed" is thereby refuted because all of these presuppositions have been shown to be problematical-hypothetical imperatives—just as, according to this approach, an attempt at justification could itself also be nothing other than this. Viewed formally, the decisive mistake for this failure lies in the confusion of the binding nature of moral norms (of categorical imperatives) with the purposive rationality of "rules of skill" (problematical-hypothetical imperatives). In contrast, if one looks at the basis of justification for this attempt then one can trace its failure back to an intellectualistic fallacy: Instead of deriving the binding nature of moral norms from the preconditions for morally responsible action, this attempt relies upon the preconditions for rational argumentation, hence upon the preconditions for our use of rationality. As is well known, such attempts are as old as the history of the efforts surrounding a justification of ethics itself. If Socrates was of the opinion that "virtue" was a form of knowledge and that no one voluntarily mistook the goal of his action, then he obviously believed that correct insight alone was the sufficient condition for morally responsible or even "good" action. Even Thomas Hobbes (*De Cive*, III, 3) still believed he could detect a "similarity" (*similitudo*) between an unjust action and a failure in argumentation. The intellectualistic fallacy that exists in Apel's attempt at justification, however, goes back to the view that one can enlarge the pragmatic idea of a "*community of investigators*" into a universal community of communication of responsibly acting persons and thus transfer Peirce's expectation of progress in knowledge to the moral idea of a unity of the human species. It must be asked whether the rationality that must be presupposed in the conception of a universally binding ethic is already to be found in the objectivity of a rational argumentation or whether it must be sought in the precondition for morally responsible action itself.

III

If, out of an attempt to justify ethics, one may expect an answer to the question as to the grounds (if any) for the universally binding quality of moral norms—as we do in fact assume throughout—then the answer, which might seem to be provided by Apel's attempt at justification, is hardly satisfactory for yet another reason. For the answer really consists only in the suggestion that, to the extent that we have no choice but to enter into arguments, we have always necessarily recognized the binding nature of universal binding norms. The fact that the necessary conditions for rational argumentation are said to be the sufficient conditions for the universally binding nature of moral norms hardly appears plausible even if one agrees with the view that any discussion of a problem is to be viewed with reference to the ideal, universal community of communication. The always "already presupposed" (putative) recognition of moral norms does indeed lead to an ideal universal communication but not really to a *reason for the validity* of moral norms, unless one wishes to elevate rationality into an end in itself or into an absolute value.[19] It appears more promising to find the answer to the question of the ground for the validity of moral norms in the preconditions for morally responsible action.

One cannot ask this question with the necessary radicalness if one has not yet clarified the fact that the binding nature of whatever norms is in no way indisputable. Norms are neither facts of nature nor analytical propositions but rather—as Kant already emphasized—synthetic a priori propositions: they demand that we limit the sphere of *possible* actions open to us, even against our wishes, to the respectively *permitted* actions, and that we do so even if, without any need to fear unwanted consequences, we were in a position to act according to our wishes. This limitation cannot be derived from the concept of our interest in action; the proposition in which this is demonstrated is thus a synthetic one. But the fact that we have to distinguish between possible and permitted actions is obviously a rule which, independently of all empirical goals, we have to take into account in our actions; that which demonstrates this is thus an *a priori* judgment. Since it refers not to the preconditions of our knowledge but rather to those of our action, it is an *a priori* practical-synthetic judgment. Yet how can it be the case that such a judgment lies at the basis of all our action? Where is the basis of its validity to be found? Do we rightly assume its validity at all?[20]

If, first, we presuppose in a thought experiment that there exist no binding norms at all which limit the sphere of possible actions open to us, then we easily recognize that, although our freedom of action would be significantly enlarged, this would also be the case for all others and that, as a result, we would also have to rely upon the protection which the validity of limiting norms nonetheless secures for us. An interest in the validity of norms is therefore definitely to be recognized, but it does not lead beyond the wish that others should, in their actions and insofar as they affect us, limit their actions with regard to norms which they take to be binding. But since each other person can employ this consideration for him- or herself, nothing is to be hoped for in this direction. Moreover, one would have cause to regard others like natural forces, independently of whether one either had an optimistic or a pessimistic opinion as to what human beings are capable of. Unpleasant though such a situation might be, there still remains the question as to how in fact our freedom of action is to be limited by norms, where indeed any limitation which appeals to one person would displease another, where in fact anyone can take a special interest in some modes of action or other. Without norms that are binding and generally followed, human activity is more strongly threatened than is the predominantly instinctive life of animals; but precisely our interest in the preservation of our unbounded freedom prevents us from accepting limitations on our freedom of action, limitations that nonetheless are necessary.

It is clear from this preliminary reflection wherein the task lies, if a specifically human form of ordered collective life is to be found: the necessary limitations to our freedom of action for the creation of an ordered collective life may not transcend that of our freedom itself. For instance, this would be the case if the order of our collective life were created solely through the application or threat of constraint—if this is possible at all—or even if it were to be enforced by individual measures or commands. The necessity for limitations and the indispensability of the claim to freedom are obviously only compatible if acceptance of the limitations can be *expected* (*zugemutet*) to be followed in principle by every human individual. The concept of legitimate expectability already excludes the fact that the possibly necessary limitations extend to what is indispensable, and thus above all to the claim to freedom itself.

1. The highest precondition for universally justifiable (*zumutbar*) limitations on our freedom is obviously that the limitation itself has the character of universality and thus can be expressed in a *rule* whose adherence is universally exactable. The creation of an ordered collective life cannot therefore be the task of a social technology which seeks to create order by direct influence upon the behavior of individuals, in such a way as if the appropriate means for the realization of a desired state of affairs were to be found and made available. (All the recommendations of a social technology would be merely problematical-hypothetical imperatives.) Rather, a universally justifiable order of human collective life can only be achieved if it rests upon the *will* of individuals to follow the limitation upon their freedom of action that is to be established by rules. Only in this case is the rule recognized as a *norm* that is to be followed. The free *recognition* of a norm, that is, one not enforced by application or threat of force, by those who are to follow it, is therefore a necessary precondition for a universally justifiable limitation upon the freedom of human individuals. Only a freely recognized norm is compatible with the indispensability of our claim to freedom.

An individual's *possible* actions are distinguished from *permitted* actions in that a *justified claim* to freedom of action is grounded with reference to the fact that it is based on a norm freely recognized by all; at the same time, other possible actions preserve the character of being not permissible. Yet this can only meaningfully take place if the same norm is freely recognized at the same time by all remaining individuals, so that those actions upon which one of them has a justified claim are always not permitted for the remaining individuals. Hence, Wittgenstein's private language argument is valid without doubt for a norm: a single individual alone cannot recognize and abide by a norm. But if justified claims only emerge out of commonly recognized norms then only such norms are universally justifiable which, in principle, impose the *same* claims and obligations upon all individuals. For an obligation is certainly nothing more than the recognition of the justified claims of another person. Therefore, only by the common recognition of a norm do human individuals enter into such a relationship to one another that they recognize one another reciprocally as justified and duty-bound actors, i.e., as *persons.* Only on this basis are they also in a position to answer to one another for their actions and to be responsible for them. Strictly speaking, one can indeed only speak of "actions" as such where one is responsible for one's deeds and where this can be *imputed* to someone. Privileges do not exclude the reciprocal recognition of persons; they too are only universally exactable on the basis of the *equal rights* of persons.

In the discussion so far of the preconditions for the reasonableness of limitations to our freedom of action, my aim has been to reconcile our indispensable claim to freedom with the necessity for limitations on freedom. It does appear that this is not only possible but also that, on this basis, both the concept of action as well as that of freedom first come into their own at all. Only persons acting responsibly are really *free;* only they are in a position not merely to act arbitrarily but indeed with justification. What previously has been termed "freedom of action" is thus really only demonstrated on the basis of the reciprocal recognition of persons who act responsibly. A further precondition can be derived from the demand for the universal expectability of norm acceptance, namely, that the limitations to our freedom of action at the same time must secure the satisfaction of universal human needs and make possible specifically human forms of interaction. If they were totally unfit for this, then their recognition could be demanded by no one. However imprecise the concepts of universal human needs as well as specific human interactions may be, and however culturally dependent their definition might in each case be, nonetheless, norms, in order to be recognized as binding, must indeed satisfy the material conditions of our life. Only by the fact that the idea of the equal rights of persons is applied to the material conditions of human life does the concept of universally justifiable *substantive norms* emerge. However, since elementary needs of life and types of interaction cannot be derived from the concept of a normative order of responsibly acting persons, but rather must be established with reference to the empirical character of human beings, the attempt at an a priori reconstruction of a universally binding morality on the basis of the legitimate expectability of norm acceptance already oversteps the boundaries of what can be demonstrated. As will be seen, there are such elementary needs of life and types of interaction, and it is difficult to imagine how the recognition of certain elementary material norms could be avoided.

Under the empirical and in particular historical preconditions of human collective life, we clearly must define how far the satisfaction of human needs and the forms of interhuman cooperation should be supported or made possible by binding norms. Cooperation in the *specification and differentiation of substantive norms* is certainly universally expectable (*zumutbar*) precisely with reference to the realization of a specific human form of life; only in this way could a concrete system of norms be created that is appropriate for ordering human collective life under given empirical-historical conditions. Since at this level in the justification of ethics, cultural and empirical variables also appear, an a priori reconstruction of a concrete system of norms is naturally quite impossible. Only the development to a specified and differentiated arrangement of a concrete system of norms belongs among the conditions of universally exactable norms. Whoever evaded them would remain at the stage of anarchistic primitivism.

The concrete, culturally conditioned, and empirical-historical conditions of life are also of significance in yet another way for the concept of universally expectable norms, namely, insofar as they define those behavioral expectations as a result of which a situation is "normal" or "abnormal": all substantive norms presuppose the existence of a "normal" situation; to the extent to which the situation no longer corresponds to the conditions under which the specified and differentiated material norms are to be valid, adherence to them is also no longer universally demanded. Whoever continued to recognize the binding nature of concrete norms in such an exceptional situation might, nonetheless, appeal to the fact that these norms are not *applicable* according to the situation of things. The reasonableness of following binding norms therefore presupposes the presence of normal (i.e., assumed from the outset in the act of recognition) conditions of applicability.

If one now surveys the whole complex of conditions under which norms, because they are universally expected, can be viewed as binding, then one already has the first part of the answer to the problem of grounding the validity of moral norms: these conditions are, as it were, *metanorms*[21] which state how the necessity for limitations upon our freedom of action can be reconciled with the irrevocable claim to self-determination for the creation of a satisfying collective human life. Insofar as moral norms fulfill these conditions, their recognition and adherence may be universally demanded, and insofar as they are recognized, they are also binding. It is thus not the act of recognition as such which justifies the binding nature of a norm but rather the significance which this act contains with regard to this system of metanorms.

Of course, a norm, a system of norms, or even norms as such would not be binding for that person who denied them recognition; he would also not be in the same situation as someone who, when driving a car, stepped both on the gas pedal and on the brake. But with the refusal to recognize norms he would at the same time renounce being recognized as a person; and being perceived as one renouncing specific norms or a system of norms he would, at the same time, be excluded from the community of those who are connected to one another by the common recognition of these norms or a specific system of norms. Thus, the following point becomes clear: Along with the voluntary self-limitation entailed by recognizing the binding nature of norms, we gain, at the same time, a status which, as rational living entities alone, we could never achieve, namely the claim to *human dignity*. For this is a title which we hold only as a being that acts freely and responsibly. If it is still necessary to reply to the question as to what it is that can indeed *motivate* us to recognize moral norms, then the answer is certainly to be found in the idea of human dignity.

2. From this survey of the conditions that must be fulfilled if norms are to be universally binding there finally emerge those basic norms whose universal recognition is to be demanded with reference to an ordered collective human existence, which also fulfills the irrevocable claim to self-determination. Anyone who is capable of doing so *should* be prepared to render account for their actions, in that he—as a person—acts responsibly, i.e., limits the sphere of all possible actions that are factually available to him to those which are permitted him with regard to the justified claims of others affected. This means that everyone as a person *should prima facie* (until there is evidence to the contrary) also recognize all others, who are capable of acting so, as persons. Furthermore, anyone capable of this *should* only act according to such rules as, at the same time, any other person could recognize as binding. For only in this case does he not claim more for himself than he is already prepared to concede to any other person. What is more, anyone *should* concede elementary material rights to any other person *prima facie* (even before he has reached an agreement concerning them with others), which no one could meaningfully relinquish. And finally, each *should* be prepared, with regard to collective human existence, to reach an agreement with all others who are prepared to do so concerning the extent, specification, and differentiation of material rights, as well as regarding cooperation in the creation of circumstances in which the substantive norms made concrete

in this way are applicable, i.e., in which adherence to them is universally binding.

The first two of these basic norms are "formal," insofar as they make the recognition of universally binding norms into a duty, without in fact already saying anything about which rights and duties result from their recognition. In contrast, the third basic norm is "substantive," but unfortunately indefinite, since, prior to all common agreement and arrangements, one may only vaguely presume which substantive rights are to be conceded to those with whom one does not already associate on the basis of commonly recognized norms. The fact that nonetheless this basic norm must be an element of a rationally justifiable universal ethics results from the reflection that otherwise the murder of natives with whom one has hitherto had no contact would not be morally reprehensible, just as conversely, without this substantive basic norm, the murder of invaders by natives would also be considered morally indifferent. Now one could indeed assert that primitive peoples who had no contact with the civilized world might well feel threatened by intruders, so that for them a situation marked by the command not to kill does not exist at all; this does not hold, however, for the situation of civilized invaders. Indefinite though these three basic norms may be, they are nonetheless in no way empty and unnecessary. The two final basic norms are also substantive norms. But they are to be distinguished from the third one by the fact that, unlike the latter, they do not first and foremost forbid something—the elementary human rights that may be derived from the three basic norms are primarily prohibitions on disobeying them—but instead mostly call for something: to cooperate in the concretization and formation of a system of substantive norms and in the creation of circumstances appropriate to them. But, as enjoining basic norms, they also generate a preparedness for duty; as to which actions in a concrete situation someone is obliged to undertake, must in this case—as in all cases that enjoin substantive norms—be capable of being decided by persons themselves with reference to their other duties and above all to their justified interests. If, however, not even the *preparedness* to which these two final basic norms refer may be demanded of persons, then it is not clear how one could morally disapprove of the behavior of the person who did not wish to participate in or even sought to prevent the creation of an order of human collective existence on the basis of universally expectable norms.

The basic norms which one can formulate at this second stage of justification of a universally binding ethics are certainly capable of further elucidation. It is for this reason that one can insist on the fact that they are neither, as Apel claims, merely procedural norms for the formation of a consensus about norms nor, as, for instance, is assumed by Welzel[22] or Rawls,[23] purely formal norms, from which substantive duties and rights cannot be derived. Despite their regrettable but unavoidable indefiniteness, we are justified in viewing them as universal demands that already possess the character of a binding nature wherever human persons confront one another.

3. One can now consider certain empirical hypotheses concerning universal human needs and interests as well as specific human interactions which would allow the formulation of elementary prohibitive norms. As will be shown, what is at issue are widely known and widely recognized basic norms. It is difficult to conceive that some kind of collective human existence could exist in which their validity is not presupposed. One can see the basis of their binding nature in the relationship that exists between the task of developing a universally expectable normative order and the general conditions of human life, at least insofar as they can be tackled or improved by human activity.

As elementary human needs and interests one might, above all, wish to consider the following three: the interest in the integrity of life and limb, in undisturbed control over things for securing the maintenance of life, and in the reproduction of human life itself. If the task of a normative order consists in protecting such elementary needs and interests, i.e., guarding their satisfaction or realization from attacks and disturbances, then one cannot see how one can avoid recognizing such elementary substantive prohibitive norms such as "You should not kill," "You should not steal," "You should not commit adultery," since a refusal to do so would certainly mean that one did not also think of laying claim to the corresponding basic rights to integrity of life and limb, to property, and to an undisturbed family order. It is certainly true that, at this stage, one cannot clearly determine how far any prohibitive norms and the relevant corresponding basic laws extend. Whether a perhaps unintended injury or the confiscation of another person's belongings falls under the first two of these prohibitive norms, and which kind of family order is subverted by the ban on "adultery," cannot be decided solely on the basis of hypotheses concerning elementary human needs and interests and their protection by means of a universally binding normative order. Even a universal consensus, which would make possible the reply to these questions, is not available. When the biblical commandment forbids killing, only the worst case is mentioned without other violent crimes being thereby rendered usually permissible. The prohibition on stealing, in any case, presupposes already a norm that regulates the legal acquisition of property in things, so that in fact only the property right to things necessary for securing the maintenance of life remains an elementary basic norm.[24] Naturally, the right to the protection of a family order is especially unspecific, since the family systems of different peoples are extremely diverse. Even if the maintenance and perpetuation of specific systems can hardly be demanded by universal binding norms, one can nonetheless derive rights and duties (e.g., with regard to the protection and rearing of children) that are universally binding on the basis of the interest in the preservation of family institutions in association with generally expectable rights and duties.

Aside from elementary needs and interests that are to be protected by binding norms, there also exist specific human forms of interaction which are just as elementary and therefore require the same protection. In the context of these reflections we can point above all to two types of interaction: the exchange of experience and the exchange of services. Since human individuals are characterized by a great capacity for learning and, at the same time, a great need to learn, one can view the interest in the exchange of experience as the foundation of a specifically human form of interaction for whose protection not merely a universal interest exists, but which could not exist at all were there not good reasons for the assumption that normally communications do not serve to mislead and to deceive. The importance of the moral ban on lying thus does not really consist in the demand to make available to others one's experiences and knowledge but rather in the condemnation of any action which is directed toward misusing the *trust* of others in communication in order to deceive them for personal ends. Since human individuals have an interest in cooperation through the exchange of services, since this can be significantly extended if the connection between a service rendered and its reward must not be simply simultaneous, and since this connection can be created by declarations of intent, then there exists a universal interest in the fact that such declarations, through which we promise future services, are actually followed out. The moral commandment to stick to a given promise rests upon the presupposition that such a promise is not a nonbinding declaration of intent but instead a binding obligation that one must maintain amidst changing circumstances if indeed this person is committed to responsible action. An insincere promise is therefore an attempt, based upon the trust of another in the fact that the binding nature of a promise is universally recognized, to gain advantages for oneself by deception. Thus, since the interest in human interaction may be assumed to be universal, the ban on lying and the command to hold to a given promise are rightly valid as universal substantive norms which are binding for all responsible actors. Just as in the case of the three previously mentioned substantive norms, which aim to protect general human interests and needs, so in the case of these two norms as well one must start out from the fact that their binding nature is necessarily recognized before any contact and agreement has taken place.

4. All the assertions put forward in the previous stage of this argument are subject to a principled reservation. As a rule, it is not clear from the outset which actions fall under the previously justified norms and which are not demanded or forbidden by them. Without special evaluative standards, it is uncertain as to whether a declaration through which we promise future services is to be evaluated as a promise or as a mere

declaration of intent; normally, one cannot see whether a communication is honest information. As indicated, the inalienability of property rests upon the clarification of the conditions of the acquisition of property, not to mention the difficulty in a concrete situation in which legally binding agreements do not exist for deciding whether a morally forbidden attack upon the integrity of life and limb or on the order of family relationships exists or not. But even if these and similar questions could be decided with reference to universally binding substantive norms, the question still remains open as to whether obedience to these norms in a given situation was also justifiable: that the command not to kill is invalid in the case of a direct attack on one's own life is accepted even under the conditions of a legal-constitutional order; but what happens if an effective constitutional order is not yet or no longer in existence? The inviolability of another's property is also suspended in constitutional circumstances where an extremely unusual crisis situation exists; but can one speak at all of a "normal" situation, if norms are not yet (or no longer) being followed? Similar doubts are conceivable with regard to the other substantive norms discussed so far.

We can thus see that binding norms are only in a position to order interhuman relationships effectively if the universally binding substantive norms are made concrete by the agreement and arrangements of individuals and if, by an ordinary adherence to these norms, a "normal" situation (i.e., a situation in which obedience to them can *prima facie* be generally assumed and expected) is created. Naturally, from the standpoint of the theoretical reconstruction of binding norms, this is an extremely complex task. In contrast, in historical reality, this task has more or less long since been satisfactorily solved so, that as a rule one can partially succeed in answering moral questions on the basis of established norms and their accepted conditions of applicability. Such endeavors presuppose the argument developed above, and this means: it must be assumed in each case that those who have recognized the specified norms agree to them and find the corresponding conditions of applicability for them at hand. In other words, norms that have been made concrete are neither *prima facie* universally binding, nor is the expectation of their being followed independent of judgments concerning the normality of the given situation. For those who do not belong to the community of those who are associated with one another by commonly recognized, concretized norms, these norms are not *prima facie* binding; and since the recognized moral norms in a community are not codified anyway, it is often unclear even among the members of the community how, for example, moral questions that arise should be answered.

Nonetheless, the claim of certain concretized systems of norms to universal recognition is not completely and from the outset incorrect. Without doubt it becomes invalid if a concrete system of norms does not even comply with the conditions of general expectability (of acceptance) because, for instance, the maxim of basic equal rights among the addresses of a norm is injured or the free recognition of the system of norms as a condition of its binding nature is not guaranteed. Numerous systems of norms in the past and the present only partially or insufficiently fulfill these conditions; hence they can be viewed as unacceptable. However, the claim to a universal binding force can also fail as a result of the primitiveness or undifferentiated nature of a normative system, if, for example, it no longer is compatible with the complexity of a developed society. Such a claim is still justifiable only if a normative system is capable of development and open to further differentiation. But this condition is only fulfilled if the concept of binding force itself permits further differentiation over and above the previously discussed framework.

5. An attempt at further differentiation already emerged in the previous discussion when a distinction was made between primary *prohibitive* (*verbietende*) norms and primary *enjoining* (*gebietende*) norms. On a superficial glance, one could gain the impression that the prohibition on lying and the enjoinment to speak the truth are equivalent. But this is deceptive: one cannot only deceive another person by lying or inform him by true communications; one can also renounce doing either the one or the other. Both the (moral) prohibition on lying and the (moral) enjoinment to truthfulness exclude two possibilities as unpermissible. Not to inform another person where this was

possible is certainly permitted by the prohibition on lying; in the enjoinment to truthfulness, however, it is not. The one *prohibition* to lie forbids the deception of another, whereas the *command* to tell the truth even makes the other's instruction into a duty. Whereas, as a rule, deception serves the personal interests of the liar, the instruction of another person may frequently damage the personal interests of the person who feels obliged to give information (e.g., in a competitive situation). However, all existing discussions of moral norms rest upon the presupposition that we are prohibited from following our own interests by moral norms to the extent that this is necessary for the creation of normatively ordered human relationships. Substantive enjoining norms which make the *furtherance* of the interests of another person even against our own interests into a duty clearly possess a status different from that of substantive prohibitive norms discussed so far.

Nevertheless, the fact that substantive enjoining norms may also lay claim to a universally binding character is shown, for instance, by the command to offer assistance to others in acute danger. Of course, here too the criterion must be the concept of general expectability of acceptance, with all the already stated difficulties and uncertainties which it carries. Fundamentally, however, we must adhere to the fact that a system of moral norms that prohibits damaging the justified interests of another must be enlarged by a system of norms which indeed requires the support of others in their efforts to satisfy elementary needs and to realize justified interests. Of course, it is precisely those needs and interests which are protected by substantive prohibitive norms and that we are obliged to support because of substantive enjoining norms, insofar as this appears to be necessary and reasonable. From this it follows that a conflict between a person's justified interests and the demand to further the interests of another is not only possible but even permanently so, for otherwise no one would be in a position to support those who were in need of such support. Hence, what can be morally universally enjoined is the *preparedness*, graduated according to criteria of nearness and urgency, to exercise solidarity with one's fellow human beings.

Nonetheless, moral prohibitive norms (in part, also moral enjoining norms) require further supplementation with regard to the security of those who wish to follow them against exploitation by others who are not prepared or less prepared to do so. Furthermore, certain justified claims are so elementary, and damage to them is thus so momentous that the enforcement of these norms by threat and the use of force must be sanctioned when necessary. As is well known, in a developed society this task falls to the *law,* and by contrast to specific moral norms that may not or are only partly legally protected, there now emerges the further task of recording and if possible codifying a system of legal norms, and of creating institutions for the generation, application, and implementation of legitimate legal norms. When in a theoretical reconstruction the necessity for creating such institutions is established, then the necessity for creating a *political state* and hence a system of public law under the conditions of the general expectability of binding norms is also established. This should all make it clear that, in the justification of ethics, specific moral norms (i.e., moral norms recognition of which and adherence to which can be made into a duty independent of their enforcement by legal-governmental sanctions) presuppose for their general validity the existence of an effective legal and governmental order; the question of the conditions for the applicability of specifically moral norms is thus, in a developed modern society, often a question about the effectiveness of legal state protection.

But moral and legal norm systems are neither the only nor the only universally binding normative systems upon which the order of human coexistence rests. Less often observed, but no less important in a developed society than in a primitive one, are the norms of civility or politeness.[25] In fact they are less fundamental insofar as, unlike morality and law, they do not have as their basis the preconditions for a normatively ordered collective existence. This means that the violation of these norms, in contrast to the violation of substantive prohibitive norms, does not place in question the normative order of collective existence as such. But, just as a satisfying normative collective order would not be possible without binding substantive enjoining norms, so too there belongs to a satisfactory order the fact that individuals are not merely recognized as responsible actors. If we first gain a claim to human dignity by our recognition of universally binding moral norms, then the recognition and adherence to the norms of politeness in interaction with others first secures us that respect which protects us from crude obtrusiveness; it preserves sensitivity to others and makes it a duty. We can assume that all human individuals have an interest in *self-respect*—not just as morally responsible actors furnished with civil rights—and in protection from insult and disparagement by unseemly treatment. It is this *amour-propre* which motivates human individuals to create and recognize specific norms of politeness in which symbolic gestures are often meaningless to outsiders but which nonetheless contain a basic supply of reciprocal respect in the form of binding norms, which are often universal, or at least extend far beyond the boundaries of specific peoples and cultures. These normative systems also supplement those of morality, relatively independently of specific moral norms—at least in a developed society. It thus becomes clear that a lie, which in a one-sided moral view would perhaps appear as a reprehensible mode of action, in certain circumstances may be respected with regard to norms of politeness. Because it intends to preserve an individual's feeling of self-respect, lying may in fact deserve praise. Furthermore, alongside these normative systems should be included those systems of decorum, honor, sanctity, or valor which from the outset only claim adherence from those who are prepared to place higher demands upon themselves and are prepared to relinquish the satisfaction of expected needs and individual interests. Without negating the idea of a universally binding morality, these normative systems highlight the limitation of what is to be achieved through the recognition of and adherence to universally binding moral norms.

Only with a glance beyond the boundaries of a rationally justifiable, universally binding ethics does the attempt to answer the question of the grounding of the validity of moral norms succeed in reaching a conclusion: moral norms are binding because they represent the foundation—and no more than

Karl-Heinz Ilting

that—of a normatively ordered human coexistence and also because in recognizing their binding nature we acquire a claim to human respect and recognition as members of the human community.

If one looks back from this vantage point at Apel's attempt to justify a rational ethics on the basis of the idea of a community of argumentation, then it becomes clear that (1) many motifs of his deliberations can be fully established within the framework of the outline developed here, (2) some motifs must be significantly relativized (such as, for instance, his overemphasis on the role of argumentation in the moral normatization of our collective existence), but (3) the idea of a community of researchers and participants in argument as an appropriate model for the description and justification of a normative system is to be rejected. But since the present observations are not to be understood as a moral undertaking but instead as an undertaking about morality, and therefore as argumentation, I can only hope that Apel will respect them as a contribution to the clarification of the questions which he has raised.

Notes

1. In this article I wish to characterize as norms only such behavioral rules which, in some sense or other, be it perhaps universally or even only within a specific group of individuals, are validly binding (i.e., not following them is regarded in some sense as reprehensible).

2. See *Towards a Tranformation of Philosophy*, London/Boston 1980, pp. 260–261: ". . . that the ethics of argumentation which is presupposed in logic . . . the logically and empirically scientific justification of opinions . . . can prove to be a *claim* made by all the members of the community of argument on all the others and therefore represents a moral duty."

3. See H. M. Baumgartner (ed.), *Prinzip Freiheit*, Freiburg/Munich 1979, p. 34.

4. This argument recalls a *topos* of the Aristotelian *protreptikos:* one must philosophize; for the person who disputes this philosophizes (see Aristotle, *Fragments*, ed. Ross, Oxford 1955, pp. 27ff.).

5. See "Kant, Hegel und das aktuelle Problem der normativen Grundlagen von Moral und Recht" in Dieter Henrich (ed.), *Kant oder Hegel?* [Stuttgarter Hegelkongress 1981], Stuttgart 1983, pp. 597–624.

6. See Funkkolleg, *Praktische Philosophie/Ethik*, Studienbegleitbrief 8, Weinheim/Baste 1981, p. 86.

The Basis of the Validity of Moral Norms

7. See K.-O. Apel, et al. (eds.), *Praktische Philosophie/Ethik, Materialien zu Funkkolleg I*, Frankfurt 1980, p. 289.

8. Apel criticizes Kant's doctrine of the categorical imperative for being "inadequate as a principle for the justification of norms" (*SBB8*, p. 83). But in so doing Apel imputes to this doctrine a task whose solution it did not claim to achieve. The categorical imperative is not a principle for the justification of norms but rather a criterion of judgment for distinguishing morally permissible and impermissible actions. Apel too does not successfully overcome this point with his "two-stage procedure for the justification of norms"; the "discursive formation of consensus" that he recommends in any case only serves the "metanorm" (corresponding to Kant's categorial imperative) as a criterion of judgment, whereas the "validity claims" that are brought into the discussion correspond to Kant's "maxims" and, just like the latter, should be tested for their moral justifiability.

Hegel's well-known objections that the doctrine of the categorical imperative rests upon a tautology (see "Über die wissenschaftlichen Behandlungsarten des Naturrechts" in G. W. F. Hegel, *Gesammelte Werke* (H. Buchner and O. Pöggeler eds.), vol. 4, Hamburg 1968, pp. 436f.) is accepted by Apel but viewed as too unjust. For whoever has agreed to safeguard another person's *property* and later refuses to give it back (perhaps because the lawful owner can produce no documents) has *ipso facto* recognized that property should exist—he wishes in fact to retain someone else's property as property—and he cannot therefore pretend that he is acting according to a universalizable maxim that no property at all should exist and, at the same time, does not wish to recognize the property of another as such. Furthermore, he has agreed to *safeguard* the property of another person, i.e., to return it upon request but nonetheless refuses to return it upon request. Moreover, he has *promised* to return the property and, at the same time, breaks his promise. However narrowly or broadly one interprets the maxim according to which he has acted, in any case he has acted according to a maxim that cannot serve as the principle of a universal law, since in this case it would transcend itself. Hegel was indeed correct when he asked: "In the light of the fact, however, that no deposit at all existed, what contradiction exists in this?" (op. cit., 436, pp. 31f.): but if no deposit existed then no one would trust his property to an embezzler and thus the latter would in no way be in a position to appropriate someone else's property in this manner. Hegel's stereotypically repeated objection to the doctrine of the categorical imperative is unfortunately one of many indices of the fact that the principles of Kantian ethics remained unclear to him for his lifetime.

By contrast, it is true that Kant did not indicate any way in which one arrived at universally binding *substantive* norms, such as the ban on lying or the enjoinment to keep a promise; he can only show that it is impossible for a contradictory mode of action to be morally permitted. I will present a justification of such substantive norms in the third stage of my attempt outlined below.

9. See *Towards a Transformation of Philosophy*, op. cit., pp. 258–260. My presentation is an attempt to reconstruct the logical structure of this text.

10. In fact, provoked by my article "Anerkennung" (as a lecture in 1971; first published in G.-G. Crau (ed.), *Probleme der Ethik—zur Diskussion gestellt*, Freiburg/Munich 1972, pp. 83–107). At that time my aim was to make clear, above all in opposition to Lorenzen and Habermas, that a purely intellectualistic justification of ethics is not possible since binding claims presuppose recognition. Apel has taken up these ideas, and completely in keeping with my interpretation, has added that, "The free acknowledgement of norms by human subjects is only a *necessary* but not a *sufficient* condition for the moral validity of norms" (*Towards a Transformation of Philosophy*, op. cit., p. 270). I have attempted to provide the answer to this problem of the sufficient condition for the existence of rational binding force in my article, "Wahrheit und Verbindlichkeit" in K. Lorenz (ed.), *Konstruktionen versus Positionen*, Berlin/New York 1979, vol. 2, p. 139.

Karl-Heinz Ilting

11. I start out from this view that no *quaternio terminorum* exists, i.e., that the middle concept of "preconditions of a community of argumentation" is not used equivocally in minor and major keys. One might indeed believe that Apel used it in the minor key in the sense of ". . . (theoretical) community of argumentation" and in the major key in the sense of ". . . (practical) community of communication"; but Apel leaves us without doubt that he wishes to establish the recognition of *moral* norms as the precondition for a purely *theoretical* discussion of a problem.

12. See on this my article, "Geltung als Konsens," in *Neue Hefte für Philosophie*, no. 10, Göttingen, 1976. In this context, Hans Albert (in *Tranzendentale Träumereien*, Hamburg 1975, p. 150) speaks of a "perversion . . . that lies in *defining* the *concept* of truth by recourse to a consensus however it is conditioned. At best, it would be meaningful to define the consensus sought, in order that it be relevant at all in this context, by recourse to the idea of truth, for otherwise it would never be clear *about what* such a consensus is striven for."

13. On this now, M. Hossenfelder, "Kants Idee der Transzendentalphilosophie und ihr Missbrauch in Phänomenologie, Historik und Hermeneutik" in I. Heidemann and W. Ritzel (eds.), *Beiträge zur Kritik der reinen Vernunft 1781–1981*, Berlin/New York 1981, pp. 332ff. It is to be hoped that this contribution is sufficiently taken into account in further discussions of this question.

14. See H. Wagner, "Kant gegen 'ein vermeintes Recht, aus Menschenliebe zu lügen'" in *Kant-Studien*, Berlin/New York 1978, pp. 92ff.

15. If, in this context, one were to evaluate the verbalization of the game of intrigue as argument, then in a poker game conscious deception is also permissible and, in principle, possible.

16. Proposition (6) goes in the direction of the problematical-hypothetical imperative of an argumentation as valid for *all* human action, to be established therefore as an assertorical-hypothetical imperative; even if this argument were valid, it would not extend beyond the hypothetical imperative.

The attempt to interpret this hypothetical imperative as a categorical imperative is to be found in *Towards a Transformation of Philosophy*, p. 270, where Apel declares that the "will to argumentation" is not "empirically conditioned" for a philosopher since it is the "the precondition for the possibility of every discussion of hypothetically posited, empirical preconditions." What is correct in this argument is the fact that one cannot achieve a goal of action if one does not fulfill a necessary precondition for its achievement. But this is indeed precisely the definition of the problematical-hypothetical imperative (of purposive-rational action): for the person who seeks to reach a freely chosen goal by following all the rules necessary attendant upon it, these rules are therefore "preconditional for the possibility," but in no way—as Apel interpolates at this point—the *transcendental* preconditions of possibility. Further, by virtue of the fact that someone wishes to achieve a goal of action "unconditionally," these rules do not become "categorical" imperatives—even where it is the case that someone could do nothing other than strive for this goal of action. For hypothetical imperatives are all "analytical" whereas a categorical imperative is synthetic: it prohibits or entails not because someone wishes to realize a goal but rather because someone wishes to achieve a goal in a manner in which not even he himself can claim universal validity.

17. See "Sprechakttheorie und Begründung ethischer Normen" in K. Lorenz (eds.), *Konstruktionen versus Positionen*, II, Berlin/New York 1979, II, p. 91.

18. This is also confirmed by Apel when he refers to the fact that one cannot meaningfully declare: "I am now lying" ("Sprechakttheorie," op. cit., II, pp. 85, 90). In fact,

The Basis of the Validity of Moral Norms

this statement, as a conscious infringement of the rules of purposive rational action, would be *absurd*. But absurdity is not a moral criterion.

19. This perspective is revealed when Apel assumes that "the ethics of argumentation ... makes logic and science a duty" (*Towards a Transformation of Philosophy*, op. cit., p. 261.)

20. On Kant's attempts to answer these questions, see my article, "Gibt es eine kritische Ethik und Rechtsphilosophie Kants?" in *Archiv für Geschichte der Philosophie*, vol. 63, 1981, pp. 325–346.

21. The term "metanorm" is used here, as in my article "Wahrheit und Verbindlichkeit" (p. 135), in a different sense than by Apel. Under "metanorm" Apel understands the basic norm of universalized reciprocity of all "claims to validity," which at the same time is to serve as the "always already recognized metanorm of the formation of a consensus concerning norms" (see "Kant, Hegel, . . ." op. cit., pp. 34f.; see *Funkkolleg, SBB*, p. 87). According to my linguistic usage, metanorms are not themselves recognized and binding norms, but rather they define the preconditions for the binding force of norms. We can dispense here with a critique of Apel's linguistic usage.

22. See *Naturrecht und materiale Gerechtigkeit*, Göttingen, 4th edition, 1962.

23. See *Theory of Justice*, Oxford 1972.

24. If, for instance, Locke or Fichte were of the opinion that labor as such bestows a property claim upon the object worked upon, then this is certainly untenable since no one can induce another person to recognize a property claim by means of the work that the former has carried out. In the context of the attempt at justification developed here, however, one may view labor for securing the means of subsistence, in association with the already justified norms, as an important title to justifying a claim to property. In my opinion, this title is much more important, for instance, than the right of *prima occupatio*.

25. See on this my article, "Sittlichkeit und Höflichkeit," in Stagl (ed.), *Aspekte der Kultursoziologie*, Berlin 1982.

7

Are Norms Methodically Justifiable? A Reconstruction of Max Weber's Reply

Hermann Lübbe

Recently, a German philosophy department invited a number of philosophers and methodologists of the social sciences to discuss the question as to whether norms were methodically justifiable. I do not dispute that aspects of this question cannot be resolved by common sense alone. On the other hand, what is at issue is evidently a question which owes its seeming relevance to the insinuation that there are those who doubt the possibility of methodically justifying norms at all. It is a question which is connected with the persistent dispute over value judgments, one which seeks to challenge those of whom one assumes that they take value judgments—in fact norms, or universal prescriptions for action—to be forms that are not constituted in a rational manner and which therefore cannot be expected from the sciences themselves. Of course, under this familiar aspect, our question as to whether norms are capable of being methodically justified is therefore likely to awaken the suspicion in the larger public sphere that philosophers and methodologists of the social sciences who raise this kind of question might, as a result of academic life, lack a sense of reality. Are norms capable of being methodically justified? How could one frame such a question? It is obvious that from parliaments to the highest courts, from party congresses to synods, permanent authorities are active, in accordance with reliable and conventional rules, in establishing norms, universal laws in fact, or statutes that are then valid for all those in the sphere of their jurisdiction. Social acceptance requires norms to be institutionally established, most often through the agreement of majorities that are competent to arrive at conclusions, and it is reasonable to assume that these majorities would not have granted their agreement if they had not taken the respective norms to be well-justified norms. To this extent, one may also assume that in the dominant public sphere in which such majorities are formed, it is a trivial fact that norms are capable of being methodically justified.

Even the more wide-ranging question of how norms are in fact justified in a way capable of producing agreement is a question without any dramatic implications for larger public circles. Nonetheless, an essential component of our political culture is indeed that one knows as a citizen which obligation to justification is appropriate, who makes recommendations in executive committees for introducing a norm, and that besides, one also knows the procedures through which norms are enacted. In stating this, I have already raised the distinction that should concern us in more detail, namely, that between the procedure for *justifying* norms and the procedure for *applying* norms or the procedure for *enacting* norms.

Whoever recommends the introduction of a norm must justify it and no parliament would accept from the government or from a party an unjustified parliamentary bill or statute. But even the methodically most thorough justification of a norm, which secures the validity of this norm on the cognitive level, does not provide *eo ipso* the social acceptance of this norm. This is in fact provided only as the result of an institutional procedure for enacting norms, of which the justification of norms is merely a part.

Naturally, it cannot be disputed that the justifications of norms, as they can typically be found in speeches introducing parliamentary bills or statutes, embody a host of defects. Yet it is more rare that no one notices this and that a political opponent does not in fact find fault with it. Fortunately, the common case of a faulty justification that no one criticizes most often occurs where all are reasonably prepared to agree to the recommendation for the introduction of a norm, so that in this case nothing is dependent upon the greater or lesser soundness of the explicit justification. If something does depend upon it, because it still has to give rise to understanding and agreement, which are lacking, then naturally one cannot accept deficiencies in justification. If they do nonetheless arise, then the reason is mostly not that the methodical, procedural requirements for the justification of a norm were not known or, for their part, were deficient. Rather, objective difficulties are what hinder us in the attempt to meet fully the well-known and recognized requirements for the justification of norms. In many instances, it is not possible to fill in completely certain gaps in our knowledge of reality that support our recommendations for norms. Hence, our prognoses concerning social behavior, for instance, which allow us to expect the desired effects of normative action, prove to be unreliable. Consequently, it is not the rules which we follow in the practice of the justification of norms that need to be overhauled, but rather the assumptions about reality that are constitutive for the rules determining such justification.

My key assertion is that, in the exoteric contexts of the processes of enacting norms that permanently and so often confront us, we do indeed constantly come across factual deficiencies in the pertinent justifications, but that it is indisputable which requirements are fundamental for the justification of norms.

Thus, why does one ask whether justifications of norms are possible and, insofar as they are possible, what do they achieve? The fact that such doubt in parliamentary practice or the activity of party program commissions does not predominate, must of course be no reason for philosophers esoterically—for their part—not to ask relevant questions. Philosophy is not merely concerned with questions that have already been posed outside its domain of inquiry. It also raises questions from a critical standpoint to remove deficiencies that one would not otherwise have noticed. To be sure, simply to question in this way what no one otherwise questions and what cannot be shown to be questionable or worthy of questioning, would be a waste of time.

Where, particularly in our public life, do the deficiencies lie which compel us to place in question the methods of how we justify norms? In a trivial manner, we are subject to the validity of many norms which should be more or less urgently changed, replaced, or removed. Yet this does not prove that our method for the justification of norms is deplorably flawed. It is sufficient that we have gained new knowledge regarding what is the case or that we consider the circumstances to have changed. Changes in norms are then called for, even for this reason alone.

In such instances, there is much that is in a sorry state but this is not because our method for justifying norms was in itself in a deplorable state. I maintain that this is our situation. If this assertion is true, then the question arises as to how it is that the methodical justification of norms could be made into a problem at all in present philosophical discussions. As far as I can see, viewed exoterically, there exists primarily a literary reason. It is not any evident calamity in the public practices of justifying norms that provokes present efforts at a methodical reconstruction of this practice, but rather the actual or putative assertions of philosophers or other intellectuals that norms are incapable of a methodical justification. In addition, there is also the interpretational claim that at least some of the deficiency in social circumstances and in political practice, which affected us and others and which still affects us, could be the practical result of the assertion that norms are incapable of a methodical justification.

It is of course Max Weber who, in this context, plays the role of the classic author of a theory that declared justification of norms impossible by analogy with the justification of assertions about reality. Accordingly, he traced the political validity of norms back to the decisions of power holders. It is the case that in Max Weber's work, we can read statements that seem to belong to such a theory. I wish to quote here one of the most cited, relevant statements. Out of Max Weber's reflections on the meaning of the so-called value-freedom of the social sciences, I wish to cite the statement in which Max Weber expresses himself on the question as to "how conflicts between several concretely conflicting ends are to be arbitrated." The culpable sentence reads: "There is no (rational or empirical) scientific procedure of any kind whatsoever which can provide us with a decision here."[1]

This is a statement that seems to confirm unambiguously what Horkheimer, as one particularly influential critic among others, accused Weber's philosophy of. For Horkheimer,[2] "practical reason" abdicates itself in this philosophy and remains as "instrumental" reason. According to Horkheimer, Max Weber did not wish to conceive of "any rationality . . . by which man can discriminate one end from another." His work is a testimony to the renunciation of "philosophy and science as regards their aspiration of defining man's goal." Subsequently, Jürgen Habermas reiterated this interpretation of Weber with the personalizing qualification "that Carl Schmitt" was "a 'legitimate pupil' of Weber's."[3]

Yet my aim here is not to clear Max Weber of such charges. If one wished to engage in any discussion of this problem, then one would also have to question whether and to what extent someone can be made responsible for the misunderstanding that he has created. My intention is to show that one does indeed misunderstand Max Weber if one interprets him in the manner which is suggested to us in the pertinent interpretations of the Frankfurt School as well as the Erlangen School.

I wish to show that Max Weber's thesis of science's inability to produce decisions in situations of normative conflict is quite compatible with the thesis of the methical justifiability of norms. If it is indeed the case—and I do assume this along with bourgeois common sense and against philosophy—that justifications of norms in our public life are everywhere practiced in a manner that does not give rise to questions or complaints, then Max Weber too can hardly have overlooked this. Although he was also a philosopher, he was not one who subscribed to a transcendental reality. If this is the case, how could Max Weber make the claims he did? How could he claim that there exists "no (rational or empirical) scientific procedure of any kind" that could provide the basis for a decision in instances of politically conflicting goals? This question may be made plausible with the help of a distinction between the procedure for justifying norms and the procedure for applying or enacting norms that was already referred to in our introductory remarks. The distinction refers to an easily overlooked ambiguity in the meaning of the word "valid" when we speak of the fact that norms are valid. What is "valid" here, on the one hand, are the norms insofar as they are well-grounded. What is "valid," on the other hand, are norms insofar as they have secured a socially effective binding force. In the first case, one could say that norms are valid in accordance with the subject matter itself or, logically, that they are justified in a deductive sense. In the second case, they are valid socially. The first form of validity is taken care of by the procedure for justifying norms; the second form of validity is taken care of by the procedure for employing norms. Both procedures are inseparable, but they are nonetheless distinguishable. This is true even in the special case of the teaching of norms. It holds for moral education that it really only reaches its goal when the pupil follows the norm—whose observation it demands— by concurring with the good grounds which support the norm. On the other hand, since Isaac's sacrifice and despite the State of Hessen's "Guidelines for the Teaching of Social Studies," moral education is not rational if it does not include teaching the capacity in certain instances for orientating one's actions toward norms that are in fact (socially) valid, even though their justification is obscure or obviously deficient. This rule is valid for the reason that the procedure for enacting norms in the case of a rule is socially more important than the soundness of the justification of the norm whose social validity is procedurally enacted. The legitimacy of the principle of the majority rests precisely upon this point. The validity of the principle of the majority in parliamentary and analogous procedures for applying norms presupposes a readiness to recognize the social validity of norms independently of whether one may also agree with these norms through the force of their justification. It is precisely this that is intended in Luhmann's formula of legitimation through procedures.

One does not need more than the distinctions made explicit here in order to reconstruct Weber's both famous and notorious thesis about the uselessness of science for normative decisions in the cases of genuinely conflicting goals. It seems to me that Weber's thesis is rendered plausible when one links it to difficulties in the practice of applying norms.

"There is," according to Weber's thesis in the version cited, "no (rational or empirical) procedure of any kind whatsoever which can provide us with a decision here." In what instance? In the case of the political existence of a conflict "between several concretely conflicting ends." From the standpoint of explicit distinctions between procedures for justifying norms and procedures for applying norms, Max Weber's thesis is plausible. Let us assume the simple, exemplary case, that the "conflicting ends," the "wished-for or intended" ends are two or more in number, that they are rights for commanding and for using objects, etc., whose universal, unlimited use destroys the object for whose sake the possession of these rights is valuable. The competition of several states in the Antarctic fishing for whales is exactly of this form, and until now this particular conflict has not been definitively resolved. With regard to several of the questionably huntable species there exists the hope that it might still be possible to resolve the conflict in good time. Is there a "scientific procedure of any kind that could provide a decision here"? Whoever answers this question in the affirmative simply confuses the pertinent procedure of the justification of the already well-known norm of preservation, which raises as an obligation the general observation of species-preserving catch quotas on the part of all participants, with the political procedure for rendering this norm socially valid in multilateral, international treaties. In this instance, too, it is of course the case that the pertinent justification of norms is a component of the procedure for the application of their social, i.e., grounded in international treaties, validity. Ecological problems have certainly enjoyed worldwide publicity for more than half a decade, and everywhere laypersons' zoological series on television with constant appeals to the preservation of animals is one of those programs with the highest ratings. In such a time as this, each awakened child of television is capable of justifying the norm with the slogan "This applies to everyone!" Observation of this norm can solve the conflict, save the remarkable sea mammal from extinction, and can secure an oil in large amounts and well into the future for the purposes of nourishment and lubrication as well as ambergris for our culture of perfumes. Over and above this, the complexities of the problem are well known to biological and marine fishery specialists and, to the extent that this is not sufficiently so, they continue to engage in research, and whole research fleets are internationally fitted out for this purpose. There is no lack of memoranda prepared for conferences and they are a constit-uent element of conference materials. Nonetheless, up to now, the already well-known norm defending the preservation of near-extinct species has still not been enacted.

The situation is precisely that which I assumed at the outset: defects in the procedures for justifying norms are in no way the problem at issue and—so far as I as a layperson can judge— not even the procedurally legitimate justification itself points to substantive deficiencies with regard to insufficiently estab-lished hypotheses concerning the assumed reality. What is in a sorry state is solely the practice of applying norms and it is obvious how little the correct justification of norms as such, which belongs to such a practice, requires something in it to be changed. It is precisely this which Max Weber made us aware of as a warning against the unwise hopes of many sci-entists. What is at issue is a decision by means of which a well-known, well-justified and thus (factually and logically) valid norm is elevated into a socially valid norm.

I do not see what one should object to in Max Weber's thesis, cited three times already, if one considers it in relation to this decision. In order to make its self-evidentness apparent, I will now cite it finally for a fourth time: "There is no (rational or empirical) scientific procedure of any kind whatsoever which can provide us with a decision here."

The validity of a norm defined by means of its justification is not identical with the social validity of that norm, and, as a rule, the former is also not suitable without further ado for bringing about the validity of the latter. The hiatus with which we are therefore concerned is, as one sees, not that of the hiatus between is and ought, which we have acknowledged in relevant discussions since David Hume, but rather—in order to speak at an analogously higher level—the hiatus between ought and intention which we have acknowledged since Soc-rates. In our exemplary instance, what they ought to do is indeed very well known to all participants. Yet they still do not want to do it with a normatively decisive effect and precisely at this point the skill of the scientific expert on the justification of norms terminates. Of course, this does not prevent him, in principle and moved by the power of his arguments, from engaging as an expert in the application of norms and slipping into the role of the pedagogue, journalist, or politician. This often takes place, sometimes even to good effect, and even Max Weber's biography demonstrates that science as a vocation and politics as a vocation—although here in our social world they are two vocations—are practicable at least temporally and within certain limits as a dual vocation. This will not prove to be the rule, and we all know of instances in which the attempt at erecting a blending of both vocations into a duty for every single scientist has ended partly in laughable and partly in institutionally destructive consequences. At the time of the First World War, this duty had already become commonplace in Germany and countless politicized professors conformed to it in the well-known public acts of demonstration of their political engagement in order that they could announce that they knew what they should do and, correspondingly, wished to do and thus did it.

I have no doubt that Weber's sarcastic portrayal of the dreadful consequences of the collapse of the distinction between the activity of justifying norms and that of applying norms also found countless examples in the phenomena of the most recent academic political short-circuiting between science and politics to which it referred. I do not thereby assume that the activity of justifying norms, which indeed I hold to be an activity of scientists too, is not compatible with political engagement for the social validity of relevant norms. Rather, it is my opinion that the specific civic duty of experts in the justification of norms is, as a rule, fulfilled precisely in the soundness of their practice of justifying norms. This is the role that is procedurally intended for them in the contexts of the activity of applying norms. Aside from highly unusual situations, a contribution to the destruction of the relevant procedure for the enactment of norms would only be achieved if the expert in the justification of norms were suddenly, instead of convincingly establishing his justifications, to throw accusations against the Soviets, the

Japanese, against all participants, that they still do not want what they nonetheless evidently should want, namely, to conclude the well-grounded catch-quota norm and henceforth to observe it.

But then should not the justification of a norm that is recognized also *eo ipso* establish its social validity? That would be all well and good and should be required. But it would again only be the already acknowledged requirement that we also ought to want what we ought to do. The hiatus between the two has been our problem since Socrates. Even Plato, who did not tolerate this hiatus, had to seek out the solution to this problem by means of procedures for the application of norms that lay above institutions. Plato's institutional solution to this problem was the fusion of institutions that, on the one hand, were devoted to the justification of norms and, on the other, to the application of norms. This meant the fusion of the republic with the academy. This is not the place to discuss why it is that attempts to fuse procedurally and erroneously the justification of norms with the application of norms in this way lead toward educational dictatorship and to an even worse terror. It suffices to bear in mind that the hiatus between ought and intention in social reality is in fact a huge one, in order to realize the significance of the establishment of special procedures for applying norms which are more than lectures from the pulpit or podium and which operate irresistibly upon individual wills. Rules of procedure, statutes, and in fact the whole system of parliamentarianism are procedures for enacting norms which presuppose that absolutely clear justificatory reports do not always force people into active practical insight. Hence, it is reasonable to take a vote on that which should be socially valid after justifying speeches and discussions and to provide the validly voted upon decision with the usual protective sanctions. In the knowledge of the fact that, in the majority of cases, the shortcomings of social life do not have their origin in the deficiencies of our procedures for justifying norms but rather in purposeful procedures for applying norms, this was the chosen object of Max Weber's political sociology.

In this attempt at a reconstruction of Weber's pertinent thesis, by means of the distinction between the factual or logical and the social validity of norms, as yet nothing has been done to answer the question as to how norms are to be justified. This does not pose a difficulty if what I assumed at the outset is true, namely, that the procedure for the justification of norms, in contrast to that of the procedures for applying and enacting norms, is unproblematical.

Is this the case? In order to answer this question we would now have to introduce and analyze a rich and representative collection of examples of successful procedures for the justification of norms—for example, those contained in parliamentary reports or similar documents. For reasons of space, I will limit myself to providing the general outline according to which the justifications of norms actually succeed in our public life. I describe this outline in such a way that I exclude myself from the criticism that I have only described the outline for the justification of norms for technical action. I will come back later to this criticism. The outline looks roughly like this:

1. One states an intention that all participants in the procedure share in harmony.

2. One describes the circumstances which evidently do not correspond to that which one harmoniously intends.

3. On the basis of theories concerning the effect of actions, one indicates those actions that would be appropriate to change circumstances in such a manner that they corresponded to the agreed-upon intention.

4. One formulates the norm which, if it were to be put into effect, would specify that all participants must act in this way.

Basically, this is so simple and obvious that it is not at all necessary to demonstrate it in examples of actual justifications, especially general public-law regulations—such as the general duty of hunters, for instance, to take out indemnity insurance.

However, the structure just outlined assumes the case of starting out by recourse to an agreed intention. Now it has become customary once more to say, recalling certain aspects of Aristotle's doctrines, that a norm that universally rules actions by subjecting that which "is" to our agreed intention, is "technical," whereas the really interesting case is that of a justification of "practical" norms. In this line of argument, one is accustomed to call a norm "practical" which in the case of a conflict in the intentions of the participants, prescribes acting in a manner that includes a conflict-resolving change in the intentions of the participants.

The distinction between dissensus with regard to an intention and consensus with regard to an intention is, of course, a powerful one and related to this it makes a difference whether we are concerned to bring about a consensus in the case of a conflict in the intentions of the participants or whether we do what accords with our agreed intention. Politics as the art of gaining agreement and technology as the art of making that which we intend to do as a result of such agreement realizable are related to these distinctions. Only I do not see that the structure of the justification of norms is also affected by them. If in fact a constraint or a readiness exists to terminate conflict between those who want diverse things from the results of conflict and replace it with an agreement instead of a trial of strength, then the only possible procedure for such agreement is this: to have recourse to a higher common intention with reference to which the conflict of intentions, insofar as it is not settled, would have to be brought to a close. But precisely this is once more the accepted starting point for the already outlined general procedure for the justification of norms, through whose observation the dominant conflict of interests would then be settled, with the effect of making successful the higher common will of those affected by this conflict. The conflict between whaling nations cited as an exemplary instance is precisely of the structure outlined. Through their present intentions they are in conflict, each seeking to make as much profit for themselves so that, as an unobserved consequence of others' intentions—and thus of all of them—the opportunity for making this profit will soon be absent for all of them. The conflict-resolving norm, which prescribes the universal observation of catch quotas that preserve species—as one can see according to my argument above—is only justifiable by starting out from higher common intentions to be still able to make a profit in the future. It is, accordingly, like any norm, "technical," namely, by its appropriateness as the means which provides what they must do, in order that they can do what they intend to do. It is not necessary to fully outline why it is that, in the exemplary case of whaling, notwithstanding the successful and also materially relatively unproblematic justification of norms, the implementation of norms gives difficulties. In short, the reason lies in the fact that the norm, if it were in fact to be socially valid, must, precisely because of this, provoke new analogous conflicts in other contexts of activity, for instance, the conflict with those whose fundamentally justified interest in the amortization of the fishing fleet or whose fundamentally justified interest in the conservation of the jobs of the seafaring inhabitants of uneconomic regions is incompatible with the reduced catch quota. There would thus begin here anew, at a higher level, the problem of the normative justification of other higher norms and in order to be able to solve it we would again need as previously the fact of a higher agreed upon will. For only then can we say what is demanded of every person in order that they can all achieve what they all agree to want, namely, in the last instance for example, to live well and in peace, and it would indeed be possible to formulate a norm of the last instance related to this last instance intention, a basic norm as one is accustomed to say nowadays, which then would be related to the above characterized intention of the last instance in the manner outlined.

There are indeed several statements known to us from the history of practical philosophy which we can interpret as the formulation of this basic norm. Nowadays, too, philosophers are at liberty to formulate such "basic norms" to which one must have recourse in the last instance in this process of progressive conflict resolution. Along with Wilhelm Kamlah one might then justifiably say: "It is required of everyone at all times to observe that their fellow human beings are needy like themselves and should be treated accordingly." What one has achieved in practice with this we can realize from the distinction between objective and social validity: what is well justified is in fact thereby not yet implemented. Accordingly, in the case of this basic norm, it seems to be true that there is no procedure for its implementation which would do more than give examples of its observance without being certain that all people would follow these examples. One is then still at liberty to provide the doctrinal dissemination of its justification which in this case too, as in all other cases of the justification of norms, is nothing more than the evidence that it is the appropriate means which provides us with what we must do in order that we can in effect want what we all want, namely, to live well and in peace. In this respect, the "basic norm" is "technical," and precisely technical in this sense was also Max Weber's assertion (properly reconstructed) that, by scientific or other rational means in "procedures of whatever kind," we are never capable of achieving anything more than analyzing the incompatibility of that which different groups want and of specifying the conditions for the compatibility as well as the means of realizing that which we peacefully want. But a second and different problem is that of establishing the social validity of that to which we have attributed an objective or logical validity.

Notes

1. M. Weber, *The Methodology of the Social Sciences* (trans. and ed. E. A. Shils and H. A. Finch), New York 1949, p. 19.

2. M. Horkheimer, *Eclipse of Reason*, New York 1974, p. 6, n. 1.

3. O. Stammer (ed.), *Max Weber and Sociology Today* (trans. K. Morris), Oxford 1971, p. 66.

8
Remarks about Rationality and Language

Herbert Schnädelbach

The "transformation of philosophy" by transcendental-pragmatic means requires the replacement of the critique of pure reason by the critique of linguistic reason. The investigation of the preconditions for the possibility of knowledge which, at the same time, can be taken as an analysis of the preconditions for the possibility of knowledge of objects, is assumed by Kant to precede the analysis of the conditions for the possibility of linguistic communication. For Kant such conditions are always already fulfilled. The critique of knowledge is completed by the critique of meaning; indeed, it is first made possible after sense-critical skepticism has placed in question its traditional foundations. In fact, it is precisely this that transforms Kant's pure reason into linguistic reason, for the "synthetic unity of apperception" that appeared to him as "understanding itself" and thus as the "highest point, to which we must ascribe all employment of the understanding, even the whole of logic, and conformably therewith, transcendental philosophy,"[1] is now to be understood as the "transcendental synthesis of linguistically mediated interpretation qua unit of agreement concerning something in a community of communication."[2]

An important step in carrying out this program is the transformation of the traditional concept of reason itself. If one wishes to interpret "reason" as a fundamental transcendental-pragmatic concept, then one can no longer follow—as did Kant—the mentalistic paradigm of an introspective psychology of capacities, and for the rest trust in the guidelines of formal logic. Any new attempt at the critique of reason immediately places that which is criticized in the sphere of linguistically mediated intersubjectivity. It is communicative competence and not capacities of consciousness that are to be investigated.[3] A formal logic orientation is inadequate because linguistic communication—in its syntactical, semantic, and pragmatic aspects—has become the "medium of transcendental reflection,"[4] and these aspects are not capable of being grasped solely by logical means. This medium of transcendental reflection is then, at the same time, its central theme; for according to Kant's model of the critique of reason, subject and medium necessarily coincide. The reason that is subjected to critique is no different than the reason of those who engage in criticism, for communicative competence must itself lay claim to this very same reason. In other words, that which is to be explicated as reason under transcendental-pragmatic preconditions is identical with that communicative competence which the transcendental pragmatist (in his attempt to analyze communicative competence) must have already acquired prior to applying. This apparently paradoxical structure distinguishes the transcendental pragmatist's "research program" from that of linguists and ethnologists; unlike for these latter two, for the transcendental philosopher it is not someone else's but his own reason that comes into focus.[5]

Reason is nowadays dealt with under the catchword of "rationality." The grounds for this must be searched for in the history of theoretical developments. The tradition of logical empiricism, in its late stage as philosophy of science, became attentive to the scandal of the "rationality gap": that is, the "rational reconstruction" of science revealed itself to be simply a privileging of the modern paradigm of rationality as such. Under these circumstances, logical empiricism preferred to abandon the expression "reason" to other intellectual traditions; it was suspected of being a metaphysical residue. For yet others, at least since Max Weber, rationality became a theme of the social sciences; most recently, the post-Wittgensteinians have returned to this concept,[6] and in this roundabout way it has now reentered the philosophical discussion. However, there are also some substantive reasons for this change in terminology. The expression "reason" is open to substantialistic interpretations, and although they were already expressly countered by Kant's doctrine of reason as the highest capacity of cognition and his critique of paralogism, reason is sometimes very difficult to distinguish from *res cogitans* in his work. Reason, understood neither as a substance nor as a fact, but as a quality, is "reasonableness," and here one would quite as easily say "rationality." A further advantage of this mode of expression lies in the fact that it prejudges substantively much less than does the term reason, which is burdened with all kinds of traditional connotations: for instance, the opposition between reason (*Vernunft*) and understanding (*Verstand*) or the etymological association of "reason" (*Vernunft*) and "understanding" (*Vernehmen*). On the other hand, nowadays "purposive rationality" and hence "instrumental reason" are frequently associated with "rationality," and the concept often gets caught in the crossfire of the general critique of rationalism. A distinction among types of rationality, such as "instrumental," "communicative," etc., usually suffices in order to counter such a *pars pro toto*.[7] And the most important advantage of the term "rationality" seems to be that its range of meaning offers less resistance to an internal differentiation of what is meant by it than would be the case with any comparable expression. If this is true and if we wish to make use of this advantage, then in the place of the philosophy of reason according to Kant's model, there emerges a transcendental-pragmatic theory of rationality, whose basic framework now appears in outline—and above all in the work of Karl-Otto Apel—but which can in no way be taken to be an undisputed theoretical program in every respect.

What follows is intended as a contribution to this program in the form of a number of provisional remarks on the problem of how it is possible by transcendental-pragmatic means to represent rationality in language: what does a critique of reason, now transformed into the critique of linguistic reason in the medium of transcendental pragmatics signify for our understanding of rationality? After a number of intuitively plausible observations on the predicate "rational," I wish to expound three theses:

1. The critique of linguistic reason as the propaedeutic part of a transcendental-pragmatic theory of rationality must start out from Kant's broader understanding of "reason," i.e., it must take into account the whole field which Kant explicates as understanding, judgment, *and* reason.

2. Given post-Kantian conditions, which also underlie the transcendental-pragmatic program, it is impossible to fully represent rationality by way of principles, rules, or norms. Accordingly, the difference between what we always already assume to be *possible* rationally and what we can explicate as *our* rationality is in principle untranscendable; "rationality" is an open concept.

3. The result is the "historicity of reason" and a "residual decisionism" in ethics. There exists no transcendental-pragmatic "First Philosophy" and hence also no communicative-ethical equivalent to the Kantian "fact of pure practical reason."

I

Viewed intuitively, the predicate "rational" stands at the intersection of two distinctions: its application can be descriptive or normative and can be intended nondispositionally or dispositionally. In the first case, we usually take rationality to be an ascertainable quality,[8] and in this way we can explain why it could become a theme of a value-free social science. At the same time, through the use of the predicate "rational," we often take up a normative or evaluative stance toward that to which this predication refers. But, at least since Schopenhauer, it is no longer self-evident that what is rational is also what is better; the traditional consensus on this, which *Lebensphilosophie* subsequently completely shattered, can today, in the age of a widespread defeatism with regard to reason, no longer be taken seriously. Whoever mentions "rationality" provokes normative dissent, and this would not be possible if the predicate "rational" admitted of no normative mode of application; not this application, but its justifications are the problem. The normative sense of the term "rational" is indeed also the reason why, in the tradition up to Kant and Hegel, the rational justifications of norms were always held to be possible and successful. Accusing Kant of a "naturalistic fallacy"[9] carries with it the danger of overlooking this. It is a characteristic of our philosophical-historical situation, and not that of German idealism, that we can no longer assert without argument that reason and rationality are what is good, standard, and binding. The fact that reason and the will to reason, reason and the interest in what is reasonable[10] were once a unity, is still evidenced in Max Weber's work, in which the imperatives of rationality represent cultural values that he is not prepared to simply dispense with—even if there exists no ultimate justification for this position.[11]

The second distinction, namely, a nondispositional and a dispositional meaning of "rational," can be traced back to the fact that whenever we take actions, statements, solutions to problems, institutional regulations, etc., to be rational—and these are all examples of nondispositional predications—what they stand for is viewed as the actualization of a potentiality for rationality which we ascribe to persons, be they individuals or collectivities. Usually, the dispositional application of "rational" expresses the ascription of such a potentiality for rationality with reference to potential acting subjects. This means that "rationality" normally belongs to persons-actions-language. Talk of "system rationality" is indeed a category mistake in Ryle's sense; at the very least, it is replaceable by "system functionality"[12] because it is no longer possible to distinguish it from the latter. The price for the representation of rationality in the thing-structure-event-language is then the complete congruence between rationality and functionality.[13] The intuitively enlightening connection between rationality and the subjectivity of action also makes us understand why the whole metaphysical tradition brought the "objective reason"[14] of the intelligible world structures into a causal relationship with a divine *nous* (reason); with the turn to the subject in modern philosophy, this connection was retained as the doctrine of the primacy of practical reason. A further consequence of this potentiality-action model of rationality is that we sometimes believe we can appeal to rationality: one cannot appeal to facts or structures but only to potentialities, i.e., demand their actualization, and the dispositional sense of "rational" provides the grammatical evidence for this commonsense conviction.

If one investigates more closely the dispositional predicate, "rational," in the context of intuitive reflections, then it is obvious that this is no simple dispositional predicate of the type "soluble" or "burnable." Whenever someone exhibits exactly the same predictable reaction under identical conditions, even if we approve of their mode of reaction and without additional information, we are inclined to call them not rational but compulsive. People are only rational if they themselves are still in control of the realization of their behavioral potential; without the rational use of reason, reason is inconceivable.[15] Rationality is at least a metadisposition, if not a disposition of a higher level.[16] This means that as a rule we only speak of rationality where the accomplishment of what is to be termed rational could also have been left undone. The distinction between nature and reason and the fallibility of the latter,[17] as well as the association of rationality with freedom and responsibility, have their roots in this. (We take a person who rejects *any* responsibility, to be not rational but unreliable; in other words, we still make him or her responsible for that fact that he or she rejects any responsibility.) As soon as we can no longer impute rationality to an objective, suprahuman subject— whether it be God or "history"—then, with the ascription of rationality, we always also imply the responsibility of a potentially rational being for itself, i.e., our own responsibility.

II

In his philosophy of reason, Kant follows such intuitions very closely; one can interpret his doctrine of the spontaneity of understanding and of practical reason as an attempt at the conceptual dissection and argumentative justification of such intuitions. The metadispositional character of rationality appears in Kant's work in the context of his doctrine of judgment. Understanding is the "capacity of rules," reason that of "principles" which are nothing other than rules of a special kind, namely, synthesizing rules for the rules of understanding, and hence metarules.[18] (In what follows, I shall make no use of the difference between rules and principles.) In contrast, judgment is the capacity of "subsumption under rules,"[19] and therefore a specific *use* of rules. If, intuitively, we must impute the rational use of rational rules to rationality, then, in the transcendental-pragmatic reconstruction of reason, we cannot remain limited to what Kant stated explicitly about understanding and reason, but rather we must include judgment too. Consequently, over and above the universals of understanding and reason, there comes into play a basic relationship of rationality to the particular, for judgment is "the capacity to think of the particular as contained within the universal."[20] In so doing, Kant deliberately distinguishes between determinant and reflective judgment, according to whether the universal is already given or whether it must first be imagined. The capacity for the rational use of rules and for subsumption, the capacity, "i.e., to distinguish whether something stands under a given rule (*casus datae legis*), or not,"[21] are, however, identical, since every use of rules takes place in individual cases. Through the specification of formal characteristics, Kant's theory of judgment thereby offers the possibility of interpreting anew the Aristotelian series of dianoetic abilities (*technē, episteme, phronesis, sophia, nous*), which are offered together in the "Nichomachean Ethics"[22] as replies to the question of the meaning of rationality. Because production and action always take place as singulars, which cannot be deduced a priori and deductively from a universal, the respective dianoetic abilities of "art" and "practical wisdom" require a synthesis of universal knowledge with knowledge of particulars. Following a long tradition Kant assigns this task to judgment.[23] Art as "a state of capacity to make, involving a true course of reasoning" and practical wisdom as "a reasoned and true state of capacity to act with regard to human goods,"[24] despite their essential relationship to the particular, belong to the capacities of reason that, along with traditional self-understanding, Kant conceived as capacities of cognition.

For him, science (*episteme*) and intellectual insight (*nous*)—as well as that combination of the two which Aristotle termed wisdom (*sophia*)—confront one another in such a manner that in them, as the capabilities of knowledge of the universal, the reference to the particular only emerges as inessential. Although subsumption takes place in logic and the sciences, for Kant logic as the organon of the sciences contains no rules of subsumption.

General logic contains, and can contain, no rules for judgment. For since general logic abstracts from all content of knowledge, the sole task that remains to it is to give an analytical exposition of the form of knowledge [as expressed] in concepts, in judgments, and in inferences, and so to obtain formal rules for all employment of understanding. If it sought to give general instructions of how we are to subsume under these rules, that is, to distinguish whether something does or does not come under them, that could only be by means of another rule. This in turn, for the very reason that it is a rule, again demands guidance from judgment. And thus it appears that, though understanding is capable of being instructed, and of being equipped with rules, judgment is a peculiar talent which can be practiced only, and cannot be taught. It is the specific quality of so-called mother wit; and its lack no school can make good.[25]

Kant then states in a famous footnote: "Deficiency in judgment is just what is ordinarily called stupidity, and for such a failing there is no remedy."[26] He also suggests terminologically a close relationship between judgment and the opposite of stupidity: "Whoever shows judgment in business is clever. If he has wit as well then he is termed intelligent."[27] The connection between judgment and intelligence, which reveals Kant to be a late Aristotelian,[28] is also to be extended to the theoretical realm, and this distinguishes him from Aristotle. Universal logic, which can only contain rules but no rules as to the application of rules, must leave open its own application; it provides no doctrine of judgment for it is only a canon but not an organon of understanding and reason. Kant's interpretation of applied logic thus implicitly brings judgment into connection with the Aristotelian *technē*. First of all, he criticizes the traditional separation of logic into theoretical and practical logic: "General logic, as a mere canon abstracting from all objects, can have no practical part. This would be a *contradictio in adjecto,* because a practical logic presupposes knowledge of a certain kind of objects to which one applied it. . . . General logic, considered as practical, can therefore be nothing more than a *technique of*

Herbert Schnädelbach

learning as such—an organon of scholastic method" and, as Kant then expresses it, to wish to teach the "doctrine of method" as "a logical art," independently of the knowledge of the sciences and their objects, is not only "futile" but even "harmful."[29]

With his doctrine of judgment as the integrating component of the capacity of "reason" in the broadest sense, Kant adhered to the Aristotelian insight that the "technical" and "phronetical" capacities of human beings to relate "dianoetically" to particulars, even when no universal rules were provided for this, are an unavoidable aspect of their rationality. The post-Kantian Aristotelians (from Hegel to Gadamer) have constantly sought to remind theoreticians of the abstract principles of reason of this. Formal logic, with its supply of universal rules, is, as a result, never capable of completely representing that which is justifiably termed rational, because it can offer no artistic rules and rules of wisdom for the application of rules; the art and wisdom of applying rules can never be taught in a doctrinaire manner, but rather can only be practiced through examples and against the background of a universal canon which excludes as inadmissible particular instances as "a cathartic of the common understanding."[30] Kant's problem and that of all transcendental philosophers who succeeded him is the following: according to which guidelines is this comprehensive concept of rationality capable of being explicated, if it cannot be those of formal logic?; how can one integrate into the transcendental theory of rationality the equivalents of judgment—of which only a critique can exist but which cannot be a part of the system of transcendental philosophy?[31] At the same time how can one wish to adhere to the a priori character of this concept of rationality which seems necessarily to exclude the sphere of application? How can one represent rationality in a priori rules, if indeed it is apparent that, for the application of rules which belong to rationality, no a priori rules can exist?

III

Kant's reply to this question consists of a change in levels of argument and a thesis; he moves over from formal to transcendental logic and states:

"Transcendental philosophy has the peculiarity that besides the rule (or rather the universal condition of rules), which is given in the pure concept of understanding, it can also specify *a priori* the instances to which the rule is to be applied. The advantage which in this respect it possesses over all other didactical sciences, with the exception of mathematics, is due to the fact that it deals with concepts which have to relate to objects *a priori,* and the objective validity of which cannot therefore be demonstrated *a posteriori,* since that would mean the complete ignoring of their peculiar dignity. It must formulate by means of universal but sufficient marks the conditions under which objects can be given in harmony with these concepts. Otherwise the concepts would be void of all content, and therefore mere logical forms, not pure concepts of the understanding."[32]

According to Kant, there does indeed exist in the context of transcendental logic a doctrine of judgment as organon: in fact the "transcendental doctrine of judgment" (ibid.); it is the "advantage"[33] of transcendental philosophy over all other disciplines. It signifies that whoever has at their disposal transcendental rules, should at the same time have at their disposal *a priori* rules for the application of rules, without requiring further rules of application for these rules for the application of rules and thereby falling into the trap of an infinite regress. An analogous situation holds for "pure practical judgment."[34] Conversely, it is also the case that without such a priori rules for the application of rules, which excludes the *regressus in infinitum,* no transcendental philosophy in the Kantian sense would be possible. It would then once more split off into a pure and an applied part and precisely would *not* be able to show that "the conditions of the *possibility of experience* in general . . ." are "likewise conditions of the *possibility of the objects of experience*" and "for this reason they have objective validity in a synthetic *a priori* judgment."[35] The a priori rules for the application of rules are the "touchstone" on which it is decided whether transcendental analysis is also in reality capable of encompassing a priori the whole realm of rationality that Kant had interpreted in the guidelines of logic as the field of operation of understanding, judgment, and reason.[36]

Now my thesis is that it is precisely the linguistically oriented transformation of transcendental philosophy into transcendental pragmatics that fundamentally excludes the complete representability of rationality in rules—and thereby in principles and norms. The transcendental pragmatist can reply that Kant himself did not do justice to this aim and, in addition, can state that the rationality of the critical enterprise, i.e., criticizing reason itself, is not to be found on the side of the reason that is criticized. In fact, the "transcendental reflection" of the amphiboly chapter of *The Critique of Pure Reason,* which at least partially deals with the method of the critique of reason itself,[37] is not mirrored in that which appears in the transcendental dialectic as the *proprium* of reason. Critical reason exhausts itself not in the logical-transcendental use of reason; indeed, the reflecting judgment is itself the organon of the "critical enterprise,"[38] and thus the mere existence of the "critique of judgment" expresses the systematic surplus of critically reflecting reason over "doctrinal" reason.[39] The fact that this is not merely a contingent defect of the Kantian system which one can view as having been overcome by Fichte or Hegel, is revealed by fundamental arguments that already arise at the threshold of transcendental philosophy's hermeneutic turn towards language against the complete representability of reason in rules. Thus, Dieter Henrich has referred to the fundamental outdatedness of any reflexive rational explication solely on the basis of its reflexive structure[40]; in this context Gerhard Frey has advanced Gödel's theorem.[41] However, I do not wish to enter into these arguments here. Rather, I wish to show that in the limited realm of theoretical reason too—which Kant believed he had thoroughly criticized—the complete representability of rationality in rules and rules for the application of rules is unattainable, and is so solely as a result of the linguistic orientation of transcendental analysis in the context of transcendental pragmatics. Along with Apel, I maintain that "transcendental-pragmatic" analysis is that analysis which deals not with communication as such in a quasi-objectivistic manner but rather deals with communication exclusively as a precondition for the possibility of philosophical reflection and hence as a very specific type of discourse.[42] In this analysis, those preconditions are investigated which the critically philosophical person, i.e., the one who questions the possibility of rational understanding, knowledge, and action, must have already assumed to be fulfilled in order to be able to raise questions at all.

Kant's claim to thoroughness can only be defended if formal logic, as autonomous theory, is suitable for the guidelines of the analysis of the use of understanding and reason. Further, it requires the success of a transcendental deduction of pure concepts of understanding that can be reconstructed according to these guidelines. If both preconditions are fulfilled then the "transcendental doctrine of judgment" and the dialectic of pure reason can be reached in analytical steps. Now if one attempts to repeat this program by transcendental-pragmatic means and, along with Kant, to cover the whole realm of theoretical rationality insofar as it makes possible scientific knowledge, then this goal of completion is forced into the unattainable distance: for language is *impure* reason, i.e., infected by the empirical and subject to contingency.[43] One cannot represent language in formal-logical rules and no transcendental deduction is possible from impure concepts of understanding; thus, there cannot exist any transition to a "transcendental doctrine of judgment" that could allow the a priori rules for the application of rules of linguistic reason to be formulated. The result is that linguistic reason is, at best, limited by given rules, yet is never really expressed through them.

However, this line of argument may still not be a satisfactory one, for it appeals only to the opposition of pure reason and language, without clearly specifying what exactly is meant by "language." The transcendental pragmatist as well does not speak so all-inclusively of "language," but rather of "communicative competence," and it seems as if rationality must now let itself be represented as a basic stock of communicative rules of competence. In addition, the transcendental-pragmatic perspective assumes that, in the investigation of this question, it is only the competence which those investigating must always already possess that is at issue. For a transcendental-pragmatic theory of rationality, in the light of this dual limitation of the field of investigation, everything rests upon the concept of competence. Chomsky had introduced this concept in "Aspects of the Theory of Syntax" (1965) in the context of his competence-performance distinction: "competence" was defined there as the knowledge of an ideal speaker-hearer of the rules of his language and his ability to make use of them; if one disregards the specific marginal preconditions that are irrelevant to linguistics, then "performance can be interpreted as the direct reflection of linguistic competence."[44] Without going into details[45] here, one can say that this concept of competence has undergone at least two additional extensions in its reception by Habermas and Apel. First, the transition from a merely linguistic competence of the production of grammatically correct linguistic entities to communicative competence leads to the integration of the dimension of action into the theory of language: communicative competence is basically the competence for communicative action.[46] Second, the competence that makes communication possible—as Apel and Habermas have shown—must also contain within itself metacommunicative competencies, because understanding in natural languages always presupposes simultaneously being in agreement about the language itself.[47] Both aspects have extremely important consequences for the theory of rationality.

Linguistic competence may be conceived of as a computer program that under ideal conditions also effectively generates performance; this can then be taken to be the "direct reflection of linguistic competence." Yet for communicative competence this model is insufficient because of the action character of performance that the transcendental pragmatist employs. Here, the actualization of competence can in no respect be interpreted according to the *stimulus-response* model as a quasi-mechanical process that, under specific antecedent conditions and in the ideal case, always runs in the same manner. This was compatible with Chomsky's theory of linguistic competence since in fact it merely defined which linguistic entities would be generated if they were spoken. However, if communicative competence is viewed as the competence for communicative action then it follows that not merely the "how" but also the "whether" of action lies in the hands of the competent speaker. Thus, at least on the basis of the assumption according to which inaction is also action, communicative competence can not only be a capacity for rule-following but must also be one of the power of disposing of rules. But a person who can fail to apply rules must also be entrusted with the capacity for the intentional disregard of rules or the creative transformation of rules; yet—as is indeed intuitively evident—these are precisely structural features of rationality as a higher level dispositional predicate to which Chomsky's competency version does not correspond. At this point, the other extension of the concept of competence asserted by Apel and Habermas can be directly added. Whoever always also has the power to dispose in principle of the communicative rules that he follows, must also be in a position to explicitly make himself understood with regard to these rules too; only in this way is "rule-changing creativity"[48] not a blind natural process. In this way, metacommunicative elements are distinguished as indispensable components of communicative competence, and they are the linguistic basis for the doctrine of original reflexivity in mentalistic theories of consciousness.[49] If one now asks what the circumstances could be for the competent speaker to creatively change rules, then the point at which the enlarged theory of competence comes into contact with the tradition of hermeneutic philosophy becomes evident. It is a fundamental thesis of hermeneutics that the application of rules and experience in this regard possess a constitutive significance for the stock of rules in question; furthermore, rules change in the course of their application and thus cannot themselves be stated without the statement of the conditions of their application; in turn, however, rules that are changed indicate yet another application of rules, and so on. This *feedback* between the rule and rule application is only a special instance of the hermeneutic circle between the whole and the parts, the universal and the particular, preunderstanding and actual understanding that in fact is not an empty or "vicious" circle since what moves in this circle—to speak in modern terms—represents a system capable of learning. This implies for the theory of rationality that it is not sufficient to unify understanding, reason, and judgment in an enlarged concept of reason as did Kant. Rather, if one operates with the model of communicative competence in the sense indicated, then one must indeed construe rationality as a complex unity of the possession and application of rules that is distinguished by interaction between its elements, and in which there is no room for a one-sided, a priori-deductive relationship between understanding/reason and judgment, competence, and performance. Viewed in this way, rationality can at least be seen as an open system of communicative competence that is not completely representable in rules—a system that, though bounded by rules, nonetheless contains rules of a type which through their competent following also permit intentional change. We cannot, on the one hand, and in opposition to Chomsky, conceive of our capacity for language as an open rule system and, at the same time and in the same perspective, wish to enclose our reason in unchangeable universal rules; because of the hermeneutic implications of this way of viewing things, we must also abandon notions of fixed communicative rules as well as rules for the application of rules in the theory of rationality.

IV

The consequence of this argument is the "historicity of reason"; this means that rationality is always also something empirical, contingent, and changeable.[50] If the factual application of rules actually applies back to the stock of rules in the manner in which the hermeneutic theorist asserts, then there exists no reason for asserting any form of competence-dogmatism. I do not see how the absolute stability of the communicative stock of rules, which suggests the well-known competence-performance distinction, is capable of being seriously advanced without quite strongly innatist premises.[51] The alternative to this is at least a general presumption of historicity with regard to all that is alleged by the transcendental-pragmatic perspective to be the stock of rules of our communicative competence and thus as the core of our rationality. Yet this suspicion is suggested not only by a mistrust of innatism but also by the two considerations outlined above on the "costs" of the hermeneutic turn in the critique of reason: the impossibility of fully apprehending the application of linguistically conceived rules of reason themselves in rules results in the fact that the difference between that which we always already lay claim to as our rationality and that which we can explicate as our rationality can never be overcome in principle. Furthermore, if we do not wish to be mentalists, we must reckon with the changeability of the rules of rationality in the course of their application.

In the transcendental-pragmatic perspective, this conclusion has the epistemological consequence that assertions about the universality of rules representing rationality can always only possess a hypothetical and never an apodictical character. Since the historical character of rules of rationality can never be completely excluded, the claim to universality also usually raised in this context can now only be permitted in a quasi-empirical sense; the transcendental predicate "necessary" must be renounced. The reasons for this become apparent if we compare Kant's procedure with that of Wittgenstein. Both start out from the fact that we cannot identify rules independently of their use. For Kant, the "logical use" of understanding and reason, i.e., their "logical function" in judgments and conclusions, are the "guidelines," revealing the rules of understanding and the principles of reason. For Wittgenstein, the inseparability of a rule and the application of a rule is the basis for the view we customarily refer to as the "use theory of meaning." In turn, this "theory" is also the key for the explanation of the "concepts of understanding, meaning and thinking."[52] The distinction between Kant and Wittgenstein is only that Kant held formal logic, interpreted as an independent theory, to be the guideline according to which a priori rules of understanding could be identified independently of their empirical use and could thus be proven in their transcendental interpretation. In contrast, Wittgenstein, in the *Philosophical Investigations*, refers to the question of thought and its rules only in the actual use of the expressions "understanding," "meaning," and "thinking" in a nonideal language, and this question is only to be stated empirically—ideal language and ideal rules of communication are, at best, a construction.[53] The rationality that is incorporated in the nonideal, contingent, changeable rules of communication is also therefore a historical rationality, because language, insofar as it is "the sole primary and ultimate organon and criterion of reason," must manage "without another credential besides tradition and use."[54] Thus, in the theory of rationality, one cannot simultaneously adhere to (a) the Kantian-Wittgensteinian inseparability of rule and rule application, (b) accept the "linguistic turn," and (c) seek to adhere to a strict apriorism in the sense of Kant's thesis of completeness. It is not merely the possible contingency of the rules of rationality themselves that leads to such a conclusion but rather the fundamental impossibility, after the hermeneutic turn in transcendental philosophy, of being able to show reconstructively the independence of such rules from an empirical use of language. Yet if transcendentally and pragmatically reconstructable reason is always merely historical reason, then there exists no transcendental-pragmatic First Philosophy.

Such reflections lead to analogous consequences for ethics. In communicative ethics, there is no place for a "pure practical judgment" that would be interpreted as the capacity of pure a priori norms of normative application. Karl-Otto Apel has replied to Habermas's criticism that in his foundation of ethics there lies a "decisionistic residual problematic" with the distinction between decision as the justification of norms (or their substitute) and the decision to apply norms and has defended the freedom of decision in the second instance as the essential element of our self-respect as human beings.[55] We can agree with this, but at the same time we should ask how it is possible, under transcendental-pragmatic presuppositions, to distinguish the justification of norms and the application of norms in such a way that the residual decisionism of the application of norms does not encroach upon their justification. A feature of the concept of a norm is that it is factually possible to deviate from it, just as it is a feature of a rule that it permits exceptions; thus, factual deviation is not the problem. Yet if we also treat seriously the transcendental-pragmatic dimension in ethics, then, because of the indissoluble association of communicative-ethical rules with empirical-historical application, no moral justification of the Kantian form can exist: practical reason, i.e., the reason brought about by the "determining ground of the will"[56] is, as communicative reason, just as much impure reason. Thus, it always necessarily also contains culturally specific and decisionistic elements: there exists no "fact of pure practical reason" but rather a "fact of historical practical reason" that is itself a historical fact. The dignity of humanity thus consists not merely—as Apel says—in the fact that we are the addressees of an obligation from which we can also withdraw; it consists equally in the burden of having to treat responsibly the principles of obligation which we find assigned to ourselves because their content is basically also dependent upon our contingent life as moral entities.

At the same time, this impure character of practical reason signifies that the sphere of rationality is broader than that of morality. The fact that we remain rational beings even if we try to escape from morally justifiable claims was expressed by Kant in his doctrine of "radical evil," which in his view consists in the free inversion of the moral order, that is, the inversion of "love of self" and "respect for the law" in the establishment of maxims of action.[57] Kant's residual decisionism consists in the thesis "that the first subjective ground for the adoption of moral maxims is unresearchable" because

since this adoption is free, the ground for it (why, for example, I have adopted an evil rather than a good maxim) must be sought for not in a natural inclination (*Triebfeder der Natur*) but rather once more in a maxim; and since this too must just as equally have its ground, but apart from the maxim no determining ground of pure arbitrariness should or could be specified, one is pushed ever further back into the series of subjective determining grounds *ad infinitum*, without being able to arrive at the first ground.[58]

The freedom of this "adoption," which above all else makes possible its imputability, is the privilege of the rational being that also remains in existence in the case of the radically evil. In fact, Kant's argument is directed against his own thesis of completeness in the context of ethics; the freedom to choose a maxim which, though it does not rule out the categorical imperative as a moral supernorm yet nonetheless renders it inapplicable, prevents this supernorm, according to the model of the "transcendental doctrine of judgment," from providing a priori for all its instances of application. The excess of rationality over morality that is thereby established is enlarged in a dramatic manner in the transcendental-pragmatic perspective, for here, in addition to that freedom of "adoption," there is to be added a stock of norms with a constitutive feed-back derived from the lived-out application of norms to the stock of norms itself. It is the case for practical rationality too that it cannot be completely represented in practical rules, i.e., norms; the concern is not one of reclaiming it merely for a fixed stock of norms and for the rest demarcating the application of norms as pre- or nonrational: the application of norms is not completely determined by any stock of norms and, in addition, through them it is only limited in a changeable manner and in a manner that renders the stock of norms itself changeable. Because practical rationality embraces all of this, the transcendental-pragmatically reformulated categorical imperative cannot be the basic norm of rationality as such.

V

In the theory of rationality it seems as if the last word lies unavoidably with historicism and relativism; but this is not the case.[59] Rationality is an imputation that is necessary and unavoidable in the transcendental-pragmatic perspective in the form of the presupposition "I am rational." The fact that in particular cases this can be false is no objection to it since, in order to be able to demonstrate it, I must once again lay claim to it: even in order to perceive our unreasonableness, we must already have trusted our reason. In contrast, what we trust as "our rationality," over and above this mere "that" of reason, stands under a suspicion of historicism that is not to be eradicated a priori. If we wish to counter this suspicion from the outset, we can no longer console ourselves with this naked "that" of rationality, without being able to say at the same time what we have consoled ourselves with. If we believe we can move immanently and in a purely a priori manner, however, from the "that" of our presupposed rationality to its "what" and to self-identification as rational beings, then we are taken in by a false inference which one can characterize, by analogy to Kant's critique of the transition from the "I think" to *res cogitans,* as the "paralogism of historical reason." Nonetheless, there exists no reason to surrender to historicism. Although the philosophy of reason, which nowadays must emerge as the theory of rationality on the guidelines of language, must not seek to exclude from itself historical elements, this is no reason for defeatism: rather, it must ask how we can conceptually combine rationality and historicity and do so without dogmatic premises and relativistic consequences. The transcendental-pragmatic "theme and medium of transcendental reflection," i.e., language itself, compels us to do this and rationality and historicity are always already unified in it. It remains to be demonstrated in what manner this is the case.

Notes

1. I. Kant, *Critique of Pure Reason* (trans. N. Kemp-Smith), London/New York 1933, B134, p. 154.

2. Karl-Otto Apel, "Der transzendentalhermeneutische Begriff der Sprache," *Transformation der Philosophie*, II, Frankfurt 1973, p. 354.

3. See ibid., pp. 352ff.; also Apel's "Noam Chomsky's Theory of Language and Contemporary Philosophy" in K.-O. Apel, *Towards a Transformation of Philosophy*, London 1980, pp. 180–224, especially pp. 201f.

4. See K.-O. Apel, "Sprache als Thema und Medium der transzendentalen Reflexion," *Transformation der Philosophie*, II, op. cit., pp. 311f.

5. In my view, the strict reflexivity of a critique of communicative competence is the sole feature which distinguishes Apel's transcendentald-pragmatic program from Habermas's universal-pragmatic program. Of course, it leads to an obviously different type of theory in the two authors' work: see K.-O. Apel, "Noam Chomsky's Theory of Language," op. cit.; also, K.-O. Apel, "Der transzendentalhermeneutische Begriff der Sprache," op. cit.; in comparison, J. Habermas, "What is Universal Pragmatics?" in *Communication and the Evolution of Society*, (trans. T. McCarthy), Boston 1979, pp. 1–68, especially pp. 26ff.

6. See B. R. Wilson (ed.), *Rationality*, Oxford 1979.

7. See K.-O. Apel, "Types of Rationality Today: the Continuum between Science and Ethics," in T. F. Geraets (ed.), *Rationality Today*, Ottawa 1979, pp. 307ff.

8. See J. Bennett, *Rationality*, London/New York 1964.

9. K.-H. Ilting, "Der naturalistische Fehlschluss bei Kant," in M. Riedel, *Rehabilitierung der praktischen Philosophie*, I, Freiburg 1972, pp. 113ff.

10. See J. Habermas, *Knowledge and Human Interests*, (trans. J. J. Shapiro), 2nd edition, Boston/London 1978, pp. 187ff.

11. See M. Weber, "Science as a Vocation," in H. H. Gerth and C. W. Mills (eds.), *From Max Weber*, New York/London 1946, pp. 129–56, especially pp. 143ff.

12. See N. Luhmann, *Zweckbegriff und Systemrationalität,* Frankfurt 1973, especially pp. 14ff.

13. See J. Habermas, *Theorie des kommunikativen Handelns,* II, *Zur Kritik der funktional-istischen Vernunft,* Frankfurt 1981, e.g., pp. 453ff.; *The Theory of Communicative Action II: A Critique of Functionalist Reason* (trans. T. McCarthy), Boston 1987.

14. See M. Horkheimer, "Zum Begriff der Vernunft," in M. Horkheimer and T. W. Adorno, *Sociologica II,* Frankfurt 1962, pp. 193ff.

15. See H. Schnädelbach, "Against Feyerabend," in H. P. Duerr, *Versuchungen I,* Frankfurt 1980, pp. 300ff.

16. See J. Bennett, *Rationality,* op. cit., pp. 21ff. and pp. 114ff.; also C. G. Hempel, "Rational Action," *Proceedings and Addresses of the American Philosophical Association,* 35, pp. 5–23.

17. Thomas Hobbes already speaks of the "priviledge of absurdity" that only befits human beings; see T. Hobbes, *Leviathan,* (ed. C. B. Macpherson), Harmondsworth 1981, p. 113.

18. See I. Kant, *Critique of Pure Reason,* op. cit., B356ff.

19. Ibid., B171.

20. I. Kant, *Critique of Judgment* (trans. J. H. Bernard), New York 1951, BXXV.

21. I. Kant, *Critique of Pure Reason,* op. cit., B171.

22. On what follows, see the sixth book.

23. On the history of the concept of "Judgment," see H.-G. Gadamer, *Truth and Method,* London 1975, pp. 39ff.

24. Aristotle, *The Nicomachean Ethics* (trans. D. Ross), New York/Oxford 1980, 1140a 20f. and 1140b 20f.

25. I. Kant, *Critique of Pure Reason,* B171f.

26. Ibid., B173.

27. I. Kant, *Anthropologie I,* para. 46; *Anthropology from a Pragmatic Point of View* (trans. V. Dowdell), Carbondale, Illinois 1978.

28. The agreement with Aristotle extends even to the examples: see B173f. and Aristotle, e.g., *Metaphysics* I, 1 and *The Nicomachean Ethics,* VI; the issue is always the relation between knowledge of a rule and experience.

29. I. Kant, *Logic,* A13; as the context indicates, "technique" is here still basically understood on the basis of *technē,* ars: see op. cit., A13ff. See *Logic* (trans. R. Harkmann & W. Schwarz), Indianapolis/New York 1974, pp. 20f.

30. I. Kant, *Critique of Pure Reason,* B77.

31. See I. Kant, *Critique of Judgment,* BXX1ff.

32. *Critique of Pure Reason,* B174f.

33. Ibid., B175.

34. I. Kant, *Critique of Practical Reason* (trans. L. W. Beck), New York 1976, A119f.

35. *Critique of Pure Reason,* B197.

36. See ibid., B360.

37. See H. Schnädelbach, *Reflexion und Diskurs. Fragen einer Logik der Philosophie,* Frankfurt 1977, pp. 90ff.

38. See G. Schonrich, *Kategorien und transzendentale Argumentation. Kant und die Idee einer transzendentalen Semiotik,* Frankfurt 1981, pp. 225f.

39. See W. Bartuschat, *Zum systematischen Ort von Kants Kritik der Urteilskraft,* Frankfurt 1972.

40. See D. Henrich, *Fichtes ursprüngliche Einsicht,* Frankfurt 1966; also his "Selbstbewusstsein" in R. Bubner, Cramer, Wiehl (eds.), *Hermeneutik und Dialektik I,* Tübingen 1970, pp. 257ff.

41. See G. Frey, *Sprache–Ausdruck des Bewusstseins,* Stuttgart 1965, pp. 38ff; also his *Theorie des Bewusstseins,* Freiburg/Munich 1980, pp. 69ff.

42. See H. Schnädelbach, *Reflexion und Diskurs,* op. cit., pp. 366ff.

43. Hamann, in his *Metakritik über den Purismus der reinen Vernunft* (1784), was in fact the first to relate the critical activity of reason back to language and thereby to introduce the hermeneutic turn into the critique of reason; the dependency of all the achievements of reason upon previous linguistic achievements of understanding is already the basic philosophical motive in Schleiermacher, who right up until the present day has been misunderstood as a "psychologist." (See M. Frank, "Einleitung" to Schleiermacher, *Hermeneutik und Kritik,* Frankfurt 1977). The hermeneutic turn towards language, under the conditions of the later nineteenth century, was subsequently experienced as the invasion of psychologism and historicism into the realm of reason, which it was believed one must hold in check with neo-Kantian "purity."

44. N. Chomsky, *Aspects of the Theory of Syntax,* Cambridge, MA 1965, p. 10.

45. See the article, "Kompetenz" in J. Ritter (ed.), *Historisches Wörterbuch der Philosophie,* vol. 4, columns 918ff.

46. As already in J. Habermas, "Vorbereitende Bemerkungen zu einer Theorie der kommunikativen Kompetenz," in J. Habermas/N. Luhmann, *Theorie der Gesellschaft oder Sozialtechnologie?,* Frankfurt 1971, pp. 101ff.

47. See K.-O. Apel, "Noam Chomsky's Theory of Language," op. cit., pp. 205ff.

48. See ibid., p. 211.

49. See H. Schnädelbach, *Reflexion und Diskurs,* op. cit., pp. 142f.

50. See on this point, H. Schnädelbach, "Zur Dialektik der historischen Vernunft" in H. Poser (ed.), *Wandel des Vernunftbegriffs,* Freiburg/Munich 1981, pp. 15ff.

Herbert Schnädelbach

51. See N. Chomsky, *Language and Mind,* New York 1968; also his *Rules and Representations,* New York 1980.

52. L. Wittgenstein, *Philosophical Investigations,* para. 81; his "use theory" states: "For a *large* class of cases—though not for all—in which we employ the word 'meaning' it can be defined thus: the meaning of a word is its use in the language." (para. 43)

53. See para. 81.

54. Hamann, op. cit., in J. Simon (ed.), *Schriften zur Sprache,* Frankfurt 1967, p. 222.

55. See K.-O. Apel, "Types of Rationality Today," op. cit., p. 334.

56. I. Kant, *Critique of Practical Reason,* A29.

57. See I. Kant, "Die Religion innerhalb der Grenzen der blossen Vernunft," B34; *Religion Within the Limits of Reason Alone* (trans. T. Greene), New York 1960.

58. Ibid., B7, footnote.

59. See on what follows, H. Schnädelbach, "Zur Dialektik der historischen Vernunft," op. cit.

9

Practical Philosophy and the Theory of Society: On the Problem of the Normative Foundations of a Critical Social Science

Albrecht Wellmer

I

The distinction between "is" and "ought" is as old as the history of human language and human institutions. Both, in fact, presuppose the existence of rules and norms; but the recognition of rules implies the distinction between that which corresponds to the rule and that which contravenes it: in short, the distinction between is and ought. The difference between the two is the *presupposition* of ethics. But an ethical question first exists when the agreement of actions with the factually valid norms of a society are no longer recognized as the final instance of a "justification" of these actions. In Western history, the problematic of justification has become radicalized in two different directions: (1) by the question of the legitimacy, i.e., of the "justice" of the norms themselves, and (2) by the question of the moral value, i.e., of the "justness" of the actors. In both cases, what is at issue is the discovery of a difference between is and ought, as it were, on a higher level of reflection: with regard to the first question what is at issue is the difference between that which as a norm is factually valid and that which as a "just" norm should be valid; with regard to the second question, at issue is the difference between the factually and normatively required relationship of actors to the norms which they follow. In short, at issue is the critique and justification of norms, on the one hand, and the evaluation of motives on the other. The fact that an internal connection exists between both questions remained hidden to neither classical Greek ethics nor to Christian ethics; both dealt with it, though in different ways and with radically diverse emphases. However, for both it may be said equally that they lay claim to a standard of the justice of norms and actions that lies beyond the standards established by factually existent norms. At this point there emerges ethics in the sense of the European philosophical tradition and thereby two problem areas: The morality of the individual is no longer guaranteed by the fact that, as it were, it incorporates within itself the institutions and norms of the community; the separation of legality and morality, and the establishment of conscience as an independent instance follow. And the norms and institutions of society cease to draw their legitimacy from their quasi-natural facticity: this means the separation of legality and legitimacy.

European moral philosophy is the working out of these two problems in the dimensions of the ethics of the individual and of political philosophy. Hegel's philosophy is the last major attempt to unify once more the realms of ethics and political philosophy that in the meantime had become separated. Hegel demonstrates the futility of a moral consciousness that has separated itself from the concrete morality of a political community; on the other hand, however, he demonstrates the futility of institutions that injure the right of subjectivity: the problem of the good life can only be solved through the reconciliation of the particular and the universal in the concrete morality of the state.

Of course, Hegel believed that this insight was only possible as the recognition of the *reality* of the moral idea in existing states. His insight that the autonomy of the individual could only be *real* on the foundation of a polis that had become rational was paid for with the illusion that the reconciliation of the particular and the universal was the truth of the Prussian state. But with the collapse of this illusion, Hegel's attempt to once more unify ethics and the theory of society was effectively discredited. It is true that Marx's critique of political economy still lived from the Hegelian problematic; but the positivistic separation of normative ethics and empirical social theory was not stopped by the subsequent history of Marxist theory. In the light of Hegel's discrediting of the moral standpoint, this nonetheless signified that a positivistically misinterpreted theory of society and history would at least tend to become the justificatory instance in normative questions. Though not in Marx, but certainly in the Marxist tradition, there recurs this phenomenal "naturalistic fallacy" of deriving is from ought. Here, semipositivistically and in a semi-Hegelian manner, an absolute demarcation of is and ought is associated with a reduction of what ought to be to what is. There is of course a dilemma here from which bourgeois science and bourgeois society also do not remain spared. More precisely, after imperialism had established itself as the heir of the bourgeois revolution, and positivism as the heir of the bourgeois enlightenment, the problematic of a not merely technical-rational but "reasonable" organization of society increasingly lost both intellectual prestige as well as moral practicability: dissolved, on the one hand, in the no-man's land of the disciplines of philosophy, sociology, and political science organized according to the division of labor; dissolved, on the other, in the organizational structures of a society whose complexity seemed no longer to offer any point of relevance for an old European concept of practical reason.

Of course, this problematic has only appeared to be dissolved. It still continues to haunt not merely the theory and practice of socialism but equally the legitimation crises of Western industrial societies and the crises of the foundations of social science. It almost seems as if the idea of practical reason allows itself to be suppressed only at the price of secondary irrationalities, be it in social, communal life, or in science. On the other hand, however, any attempt to restore the validity of an idea of practical reason in the empirical social sciences in an epoch that has been rendered scientistic, must appear *prima facie* as a sacrilege to the criterion of the rationality of a science which had laboriously enough emancipated itself from the normative modes of thought of social *philosophy* and the *philosophy* of history. With the nervous reactions of a scientific conscience that has become sensitive, such an attempt almost unavoidably conjures up the three interconnected associations, already present in Hegel, of dogmatism, utopia, and terror.

Therefore, the attempt to bring together once more practical philosophy and empirical social science in fact requires a justification. Now it would indeed be presumptuous to attempt such a justification within this brief space. In the last fifteen years an extensive discussion on these topics has built up. And here indeed I am thinking of criticisms of both the empiricist thesis of value-freedom as well as of attempts to rehabilitate a substantive concept of practical rationality from a philosophy of science and a political standpoint. I will refer here only to the constructive theory of ethics and science of the Erlangen School; within analytical philosophy, to the theoretical contributions of John Rawls and Charles Taylor; as well as of the attempt at a foundation of social science on the basis of the communications theory of Jürgen Habermas and Karl-Otto Apel. All these theories and theoretical contributions seem to have in common the attempt to rehabilitate a concept of practical reason that was incorporated into the European tradition of moral philosophy from Plato to Hegel, without forgetting the irrevocable gap that separates us from this tradition; a gap that one could characterize with the catchphrase "the end of metaphysics," but which can be more appropriately characterized by three other turning points: (1) the supersession of a philosophical critique of false consciousness by an empirical-theoretical critique of this false consciousness: Marx and Freud, (2) the penetration of a now empirical social science into the life-context of society, and (3) the analytical-linguistic turn in philosophy.

In what follows, I will take up Jürgen Habermas's attempt at a foundation of social science on the basis of communications theory because I hold it to be the most comprehensive and convincing of the attempts at the reconstruction of practical reason from a philosophy of science and political standpoint. Habermas's theory begins with the so-called "Critical Theory" of the Frankfurt School; but, with the attempt at a linguistic-analytical foundation of ethics and social theory, it goes decisively beyond it. In association with recent developments in linguistics and linguistic philosophy, Habermas has outlined a universal-pragmatic theory of language that is to take over the role of a "metatheoretical" foundation for the social sciences. At the level of this theory of language, he reconstructs the traditional ideas of truth, freedom, and justice as reciprocally interrelated, quasi-transcendental, fundamental norms that, as it were, enter constitutively into the structure of linguistic communication. Habermas has undertaken the explication of these fundamental norms in the form of a discourse theory of truth on the one hand and a communicative ethics on the other. The justification and clarification of the ideas of unconstrained reciprocal recognition among autonomous human subjects gained in this way and a communication between them freed from internal and external restrictions should, according to Habermas, serve at the different levels of social scientific theory formation to bring the connection between empirical analysis and normative presuppositions into the construction of theoretical categories and basic assumptions. In this project, the main point, above all, is the progressive "concretization" of abstract categories, as it were, in the passage through the different strata of social scientific theory formation.

At this point, I wish to discuss the core notion of Habermas's construction, namely, the discursive or dialogical-ethical reformulation of a concept of "practical" or "normative" truth.[1] In terms of this construction, norms and institutions are "true," i.e., "legitimate" or "just," which can find recognition in an unconstrained discourse of all those affected by them, or, as we can also say, concerning which a "radical" consensus of all those concerned could be attained. In terms of this elucidation, we can also speak of a *discursive* or *consensual* principle of practical truth or of a discursive concept of legitimacy. The universal pragmatic *justification* of such a discursive principle is the justification of the thesis that everywhere, where practical questions are argued about, such a principle must necessarily already be recognized at least in principle by the participants in argumentation. To say of such a discursive principle that it characterizes the ultimate normative foundation of the social sciences thus includes the thesis that according to this idea of practical truth the social scientist is always from the outset bound up with his or her object.

II

In order to establish the boundaries of the following discussions, I wish first of all to refer to four central objections that can be made against such a discursive principle:

1. The philosophy of science objection: The discursive principle is exposed to the objection that it places in question a fundamental principle of modern science, namely, the separation of "facts" and "norms" and thereby questions the principle of "value-freedom."

2. The hermeneutic objection: The discursive principle is exposed to the objection that the basic norms of practical rationality to which validity is attributed are *empty* and that their application therefore necessarily leads to dogmatism.

3. Social theory's objection: The objection is raised against the discursive principle that the concept which is implicit in it of a "rational" organization of society is mythological; the social realization of such a principle could thus only lead to terror, anarchy, or a refeudalization of society.

4. The objection to theoretical justification: This objection declares that a universal-pragmatic justification of a discursive principle is impossible, if we do not wish to fall back upon three forms of justification that have all been equally discredited—the naturalistic, the transcendental, or the speculative.

These four objections, which come from quite different directions, nonetheless coincide on one point: The capacity for truth in the realm of practical questions is disputed and thereby, at the same time, the possibility of social theories which, as empirical-scientific theories, could produce at the same time a practical-critical, i.e., a normative knowledge of society.

In what follows, I wish to discuss the first and fourth of the four objections outlined above only briefly, but the second and third more fully. In a contribution whose subtitle addresses the problem of the normative foundations of a critical social science, this balance of emphasis requires a justification. I believe that all four problems refer directly and to an equal extent to the question of the normative foundations of social science. But in the space of a single contribution, it is not possible to deal fully with all four problems to an equal extent. I have therefore decided upon the above choice because it seems to me that the most decisive critique of the attempt at a restoration of the connection between practical philosophy and empirical social science today comes from the camp of those who either associate the utopian implications in a rehabilitated concept of practical reason with terror or anarchy, or who raise the objection either of dogmatism or irrelevancy against the claim to objectivity contained in this concept. Both critics are Hegelians who have lost Hegel's trust in the power of reason and who now merely hold on to his critique of the Enlightenment.

III

I commence with a brief discussion of the so-called problem of value-freedom. The core of the postulate of value-freedom, formulated by Max Weber and in the empirical social sciences to a large extent and for a long time afterwards gaining more or less unproblematic recognition, states the following: Social science, insofar as it is science, is concerned with the establishment and explanation of empirical facts and regularities. Insofar as the social scientist adopts an evaluative position, he or she abandons his or her role of social scientist; for value judgments or normative statements cannot be derived from the ascertainment of facts; instead, in the last instance, they are the expression of value-*decisions* that are not rationally justifiable. Of course, it cannot be avoided that the value-premises of the scientist condition his or her choice of problem and their criteria of relevancy; but the *validity* or his or her results, when he or she proceeds in a strictly scientific manner, are independent of his or her (or anybody's) value-premises. Likewise, value judgments may not be derived from the scientist's empirical findings.

This classic version of the postulate of value-freedom has been criticized primarily from three different directions. In the first case, the critique takes its starting point from an analysis of the normative presupposition of scientific procedure itself; this type of critique has, in my opinion, been worked out most systematically by supporters of a constructive ethics and philosophy of science.[2] In the second case, the critique places in question the possibility of a value-free theoretical language in the social sciences and, at the same time, thus challenges the thesis that normative statements cannot be derived from the descriptive statements of the social sciences; this type of criticism has been developed in a convincing manner by, for instance, Charles Taylor.[3] In the third case, the critique emerges from a *radicalization* of the postulate of value-freedom—namely, from the thesis that the object of social science contains as it were in itself a nonarbitrary standard of evaluation; therefore, the social scientist, for instance in the analysis of alien cultures, also places in question the normative presuppositions of his or her scientific activity, for otherwise the evaluations implicit in these normative presuppositions (i.e., the scientist's criteria of rationality) would render impossible an appropriate description of particular cultures. This position has been advanced with great rigor by Peter Winch.[4] It seems as if it represents a radical antithesis to the first type of critique.

Allow me to briefly elucidate these three positions which *prima facie* are apparently not reducible to a common denominator:

1. The constructive ethics and philosophy of science analyzes the connection between the basic norms of scientific rationality and the basic norms of rational behavior or rational speech. If such a connection between the norms of scientific rationality and nonarbitrary basic norms of rational behavior can be construed, then the standards that must necessarily be recognized by the scientist *qua* scientist already also contain a nonarbitrary standard for the normative evaluation of institutions and systems of action.

2. Taylor's critique of the postulate of value-freedom moves in a complementary direction. Partly by taking up Gunnar Myrdal's well-known works on value problems, Taylor demonstrates that the categorical frames of reference of social scientific theories necessarily prejudge both specific gamuts of possibilities as well as a specific "value-slope." Taylor demonstrates from examples such as modern theories of democracy the interdependency of values and facts embedded in them here: the value-premises of the researcher prejudge the range of variation for empirical analyses; at the same time, the empirical results of the researcher's analyses prejudge evaluations in the sense of the internal "value-slope" of the researcher's theory. Hence there exists in the categorial reference system of theories themselves an embedded unavoidable connection

between the establishment of facts and normative statements. Even if it is not the task of the social scientist *to express* value judgments, the facts *themselves* speak, as it were, a normative language.

3. Finally, Winch's thesis, which he has developed by drawing upon the analyses of language games in the later Wittgenstein, amounts to the critique of a social science that appears to proceed in a value-free manner, which as it were, projects its own criteria for rationality upon its object. His line of argument can be described roughly as follows: Social life-worlds are basically symbolically structured. Thus they cannot be appropriately described without recourse to the self-interpretation and criteria of rationality of those who act within them. But, insofar as, for instance, the anthropologist "slips in" the norms of rationality of *his or her* culture into the description of alien cultures, the anthropologist subsumes their central concepts into a coordinating network that is alien to them, i.e., into a system of logical relations that are alien to them, and in so doing, obstructs a genuine understanding of them. In the light of the norms of one's own culture, the anthropologist must therefore exercise a kind of "*epoché*"* in order to describe an alien culture appropriately, i.e., in terms of the standards that are embedded in it.

I wish, first of all, to take up the last aspect of Winch's position. Winch associates a thoroughly *practical* interest with this position. He believes that out of the analyses of alien cultures we can gain a perspective from which we can critique our own scientized culture. Yet this would be impossible if, in the analysis of alien cultures, we always allowed our own understanding of rationality to enter into the description of facts: indeed, in this way—on logical grounds—the empirical facts could only always confirm our normative prejudices. Of course, the practical interest that is expressed in Winch's position indicates that the latter cannot consistently be interpreted in the sense, as it were, of a hermeneutically developed positivism. In fact, Winch must assume the possibility of the "translation" of an alien language game into that of the particular one of the

---

*E. Hurserl's term for "bracketing" one's presuppositions—Eds.

researcher and hence, put hermeneutically, must assume the possibility of a "fusion of horizons" in the sense of a critical application of anthropological knowledge to the cultural situation of the anthropologist. In so doing, however, he unavoidably places both cultures in the space of a truth reference that is *common* to both. But even if one does not concede this, then there results from the reflection just outlined the fact that a consistently held hermeneutic position in Winch's sense *need* not stand in contradiction to the first of the outlined critiques of the postulate of value-freedom; that critique, may I remind you, asserted that practical questions are capable of truth.

A grounding for the social sciences on the basis of a theory of communications in the sense outlined at the outset of this contribution can in fact only be understood as the attempt to unite the three positions sketched here which commence from a critical stance vis-à-vis the postulate of value-freedom. Along with Winch, it assumes that social scientific analyses must start out from the self-interpretations of actors and that symbolically organized social systems *in themselves* have a relationship to truth. Along with Taylor, it commences from the fact that "value-judgments" enter unavoidably into the categorical systems of social scientific theories and hence manifest themselves in their empirical analyses. Finally, along with constructive ethics, it asserts that practical questions are capable of truth. Under these presuppositions, the problem of objectivity of the social sciences is evidently now placed in a completely new form: If, in fact, the truth capacity of both empirical-theoretical as well as normative-practical questions is asserted; if, furthermore, an interdependency between the decision of practical-normative and empirical-theoretical, in short, between "descriptive" and normative claims to validity is asserted, then the irreducible pluralism of ultimate value-decisions, at the same time as the irreducible pluralism of categorical predecisions, is placed in question. There then exists, in fact, a continuum of rational discourse that embraces to an equal extent normative, empirical, and categorial problems of decision. This means, however, that the concept of "objectivity" in the social sciences can still only be sufficiently clarified with reference to all three levels of discourse.

IV

I wish to leave these rather thesis-like comments on the problem of value-freedom and objectivity as they stand. Indirectly, though, the comments that follow can be understood as an elucidation and defense of the attempt at a solution from the standpoint of a theory of communication. What is at issue here is the question as to the *meaning* of this *discursive principle* that forms the core of the attempt at a justification from the standpoint of a theory of communication, and indeed as to the extent that this principle should not merely characterize the normative basis of social science but also the normative horizon of the society in which we live. Understood in the latter sense, the discursive principle denotes a principle of democratic legitimacy; in so doing, it directly connects the concept of legitimacy with that of "practical truth." In terms of this principle, institutions and power become *legitimate* only if their claim to recognition can be grounded in an unconstrained consensus reached by means of domination-free discourse. Institutions and forms of constitution and exercise of power that are "legitimate" in this sense are "justified," "just," and "rational." According to Habermas, this concept of legitimation represents the critical reconstruction of a type of legitimation that came to dominate in the bourgeois revolutions of the modern period, and which he characterizes as "the procedural type of legitimacy of modern times."[5] The model that is based upon this type of legitimacy is developed most clearly in the contractual constructions of modern natural law: it is the model of an unconstrained agreement between free and equal persons. Typical for this type of legitimacy, at least in its reconstructed form, is that in it all the presuppositions of substantively or ontologically grounded truths concerning the correct order of society are abandoned and only the *form* of the process of reaching agreement and consensus is made the criterion of normative rightness. But this means that now no longer only, as for instance in Plato, a consensus of all rational persons is necessarily anticipated in the determination of that which is just; rather, conditions are now normatively distinguished under which a rational, i.e., discursively orientated, consensus would be factually possible.[6]

In what follows, I wish to elucidate the meaning of this formal principle of legitimacy, in that I show, first, in what sense it "transcends" both the contractarian idea of modern natural law and Kant's formal ethics, and in that I then discuss, the second and third objections outlined at the outset.

I wish to commence with a clarification of these two objections. Both of them may be brought together with arguments that are already to be found in Hegel—and in fact in his critique of the moral standpoint, on the one hand, and in his critique of natural law concepts of democracy on the other; these are arguments which have been taken over by hermeneutic philosophy in the one case and by systems theory in an appropriately modified form in the latter.

The first objection states that, in the idea of a domination-free discourse, we only appear to have gained a standard of legitimacy that lies beyond the facticity of historically realized legal and moral systems and that, as it were, supplies us with an objective criterion for the judgment of factual valid norms and institutions; whereas in reality precisely the formal character of this idea makes it functional for the most arbitrary of contents and opinions. The idea of domination-free communication owes its attraction, as it were, to an undestroyed "transcendental" illusion that may well be anchored deep in the grammar of our language; precisely in its situationless character it produces the illusion of a fixed place, an Archimedean point as it were, from which we can if not practically unhinge the historical world then indeed judge it as a whole. The attempt to apply this norm—whether it be in theory or in social practice—would in reality, however, be synonymous with the attempt such as Baron Münchhausen's to pull oneself from the swamp with one's own hair. Translated into theoretical practice, the result of such an attempt could only be an uncritical absolutization of arbitrary or fortuitously recognized social standards. Translated into social practice, the corresponding result would be terror, arbitrariness, or anarchy—consequences which Hegel had already characterized as the necessary result of the attempt to translate moral idealism or the democratic postulate of equality of natural law into social practice.

The second objection asserts that the discursive-ethical principle of consensus rests upon an untenable methodological individualism; in fact, upon the attempt to construe the concept of a rational organization of social *systems* from a concept of practical rationality that only possesses relative significance at the level of individuals and their face-to-face interaction, freed as it were from institutions. For Hegel this argument implies that the idea of a rationality of the totality, "permeating" through the insight and recognition of single individuals and mediated by them, can only be conceived as the concrete rationality of an organic, self-organized state which, as something always already confronting subjective consciousness and, at the same time, first constituted by them, can be recognized only subsequently as the spirit of its spirit. Compared to the concrete rationality and morality of the state, the subject consciousness always arrives too late: precisely this belongs to its concept as that of a single individual. The individual consciousness can therefore indeed make this rationality its own through insight; but it cannot claim to bring it forth from itself. Against this, the argument in the context of a systems theory liberated from old European illusions, states that the concept of a practical rationality only has a limited functional meaning *within* social systems and is not applicable to them as a whole.

V

In the light of the structural similarity of the discursive principle with the contractual constructions of natural law on the one hand, and with Kant's formal ethics on the other, it is no coincidence that the most important objection to this principle as a rule may be placed in relation to arguments that are already to be found in Hegel. Here, I wish to advance the thesis that the historical-theoretical and political constellations, under which *we* discuss a formal principle of democratic legitimacy, cannot be projected back to those constellations that lay at the basis of Hegel's critique of Kant and of natural law.

The following may be stated by way of provisional justification of this thesis. The discourse principle, in the sense outlined here, presupposes a critique of Kant in a different sense than that which Hegel had in mind. Furthermore, it presupposes a metacritique of the Hegelian critique of natural law, broadly in the sense in which such a metacritique can be derived from

Marx's critique of political economy. In Kant's ethics and philosophy of law one can show that a dialogical principle of practical truth, which is contained in both and links both together, is suspended at decisive places, in part on grounds *internal* and *external* to the system, in favor of a merely logical formalism.

The grounds *internal* to the system are responsible for the fact that Kant developed the formal basic principle of his ethics, expressed in the categorical imperative, only in the sense of a *logical* and not a *procedural* formalism; in other words, they are responsible for the fact that Kant developed the categorical imperative as the basic principle of a *monological* ethics.[7] The grounds *external* to the system are responsible for the fact that in his legal philosophy—i.e., in his "rational-law" interpretation of natural-law contractual constructions—Kant dogmatically restricted a planned *discursive* model of freedom and equality by deriving it from a *market* model of freedom and equity taken over from the tradition of natural law. The connection that is constructed by natural law theory between freedom, equality, and private property gives the discursive-ethically organized Kantian legal philosophy a content derived to a certain extent from outside: The discursive model of freedom and equality is a priori reduced to a degree of freedom allowed by a market model of freedom and equality. Indeed, it is not merely the formal character (in the negative sense) of his ethics which is connected with this double limitation of Kantian moral and legal philosophy; the absence of a convincing connection between "morality" and "legality" is also tied to these limitations.

If one attempts to think through Kant's philosophy in the light of the critique just outlined—i.e., in the sense of the development of a dialogical principle of practical truth planned by Kant but which ultimately remained suppressed by him—then this implies at the same time the attempt to go beyond Kant *in a different direction* than, for instance, did Hegel. Hegel's critiques of Kant and of the contractarian construction of natural law thereby, at least in part, lose their foundation. In addition another factor appears: the critique of the Kantian version of natural law just outlined applies equally to Hegel as well as to Kant.

In fact, Hegel's critique of the contractual constructions of the state—still defended by Kant—itself still presupposes that natural-law property construction which I have characterized above as the limit to Kant's legal philosophy. This means that Hegel's critique of the contract theory of the state first gains its precise meaning in connection with its *justification* of a depoliticized version of natural law. Simplified somewhat, one could describe the state of affairs that is in question here in the following manner: Hegel had a more realistic interpretation of bourgeois society than did his predecessors in natural law theory. He already recognized that the emergence and sharpening of an opposition of social classes was a necessary social consequence of the capitalist mode of production. He thus had every reason to doubt the possibility of a harmony of self-interest and public interest in the framework of a bourgeois democracy founded upon private property. Above all, he saw that the special interests of the property owner supported by the bourgeois legal order were a *particular* interest, in the sense that their realization was unavoidably bound up with the production of a class of nonproperty owners. In this case, however, a "reconciliation of the particular and the universal" was no longer to be expected from the bourgeoisie, elevated in the democratic state into political citizens. Therefore, Hegel was unable to bring together under the same cover two notions that belong together in modern natural law and in Kant's work: namely, the notion of the freedom and equal rights of property owners, on the one hand, and the notion of political freedom and equality, on the other. Nevertheless, for Hegel, the constitution of bourgeois society signified an untranscendable final stage in the history of the emancipation of humanity. For this reason it required "transcendence" in a state independent of antagonistic interests, a state which brought injured rationality to its aid. Hegel, in a characteristic manner, could of course only exemplify this transcendence of bourgeois society in the substantive morality of the state, in an already anachronistic state in terms of world history—the Prussian constitutional monarchy. The power of this state, unchecked by its citizens, remained—contrary to Hegel's intentions—the sign of a transcendence that is not dialectical but enforced.

It was Marx who first followed an alternative way sympathetic to Hegel's analysis, in that he already commenced the critique on that level upon which Hegel, still in good faith, had continued the tradition of natural law: namely, that of "abstract right." Marx's critique of the ideology of equivalent exchange may be understood as a critique of the legitimating function of the connection, asserted in natural law, between freedom, equality, and private property. This connection is shown by Marx's analysis of the deep structure of equivalent exchange to be both real and illusory. It is therefore no coincidence that it conditions the self-understanding of the revolutionary bourgeoisie. As a "necessary illusion," bound up with the material foundations of bourgeois society, it represents in fact the naturally given basis for legitimating the domination of the bourgeois class.

The critique of political economy destroys the ideological illusion inherent in the connection between freedom, equality, and private property by an analysis of the capitalist mode of production which simultaneously advances in three directions, corresponding to the nexus already built into bourgeois theory between the conceptions of the *structure, genesis,* and the *developmental perspectives* of this mode of production. In contrast to the theories of modern natural law and of classical political economy, Marx's theory signified at the same time a radical *historicization* of the bourgeois mode of production; with the illusion of justice this mode of production equally takes on the illusion of naturalness. Thus, Marx contrived to demonstrate that the capitalist system in all three temporal dimensions—in the light of its contemporary structure, its prehistory, and its developmental possibilities—did not merely *fortuitously* deviate, i.e., because of external reasons, from the norm of domination-free intersubjectivity, which bourgeois theorists had seen realized in a market model based on free exchange between legally equal proprietors. In fact, Marx showed three things:

1. A system of universal freedom and equality based on exchange relations between private property owners necessarily presupposes the opposition of wage-labor and capital. Thus, it represents—despite its ideological claim—a form of class domination.

2. The natural law derivation of a connection between work, property, and legal equality—and this means the reconstruction of the bourgeois order of property in the sense of a norm of domination-free intersubjectivity—is not merely false historically; rather, it is—and this applies to the Hegelian transformation of natural law into "the law of reason"—also false in the sense of a *logical* construction. The realization of bourgeois legal equality—in the sense of a system of fully developed equivalent exchange—in fact presupposes the *separation* of work from property. A historical perspective is thereby rehabilitated which can appropriately take account of those elements of force which entered into the constitution of bourgeois private property.

3. According to its internal logic, the development of the capitalist mode of production in no way leads to a procurement of the welfare of all through the egotism of individuals; i.e., the logic of the motion of capital permits no advance toward a society that would at the same time be capitalist *and* just, in the sense of the natural-law legitimating principle of an agreement of free and equal persons. Rather, it sets free a process of capital of concentration, crises, and mass poverty which only after the supersession of bourgeois property could be brought under the rational control of the associated producers.

The critique of political economy destroys the illusion of the absence of force which is inherent in the system of equivalent exchange and hence at the same time in the bourgeois system of freedom and equality. I wish to put forward the thesis that Marx's critique only has meaning if one understands it as an *immanent* critique of bourgeois class society. The ideology of equivalent exchange in fact obtains its legitimating force from the illusion, associated with it, of an order of social relations between individuals free of force. Hence, it may be asserted that the critique of political economy *as* the critique of ideology lives from the implicit reference precisely to that idea of domination-free reciprocal recognition whose realization the bourgeois system of freedom and equality claimed to be. Yet it follows directly from this that the communism of a classless society propagated by Marx may only be legitimated from the context of Marx's critical theory in the sense of a *radicalization and supersession* of bourgeois democracy, that is, in the sense of a natural law severed, as it were, from the foundation of bourgeois private property.

VI

These brief allusions to the reception and critique of natural law in the theories of Kant, Hegel, and Marx, as well as my references to the problem of a "formal" ethics in Kant, should make clear that the inherently formal character of a discursive-ethical principle of consensus (1) must be conceived in the sense of a *dialogical* interpretation—or "transcendence"—of the Kantian moral principle, and that (2) it must be understood against the background of an ideological critique of modern natural law, whose premises still underline the universalistic legal theory of Kant as well as the treatment of "abstract law" by Hegel. Both theories first gain their specific content from the a priori legitimation of a bourgeois order of property and, linked with this order, the extraction of a sphere of pure strategic interactions from the realm of the possible discursive process of will-formation. Hegel's critique of the political interpretation of the natural law postulate of equality still presupposes its "basis," namely, a concept of property continued in natural law terms. With this is associated the necessity and, at the same time, the failure of Hegel's attempt to demonstrate the concrete universal of particular state orders as the immanent truth of the universalistic moral and legal principles that are "transcended" in them. In contrast to Kant's legal theory, Marx's critique of natural law refers to a quite different point than did Hegel's critique of natural law. In fact, it places the starting point of Hegel's legal construction and thereby the presuppositions of Hegel's critique itself in question. At the same time, however, its signifies a partial rehabilitation of Kant's theory; for it destroys the illusion of an already achieved reconciliation of the particular and the universal and thereby makes the production of the rationally universal once more into a historical *problem.*

Now the discursive-ethical principle of consensus represents the attempt to define anew the truth of ethical and juridical universalism in Kant or in natural law. And the critique of Kant and of natural law, implicit in this attempt, runs in a certain sense *in opposition* to Hegel's critique. In particular, it is now disputed that the bourgeois principle of property represents the core truth of universalistic formal law, and precisely because of this, the connection between universalistic ethics and the contractual constructions of natural law, asserted by Kant and disputed by Hegel, can be made intelligible on a new basis. Although a discursive-ethical principle of consensus is no less formal than the disputed legal and moral principles, it thus also allows, at the same time, the form-content problem to appear in a new light. One might make clear the distinction in the following way. The intentional determination of an actor in the sense of the categorical imperative is a basically monological process; but since concrete contents of action cannot be derived without further ado from a formal principle, determinations of content must derive from other sources, and indeed, as it were, behind the backs of actors. The content could just as easily be provided from an uncritical recognition of socially valid norms as it could from them more or less arbitrarily being placed in question: The counterfactually assumed "realm of ends" is just as identical with the existing social reality as it is absolutely different from it. In contrast, a discursive-ethical principle of consensus proceeds *dialogically.* It does indeed require from us more than merely the solitary decision as to whether we were prepared to make a maxim of our will into the principle of a universal legislation. Instead, it refers to the practice of dialogue as the sole possible procedure through which we can discover whether we can recognize both a norm and the interpretations of our needs that enter into it as correct and thus also, in a rational manner, whether we should recognize it. A discursively arrived-at consensus, however, can be compared with an agreement of free and equal persons. Herein lies the analogy to the contractual constructions of natural law, as long as one understands this not in the sense of a myth of origins but rather in the sense of a standard legitimacy for bourgeois society. Yet, in turn, the discursive principle is distinguished from these contractual constructions by the fact that it does not establish in advance the contents of a possible rational consensus and thereby, at the same time, substantive criteria for a distinction between what is "reasonable" and what is "unreasonable," but rather, conversely elevates the discursive procedure itself into the criterion for the rationality of any possible consensus.

The sole content that can be characterized as normative and which is provided from such a principle of consensus exists in the formal structure of a dialogical relationship between the individuals that we can describe as a relationship of domination-free reciprocal recognition. In this, I believe, a fundamental Kantian intention is better realized than Kant himself was able to do in his ethics: namely, the elaboration of a *formal* determination as the solely a priori realizable content of moral consciousness. Yet now what is at issue is no longer the form of a relationship of the acting human subject to him or herself, but rather the form of an intersubjective relationship that is, at the same time, a practice of dialogue. In this way, at the same time, what is avoided is that the recourse to mere facticity (as in Kant)—either to current norms or to the fortuitous needs, interests, and interpretations of individuals—becomes the mode of mediation of form and content that cannot be questioned because it takes place behind our backs. *All* dimensions of social facticity now become incorporated into the movement of possible critique and possible discursive transformation.

VII

After this preliminary clarification, I now wish to discuss the two objections referred to above against a discursive-ethical principle of consensus. I will repeat them briefly:

1. Such a principle of consensus only appears to supply us with an "objective" standard, i.e., due independent of the current historical facticity of recognized norms, needs, and interpretations, for the judgment of factual social circumstances.

2. A principle of consensus based on the theory of discourse, understood as a principle of democratic legitimacy, represents a "category mistake": social systems as a whole do not permit themselves to be "discursively reconstructed" through a discourse that, as it were, has become total; rather its discursively indestructible and discursively unreconstructable facticity is every time the precondition for the possibility of *partial* dis-

course. To ignore this state of affairs means to conjure up terror at the same time as utopia.

The two objections may be understood as two complementary aspects of a suspicion of meaninglessness raised against the principle of discourse. If it were possible to refute the two objections then this would signify, at the same time, an indirect confirmation that Hegel's *justified* objection to Kant and natural law no longer applies to a discursive-theoretical principle of consensus. I wish to attempt to show what such a confirmation could look like.

Permit me, first of all, to attempt to make clear the real core of the second objection. The objection states that a principle of consensus represents no possible form of organization of the social processes of will-formation and the decision-making process. In particular, one could argue roughly as follows[8]: societies can only exist insofar as competencies for decisions and procedures for deciding are defined and recognized as legitimate—and in fact this is all the more the case the more complex the particular societies are. In this way, institutional boundary conditions are always already pregiven under which, at all events, limited practical discourses can take place that can lead to valid decisions. Such discourses are basically limited: not only—as a rule—with regard to the number of participants, but also in thematic and temporal respects. It is necessary to come to decisions for, apart from the case of scientific discussions, questions of validity cannot be left open: one or another norm is valid. Therefore, the necessity of coming to a decision has priority over any postulate of consensus. From this there also exists the necessity for procedural rules that first of all make it possible to come to *valid* decisions. The production of substantive consensus remains more or less fortuitous. In principle, then, nothing would change in this if one could commence from an actually produced consensus concerning basic norms and procedural rules (for instance, in the sense of natural law contractual constructions) that make the principle of parliamentary majority decisions themselves into the content of an original consensus. For such a consensus does not suffice to guarantee a consensual legitimation of derived or procedurally legitimated decisions in the sense of a principle of discourse. In order to understand this, one only needs to point out that the consensus concerning procedural rules must remain bound up with the presupposition that the procedurally legitimate decisions lead to an appropriate concretization of originally abstract *substantive* basic norms. In other words, the original consensus contains within itself no guarantee that a disagreement concerning the *meaning* of this consensus which emerges at a later level of the decision-making process will necessarily be avoided; and in case such as disagreement emerges, it requires once more a procedurally legitimated instance that corresponds to a decision, even if no consensus can be attained (and in fact, again, simply because a nondecision would also be a decision). Hence, one could speak of a logical primacy of deciding or of *being* decided over against *consenting*; similarly, just as the metainstitution of language and the institutions of social interaction always already are prior to any possible discourse, so is any possible discursive consensus always already decided upon in advance. Therefore, the decision cannot wait for the consensus. For this reason, although it is indeed possible to introduce discursive procedures into decision-making processes, one cannot, however, organize the social process of will-formation and decision making as a whole according to the principle of the discursive orientation towards consensus. The only conceivable social realization of such a principle would be either a realm of pure rational beings (angels) or a social state of nature in the most pregnant sense of the word, i.e., in each case, the transcendence of society as a *human* one: either the transcendence of its finite nature or the transcendence of its (finite) rationality.

Yet I wish to maintain that this whole line of argument itself rests upon a "category mistake"; namely, upon a confusion of two levels of investigation: on the one hand that of a *principle of legitimacy* and, on the other, that of the concrete social *forms of organization*.[9] In order to refute the second of the objections outlined above, it would thus be sufficient to make *this* distinction perfectly clear. In order to do this it must be demonstrated that the principle of discourse contains a standard for the critique of concrete social forms of organization that is not empty, even though it itself does not already express an ideal social form of organization. In order to carry out this demonstration, I wish first of all to refer to the operational features of the principle of consensus. As is easy to see, this principle is not to be equated with the Platonic utopia of the good ruler who realizes in an anticipatory manner the consensus of all reasonable people. Indeed, it does not release us, under the pressure of coming to a decision, from the necessity of antici- pating in each case a rational consensus; at the same time, however, it refers us to *real* discourses or consensuses to be aimed for in the future as the sole instance of a possible testing and justification of our anticipations. What is assumed here as the norm of truth is not a monologically anticipatable consen- sus of all rational people—which can therefore just as easily fail to appear as a factual consensus—but a rational consensus, aimed for dialogically, of *all* people. Thus, the principle of consensus compels us to treat *all* beings gifted with language, if not already as rational then indeed sub specie as beings capable of rationality.

But the fact that the principle of consensus represents a norm of legitimacy, without already providing ready to hand an organizational principle for social processes of decision- making, can be made clear in the following way. Public dis- courses affect institutionally regulated processes of decision- making, and in fact they do so already in bourgeois society. According to the bourgeois-liberal model of the public sphere, discourses that are public and free from sanctions should be a means of *enlightenment* in a dual sense: the individual should learn in them, as Kant formulated it, "to serve his or her understanding without the direction of another," and, at the same time, through such discourses political institutions should be placed under the constraint of legitimation. Although such discourses, as Kant knew equally well, already presuppose the institutions of bourgeois law, they nonetheless represent a mode of discursive will-formation that cannot be made to co- incide with the institutionalized procedures of legislative, ju- ridical, and administrative decisions.

What is at issue with regard to our present reflections is not, for me, the question as to how far the bourgeois public sphere ever fulfilled the functions which were imputed to it. Rather, what concerns me is the internal *logic* of a discursive model of freedom and equality. Yet after we have already clarified the fact that processes of discursive will-formation and institutionally regulated decision-making procedures, although parts of a *single* system of institutions and related to one another, nonetheless represent two levels of the social life-process that are structurally distinct from one another, the question of the institutional "representability" or "realizability" of the principle of discourse takes on a new meaning. Now indeed it is a question as to whether conditions are conceivable under which, on the basis of a consensus concerning basic norms—that is, basic norms of freedom and equality as well as procedural norms of collective will-formation—procedurally "legitimate" decisions, although they do not unconditionally *emerge* out of discursively arrived-at consensuses of all those concerned, do nonetheless *stand the test* in an unconstrained discourse of all those concerned. In order that such a thing is possible, the discourse of those concerned, whether it is real or anticipatory, must, of course, be "included" in the institutionalized decision-making procedures; and that is only possible if these procedures have already entered into the medium of a public discourse that, even though not itself a decision-making *procedure,* nonetheless makes discursive rationality in the decision-making processes possible. Yet, it is at least not unthinkable that legally valid decisions "reach" an anticipated consensus of all concerned and that the particular anticipations stand the test in actual discourse. Nevertheless, the acceptance of a principle of consensus does not oblige us to accept the real possibility of such an "ideal state" of society. Rather, it enables us to give a legitimate meaning to a distinction which was already accepted in natural law contract theories but was never satisfactorily worked out: namely, the distinction between the legitimacy of basic norms, which arises out of a consensus of all as free and equal persons, and the inferred legitimacy of norms that prove not to be capable of achieving a consensus. From a purely procedural viewpoint, this distinction, as I have indicated above, leads to paradoxical situations: it does not exclude either the possibility of a "tyranny of the majority" or that of a self-transcendence of democracy. From the viewpoint adopted here, however, the distinction can be justified in this manner: Since, in fact, the basic consensus is at the same time a consensus concerning the principles of discursive will-formation—and this means concerning the connection between discourses and decision-making procedures—it is at the same time a consensus with regard to how one deals with unresolved dissent; to assume the continual existence of this basic consensus thus also means to assume that those who dissent know themselves to be recognized in their basic rights. The fact that this *must* be the case cannot of course be logically imputed from contractual constructions; I believe that John Rawls was mistaken on the point, when he attempted once more to justify the structure of a "just" society in the sense of the contractual constructions of natural law. In fact, quite apart from the principle of consensus itself, we can in reality not construe a priori the content of such a basic consensus, since as a practical relationship between individuals it could only emerge out of their concrete historical situation. We can say what it means to assume such a consensus: namely, that individuals know their common interests as recognized in the institutions of society and thereby at the same time recognize one another reciprocally as free and equal persons; but we could not say what its concrete content was. Nonetheless, we can at least say that, under the preconditions assumed here, the dialectical connection of abstract law, morality, and ethical life construed by Hegel loses its foundation. One might say that the principle of discourse indicates the anticipation of a state of affairs in which the three spheres of law coincide: i.e., a state of affairs in which a discursive reality that has become a moral "custom" has its direct counterpart in the norms and institutions of society, whereas, conversely, the legal norms have gained an immediate moral content. Of course, this also means that one may only speak of a generalized domination-free discourse if the basic institutions of society already corresponded to the principle of consensus, i.e., if that practical relationship between individuals was produced and institutionally secured which is the presupposition of a generalized unconstrained discourse. This distinctive homologous relationship of law, morality, and ethical life thus also indicates the real utopian horizon that is to be found in a discursive-theoretical principle of consensus. John Rawls was thus correct when, in his *Theory of Justice*, he sought to develop this anticipated homology in the concept of practical reason.

In particular, in a kind of "retranslation" of Hegel's insights into a Kantian system of reference, Rawls made clear that the specific necessity of a "self-stabilizing" society, which has become just in the sense of a convergence of the "good" with the "just" life, results from the assumption of a basic consensus that has become an institutional reality. Yet this is nothing other than Hegel's idea of the reconciliation of the particular and the universal in the concrete ethical life of the state. As in Hegel, so here too it is also the case that the rationality of individuals would be formed automatically in the framework of a rational universal: only that they, the individuals, do not need to be speculative philosophers—one might add, not systems-theorists or party functionaries either—in order to see the rationality of the totality. Rather, the reconciliation of the particular and the universal becomes one of experience and insight available to any rational person.

Yet does not this notion in fact sound like a bad utopia? I would reply that it is no more or no less utopian than the concept of practical reason itself. The principle of discourse signifies that utopia which we enter into as long as we grant to all human beings the right to demand justifications—not justifications for everything, but certainly justifications for those decisions and norms that demand something from them. What is at issue here is not a new idea. We are concerned with the reformulation of an old idea, to which we arrive if we eliminate all those substantive premises which are associated in the history of political philosophy with the idea of practical reason. These substantive premises are usually concerned with a "naturalization" and hence the legitimation of social differences or relations of domination: whether it be a concern with denying slaves, people of color, or women the capacity of reason or with a "naturalization" of the bourgeois order of property. In all these instances, what is at issue is a restriction of the possibilities for discourse, or, perhaps one should say, the legitimation of the socially effective restrictions upon possible discourse. The specific formality and, at the same time, radicality of a discursive-ethical principle of consensus arises out of the destruction of all these premises that substantively circumscribe the concept of practical reason.

VIII

Now it is clear that one cannot directly derive what we should do here and now from a concept of practical reason. This also holds for the principle of discourse. The principle of discourse can only provide a *direction*. It requires the expansion of the realm of discursive rationality up to those limits that—if they indeed exist—we can discover only through historical practice. If today, in contrast, the obsolescence of the concept of practical reason is asserted by systems theory, then I believe what is at issue is a new form of legitimation of the restriction of discourses: in place of substantive premises, such as still limited the possibilities of discursive rationality in the contractual constructions of natural law, there steps a radical questioning—because it itself has become formal—of a concept of practical reason that has become formal. Yet whatever may be the uses of systems theory for a reformulation of the problem of democratic organizational forms that is appropriate to the complexity of modern societies (and I surmise that its usefulness is not small), the idea of practical reason may only be *superseded* at the price of a self-incapacitation of individuals acting in society.

I have also indicated here the practical grounds which today could cause us to start out from that level of abstraction upon which alone a concept of practical reason could be explicated. These reasons are associated with the apparent obsolescence of the idea of practical reason: an apparent obsolescence which is only theoretically ratified by systems theory but which, as a systematically produced—i.e., ideological—illusion, belongs to the contemporary aggregate state of industrial societies. In this, there is expressed a particular "dialectic of Englightenment," which from a specific stage of human emancipation onward seems to threaten the foundations and presuppositions of emancipation itself. In the light of this, the abstract explication of those anticipations that are included in the idea of practical reason gains its meaning as part of an attempt to cause us to reflect upon the foundations of collective human existence which have been called into question.

Of course, this in no way changes the fact that the practical problem in the idea of practical reason—if indeed we still trust

Albrecht Wellmer

in such an idea—is, as Hegel quite correctly saw, the problem of its *mediation* with the concrete situation of particular actors and their society. Hegel solved this problem insofar as he sought to demonstrate that it *is* always already solved; the assertion of the contrary only testifies to the moral vanity of individuals. Can we reject Hegel's answer without incurring his critique of the "moral standpoint"? With this question I return to the second of the objections outlined above, the "hermeneutic" objection.

This objection[10] maintains that, with the idea of a "domination-free discourse," we only appear to have gained an objective standpoint by which we can "measure" the practical rationality of individuals or societies. In reality, it would be an illusion to believe that we could emancipate ourselves from the normatively laden facticity of our historical situation with the norms and criteria of rationality handed down within it, in order to view history as a whole and our position within it, as it were, "from the outside." An attempt in this direction could only end in theoretical arbitrariness and in practical terror. This objection is to be taken seriously. However, if one interprets it as an objection to the position advanced here, then it must be demonstrated once more that it rests upon a "category mistake."

Allow me to expand briefly upon this. If I understand it correctly, the problem of the mediation or "concretization" of an ideal of practical reason is placed upon three different levels: (1) that of actors, (2) that of a critical social science, and (3) that of a reconstruction of evolutionary or developmental processes. I shall at once justify why I distinguish these latter two levels from one another.

First of all, with reference to the situation of actors, it is indeed the case that it requires particular concrete analyses from which alone the normative significance and the factual possibilities of a situation can result. The principle of discourse does not supply us with a standard that we merely need to apply to reality. Yet, for their part, the possibility of concrete analyses can be independent once more from a knowledge of the total societal contexts that can only be gained, in a verified form, by means of a critical social science. Of course, it must be pointed out here that this too can never definitively solve the "problem of mediation" for human actors: concrete instructions for action can never be derived from theories. In a situation of theoretically unresolvable historical ambiguity, no one can ultimately relieve the actors of the risks involved in the attempt to act correctly in accord with a universal that is still to be realized rationally. Of course, the actors could know *this*; and this knowledge concerning an unresolvable core of ignorance might perhaps make them immune against dogmatism and blind faith.

A different kind of problem presents itself on the second "level of mediation," that of a critical social science. Here what is at issue is the choice of appropriate theoretical categories and the question as to the possibility of a critique of false consciousness. Once more, the principle of discourse supplies no "standard." Rather, there is provided only a direction, that for the rest exempts us not from the necessity of an "immanent" procedure. Its metatheoretical status is expressed in the fact that it makes possible a new definition of the problem of truth and objectivity without offering a guarantee of truth and objectivity.

The principle of discourse first gains an immediate theoretical status at the third level, that of a reconstruction of evolutionary and developmental processes in the sense of a reconstruction of the *logic* of developments.[11] Here, the principle of discourse in fact enters directly into the reconstruction of a series of logically sequential "stages" of moral or institutional "rationality," whereby, in accord with the normatively indicated endpoint, it characterizes such a series of stages in the light of their formal structure. In these theories, a genuinely new relationship is provided between moral philosophy and empirical science, a state of affairs which first occurred to the genetically oriented moral psychologists in the Piaget school. In these theories, one is indeed directly concerned with an object of investigation which no longer can be grasped in relation to the traditional distinction between norms and facts: the "logic," whose reconstruction is at issue, signifies both an empirical and a normative relationship. Yet I believe that this expresses the fact that here structures are dealt with whose normative meaning at the same time signifies the elementary survival conditions of a species that reproduces itself via linguistic symbols. Thus, one could also say that the principle of discourse expresses the connection between those conditions of survival for a form of existence that is caught between the boundaries of birth and death in a net of symbolic interactions and the utopia of the good and just life.

Yet up to now it still has not been clarified whether a discursive-ethical principle of consensus thus becomes positively "empty" if one attempts to defend it, in the sense indicated above, against hermeneutic objections. It was no coincidence that in my reflections I commenced from formulations of this principle as they are to be found in Habermas's work; one might thus expect that I would discuss it here in the form developed by Habermas within the framework of a theory of "universal pragmatics," in which a stronger claim seems to be bound up with it than the one which I have advanced here. I wish to explain briefly why I have chosen another path.

In his reflections on the consensus theory of truth, Habermas starts out from the following problem: a factual consensus does not *eo ipso* also have to be unconstrained, i.e., a rational consensus; thus, a factual consensus could be the expression of the "structural domination" embodied in the institutions of a society. The question then is: How can we distinguish a "rational" or "illusion-free" consensus from an irrational or fallacious one? Only if criteria can be provided according to which we can meet such a distinction, can a consensus theory of truth imply more than the reformulation of a relativistic concept of truth. As is well known, Habermas answers this question in such a way that he has recourse to the structural preconditions of "ideal speech situations." According to him, a consensus would be rational and hence "true" if it took place or were to stand the test under the conditions of an ideal speech situation. Habermas infers that each time when we enter into a discourse or when we produce a discursive agreement, we must assume that the conditions for an ideal speech situation are fulfilled. Such conditions are in particular: a systematic distribution of chances to apply different classes of speech acts and freedom of movement in the change of levels of discourse.[12]

Now it seems to me that such a recourse to the structural features of ideal speech situations or unconstrained discourses would only be meaningful for the purposes of a distinction between rational and irrational consensuses if one could view these structural features as independent, as it were, operationalizable criteria of the rationality or unconstrained nature of discourses for an observer not participating in a particular discourse.[13] Yet precisely this, however, is not the case. In fact, in order to be able to meaningfully apply these criteria we must always have already understood something of the concrete structure and substantive constellation of specific discursive situations. If, for instance, taking a simple case, someone permanently remains silent, then this must not *eo ipso* be a sign of asymmetrically distributed chances of speaking. Instead, we could only draw an appropriate conclusion if, counterfactually, we could supply the arguments or modes of behavior that we would expect under the given circumstances from a rational participant in discourse. Similarly, the question as to whether freedom of movement is achieved in the change in levels of discourse cannot be decided without a preunderstanding as to the places at which a change in the levels of discourse would be meaningful or necessary (something like rationality or irrationality does exist also with regard to the change in levels of discourse). In other words, *formal* criteria can only be applied on the basis of a *substantive* preunderstanding; and this means that our operative understanding of rationality, as it were, cannot be procured by the provision of the formal structure of unconstrained discourse. It is certainly true that a suppression of pertinent arguments, regardless of who voices them, is not permitted in a rational discourse. An unconstrained discourse is only realized where only the constraint of the better argument dominates. Whether that is the case or not, however, cannot be decided by the application of formal criteria for unconstrained discourse.

These reflections may be summarized as follows: The structural features of an ideal speech situation supply *no sufficient* criterion for the rationality of discourses. The fact that this criterion is insufficient is merely another expression of the fact that it is not *applicable independently* of the understanding and judgment of discourse situations, i.e., without calling to its aid additional criteria (of the rationality of arguments and behavior).

The structural features of an ideal speech situation could thus only be valid as the sufficient conditions for the rationality of consensus produced in such situations if one could so interpret them that structural features of the communicative competence of the ideal speaker were already codefined through them. Yet quite apart from the question as to what meaning the concept of an "ideal" communicative competence could have, this would only be possible if, with regard to the formal structural feature, more was already implied than is explicitly expressed in them. But this means that they must be interpreted, proceeding from the preunderstanding of the "rationality" of speakers that is not obtainable through the *explicit* structural descriptions of ideal speech situations.

Yet if the structural features of ideal speech situations represent no sufficient or independently applicable criterion for the rationality of discourses (or of discursively produced consensuses), then it is evident that they can be interpreted neither in the sense of a "metanorm" for the organization of collective processes of will-formation nor in the sense of an ideal standard for the judgment and critique of actual forms of life. Nevertheless, it seems clear to me that we also do not *need* standards of this kind. To claim that a consensus is rational indeed means to assume that it rests upon insight (upon the force of arguments) and not upon deception, self-deception, manipulation, or internalized repression; nonetheless, we can never achieve more than a *factual* consensus. To doubt the rationality of a factual consensus thus means either that specific, substantive, counterarguments can be advanced, or it means that doubt will be expressed as to the rationality of those consenting; but what we mean by the "rationality" or "autonomy" of speakers cannot be sufficiently grasped with the aid of the structural features of an ideal speech situation. Therefore, in hidden doubts of this kind there is always a hypothesis which can ultimately only be tested by producing a new "rational" consensus—a state of affairs out of which those consenting can recognize as such their previous lack of rationality.

In my reflections up to now, I have so far excluded the question in what sense a communicative ethics can be found on the level of universal- or transcendental-pragmatic analyses (see section IX below), not least because of the difficulties just indicated in the concept of an ideal speech situation. In other words, I have left open the question as to how the transition is to be understood from the simple recognition of the fact that in intersubjectively intended normative validity claims a consensus based on the insight of all "rational persons" is anticipated counterfactually, to the recognition of the universalistic principles of a dialogical ethics. The latter presupposes that every being capable of language is recognized as a potentially rational being and that, over and above this, the *meaning* of normative claims to validity are related solely to a relationship of unconstrained reciprocal recognition between rational beings (which, by the way, does not rule out that normative obligations of rational persons also exist vis-à-vis nonrational creatures). Under these preconditions—viewed historically, by no means trivial ones—an unconstrained consensus concerning such norms and institutions which block the chances of an *expansion* of rational self-determination and discursive will-formation is thus no longer capable of being *simulated*. Autonomy—even if it is only assumed counterfactually—and the will to autonomy cannot be separated from one another. Hence, the presuppositions of a universalistic ethics form the framework in which belief in the constitutional inferiority of a specific class of human beings (slaves, women, workers, blacks) is exposed as the ideology of domination and in which the struggles of these constituencies for recognition as possessors of equal rights can develop just like a struggle for the enlargement of the realm of democratic will-formation. The democratic principles of legitimacy emerged out of such struggles. The radicalization of these principles of legitimation into a principle of discourse in the sense adopted here arises out of the critique of those limitations that were still bound up with these principles in the tradition of natural law (see section III).

The idea of a social order that rests upon a factually unconstrained consensus of all is nonetheless certainly not "empty"; at the same time, nothing direct can be deduced about the legitimacy of particular social institutions from it. This already arises solely from the fact that we can never derive from principles that which is *possible* and that which is not in concrete historical situations. The refutation of the hermeneutic objection is thus, in my opinion, so simple because this objection can actually only be directed against an objectivistic misunderstanding of practical principles. In fact, one would misunderstand the role of such principles if one interprets them either directly as organizational principles or if one believed one could "deduce" from them evaluations of institutions or directives for action. If one makes this clear, then it also becomes intelligible why it is often difficult to decide whether relevant controversies really contrast the question of the normative presuppositions of a critical social science or rather, instead, their concrete, substantive assertions. Yet, I repeat, with regard to this, that the recourse to a discursive principle of practical truth can certainly never guarantee the truth and objectivity of social scientific statements, and that just as little, however, can hermeneutic objections meet the attempt to clarify the preconditions for the possibility of a critical social science by recourse to a concept of practical truth.

IX

In conclusion, I wish to return once more to the question of the *justification* of a discursive-ethical principle of consensus that has hitherto only been briefly touched upon. It may appear strange that I have saved this question for my concluding remarks. Nonetheless, there is expressed in this a difficulty; in fact I believe that it still remains to be clarified what we wish to understand by "justification," and what gain in knowledge we can expect from such a justification. Instead of dealing with these questions in detail, I wish to restrict myself to some suggestions.

First of all, it seems to me that the problem of justification, where what is at issue is the justification of a principle of discourse, is in a certain sense ambiguous. Thus, I believe that the reflections engaged in here belong just as much to the context of justification of a principle of discourse as, for instance, does the attempt to justify a principle of discourse— "transcendental-pragmatically"—by the presentation of the meaning of normative claims to validity and their implications. Yet, over and above this, it seems necessary to distinguish in another sense as well between different "levels" of possible justification. For instance, at the level of abstraction of transcendental or universal-pragmatic analysis, a communicative ethics can only be justified in the sense of an explication of the formal connection between normative claims to validity and discourses. Yet, at this level of abstraction, one actually only arrives at universalistic principles because one has already abstracted from all differences between speakers, i.e., from all concrete determinations, by the choice of the reference system. Now this choice of an abstract reference system itself seems to possess an ambiguous meaning: insofar as it is motivated by the interest in the development of a universal theory of language, the relevant statements for beings capable of language must have validity "as such." If, from this viewpoint, one investigates which norms speakers *qua* speakers must always already have recognized, then one cannot justify much more than, for example, a universal norm of "veracity" and the like. Yet one can also understand the choice of a reference system at the abstraction level of universal pragmatics in a different way: namely, as grounded in the interest in reconstructing a system of rules that will be recognized by speakers of a *specific kind*—precisely those speakers who, as moral subjects, have completed *practically* the transition to a level of abstraction that corresponds to the level of abstraction of universal pragmatics. Simplifying somewhat, one might say that the transition to a universalistic ethics occurs at the place where acting subjects themselves choose this level of abstraction as the appropriate one for moral questions. This choice signifies a transformation of the attitude of acting individuals to one another and to themselves. But in this instance, the "justificatory achievement" of universal pragmatic analysis becomes deficient in another sense: such an analysis cannot in fact justify precisely that "step in abstraction" which marks the transition to a universalistic ethics, because it methodically presupposes it.[14]

For the reason just advanced, I am of the opinion that a transcendental (or universal) pragmatic *ultimate justification* of a communicative ethics is not possible. Rather, it appears that formal attempts at justification must always already make use of presuppositions which emerge out of the educative process of the speaker and which cannot be fully eradicated in analytical-linguistic arguments. Hence, it may be that the reconstruction of this educative process itself still belongs to the

Albrecht Wellmer

justification of its results. This would mean that, in the justification of universalistic principles, the history of their elaboration—in the sense of a history of institutions and revolutions as well of the development of moral consciousness and self-identity—is their constituent element.

In terms of a reply to the question of the "justifiability" of a principle of discourse, these reflections may appear unsatisfactory. But this could also lie in the fact that the question of justification was associated with a false expectation. In fact, it seems to be the case that the justification, which we should here disclaim, belongs to those kinds of justifications through which nothing in our understanding of the world or ourselves is changed. Yet in this there always lies the suspicion that we have asked a wrong question.

Notes

1. See, for instance, J. Habermas, "Vorbereitende Bemerkungen zu einer Theorie der kommunikativen Kompetenz," in J. Habermas/N.Luhmann, *Theorie der Gesellschaft oder Sozialtechnologie?*, Frankfurt 1971; his "Wahrheitstheorien" in H. Fahrenbach (ed.), *Wirklichkeit und Reflexion. Festschrift für Walter Schulz*, Pfullingen 1973; "Legitimation Problems in the Modern State" in J. Habermas, *Communication and the Evolution of Society* (trans. T. McCarthy), Cambridge, MA/London 1979, pp. 178–206; J. Habermas, *Legitimation Crisis* (trans. T. McCarthy), Cambridge, MA/London 1976, especially part III: "On the Logic of Legitimation Problems."

2. See on this point also K.-O. Apel, "The *apriori* of the communication community and the foundations of ethics" in K.-O. Apel, *Towards a Transformation of Philosophy*, (trans. G. Adey and D. Frisby), London 1980, pp. 225–300. See on this P. Janich/F. Kambartel/J. Mittelstrass, *Wissenschaftstheorie als Wissenschaftskritik*, Frankfurt 1974; P. Lorenzen, "Szientismus versus Dialektik" in F. Kambartel (ed.), *Praktische Philosophie und Konstruktive Wissenschaftstheorie*, Frankfurt 1974.

3. See C. Taylor, "Neutrality in Political Science," in P. Laslett and W. G. Runciman (eds.), *Philosophy, Politics and Society* (Third Series), Oxford 1967, pp. 25–57.

4. See P. Winch, "Understanding a Primitive Society," *American Philosophical Quarterly*, 1, 1964, pp. 307–324.

5. J. Habermas, "Legitimation Problems in the Modern State," op. cit., p. 185.

6. See on this point, the controversy between J. Habermas and R. Spaemann in R. Spaemann, *Zur Kritik der politischen Utopie*, Stuttgart 1977.

7. In my opinion, John R. Silber (in "Procedural Formalism in Kant's Ethics," *Review of Metaphysics*, 18, 2, 1974) has convincingly shown that one can indeed interpret Kant's ethics in the sense of a "procedural formalism." But even if one accepts Silber's

Practical Philosophy and the Theory of Society

interpretation, one cannot view as a coincidence the fact that Kant did not explicitly develop the categorical imperative as the basic principle of a *dialogical* ethics.

8. Arguments of the type described in stylized form in what follows are to be found recently, for instance, in H. Lübbe, "Dezisionismus. Zur Geschichte der politischer Theorie der Entscheidung" in A. Müller (ed.), *Gesellschaftliche Entscheidungsvorgänge,* Basle 1977; H. Lübbe, "Warnung vor Ideologiediskussionen" in H. Baier (ed.), *Freiheit und Sachzwang. Beitrage zu Ehren Helmut Schelskys,* Opladen 1977; [See also, H. Lübbe, "Are Norms Methodically Justifiable? A Reconstruction of Max Weber's Reply," in this volume. Eds.]; R. Spaemann, *Zur Kritik der politischen Utopie,* op. cit., or H. Weinrich, "System, Diskurs, Didaktik und die Diktatur des Sitzfleisches" in K. Eder et al., *Theorie der Gesellschaft oder Sozialtechnologie, Theorie Diskussion, Supplement 1,* Frankfurt 1973.

9. See J. Habermas, "Die Utopie des guten Herrschers. Eine Antwort an R. Spaemann" in *Kultur und Kritik,* Frankfurt 1973, p. 382.

10. See, for instance, H. G. Gadamer, "Replik" in K.-O. Apel et al., *Hermeneutik und Ideologiekritik,* Frankfurt 1971, especially pp. 315f.

11. See on this point, J. Habermas, *Communication and the Evolution of Society,* op. cit.; R. Döbert, *Systemtheorie und die Entwicklung religiöser Deutungssysteme,* Frankfurt 1973; K. Eder, *Die Entstehung staatlich organisierter Gesellschaften,* Frankfurt 1976.

12. See J. Habermas, "Vorbereitende Bemerkungen zu einer Theorie der Kommunikativen Kompetenz," op. cit., pp. 136ff.; J. Habermas, "Wahrheitstheorien," op. cit., pp. 252ff.

13. And, of course, naturally this does not apply to Habermas. For instance, he expresses himself as follows in reply to R. Spaemann: "The consensus theory of truth does indeed justify the truth capacity of practical questions; but at the same time it is fallibilistic because it excludes an external criterion of truth; we can never possess the certainty that an empirical utterance that we make with the intention of a discourse actually satisfies the preconditions for an ideal speech situation" ("Die Utopie des guten Herrschers. Eine Antwort an R. Spaemann" in J. Habermas, *Kultur und Kritik,* op. cit., p. 381). For this reason, I am also not of the view that the hermeneutic objection to Habermas's intentions actually holds. In any case, I am doubtful whether these intentions are capable of being sufficiently expressed through a reconstruction of the concept of truth centering around the concept of the ideal speech situation. The following critical remarks on the concept of the ideal speech situation are to be understood in this sense.

14. The distinction which I have just confronted in no way corresponds to the distinction between "transcendental pragmatics" (Apel) and "universal pragmatics" (Habermas). However, I see the first of the problems referred to (that of the unspecific character of reconstructed basic norms) above all in Apel's position (see especially K.-O. Apel, "Sprechakttheorie und transzendentale Sprachpragmatik zur Frage ethischer Normen" in K.-O. Apel (ed.), *Sprachpragmatik und Philosophie,* Frankfurt 1976). In contrast, Habermas has himself expressed serious reservations concerning the idea of transcendental-pragmatic "ultimate justifications" (see J. Habermas, "What is Universal Pragmatics?" in J. Habermas, *Communication and the Evolution of Society,* op. cit., especially pp. 21ff.).

Afterword

Communicative Ethics and Current Controversies in Practical Philosophy

Seyla Benhabib

The essays in this volume present the first English collection on the program of a "communicative" or "discourse" ethics and document the lively controversy this idea has led to in the last decade. Like the Explanation vs. Understanding controversy, the dispute concerning communicative ethics is informed both by the Anglo-American and Continental traditions of thought and reflects a provocative interaction between the two. Communicative ethics, as formulated by Karl-Otto Apel and Jürgen Habermas, has been influenced by the work of such moral philosophers as Kurt Baier, Alan Gewirth, H. M. Hare, Marcus Singer, and Stephen Toulmin on moral reasoning and universalizability in ethics.[1] Above all, however, it is in John Rawls's neo-Kantian constructivism and Lawrence Kohlberg's cognitive-developmental moral theory that Apel and Habermas have found the most kindred projects of moral philosophy in the Anglo-American world.[2]

The central insight of communicative or discourse ethics derives from modern theories of autonomy and of the social contract, as articulated by John Locke, Jean Jacques Rousseau, and in particular by Immanuel Kant. Only those norms and normative institutional arrangements are valid, it is claimed, which individuals can or would freely consent to as a result of engaging in certain argumentative practices. Apel maintains that such argumentative practices can be described as "an ideal community of communication" (*die ideale Kommunikationsgemeinschaft*), while Habermas calls them "practical discourses."

Both agree, however, that such practices are the only plausible procedure in the light of which we can think of the Kantian principle of "universalizability" in ethics today. Instead of asking what an individual moral agent could or would will, without self-contradiction, to be a universal maxim for all, one asks: what norms or institutions would the members of an ideal or real communication community agree to as representing their common interests after engaging in a special kind of argumentation or conversation? The procedural model of an argumentative praxis replaces the silent thought-experiment enjoined by the Kantian universalizability test.

These essays appear at a point when the mood concerning neo-Kantian, procedural, and formalistic ethical theories on both sides of the ocean is probably best captured by the following statement of Stanley Hauerwas and Alasdair MacIntyre:

This is not the first time that ethics has been fashionable. And history suggests that in those periods when a social order becomes uneasy and even alarmed about the weakening of its moral bonds and the poverty of its moral inheritance and turns for aid to the moral philosopher and theologian, it may not find these disciplines flourishing in such a way as to be able to make available the kind of moral reflection and theory which the culture actually needs. Indeed on occasion it may be that the very causes which have led to the impoverishment of moral experience and the weakening of moral bonds will also themselves have contributed to the formation of a kind of moral theology and philosophy which are unable to provide the needed resources.[3]

If this statement can be viewed as a fairly accurate indication of the *Zeitgeist* concerning ethical theory today, as I believe is the case, then this certainly does not bode well for yet another program of ethical universalism and formalism. Such ethical formalism is considered a part of the Enlightenment project of rationalism and of the political project of liberalism, and it is argued that precisely these intellectual and political legacies are an aspect, if not the main cause, of the contemporary crisis. If communicative or discourse ethics is to be at all credible, therefore, it must be able to meet the kind of challenges posed by MacIntyre and Hauerwas.

In this afterword I would like to acknowledge this challenge and anticipate a set of objections and criticisms which can be pressed against communicative ethics from a standpoint which I will roughly describe as "neo-Aristotelian" and "neo-Hegelian." Since Aristotle's criticism of Plato's theory of the good and of the ideal state in his *Nicomachean Ethics* and *Politics*,[4] and since Hegel's critique of Kantian ethics in his various writings,[5] formalist and universalist ethical theories have been continuously challenged in the name of some concrete historical-ethical community or, in Hegelian language, of some *Sittlichkeit*. In fact, Apel and Habermas admit that one cannot ignore the lessons of Hegel's critique of Kantian morality.[6] Whether they have successfully integrated these lessons into communicative ethics, however, is worth examining more closely.

In recent discussions "neo-Aristotelianism" has been used to refer to three, not always clearly distinguished, strands of social analysis and philosophical argumentation. Particularly in the German context, this term has been identified with a neoconservative social diagnosis of the problems of late-capitalist societies.[7] Such societies are viewed as suffering from a loss of moral and almost civilizational orientation, caused by excessive individualism, libertarianism, and the general temerity of liberalism when faced with the task of establishing fundamental values. Neither capitalist economic and societal modernization nor technological changes are seen as basic causes of the current crisis; instead political liberalism and moral pluralism are regarded as the chief causes of this situation. From Robert Spaemann to Allan Bloom, this position has found vigorous exponents today.

The term "neo-Aristotelian" is also frequently used to designate the position of thinkers like Alasdair MacIntyre, Michael Sandel, Charles Taylor, and Michael Walzer, who lament the decline of moral and political communities in contemporary societies.[8] Unlike the neoconservatives, the "communitarian" neo-Aristotelians are critical of contemporary capitalism and technology. The recovery of "community" need not only or even necessarily mean the recovery of some fundamentalist value-scheme; rather, communities can be reconstituted by the reassertion of democratic control over the runaway megastructures of modern capital and technology. The communitarians share with neoconservatives the belief, however, that the formalist, ahistorical, and individualistic legacies of Enlightenment thinking have been historically implicated in developments which have led to the decline of community as a way of life. Particularly today, they argue, this Enlightenment legacy so constricts our imagination and impoverishes our moral vocabulary that we cannot even conceptualize solutions to the current crisis which would transcend the "rights-entitlement-distributive justice" trinity of political liberalism.

Finally, "neo-Aristotelianism" refers to a hermeneutical philosophical ethics, centered around the Aristotelian understanding of *phronēsis*. Hans-Georg Gadamer was the first to turn to Aristotle's model of *phronēsis* as a form of contextually embedded and situationally sensitive judgment of particulars.[9] Gadamer so powerfully synthesized Aristotle's ethical theory and Hegel's critique of Kant that after his work the two strands of argumentation became almost indistinguishable. From Aristotle's critique of Plato, Gadamer extricated the model of a situationally sensitive practical reason, always functioning against the background of the shared ethical understanding of a community.[10] From Hegel's critique of Kant, Gadamer borrowed the insight that all formalism presupposes a context that it abstracts from and that there is no formal ethics which does not have some material presuppositions concerning the self and social institutions.[11] Just as there can be no understanding which is not situated in some historical context, so there can be no "moral standpoint" which would not be dependent upon a shared ethos, be it that of the modern state. The Kantian moral point of view is only intelligible in light of the revolutions of modernity and the establishment of freedom as a principle of the modern world.

These three strands of a neoconservative social diagnosis, a politics of community, and a philosophical ethics of a historically informed practical reason, form the core elements of the contemporary neo-Aristotelian position. Here I shall be concerned with neo-Aristotelianism less as a social diagnosis or as a political philosophy but more as a philosophical ethics.

Let me now formulate a series of objections to communicative ethics. Some version of these has been voiced by thinkers inspired by Aristotle and Hegel against Kantian-type ethical theories at some point or another. My goal will be to show that these objections have not succeeded in delivering a *coup de grâce* (a blow of mercy) to a dialogically reformulated universalist ethical theory. A serious exchange between such a universalist ethical theory, which suffers neither from the methodological individualism nor from the ahistoricism of traditional Kantian ethics, and a hermeneutically inspired neo-Aristotelianism can lead us to see that some traditional oppositions and exclusions in moral philosophy are no longer convincing. Such oppositions as between universalism and historicity, an ethics of principle and judgment in context, or ethical cognition and moral motivation, within the confines of which much recent discussion has run, are no longer compelling. Just as it is not the case that there can be no historically informed ethical universalism, it is equally not the case that all neo-Aristotelianism must defend a conservative theory of communal ethics. Here I am concerned to indicate how such false oppositions can be transformed into a more fruitful set of contentions between two types of ethical theorizing which have marked the Western philosophical tradition since its beginnings in Socrates's challenge to the Sophists and his condemnation to death by the city of Athens.

1 Skepticism Toward the Principle of Universalizability. Is it at Best Inconsistent and at Worst Empty?

Hegel had criticized the Kantian formula, "Act only on that maxim through which you can at the same time will that it should become a universal law," on numerous occasions as being inconsistent at best and empty at worst.[12] Hegel argued that the test alone whether or not a maxim could be universalized could not determine its moral rightness. As he pointed out in his early essay on *Natural Law*, whether or not I should return deposits entrusted to me is answered in the affirmative by Kant with the argument that it would be self-contradictory to will that deposits should not exist. The young Hegel answers that there is no contradiction in willing a situation in which deposits and property do not exist, unless of course we make some other assumptions about human needs, scarce resources, distributive justice, and the like. Out of the pure form of the moral law alone, no concrete maxims of action can follow and if they do, it is because other unidentified premises have been smuggled into the argument.[13]

In view of this Hegelian critique, which continues to influence discussions of Kantian ethics even today,[14] the response of Kantian moral theorists has been twofold: first, some have accepted Hegel's critique that the formal procedure of universalizability can yield no determinate test of the rightness of maxims; they admit that one must presuppose some minimally shared conception of human goods and desires as goals of action, and must test principles of action against this background. This line of response has weakened the Kantian distinction between autonomy and heteronomy by accepting that the goals of action may be dictated by contingent features of human nature rather than by the dictates of pure practical reason alone. John Rawls's list of "basic goods," which rational agents are supposed to want whatever else they also want, is the best example of the introduction of material assumptions about human desires into the universalizability argument. The test of universalizability is not about whether we want these goods but rather about the moral principles guiding their eventual distribution.[15] Other Kantian moral philosophers, and most notably among them, Onora O'Neill and Alan Gewirth, have refused to jettison the pure Kantian program, and have attempted to expand the principle of the noncontradiction of maxims by looking more closely at the *formal features of rational action*. O'Neill, for example, distinguishes between "conceptual inconsistency" and "volitional inconsistency" in order to differentiate among types of incoherence in action.[16] "The nonuniversalized maxim," she writes, "embodies a conceptual contradiction only if it *aims* at achieving mutually incompatible objectives and so cannot under any circumstances be acted on with success."[17] Volitional inconsistency, by contrast, occurs when a rational agent violates what O'Neill names "Principles of Rational Intending."[18] Applying universalizability to maxims of action both to test their conceptual consistency and their volitional consistency avoids, according to O'Neill, "the dismal choice between triviality and implausible rigorism."[19] In a similar vein, Alan Gewirth expands on the idea of the "rational conditions of action" in such a way as to generate nontrivial and intersubjectively binding maxims of moral action from these.[20]

Both strategies have problems: in the first case, by allowing material presuppositions about human nature and desires into the picture, one runs the risk of weakening the distinction between Kantian and other types of utilitarian or Aristotelian moral theories. The result is a certain eclecticism in the structure of the theory. The second position runs a different danger: by focusing exclusively on the conditions of rational intending or acting, as O'Neill and Gewirth do, one can lose sight of the question of intersubjective moral validity. After all, the Kantian principle of universalizability is formulated in order to generate morally binding maxims of action which all can recognize. As Alasdair MacIntyre shows in his sharp critique of Gewirth, from the premise that I as a rational agent require certain conditions of action to be fulfilled, it can never follow that you have an *obligation* not to hinder me from enjoying these conditions.[21] The grounds for this obligation are left unclear; but it was precisely such grounds that the universalizability requirement was intended to produce. Put in terms which are those of Apel and Habermas, the analysis of the rational structure of action for a single agent produces an *egological* moral theory which cannot justify intersubjective moral validity. Instead of asking what I as a single rational moral agent can intend or will to be a universal maxim for all without contradiction, the communicative ethicist asks: what principles of action can we all recognize or agree to as being valid if we engage in practical discourse or a mutual search for justification?

With this reformulation, universalizability is defined as an intersubjective procedure of argumentation, geared to attain communicative agreement. This reformulation brings with it several significant shifts: instead of thinking of universalizability as a test of *noncontradiction,* we think of universalizability as a test of *communicative agreement.* We do not search for what would be nonself-contradictory but rather for what would be mutually acceptable for all. Furthermore, there is also a shift from the model of the goal-oriented or strategic action of a single agent intending a specific outcome to the model of *communicative action* which is speech and action to be shared with others.

What has been gained through this reformulation such as to counter the Hegelian objection? Have we not simply pushed the problem from one procedure onto another? Instead of deriving moral principles from some procedure of conceptual or volitional coherence, do we not simply derive them now from our definition of the conversational situation? Theorists can construct or design conversations to yield certain outcomes: the preconditions of conversation may guarantee that certain outcomes will result.[22] In an earlier article I formulated this problem as follows: either models of practical discourse or the ideal communication community are defined so minimally as to be trivial in their implications or there are more controversial substantive premises guiding their design, and which do not belong among the minimal conditions defining the argumentation situation, in which case they are inconsistent.[23] We are back to the "dismal choice" (O'Neill) between triviality or inconsistency.

I now believe that the way out of this dilemma is to opt for a strong and possibly controversial construction of the conversational model which would nonetheless be able to avoid the charges of dogmatism and/or circularity.[24] My thinking is as follows: what Habermas has previously named the conditions of an "ideal speech situation," and which in the essay "Discourse Ethics: Notes on a Program of Philosophical Justification" are called the "universal and necessary communicative presuppositions of argumentative speech,"[25] entail, in my opinion, strong ethical assumptions. They require of us: (1) that we recognize the right of all beings capable of speech and action to be participants in the moral conversation—I will call this the *principle of universal moral respect;* (2) these conditions further stipulate that within such conversations each has the same symmetrical rights to various speech acts, to initiate new topics, to ask for reflection about the presuppositions of the conversation, etc. Let me call this *the principle of egalitarian reciprocity.* The very presuppositions of the argumentation situation then have a normative content that precedes the moral argument itself. But can one then really avoid the charges of circularity and dogmatism?

One of the central disagreements between Apel and Habermas concerns precisely this issue of the justification of the constraints of the moral conversation. Apel maintains that:

> If, on the one hand, a presupposition cannot be challenged in argumentation without actual performative self-contradiction, and if, on the other hand, it cannot be deductively grounded without formal-logical *petitio principii*, then it belongs to those transcendental-pragmatic presuppositions of argumentation that one must always (already) have accepted, if the language game of argumentation is to be meaningful.[26]

For Apel, the principle that all beings capable of speech and action are potential members of the same communication community with me, and that they deserve equal and symmetrical treatment are two such conditions.

In view of this Apelian strategy of fundamental grounding or *Letztbegründung*, Habermas argues that such a strong justification of communicative ethics cannot succeed and may not even be necessary. Rather than viewing the normative constraints of the ideal communication community as being "disclosable" via an act of transcendental self-reflection, Habermas argues that we view them as "universal pragmatic presuppositions" of speech acts corresponding to the know-how of competent "moral" agents at the postconventional stage. But as Thomas McCarthy has pointed out there is no univocal description of the "know-how" of moral actors who have reached the postconventional stage of moral reasoning.[27] Habermas's description of this know-how is one among many others like those of John Rawls and Lawrence Kohlberg. At the stage of postconventional moral reasoning, reversibility, universalizability, and impartiality, under some description, are all aspects of the moral point of view, but the real point of philosophical contention is the acceptable or adequate description of these formal constraints. The appeal to moral psychology and development brings no exemption from the justificatory process. Lawrence Kohlberg was wrong in thinking that the "ought" can be deduced from the "is." The formal structure of postconventional moral reasoning allows a number of substantive moral interpretations, and these interpretations always take place by presupposing a hermeneutic horizon.

As opposed to Apel's strategy of *Letztbegründung* and Habermas's strategy of a "weak transcendental argument," based on the rational reconstruction of competencies, I would like to plead for a "historically self-conscious universalism." The principles of universal respect and egalitarian reciprocity are our philosophical clarification of the constituents of the moral point of view from within the normative hermeneutic horizon of modernity. These principles are neither the *only allowable* interpretation of the formal constituents of the competency of postconventional moral actors nor are they unequivocal transcendental presuppositions which every rational agent, upon deep reflection, must concede to. These principles are arrived at by a process of "reflective equilibrium" in Rawlsian terms, whereby one, as a philosopher, analyzes, refines, and judges culturally defined moral intuitions in light of articulated philosophical principles. What one arrives at the end of such a process of reflective equilibrium is a "thick description" of the moral presuppositions of the cultural horizon of modernity.

At one level, of course, the intuitive idea behind universalistic ethics is very ancient, and corresponds to the "Golden Rule" of the tradition—"Do unto others as you would have others do unto you." Universalizability enjoins that we reverse perspectives among members of a "moral community"; it asks us to judge from the other's point of view. Such reversibility is essential to the ties of reciprocity that bind human communities together. All human communities define some "significant others" in relation to which reversibility and reciprocity must be exercised—be they members of my kin group, my tribe, my city-state, my nation, my coreligionists. What distinguishes "modern" from "premodern" versions of universalistic ethical theories is the assumption of the former that the moral community is coextensive with all beings capable of speech and action, and potentially with all of humanity. In this sense, communicative ethics sets up a model of moral conversation among members of a modern ethical community, for whom the theological and ontological basis of the inequality among humans has been radically placed into question.

This is not an admission of dogmatism in favor of modernity, for even this "dogma" of modernity, if you wish, can be challenged within the moral conversation itself. The racist, the sexist, or the bigot can challenge the principle of universal moral respect and egalitarian reciprocity within the moral conversation, but if they want to establish that their position is right not simply because it is mighty, they must convince with argument that this is so. The presuppositions of the moral conversation can be challenged within the conversation itself, but if they are altogether suspended or violated then might, violence, coercion, and suppression follow. One thus avoids the charge of circularity: by allowing that the presuppositions of the moral conversation can be challenged within the conversation itself, they are placed within the purview of questioning. But insofar as they are pragmatic rules necessary to keep the moral conversation going, we can only bracket them in order to challenge them but we cannot suspend them altogether. The shoe is really on the other foot. It is up to the critic of such egalitarian universalism to show, with good grounds, why some individuals should be effectively excluded from the moral conversation.

Of course, our moral and political world is more characterized by struggles unto death among moral opponents than by a conversation among them. This admission reveals the fragility of the moral point of view in a world of power and violence, but this is not an admission of irrelevance. Political ideologies as well as more subtle forms of cultural hegemony have always sought to make plausible the continuation of violence and power to those who most suffered from their consequences. When such ideology and hegemony no longer serve to justify such relations, then struggles unto death for moral recognition can follow. As a critical social theorist, the philosopher is concerned with the unmasking of such mechanisms of continuing political ideology and cultural hegemony; as a moral theorist, the philosopher, has one central task: to clarify and justify those normative standards in the light of which such social criticism is exercised.[28]

Let us return once more to the Hegelian objection: can a universalist ethical theory, which views universalizability in ethics as a moral conversation governed by certain procedural constraints, avoid the "dismal choice" (O'Neill) between triviality or inconsistency? Hegel's critique assumes but does not clarify a distinction between universalizability as a procedure for testing and universalizability as a procedure for generating maxims. As a procedure for testing the intersubjective validity of moral principles and norms of action, communicative ethics is neither trivial nor inconsistent; as a procedure for *generating* valid principles of action, the model of moral conversation is a necessary but insufficient test case that requires, in any given instance, adequate contextualization. In other words, we can say of a course of action, the principle of which has passed the test of conversational universalizability, that it is morally permissible, but also assert that it was the wrong thing to do under the circumstances. The universalizability test should produce standards of what is morally permissible and impermissible in general; however, such tests are by no means sufficient to establish what is morally meritorious in any given context.

Habermas formulates the test of universalizability thus:

... unless the consequences and side effects which the general observance of a controversial norm can be expected to have for the satisfaction of the interests of *each individual* can be *freely* accepted by all.[29]

What we are asking is not whether from this procedure the moral theorist can deduce concrete moral principles guiding action. The adoption of "all contents," writes Habermas, "no matter how fundamental the action norm involved may be, must be made dependent on real discourses (or advocatory discourses conducted as substitutes for them.)"

Even if this principle of universalizability is not intended to generate concrete principles or norms of action, can it serve as a test procedure for determining what is morally permissible and impermissible? As a test procedure "U" enjoins us to engage in a counterfactual thought-experiment in which we enter into conversation with all who would be potentially affected by our actions. Let us consider some standard moral maxims to assess what has been gained by this reformulation. Take the example used by Kant, "deposits once made must be returned for otherwise there would be no property." The relevant question is: does the principle "there ought to be property" satisfy the test that "the consequences and side effects which the general observance of a controversial norm can be expected to have for the satisfaction of the interests of *each individual* be *freely* accepted by all?" The answer is that both the existence of property relations and its opposite can be adopted as a collective maxim of their actions by moral actors, if the consequences of such arrangements for the satisfaction of the interests of each can be freely accepted by all. In other words, the existence or nonexistence of property relations cannot be determined via a moral deduction. Contrary to what Kant assumed, as long as they serve the satisfaction of the interests of each individual and this can be freely accepted by all, numerous forms of property arrangements are morally permissible. Kant was wrong in attempting to generate a categorical imperative to uphold property relations; what is at stake is not property as such but other moral values like general welfare and the correct mode of dispensing of scarce resources. To this extent, the universalizability procedure in communicative ethics upholds Hegel's critique of Kant.

Yet, as formulated by Habermas, "U" also leads to morally disturbing and counterintuitive consequences. Take the maxim, "Do not inflict unnecessary suffering." Whether or not we are to inflict unnecessary suffering is to be determined by whether the consequences and side effects which the general observance of a controversial norm can be expected to have for the satisfaction of the interests of each individual can be freely accepted by all. Can we imagine a situation in which it would be in the interests of each individual and freely accepted by them that they would be not only perpetrators but receivers of unnecessary suffering? The answer to this question appears to depend on an equivocation concerning "interests." Suppose there are masochists and sadists among us who interpret their interests as consisting precisely in the opportunity to inflict and receive such suffering. Are we ready to say that under these conditions *Neminem laede* ceases to be a morally valid principle?

In other words, what appears to be the virtue of "U" in the property example, i.e., its indeterminacy, is its weakness in the second case. But the least that a universalist ethical theory ought to do is to cover the same ground as what Kant had described as "negative duties," i.e., duties not to violate the rights of humanity in oneself and in others. Yet "U" does not appear to do this.

I believe the difficulty is that Habermas has given "U" such a *consequentialist* formulation that his theory is now subject to the kinds of arguments that deontological rights theorists have always successfully brought against utilitarians. Without some stronger constraints about how we are to interpret "U," we run the risk of regressing behind the achievements of Kant's moral philosophy. The categorical imperative proves as morally impermissible what Kant names "negative duties": not to lie, not to harm, not to cheat, or otherwise violate the dignity of the human moral person. Positive moral duties cannot be deduced from the universalizability test alone but require contextual moral judgment in their concretization.[30] I have suggested above that the communicative ethics version of "U" must likewise deliver criteria for distinguishing among the morally permissible and the morally impermissible; nonetheless, this distinction alone does not yield adequate criteria of the morally right or virtuous or appropriate action under concrete circumstance.

Albrecht Wellmer, Agnes Heller, and Otfried Höffe have all recently expressed stronger criticisms of communicative ethics: even as a test procedure for what is intersubjectively permissible, "U," they argue, is either too indeterminate or too complex or too counterfactual. In Heller's sharp formulation: "Put bluntly, if we look to moral philosophy for guidance in our actions here and now, we cannot obtain any positive guidance from the Habermasian version of the categorical imperative. Rather, what we could get is a *substantive limitation* placed on our intellectual intuitions: we, as individuals, should only claim universal validity for those moral norms which we can assume would be accepted by everyone as valid in an ideal situation of symmetric reciprocity."[31] Albrecht Wellmer writes: "If we interpret 'U' as an explication of our preunderstanding of moral validity, then this means that in our moral convictions and in our moral judgments, only such judgments must be involved that the consequences and side effects which the general observance of a specific norm would have for each individual could be *freely* (*zwangslos*) accepted by all. This, however, so it appears to me, would make justified moral judgment a total chimera (*ein Ding der Unmöglichkeit*)."[32]

Heller argues that the Habermasian theory cannot be saved for it is in effect a theory of "legitimation rather than one of validation."[33] Wellmer recommends that we interpret the ideals of "rational consent" or "agreement" as regulative principles, but that in the solution of *real* moral problems under real moral *conditions,* we can "only think of what the reasonable person or those competent judges or those affected by our actions *would* say if they were sufficiently reasonable, good willing and competent in judgment."[34] I think Wellmer's response weakens the distinction between justification and contextualization. While I agree that such contextualization is absolutely crucial for *moral* judgment in real situations, I think his response makes the test of the validity of moral judgment a matter of *phronēsis* alone. I am interested in seeing whether there is anything at all, any guidelines, in the procedure of discourse ethics that could place a "substantive limitation on our intellectual intuition," in the way of necessary but insufficient criteria. Heller considers the placing of such limitations alone too minimal an achievement for moral theory. In my opinion, however, it would be quite sufficient for a universalist moral theory which is self-conscious about the historical horizon of modernity within which it is situated, if it succeeded in placing such a substantive limitation on our intuitions.

I want to suggest that "U" is actually redundant in Habermas's theory and that it adds little but consequentialist confusion to the basic premise of discourse ethics. "D" states that only those norms can claim to be valid that meet (or could meet) with the approval of all concerned in their capacity as participants in a practical discourse. "D," together with those rules of argument governing discourses, and the normative content of which I summarized as the principles of universal moral respect and egalitarian reciprocity, are in my view quite adequate to serve as the only universalizability test.

The chief difference between my proposal and Habermas's is that for him "U" has the effect of guaranteeing consensus. Without having their interests violated, all could freely consent to some moral content. But the difficulty with consent theories is as old as Rousseau's dictum—"On les forcera d'être libre." Consent alone can never be a criterion of anything, neither of truth nor of moral validity; rather, it is always the rationality of the procedure for attaining agreement which is of philosophical interest. We must interpret consent not as an end-goal but as a process for the cooperative generation of truth or validity. The core intuition behind modern universalizability procedures is not that everybody could or would agree to the same set of principles, but that these principles have been adopted as a result of a procedure, whether of moral reasoning or of public debate, which we are ready to deem "reasonable and fair." It is not the *result* of the process of moral judgment alone that counts but the process for the attainment of such judgment which plays a role in its validity and, I would say, moral worth. Consent is a misleading term for capturing the core idea behind communicative ethics: namely, the processual generation of reasonable agreement about moral principles via an open-ended moral conversation. It is my claim that this core intuition, together with an interpretation of the normative constraints of argument in light of the principles of universal respect and egalitarian reciprocity, are sufficient to accomplish what "U" was intended to accomplish, but only at the price of consequentialist confusion.

Let us return once more to the principle, "Do not inflict unnecessary suffering" to test this claim.[35] According to my formula, we are to imagine whether if I and all those whose actions would affect me and by whose actions I would be affected were to engage in a moral conversation, governed by the procedural constraints of universal respect and egalitarian reciprocity, we could adopt this as a principle of action. By adopting the infliction of unnecessary suffering as a norm of action, however, we would in effect be undermining the very idea of a moral dialogue in the first place. But it would be absurd to want to adopt as valid or correct a principle of action—the infliction of arbitrary suffering—such as would impair or jeopardize the very possibility of an ongoing conversation among us. Since such ongoing moral conversation involves sustaining relations of universal respect and egalitarian reciprocity, if we all were to engage in the infliction of unnecessary suffering among ourselves we would undermine the very basis of our ongoing moral relationship. In this sense, universalizability is not only a *formal procedure* but involves the utopian projection of a way of life as well.

There is an interesting consequence here: when we shift the burden of the moral test in communicative ethics from consensus to the idea of an ongoing moral conversation, we begin to ask not what all would or could agree to as a result of practical discourses to be morally permissible or impermissible, but what would be allowed and perhaps even necessary from the standpoint of continuing and sustaining the practice of the moral conversation among us. The emphasis now is less on *rational agreement,* but more on sustaining those normative practices and moral relationships within which reasoned agreement *as a way of life* can flourish and continue.

2 The Right and the Good

Sympathetic critics of communicative ethics have persistently pointed out that this project formulates more a model of *political legitimacy* than one of *moral validity*. To ask whether certain normative institutional arrangements would or could be freely adopted by all as being in their common interests, it is argued, is precisely to continue the central idea of the modern natural right and social contract traditions from Locke and Rousseau to Kant.[36] While many agree that such a principle of rational consent is fundamental to the modern ideas of democratic legitimacy and justice, equally many contest that it can serve as a moral procedure that would be relevant in guiding individual action and judgment.

I have argued above that on my interpretation, the basic principle of discourse ethics together with the normative constraints of argumentation can serve as "substantive tests" of our moral intuitions. Furthermore, if we do not want to jettison the distinction between *contextualization* and *justification* in ethics altogether, we can still preserve the model of a moral conversation taking place under the constraints of discourse as a limiting test for our intuitions of the morally permissible and impermissible. Clearly then whether discourse ethics is a model of legitimacy or one of moral validity will depend on what implications and usefulness we think this model has for guiding individual moral action and judgment. Precisely because I think that it can have such implications when interpreted properly, I also want to suggest that, at this stage of the debate, the critics' arguments are not convincing.

Whereas some critics of discourse ethics want to regard it as a program of political legitimacy rather than as one of moral validity, others of a more neo-Aristotelian persuasion argue that no principles of legitimacy can be formulated without presupposing some substantive theory of the good life. Quite in line with Hegel's critique of Kant, these contemporary Aristotelians and especially communitarian critics of liberalism maintain that the very idea of a *minimal-universalist* ethic, which would be supposedly "neutral" vis-à-vis the multiplicity of ethical life-forms, is untenable. Charles Taylor's objections to communicative ethics have followed this line of argument.[37] I want to name this the issue of the "right" vs. the "good."

From the outset, however, we must distinguish between the liberal-communitarian version of this controversy on the one hand, and the controversy as it applies to communicative ethics on the other. The first controversy concerns whether liberal principles of justice, as formulated by John Rawls and Ronald Dworkin in particular, are "neutral," in the sense of allowing the coexistence of many forms of life in the polity, or whether these principles both presuppose and privilege a specific way of life—let us say an individualist one, centered around the virtues of the rule of law at the expense of solidarity, of privacy at the expense of community, and of justice at the expense of friendship. While liberals continue to aspire to such neutrality, communitarians insist on the illusory quality of their search.[38]

This debate between liberals and communitarians cannot be simply extended to communicative ethics, for the obvious reason that neither Apel nor Habermas have developed a normative theory of justice out of communicative ethics, although communicative ethics has definite institutional implications (see section 3 below). When applied to communicative ethics, the issue of the "right" vs. the "good" concerns not so much the alleged neutrality or non-neutrality of principles of justice, as it does the very basis of the distinction between "justice" and the "good life" within ethical theory itself.

The defense of a deontological outlook in Habermas's theory takes a different form than what we encounter in Rawl's *Theory of Justice*.[39] Whereas Rawls distinguishes between justice as the basic virtue of a social system and the domain of moral theory at large in which a full theory of the good is at work,[40] Habermas is committed to the stronger claim that after the transition to modernity and the destruction of the teleological worldview, moral theory in fact can only be deontological and must focus on questions of justice. Following Kohlberg, he insists that this is not merely a historically contingent evolution, but that "judgments of justice" do indeed constitute the hard core of all moral judgments. Habermas writes: "Such an ethic . . . stylizes questions of the good life, and of the good life together into *questions of justice,* in order to render practical questions accessible to cognitive processing by way of this abstraction."[41] It is not that deontology describes a kind of moral theory juxtaposed to a teleological one; for Habermas, deontological judgments about justice and rights claims define the moral domain insofar as we can say anything cognitively meaningful about this.

How can we in fact defend the thesis that judgments of justice and right constitute *the moral domain?* I can see two distinct arguments in Habermas's work on this issue. First, Habermas assumes that only judgments of justice possess a clearly discernible formal structure and thus can be studied along an evolutionary model.[42] Judgments concerning the good life are amorphous and do not lend themselves to the same kind of formal study. But of course this observation, far from justifying the restriction of the moral domain to matters of justice, could also lead to the conclusion that one needed to develop a less formalistic ethical theory. This is a view which has been successfully defended by Bernard Williams in his

Ethics and the Limits of Philosophy and by Charles Taylor in various articles.[43]

Second, Habermas maintains that the evolution of judgments of justice is intimately tied to the evolution of self-other relations. Judgments of justice reflect various conceptions of self-other relations, which is to say, that the formation of self-identity and moral judgments concerning justice are intimately linked. This is because justice is the social virtue par excellence.[44]

Again, however, it can be objected that the evolution of self-other relations must also be accompanied by the development of self-understanding and self-evaluation, and if justice is the sum of *other-regarding* virtues par excellence, this still does not preclude the consideration of *self-regarding* virtues and their significance for moral theory. If one understands Habermas's defense of deontological ethics as a claim concerning the *appropriate object domain* of moral theory, then I can see no plausible arguments in favor of such a restrictive view of what moral theory can hope to accomplish.

I concur then with communitarian critics of deontology like Bernard Williams, Charles Taylor, and Michael Sandel only to the extent that viewing justice as the center of morality unnecessarily restricts the domain of moral theory, thus distorting the nature of our moral experiences. But a universalist and communicative model of ethics need not be so strongly construed. Such a theory can be understood as defending a "weak" deontology; this means that valid moral norms must be able to stand the test of discursive justification. Since practical discourses do not theoretically predefine the domain of moral debate and since individuals do not have to abstract from their everyday attachments and beliefs when they begin argumentation, however, we can accept that not only matters of justice but those of the good life as well will become thematized in practical discourses. A model of communicative ethics, which views moral theory as a theory of argumentation, need not restrict itself to questions of justice. I see no reason as to why questions of the good life as well cannot become subject matters of practical discourses. It may very well be that discourses will not yield conceptions of the good life equally acceptable to all;

yet there is a difference between assuming a priori that certain matters are questions of the good life and therefore inappropriate matters of moral argument, and between assuming that a moral community will establish a line between individual conceptions of the good to be pursued freely and shared norms and values to be cultivated collectively. It is crucial that we view our conceptions of the good life as matters about which intersubjective debate is possible, even if intersubjective consensus, let alone legislation, in these areas remains undesirable. However, only through such argumentative processes can we draw the line between issues of justice and of the good life in an epistemically plausible manner, while rendering our conceptions of the good life accessible to moral reflection and moral transformation.

Of course, this is a far weaker result than may be preferred by a strong teleologist like Alasdair MacIntyre but it remains for such a teleologist to show that under conditions of modernity one can indeed formulate and defend a univocal conception of the human good. So far Habermas is right: under conditions of modernity and subsequent to the differentiation of the value spheres of science, aesthetics, jurisprudence, religion, and morals we can no longer formulate an overarching vision of the human good. Indeed, as Alasdair MacIntyre's definition of the good life, namely, "the life spent in seeking the good life for man"[45] very well reveals, as moderns we have to live with varieties of goodness. Whether the good life is to be fulfilled as an African famine relief fighter, a Warsaw ghetto resistant, a Mother Teresa, or a Rosa Luxemburg ethical theory cannot prejudge; at the most modern moral theory provides us with some very general criteria by which to assess our intuitions about the basic validity of certain courses of action and the integrity of certain kinds of values. I regard neither the plurality and variety of goodness with which we have to live in a disenchanted universe nor the loss of certainty in moral theory to be a cause of distress. Under conditions of value differentiation we have to conceive of reason not in the image of a homogeneous, transparent glass sphere into which we can fit all our cognitive and value commitments, but more as the light shed by bits and pieces of dispersed crystals whose contours shine out from under the rubble.

3 On the Distinction Between Justice, Morality, and Politics

The neo-Aristotelian and neo-Hegelian insistence on the centrality of a shared ethos or of a concrete *Sittlichkeit* in the conceptualization and resolution of moral questions, has unavoidable implications in the domain of political action as well. If this shared ethos and this *Sittlichkeit* are viewed not primarily as the unavoidable hermeneutical horizon over and against which moral questions and problems can be formulated, but if they are considered the normative standard in light of which to assess individual actions, then morality becomes subordinated to the collective ethos of a community.

As the young Hegel wistfully wrote of the polis,

As freemen the Greeks and Romans obeyed laws laid down by themselves, obeyed men whom they had themselves appointed to office, waged wars on which they had themselves decided, gave their property, exhausted their passions, and sacrificed their lives by thousands for an end which was their own ... In public as in private and domestic life, every individual was a free man, one who lived by his own laws. The idea (*Idee*) of his country or of his state was the invisible and higher reality for which he strove, which impelled him to effort; it was the final end of *his* world or in his eyes the final end of *the* world, an end which he found manifested in the realities of his daily life or which he himself cooperated in manifesting and maintaining.[46]

Undoubtedly, this idealization of the Greek polis has to be viewed today more in light of German romantic attitudes toward Greek antiquity than judged as a historically accurate depiction of Greek society. As the mature Hegel himself recognized, the rights of subjective welfare and conscience are among the constituents of the moral freedom of the individual, and the individuals' pursuits of various conceptions of the good can never be wholly integrated within a concrete ethical totality. The split of ethical life into the family, civil society, and the state under conditions of modernity also means that potentially the dictates of individual conscience and welfare on the one hand and the claims of institutions, like the family, market, and the state, can always clash. In a famous passage of the *Philosophy of Right* Hegel defended the rights of Anabaptists and Quakers to refuse military service in the modern state on the grounds that the state is strong enough to allow for dissent without crumbling in the face of it.[47] However, both in his theory of representative institutions and even more so in his reflections on war and world history, Hegel made the "self-preservation" of the universal the *normative* goal to which morality had to be subordinated. Politics, understood as the sphere governed by the dictates of the self-preservation and the welfare of collectivities, is juxtaposed by the mature Hegel to the "abstract cosmopolitanism" and "universalism" of Kantian ethics.

In contemporary debates one can recognize this Hegelian antecedent in two charges which are frequently leveled against communicative ethics. First, communicative ethics is said to lead to anti-institutionalist and fundamentally anarchistic consequences in political life[48]; second, communicative ethics is said to be "moralistic" to the point of complete utopianism in the domain of politics. Imagine conducting a practical discourse on matters of international relations, state security, maybe even banking and fiscal policy under the constraints of an ideal speech situation! The strategic and instrumental relation of the parties to each other is so fundamentally constitutive of these macroinstitutions of political life that the kind of moralistic utopianism advocated by partisans of discourse ethics, so argues the political realist, would only result in confusion and insecurity. In the domain of politics realism, enlightened by an ethics of responsibility, in the Weberian sense, is the best approach (see Herman Lübbe's essay in this volume).

In the face of the charge of anti-institutionalism it must be said that the discourse ethics is not a theory of institutions, although it has institutional implications. Whether we interpret them as principles of legitimacy or as principles of moral validity neither "D" nor "U" can yield a concrete theory of institutions, but they have institutional implications.[49] Institutionalist thinkers like Lübbe and Niklas Luhmann maintain that upholding any concrete institutions to the demands of such rational consensus would make life impossible. Within the constraints of institutions, decision procedures, limited by space and time and scarce resources, must be respected. To hope for the rational consensus of all under these circumstances would paralyze institutional life to the point of a breakdown.

This objection is justified, but it confuses levels: the discourse theory does not develop a positive model of functioning institutions, which after all will always be subject to time-space constraints as well as to those of scarce resources and personnel. The discourse theory develops a normative and critical criterion by which to judge existing institutional arrangements, insofar as these current arrangements suppress a "generalizable interest." This appeal to the "suppressed generalizable interest" need not be read along Rousseauian lines.[50] In complex societies, it is doubtful that there could be a definition and specification of the suppressed generalizable interest which would meet with the consent of all. But one can use this criterion as a critical yardstick by which to uncover the under-representation, the exclusion and silencing of *certain kinds* of interests. In other words, it is not so much the identification of the "general interest" which is at stake, as the uncovering of those partial interests which represent themselves as if they were general. The assumption is that institutions can function as channels of illegitimate exclusion and silencing, and the task of a critical discourse theory is to develop a moral presumption in favor of the radical democratization of such processes.

What institutionalists neglect is that power is not only a social resource to be distributed, say like bread or automobiles. It is also a sociocultural grid of interpretation and communication. Public dialogue is not external to but constitutive of power relations: paraphrasing Nancy Fraser, there are officially recognized vocabularies in which one can press claims; idioms for interpreting and communicating one's needs; established narrative conventions for constructing individual and collective identities; paradigms of argumentation accepted as authoritative in adjudicating conflicting claims; the repertory of available rhetorical devices, and the like.[51] These constitute the "metapolitics of institutional dialogue," and as a critical theorist, one is interested in identifying those social relations, power structures, and sociocultural grids of communication and interpretation at the present which limit the identity of the parties to the dialogue, which set the agenda for what is considered appropriate or inappropriate matter for institutional debate, and which sanctify the speech of some over those of others as being the language of the public.

Certainly this is not the only point of view from which to understand and evaluate institutions: justice, efficiency, stability, and predictability are also relevant criteria. To assume though that all discourses of legitimacy are counterproductive or anarchistic is to disguise political authoritarianism as a post-Enlightenment critique of the Enlightenment.

In his essay, "Is the Ideal Communication Community a Utopia?," Karl Otto-Apel deals extensively with the question of the utopian content and implications of communicative ethics (in this volume). In his view, it would be utopian in the negative sense of extreme irrelevance to demand that all instances of strategic action, whether individual or collective, be governed by the norms of communicative action, aimed at achieving mutual understanding and reciprocity. Nonetheless, it is both a moral and a political question to ask what the limits of individual and collective strategic action are, and to reflect on how to mediate between the requirements of self-interest on the one hand and the moral principles of mutual and cooperative understanding on the other. Once we restate the problem in this fashion, a whole range of interesting considerations begin to emerge. The stark opposition between political utopianism and political realism is softened. Communicative ethics anticipates nonviolent strategies of conflict resolution as well as encouraging cooperative and associative methods of problem solving. It is a matter of political imagination as well as collective fantasy to project institutions, practices, and ways of life which promote nonviolent conflict resolution strategies and associative problem solving methods. Far from being utopian in the sense of being irrelevant, in a world of complete interdependence among peoples and nations, in which the alternatives are between nonviolent collaboration and nuclear annihilation, communicative ethics may supply our minds with just the right dose of fantasy such as to think beyond the old oppositions of utopia or realism, containment or conflict. Then, as today, we still can say, "L'imagination au pouvoir"!

4 On The Problem of Moral Motivation and Character

A major weakness of cognitive and proceduralist ethical theories since Kant has been their reductionist treatment of the emotional and affective bases of moral judgment and conduct. Twentieth-century neo-Kantian ethical theories have by and large rejected Kant's dualistic moral psychology, and his repressive treatment of sensuality and the emotions, all the while retaining the distinction between "action done from the motive of duty" and "self-regarding actions." Nevertheless, this rejection of the Kantian treatment of the emotional and affective basis of ethics has not meant paying renewed attention to these issues. In recent years, it has been philosophers like Amelie Rorty, Martha Nussbaum, Annette Baier, and Lawrence Blum on this side of the ocean and Ursula Wolff in Germany, as well as feminist moral theorists like Virginia Held and Sara Ruddick, who have developed a rich and significant body of work, analyzing moral emotions and moral character.[52] Does the neglect of these issues by advocates of communicative ethics so far point not just to a weak spot in the theory but maybe to a blind spot altogether?

I would like to suggest that very often ethical cognitivism has been confused with ethical rationalism, and the neglect of the affective and emotive bases of ethics is a result of the narrow "rationalism" of most neo-Kantian theories. By "ethical cognitivism" I understand the view that ethical judgments and principles have a cognitively articulable kernel, that they are neither mere statements of preference nor mere statements of taste but that they imply validity claims. These claims can be stated as: "X is right," where by X is meant a principle of action or a moral judgment, meaning "I can justify to you with good grounds why one ought to respect, uphold, agree with X." In this sense, ethical cognitivism is opposed to ethical decisionism that reduces such principles and judgments to an "I will" which cannot be further questioned. Ethical cognitivism is also opposed to ethical emotivism that conflates statements like "Child molesting is wrong" with claims like "I like Haägen-Dasz ice cream."

By "ethical rationalism," by contrast, I mean a theoretical position which views *moral judgments* as the core of moral theory, and which neglects that the moral self is not a moral geometer but an embodied, finite, suffering, and emotive being. We are not born rational but we acquire rationality through contingent processes of socialization and identity formation. Neo-Aristotelians as well as feminist theorists in recent years have argued that we are children before we are adults, and that as human children we can only survive and develop within networks of dependence with others, and that these networks of dependence constitute the "moral bonds" that continue to bind us even as moral adults. In Virginia Held's words, by ignoring the genealogy of the moral self and the development of the moral person out of a network of dependencies, universalist theorists often view the moral agent as the autonomous, adult male head of household, transacting in the market place or in the polity with like others.[53] Since Rousseau the demand has been to make "l'hômme" whole again, either by making him wholly a "Burgher" or by making him a "citôyen."

This "rationalist" bias of universalist theories in the Kantian tradition has at least two consequences: first, by ignoring or rather by abstracting away from the embedded, contingent, and finite aspects of human beings, these theories are blind to the variety and richness as well as significance of emotional and moral development. These are viewed as processes preceding the "genealogy" of the adult moral self; they seem to constitute the murky and shadowy background out of which the light of reason emerges.

Second, the neglect of the contingent beginnings of moral personality and character also leads to a distorted vision of certain human relationships and of their *moral texture,* precisely because universalist and proceduralist ethical theorists confuse the moral ideal of autonomy with the vision of the self "as a mushroom" (Hobbes).[54] Far from being a description of the "moral point of view," state of nature abstractions as well as visions of the "original position" are projections of the ideal of moral autonomy which only reflect the experience of the male head of household. But let us proceed cautiously here: I am *not* arguing that a truly universalist articulation of the moral point of view, one that includes the experiences of women and children, mothers and sisters, as well as brothers and fathers is not possible. The gender-blindness of much modern and contemporary universalist theory, in my opinion, does not compromise moral universalism as such, it only shows the need to judge universalism against its own ideals and to force it to make clear its own unjustified assumptions.

Current constructions of the "moral point of view" so lopsidedly privilege either the *homo economicus* or the *homo politicus* that they exclude all familial and other personal relations of dependence from their purview. While to become an autonomous adult means asserting one's independence vis-à-vis these relations, the process of moral maturation need not be viewed along the fictive model of the nineteenth-century boy who leaves home to become "a self-made man" out "yonder" in the wide, wild world. Moral autonomy can also be understood as growth and change, sustained by a network of relationships. Modern and contemporary constructions of the moral point of view are like the distorting lens of a camera: if you focus too badly, the scene in front of you not only becomes murky but can lose contours altogether and become unrecognizable. Likewise, the construction of those moral procedures which are to act as "substantive limits on our intuitions" must not be so out of focus that by looking through them, we lose the moral contours and moral textures of such personal relationships. Moral vision is a moral virtue, and moral blindness implies not necessarily an evil or unprincipled person, but one who cannot see the moral texture of the situation confronting him or her.[55] Since the eighteenth century, ethical rationalism has promoted a form of moral blindness with respect to the moral experience and claims of women, children, and other "nonautonomous others," as well as rough handling the moral texture of the personal and the familial.

Communicative ethics, in my view, is a form of ethical cognitivism which has so far been presented as a form of ethical rationalism. Particularly the claim, discussed above, that judgments of justice constitute the hardcore of all moral theory is an instance of such rationalism. As I have argued above (see section 2), even from within the constraints of a discourse theory, this hard distinction between judgments of justice and those of the good life cannot be sustained. Neither can the privileging of moral judgments to the neglect of moral emotions and character. There is a curious inconsistency here. The theory of communicative competence develops a post-Enlightenment conception of reason and views reason as the contingent acquisition of beings capable of language and action to articulate and sustain intersubjective validity claims.[56] The theory of communicative ethics, however, more often than not seems to perpetuate the Enlightenment illusions of the rational moral self as an isolated moral geometer.

If this is so, how can I maintain, as I also did in the first part of this essay, that the model of a universalist moral dialogue, envisaged in accordance with the formal constraints of discourses, can serve as a defensible version of the "moral point of view"? My answer is that the less we view such discourses along the model of public fora or courts of appeal, and the more we understand them as the continuation of *ordinary moral conversations* in which we seek to come to terms with and appreciate the others' point of view, the less do we submit to the distorting lens of procedural universalism. To argue that the counterfactual ideals of reciprocity, equality, and the "gentle force of reason" are implicit in the very structures of communicative action, is to argue that the "moral point of view" articulates more precisely those implicit structures of speech and action within which human life unfolds. Each time we say to a child, "But what if other kids pushed you into the sand, how would you feel then?", and each time we say to a mate, or to a relative, "But let me see if I understand your point correctly," we are engaging in moral conversations of justification. And if I am correct that it is the process of such dialogue, conversation, and mutual understanding, and not consensus which is our goal, discourse theory can represent the moral point of view without having to invoke the fiction of the *homo economicus* or *homo politicus*. To know how to sustain an ongoing human relationship means to know what it means to be an "I" and a "me," to know that I am an "other" to you and that likewise, you are an "I" to yourself but an "other" to me. Hegel had named this structure that of "reciprocal recognition." Communicative actions are actions through which we sustain such human relationships and through which we practice the reversibility of perspectives implicit in adult human relationships. The development of this capacity for reversing perspectives and the development of the capacity to assume the moral point of view are intimately linked. In the final analysis, universalizability requires us to practice the reversibility of standpoints by extending this to the viewpoint of humanity. Such a capacity is essential to being a good partner in a moral conversation, and is itself furthered by the practice of moral conversation. In conversation, I must know how to listen, I must know how to understand your point of view, I must learn to represent to myself the world and the other as you see them. If I cannot listen, if I cannot understand, and if I cannot represent, the conversation stops, develops into an argument, or maybe never gets started. Discourse ethics projects such moral conversations, in which reciprocal recognition is exercised, onto a utopian community of humankind. But the ability and the willingness of individuals to do so begins with the admonition of the parent to the child: "What if others threw sand in your face or pushed you into the pool, how would you feel then?"

5 Judging in Context vs. Principled Rigorism

The last issue I would like to treat in this afterword is the problem of *phronēsis* or practical wisdom concerning particulars. Aristotle saw this as the crowning achievement of moral *paideia* and character. A common criticism of Kantian-type ethical theories is that they substitute an ethical rigorism of principles for the art of moral judgment.[57] Justifiable as this critique may be, the discussion concerning moral judgment by either group of contenders in this debate has not advanced very far. The metaphor of the "archer hitting the mark," the language of moral insight and blindness, still dominate many recent treatments of the issue. If we can register a certain impatience with neo-Aristotelians in this respect, we must also admit that distinguishing between "justification" and "contextualization" cannot exempt the discourse theorists from analyzing what it is that we do when we supposedly contextualize moral principles and how this activity is related to the work of judging.[58] Obviously, there is a difference between the contextual application of a cookbook recipe in the environment of our kitchens, given the ingredients and the utensils we have, and the so-called "contextualization" of moral principles. If the discourse model is to succeed in acting as "a substantive limit on our intuitions" of the morally permissible and impermissible as well as guiding us in our vision of the morally required, we must be able to suggest how the procedural model of the moral conversation developed so far is involved in the process of moral judgment.

I would like to suggest that if there are certain moral and cognitive skills involved in reaching perspicacious, appropriate, sensitive, and illuminating judgments that they may bear a "family resemblance" to the conversational skills and virtues involved in the ongoing practice of moral dialogue and discourse. There is a cardinal requirement of contextual judgment, which most theorists, from Immanuel Kant to Hannah Arendt, who have developed the problem of judgment have suggested, and this is the ability, in Hannah Arendt's words, for "representative thinking":

The power of judgment rests on a potential agreement with others, and the thinking process which is active in judging something is not, like the thought process of pure reasoning, a dialogue between me and myself, but finds itself always and primarily, even if I am quite alone in making up my mind, in an anticipated communication with others with whom I know I must finally come to some agreement. From this potential agreement judgment derives its specific validity. This means, on the one hand, that such judgment must liberate itself from the "subjective private conditions," that is, from the idiosyncracies which naturally determine the outlook of each individual in his privacy and are legitimate as long as they are only privately held opinions but which are not fit to enter the market place, and lack all validity in the public realm. And this enlarged way of thinking, which as judgment knows how to transcend its individual limitations, cannot function in strict isolation or solitude; it needs the presence of others "in whose place" it must think, whose perspectives it must take into consideration, and without whom it never has the opportunity to operate at all.[59]

In Kant's discovery of the "enlarged mentality" in his theory of reflective judgment, Arendt saw a model for the kind of intersubjective validity which judgments had to be submitted to in the public realm. Judgment involves the capacity to represent to oneself the multiplicity of viewpoints, the variety of perspectives, the layers of meaning, etc., which constitute a situation. This representational capacity is crucial for the kind of sensitivity to particulars, which most agree is central for good and perspicacious judgment. The more we can identify the different viewpoints from which a situation can be interpreted and construed, the more we will have sensitivity to the particularities of the perspectives involved. Put differently, judgment involves certain "interpretive" and "narrative" skills, which, in turn, entail the capacity for exercising an "enlarged mentality." This "enlarged mentality" corresponds precisely to the reversibility of perspectives which the discourse theory enjoins. The link then between a universalist model of moral conversation and the exercise of judgment is this capacity for reversing moral perspectives, or what Kant and Arendt name the "enlarged mentality." Let me suggest in more detail why the narrative and interpretive skills involved in judging entail reversibility of moral perspectives.[60] Moral judgment is crucial in at least three domains of moral interaction: the assessment of one's duties; the assessment of one's specific course of action as fulfilling these duties; and the assessment of one's maxims as embodied, expressed, or revealed in actions.

In the assessment of duties, we are concerned with recognizing a particular situation as being one that calls for a specific kind of moral duty. How do we know that this human situation calls for the duty of honesty, or the virtue of loyalty or of generosity? What is it about a particular human situation that will allow us to identify it as being of a certain kind? I would like to suggest that here moral judgment is concerned first with the identification of human situations and circumstances as being "morally relevant." By "morally relevant" I mean a situation or circumstance so defined that it would lead us to recognize a prima facie moral duty to act in a certain way. While it is precisely the mark of one who has good moral judgment that she identifies this as being a situation of loyalty, of generosity, of courage, or of integrity, whatever else such judgment takes, it most certainly must involve the capacity for representative thinking or the reversibility of moral perspectives. Only one who is able imaginatively to represent to herself the variety and meaning of the human perspectives involved in a situation can also identify its moral relevance. For moral relevance in this context means understanding the moral descriptions and expectations and interpretations that make up the narrative fabric of a human story.

What about the assessment of one's action? Whereas in the case of assessing moral duty we ask, in what ways is this situation morally relevant for me, now we are asking, "What is it that I must do to fulfill my duty to act morally once I have recognized it?" In other words, what I do, which course of action I choose, involves some interpretive ability to see my act under various act descriptions and to anticipate how, while action A may be viewed as one of generosity, action B may be viewed as one of overbearing solicitude. I must have enough moral imagination to know the possible act descriptions or narratives in light of which an act embodying a maxim can be considered. Determining the identity of a moral action entails the exercise of moral imagination; this activates our capacity for imagining possible narratives and descriptions in light of which our actions can be understood by others. Again, such moral imagination involves representative thinking, namely, the capacity to take the standpoint of others involved into account and to reason from their point of view.

Finally, let us look at the concretization of one's maxim, or principle of duty, via a concrete action. There is often a clash between the moral intentions or principles guiding an agent and the interpretation of this by the world, once they are embodied in actions. In formulating moral intentions and maxims—"I recognize that I must be generous now," "Honesty is always my policy"—we project ourselves, our narrative history, into the world, and we want to be recognized as the doer of such and such. We identify our moral intentions and principles in terms of a narrative of which we ourselves are the author. This narrative also anticipates the meaning that such projection may or will have in the eyes of others. Assessing one's moral intentions and maxims, therefore, requires understanding the narrative history of the self who is the actor; this understanding exhibits both self-knowledge and knowledge of oneself as viewed by others. The narrative capacity for projecting a course of action, which exhibits and embodies our moral intentions and maxims, requires sensitivity to the many perspectives and interpretations in light of which our narrative and personal story will be construed. This means once more that reversibility of perspectives or the capacity for representative thinking are central in such formulations.

What I have suggested so far is that if we view discourses as a procedural model of conversations in which we exercise reversibility of perspectives either by actually listening to all involved or by representing to ourselves imaginatively the many perspectives of those involved, then this procedure is also an aspect of the skills of moral imagination and moral narrative which good judgment involves whatever else it might involve. I do not therefore see a gulf between moral intuition guided by an egalitarian and universalist model of moral conversation and the exercise of contextual judgment. Quite to the contrary, the kinds of interpretive and narrative skills I discussed above can also be easily used for "amoral" purposes.

The exercise of good judgment can also mean manipulating people—presumably good administrators, politicians, therapists, social workers, and even teachers of young children all exercise "good judgment," not always for the sake of moral reciprocity or with respect to enhancing the moral integrity of the one about whom such judgment is exercised. Moral judgment alone is not the totality of moral virtue. Here as well we need a "substantive limit" on our intuitions: only judgment guided by the principles of universal moral respect and reciprocity is "good" moral judgment, in the sense of being ethically right. Judgments which are not limited by such principles may be "brilliant," "right on the mark," "perspicacious," but also immoral or amoral. Saying this, however, is not to say that in a fragmented universe of value we are never in the situation of juggling moral principles against other political, artistic, and administrative ends. Kantian theories have paid little attention to this "fragmentation of value," and to the consequences which the fine tuning and balancing of our moral commitments with other value commitments have for the conduct of our lives.

Here, we reach a frontier where moral theory flows into a larger theory of value, and I would say, into culture at large. Morality is a central domain in the universe of values which define cultures, and it is cultures which supply the motivational patterns and symbolic interpretations in light of which individuals think of narrative histories, project their visions of the good life, interpret their needs, and the like. Moral theory finds this material, so to speak, "given." Thus, moral theory is limited on the one hand by the macroinstitutions of a polity, politics, administration, and the market, within the limits of which choices concerning justice are made. On the other hand, moral theory is limited by culture, its repertory of interpretations of the good life, personality, and socialization patterns. These two domains form the larger ethical context of which morality is always but an aspect. Yet the relation between morality and this larger ethical context is not what neo-Aristotelians and the young Hegel would like us to think it is. Under conditions of modernity, as the old Hegel knew, the moral point of view always judges the institutions of which it is a part; and the modern individual exercises autonomy in distancing him or herself from the given cultural interpretation of social roles, needs, and conceptions of the good life. In this sense the dispute between discourse theorists and neo-Aristotelians and neo-Hegelians is at its heart a dispute about modernity; it is a dispute about whether modern moral theory since Kant has been an accomplice in the process of disintegration of personality and the fragmentation of value which is said to be our general condition today.[61] My intervention in this debate intended to show that, judged from within the confines of moral theory, and without delving into this larger issue about modernity and its discontents, the debate between neo-Aristotelians/neo-Hegelians and discourse theorists is still very much continuing. Although it is too trite to think that all philosophical debates lead to good endings, my own personal sense at this stage is that this confrontation has invigorated rather than weakened contemporary moral theory.

Notes

I would like to thank my colleagues Kenneth Baynes and Dick Howard for their illuminating criticisms of an earlier draft. A shorter version of this essay appeared in *The Philosophical Forum*, special double issue on "Hermeneutics in Ethics and Social Theory," ed. by Michael Kelly, vol. 21, nos. 1–2 (Fall–Winter 1989–90), pp. 1–32.

1. See Kurt Baier, *The Moral Point of View*, abridged ed. (New York: Random House, 1965); Alan Gewirth, *Reason and Morality* (Chicago: University of Chicago Press, 1978); H. M. Hare, *Freedom and Reason* (Oxford: Oxford University Press, 1963); Marcus Singer, *Generalizability in Ethics. An Essay in the Logic of Ethics with the Rudiments of a System of Moral Philosophy* (New York: Alfred Knopf, 1961); Stephen Toulmin, *The Place of Reason in Ethics* (Cambridge: Cambridge University Press, 1953).

2. See John Rawls, *A Theory of Justice,* 2d printing (Cambridge, MA: Harvard University Press, 1972); John Rawls, "Kantian Constructivism in Moral Philosophy: The Dewey Memorial Lectures 1980," *Journal of Philosophy,* 77 (September 1980), pp. 515–572; Lawrence Kohlberg, *Essays on Moral Development,* vol. 1 and *The Psychology of Moral Development,* vol. 2 (San Francisco: Harper and Row, 1984).

3. Alasdair MacIntyre and Stanley Hauerwas, *Revisions* (Notre Dame: University of Notre Dame Press, 1983), p. vii. For a general discussion of this context, see also Fred Dallmayr's "Introduction," this volume.

4. Aristotle, in *The Basic Works of Aristotle,* ed. and trans. by Richard McKeon (New York: Random House, 1945).

5. For Hegel's early critique of Kant, see "The Spirit of Christianity and its Fate," in G. W. F. Hegel, *Early Theological Writings,* T. M. Knox, trans. (Philadelphia: University of Pennsylvania Press, 1971), pp. 182–302; G. W. F. Hegel, *Hegel's Phenomenology of Spirit,* trans. by A. V. Miller (Oxford: Clarendon Press, 1977), ch. 6, section C; *Hegel's Philosophy of Right,* trans. by T. M. Knox (Oxford: Oxford University Press, 1973), 40, Addition, pp. 39ff.; Hegel, *Science of Logic,* A. V. Miller, trans. (New York: Humanities Press, 1969), pp. 133ff.

6. Karl-Otto Apel, "Kant, Hegel und das aktuelle Problem der normativen Grundlagen von Moral und Recht," in *Diskurs und Verantwortung* (Frankfurt: Suhrkamp, 1988), pp. 69–103; Apel, "Kann der postkantische Standpunkt noch einmal in substantielle Sittlichkeit aufgehoben werden? . . ." in ibid., pp. 103–154; Jürgen Habermas, "Moralität und Sittlichkeit. Treffen Hegels Einwände gegen Kant auch auf die Diskursethik zu?" in *Moralität und Sittlichkeit. Das Problem Hegels und die Diskursethik,* ed. by W. Kuhlmann (Frankfurt: Suhrkamp, 1986), pp. 16–38.

7. Herbert Schnädelbach, "Was ist Neoaristotelismus?" in *Moralität und Sittlichkeit,* W. Kuhlmann, ed., pp. 38–64; English trans. as "What is Neo-Aristotelianism?" in *Praxis International,* vol. 7, no. 3/4 (October-January 1987), pp. 225–238.

8. For an excellent survey of the various strands of neo-Aristotelianism in contemporary discussions, and in particular for the serious differences between German and

Anglophone neo-Aristotelian trends, see Maurizio Passerin d'Entrèves, "Aristotle or Burke? Some Comments on H. Schnädelbach's 'What is Neo-Aristotelianism?'," in *Praxis International*, vol. 7., nos. 3/4 (October 1987–January 1988), pp. 238–246. I discuss communitarian philosophies in "Autonomy, Modernity and Community. An Exchange Between Communitarianism and Critical Social Theory," in *Zwischenbetrachtungen im Prozess der Aufklärung*, ed. by A. Honneth, T. A. McCarthy, Claus Offe, and Albrecht Wellmer (Frankfurt: Suhrkmap, 1988), pp. 373–395.

9. Hans-Georg Gadamer, *Truth and Method* (New York: Seabury Press, 1975).

10. Gadamer, "Hermeneutics as Practical Philosophy," in *Reason in the Age of Science*, trans. by Frederick G. Lawrence (Cambridge, MA: The MIT Press, 1981), pp. 88–113. I have not included Hannah Arendt's work under this categorization, because in matters of moral as opposed to political philosophy Arendt remained a Kantian thinker. I deal with some aspects of this admittedly not generally shared interpretation of Hannah Arendt's work in my "Judgment and the Moral Foundations of Politics in Hannah Arendt's Thought," in *Political Theory*, vol. 16, no. 1 (February 1988), pp. 29–53.

11. See Hans-Georg Gadamer, "Hegel's Philosophy and its Aftereffects until Today," and "The Heritage of Hegel," in *Reason in the Age of Science*, pp. 21–38 and 38–69; and Gadamer, *Hegel's Dialectic*, trans. by P. Christopher Smith (New Haven: Yale University Press, 1976).

12. I. Kant, *Grundlegung der Metaphysik der Sitten*, trans. by H. J. Paton as *The Moral Law* (London: Hutchinson, 1953), p. 421.

13. G. W. F. Hegel, *Natural Law*, trans. by T. M. Knox and introd. by H. B. Acton (Philadelphia: University of Pennsylvania Press, 1975), pp. 77–78.

14. For some recent considerations on Hegel's critique of Kantian ethics, see Jonathan Lear, "Moral Objectivity," in *Objectivity and Cultural Divergence*, ed. by S. C. Brown (Cambridge: Cambridge University Press, 1984), pp. 153–171.

15. The Kantian principle of universalizability does not, of course, dictate any specific content to the principles of justice; rather, it is operative in the construction of the "original position," as the privileged moral vantage point from which to enter into deliberations about matters of justice. See Rawls, *A Theory of Justice*, passim.

16. Onora O'Neill, "Consistency in Action," in *Morality and Universality*, ed. by Nelson T. Potter and Mark Timmons (Dordrecht: D. Reidel Publishing, 1985), pp. 159–186.

17. Ibid., p. 168.

18. Ibid., p. 169.

19. Ibid.

20. See Alan Gewirth, *Reason and Morality* (Chicago: University of Chicago Press, 1978), pp. 48–129.

21. Alasdair MacIntyre, *After Virtue* (Notre Dame: University of Notre Dame Press, 1984), p. 67.

22. See Michael Walzer, "A Critique of Philosophical Conversation," in *The Philosophical Forum*, vol. xxi, nos. 1–2 (Fall–Winter 1989–90), pp. 182–197.

23. S. Benhabib, "The Methodological Illusions of Modern Political Theory: The Case of Rawls and Habermas," in *Neue Hefte für Philosophie*, no. 21 (Spring 1982), pp. 47–74.

24. I have developed this argument more extensively in "Liberal Dialogue vs. A Discourse Theory of Legitimacy," in *Liberalism and the Moral Life*, ed. by Nancy Rosenblum (Cambridge, MA: Harvard University Press, 1989), pp. 143–157.

25. J. Habermas, "Diskursethik. Notizen zu einem Begründungsprogramm," in *Moralbewusstsein und kommunikatives Handeln* (Frankfurt: Suhrkamp, 1983), pp. 96–97; English translation in this volume.

26. K.-O. Apel, "The Problem of Philosophical Fundamental Grounding in Light of a Transcendental Pragmatics of Language," in K. Baynes, J. Bohman, and T. A. McCarthy, eds. *After Philosophy* (Cambridge, MA: The MIT Press, 1987), p. 277.

27. T. McCarthy, "Rationality and Relativism. Habermas's Overcoming of Hermeneutics," in Thompson and Held, eds. *Habermas: Critical Debates* (Cambridge, MA: The MIT Press, 1982), p. 74.

28. The metastatus of such criticism—whether such social criticism needs to be philosophically grounded in some generally acceptable system of norms or whether it can be exercised immanently, by internally appealing to, critiquing, or debunking the norms of a given culture, community, and group—is what sharply divides social theorists like Habermas and Michael Walzer. Given also the large area of substantive agreement among them upon the need for the radical-democratic reconstruction of late-capitalist societies, it is worth pursuing what status these metaphilosophical disagreements—immanent or transcendental; relativist or universalist—have. For Walzer, see *Interpretation and Social Criticism* (Cambridge, MA: Harvard, 1987).

29. In this volume, p. 90.

30. See Barbara Herman's excellent discussion, "The Practice of Moral Judgment," in *The Journal of Philosophy* (August 1985), pp. 414–436.

31. Agnes Heller, "The Discourse Ethics of Habermas: Critique and Appraisal," in *Thesis Eleven*, no. 10/11 (1984–85), pp. 5–17, here p. 7; see also Albrecht Wellmer, *Ethik und Dialog. Elemente des moralischen Urteils bei Kant und in der Diskursethik* (Frankfurt: Suhrkamp, 1986); Otfried Höffe, "Kantian Skepticism Toward the Transcendental Ethics of Communication," in this volume.

32. Wellmer, *Ethik und Dialog*, p. 63. My translation.

33. Heller, "The Discourse Ethics of Habermas," p. 8.

34. Wellmer, *Ethik und Dialog*, p. 64.

35. Wellmer also discusses this principle in ibid., pp. 65ff. Wellmer's argument is that since the universal adherence to this norm would eliminate precisely those cases like the legitimate right to self-defense and justified punishment, the discourse ethics is obliging us to think of what is morally right only in relation to counterfactual ideal conditions and not real ones. Wellmer concludes that the conditions of action suggested by "U" can properly be thought of as those appropriate for a "kingdom of ends." But the fact that in actual life we must always make justified exceptions to such general moral rules has little to do with the question whether our moral theory is able to justify

Seyla Benhabib

what we intuitively know to be a right moral principle, i.e., in this case not to inflict unnecessary suffering.

36. See Wellmer, ibid., pp. 121–122; Heller, "The Discourse Ethics of Habermas," p. 9.

37. Charles Taylor, "Die Motive einer Verfahrensethik," in *Moralität und Sittlichkeit*, W. Kuhlmann, ed., pp. 101ff.

38. See Michael Sandel, "Introduction," to *Liberalism and its Critics*, Michael J. Sandel, ed. (New York: New York University Press, 1984), pp. 1–13.

39. Part of the discussion which follows has appeared in S. Benhabib, "Autonomy, Modernity and Community: An Exchange Between Communitarianism and Critical Social Theory," pp. 377–79.

40. John Rawls, *A Theory of Justice*, pp. 398ff.

41. J. Habermas, "A Reply to My Critics," in *Habermas: Critical Debates*, J. Thompson and D. Held, eds., p. 246.

42. Habermas, "Ego Development and Moral Identity," in *Communication and the Evolution of Society*, trans. by T. McCarthy (Boston: Beacon Press, 1979), pp. 78ff.

43. See Bernard Williams, *Ethics and the Limits of Philosophy* (Cambridge, MA: Harvard University Press, 1985); Charles Taylor, *Philosophy and the Human Sciences*, vol. 2 of *Philosophical Papers* (Cambridge: Cambridge University Press, 1985), pp. 23–247.

44. Habermas, "Moralbewusstsein und kommunikatives Handeln," in *Moralbewusstsein und kommunikatives Handeln*, pp. 144ff.

45. MacIntyre, *After Virtue*, p. 204.

46. Hegel, "The Positivity of the Christian Religion," in *Early Theological Writings*, p. 154.

47. Hegel, *Philosophy of Right*, Note to para. 270, pp. 168–69.

48. See Robert Spaemann, "Die Utopie der Herrschaftsfreiheit," in *Merkur*, no. 292 (August 1972), pp. 735–752; Niklas Luhmann and J. Habermas, *Theorie der Gesellschaft oder Sozialtechnologie-Was leistet die Systemforschung?* (Frankfurt: Suhrkamp, 1976).

49. For a provocative consideration of the implications of discourse theory for a critical theory of new social movements in Western and Soviet-type societies, see Andrew Arato and Jean Cohen, *Civil Society and Social Theory* (Cambridge, MA: The MIT Press, forthcoming).

50. I have dealt with the difficulties of the concept of the "suppressed generalizable interest" extensively in *Critique, Norm and Utopia* (New York: Columbia University Press, 1986), pp. 310ff.

51. Nancy Fraser, "Toward a Discourse Ethic of Solidarity," *Praxis International*, vol. 5, no. 4 (January 1986), p. 425.

52. See Amelie Rorty, "Community as the Context of Character," part four in *Mind in Action. Essays in the Philosophy of Mind* (Boston: Beacon Press, 1988), pp. 271–347; Martha Nussbaum, *The Fragility of Goodness* (Cambridge: Cambridge University Press,

1986); Annette Baier, "What do Women Want in Moral Theory," *Nous*, no. 19 (1985), pp. 53–63, and A. Baier, "Hume. The Women's Moral Theorist?" in *Women and Moral Theory*, ed. by E. F. Kittay and Diana T. Meyers (New Jersey: Rowman and Littlefield, 1987), pp. 37–56; Lawrence Blum, *Friendship, Altruism and Morality* (London: Routledge and Kegan Paul: 1980); Ursula Wolff, *Das Problem des moralischen Sollens* (Berlin and New York: de Gruyter, 1983); Virginia Held, "Feminism and Moral Theory," in *Women and Moral Theory*, E. F. Kittay and Diana T. Meyers, eds.; Sara Ruddick, *Maternal Thinking* (Boston: Beacon Press, 1989).

53. Virginia Held, "Feminism and Moral Theory," pp. 114ff.

54. I have discussed the gender-bias of modern conceptions of autonomy in "The Generalized and the Concrete Other: The Kohlberg-Gilligan Controversy and Moral Theory," in *Women and Moral Theory*, Kittay and Meyers, eds., pp. 154–178; reprinted in Benhabib and Cornell, eds. *Feminism as Critique* (Minnesota: University of Minnesota Press, 1987), pp. 77–96.

55. See Amelie Rorty, "Virtues and the Vicissitudes," in *Mind in Action*, pp. 314ff.

56. See, in particular, Herbert Schnädelbach's reflections in "Remarks About Rationality and Language," in this volume.

57. For a recent statement of the hermeneutic critique of ethical theory from this point of view, see Ronald Beiner, "Do We Need a Philosophical Ethics? Theory, Prudence and the Primacy of Ethos?", *The Philosophical Forum*, vol. xx, no. 3 (Spring 1989), pp. 230ff. See also Alessandro Ferrara for an incisive probing of discourse ethics from this viewpoint, "Universalisms: Procedural, Contextualist and Prudential," *Philosophy and Social Criticism*, vol. 14, nos. 3–4, pp. 243–271.

58. See Habermas, "Moralbewusstsein und kommunikatives Handeln," pp. 187ff., where the work of Norma Haan and Carol Gilligan is discussed; Apel, "Kann der postkantische Standpunkt der Moralität noch einmal in substantielle Sittlichkeit aufgehoben werden?", pp. 103ff.

59. Hannah Arendt, "The Crisis in Culture," in *Between Past and Future. Six Exercises in Political Thought* (New York: Meridian, 1961), pp. 21–22.

60. For a more detailed presentation of the following argument, see S. Benhabib, "Judgment and the Moral Foundations of Politics in Hannah Arendt's Thought," *Political Theory*, vol. 16. no. 1 (February 1988), pp. 34ff.

61. I have dealt with the types of responses to modernity among contemporary social theorists in "Autonomy, Modernity and Community. An Exchange Between Communitarianism and Critical Social Theory."

Contributors

Karl-Otto Apel is Professor of Philosophy at the University of Frankfurt. He is author of *Die Idee der Sprache in der Tradition des Humanismus* (1963), *Der Denkweg von Charles S. Peirce* (1975), and especially of *Transformation der Philosophie*, volume 1: *Sprachanalytik, Semiotik, Hermeneutik*, volume 2: *Das Apriori der Kommunikationsgemeinschaft* (1973). Some of the essays in these two volumes have been translated into English as *Towards a Transformation of Philosophy* (Routledge & Kegan Paul, 1980). Also available in English is *Understanding and Explanation: A Transcendental-Pragmatic Perspective* (MIT Press, 1984). More recently he has published *Diskurs und Verantwortung: Das Problem des Übergangs zur postkonventionellen Moral* (1988), in addition to editing with Dietrich Böhler three volumes of *Funkkolleg Praktische Philosophie/Ethik* (1980, 1984).

Jürgen Habermas is Professor of Philosophy at the University of Frankfurt, after serving as Director of the Max-Planck Institute in Starnberg. Among his most important publications in English are *Knowledge and Human Interests* (1971), *Theory and Practice* (1973), *Legitimation Crisis* (1975), *Communication and the Evolution of Society* (1979), and *The Theory of Communicative Action*, two volumes (1984 and 1987). More recently these works have appeared in English: *The Philosophical Discourse of Modernity: Twelve Lectures* (MIT Press, 1987); *On the Logic of the Social Sciences* (MIT Press, 1988); *The Structural Transformation of the Public Sphere* (MIT Press, 1989); and *Moral Consciousness and Communicative Action* (MIT Press, 1990).

Dietrich Böhler is Professor of Philosophy at the Free University in Berlin. Among his publications are *Metakritik der Marxschen Ideologiekritik* (2nd ed., 1972); *Rekonstruktive Pragmatik: Von der Bewusstseinsphilosophie zur Kommunikationsreflexion* (1985). In close collaboration with Karl-Otto Apel he has also published three volumes of *Funkkolleg Praktische Philosophie/Ethik* (1980, 1984) together with three volumes of *Studientexte* (1984).

Robert Alexy is Professor of Jurisprudence at the University of Göttingen. He is the author of *Theorie der juristischen Argumentation* (1978), which appeared in English as *A Theory of Legal Argumentation* (Oxford University Press, 1989).

Otfried Höffe is Professor of Social and Political Philosophy at the University of Fribourg (Switzerland). Among his publications are *Strategien der Humanität: Zur Ethik öffentlicher Entscheidungsprozesse* (1975); *Ethik und Politik* (1979); *Sittlich-politische Diskurse* (1981); and most recently *Politische Gerechtigkeit: Grundlegung einer kritischen Philosophie von Recht und Staat* (1988).

The late *Karl-Heinz Ilting* was Professor of Philosophy at the University of Saarbrücken. A renowned Hegel scholar, he edited or coedited G. W. F. Hegel, *Vorlesungen über Rechtsphilosophie, 1918–31* (1973), *Naturphilosophie* (1982), and *Die Philosophie des Rechts* (1983). He also published *Naturrecht und Sittlichkeit* (1983) together with numerous articles on Aristotle, Hobbes, and Hegel.

Hermann Lübbe is Professor of Philosophy and Political Theory at the University of Zurich. Among his publications are *Bewusstsein in Geschichten: Studien zur Phänomenologie der Subjektivität* (1962); *Politische Philosophie in Deutschland* (1963); *Praxis der Philosophie, Praktische Philosophie, Geschichtstheorie* (1978); *Philosophie nach der Aufklärung* (1980); *Der Mensch als Orientierungswaise* (1982); *Handlungssinn und Lebenssinn* (1987); *Wissenschaften und ihre kulturellen Folgen* (1987); and *Anfang und Ende des Lebens als normatives Problem* (1988).

Herbert Schnädelbach is Professor of Philosophy and Social Theory at the University of Hamburg. Among his publications are *Erfahrung, Begründung und Reflexion* (1971); *Geschichtsphilosophie nach Hegel* (1974); *Reflexion und Diskurs* (1977); and *Vernunft und Geschichte* (1987). His *Philosophie in Deutschland 1831–1933* (1983) has been translated into English as *Philosophy in Germany 1831–1933* (Cambridge University Press, 1984).

Albrecht Wellmer is Professor of Philosophy at the University of Konstanz. He is the author of *Kritische Gesellschaftstheorie und Positivismus* (1969), which has been translated into English as *The Critical Theory of Society* (Continuum Books, 1971). Among his more recent publications are *Zur Dialektik von Moderne und Postmoderne: Vernunftkritik nach Adorno* (1985) and *Ethik und Dialog* (1986). A collection of his recent essays under the title *In Defense of Modernity* is forthcoming from MIT Press.

Index

Studies in Contemporary German Social Thought
Thomas McCarthy, General Editor